The Booker T. Washington Collection

THE NEGRO PROBLEM

UP FROM SLAVERY

THE FUTURE OF THE AMERICAN NEGRO

THE HISTORY OF SLAVERY

3 in 1 © 2019

Printed in the United States.

Washington, Booker T., et al.

The Booker T. Washington Collection: The Negro Problem, Up from Slavery, The Future of the American Negro, The History of Slavery / Booker T. Washington, et al. - 1st ed.

1. History.
2. African-American Studies.

CONTENTS

INTRODUCTION

"In all things that are purely social we can be separate as the fingers, yet one as the hand in all things essential to mutual progress".[1]

-- Booker Washington (said it in a speech in Atlanta, 1893)

Washington, in full, Booker Taliaferro Washington, being the surname Taliaferro from Italian origin, meaning "cut iron" (talia ferro), and Washington coming from his stepfather's first name, was born in 1856 in Virgina and died in 1915 in Alabama. He first worked when he was 9 years old at salt furnaces and later in a coal mine. He was a servant for Viola Ruffner, who taught him how to read. He later became an educator and reformer, the first president of a school that is now the Tuskgee University and, according to different encyclopedias, such as Britannica and Virgina, the most influential spokesman for black Americans between 1895 and 1915.

Washington was born on a plantation near Hales Ford, Va., about twenty-five miles east of the city of Roanoke, in a region which, now almost deserted, was in slavery days a flourishing tobacco country. It was while he was living there that he was awakened one morning to find his mother kneeling on the earth floor of the little cabin in which they lived, praying that "Lincoln and his armies might be successful and that one day she and her children might be free." It was here a little later on, as he tells us in the book *Up From Slavery* that he heard the announcement that he and all the other slaves were free.

"I recall," he says, "that some man who seemed to be a stranger and who was undoubtedly a United States official, made a little speech and then read a rather long paper—the Emancipation Proclamation, I think. After the reading we were told that we were all free and could go where we pleased. "My mother, who was standing by my side, leaned over and kissed her children,

---

[1] Du Bois, Martinsburg newspaper editor J. R. Clifford, and others formed the Niagara Movement, to counter Washington's philosophy.

while tears of joy ran down her cheeks. She explained to us what it all meant; that this was the day for which she had so long been praying, but fearing she would never live to see. "For some minutes," he continues, "there was great rejoicing, and thanksgiving and wild scenes of ecstasy. But there was no feeling of bitterness. In fact, there was pity among the slaves for our former owners. The wild rejoicing of the emancipated colored people lasted but a brief period, for I noticed that by the time they returned to their cabins there was a change in their feelings. The great responsibility of being free, of having charge of themselves and their children, of having to plan for themselves and their children, seemed to take possession of them. To some it seemed, now that they were in actual possession of it, freedom was a more serious thing than they had expected to find. Gradually one by one, stealthily at first, the older slaves began to wander back to the 'big house' to have whispered conversations with their former owners as to their future."

Thus it was that freedom came to Washington and so it came, perhaps, to some three and one-half millions of others on their plantations throughout the South.

Shortly after the "surrender," young Washington made a long journey across the mountains with his mother to West Virginia where his stepfather was then living, and it was in Malden he grew up to young manhood. Malden is situated in the mining region of West Virginia, and after a time young Washington went to work in the mines. It was while he was working down in the coal mines of West Virginia that he one day overheard one of the miners reading from a paper concerning a school at Hampton, Virginia, where a black man would be given a chance to work his way through school. He determined at once that he would seek out and find that school. So it was that a few months later he set out afoot across the mountain in the direction of Richmond to find his way to Hampton Institute. In his remarkable biography he has described how he made that journey; how he arrived hungry and penniless in the city of Richmond; how he slept for several nights under the sidewalk in Richmond until he was able to earn enough money to reach the famous school of which he had read.

At the time that young Washington entered Hampton Institute, General Armstrong, the founder of the school, was engaged in a great and interesting experiment. His purpose was to create a school which would give the sons of the freedmen education in character as well as in books. Booker Washington saw that this education was the thing above all others that the masses of the black man people needed at this time, and realized better than any other of the graduates of the institution the significance and bearing of the work that General Armstrong was trying to do. He made up his mind then that he would go out into some part of the South and establish a school which would do for other members of his race what Hampton had done for him. His opportunity came when a call came to Hampton for a man to take charge of a school at Tuskegee, Alabama. It was thus in 1881 that the famous Tuskegee Institute came to be started.

This school, which was started on July 4, 1881, in a little shanty church, with one teacher and thirty students, has grown in his life and later became a University.

In 1895 Mr. Washington was invited to speak at the Atlanta Cotton States Exposition on Negroes Day. In that speech he made an appeal for peace between the races, and formulated a program for mutual cooperation between black and white which has been the basis of all his efforts since that time.

From that time on his fame has grown steadily, both in this country and abroad. In 1896 Harvard University conferred upon him the honorary degree of Master of Arts for service in the education of his race. He has received numerous other honors since that time and has spoken in every state of the Union in favor of Negro education. A few years ago when he went abroad he was invited to dinner by the King of Denmark. In April, 1912, there was held under his leadership at Tuskegee an international conference on the Negro to which representatives came from many parts of Africa as well as the West Indies and South America. The result of this was a plan to form a permanent international organization to study the Negro problem in all parts of the world and hold meetings triennially.

Born in a slave hut, he began working at nine after emancipation, first in a salt furnace and later in a coal mine. From this humble start, he was selected to head a new normal school for African Americans at Tuskegee and later in 1896 he was the first African American to receive a honorary degree from Harvard University. In 1901, he became the first African American to dine in the White House.

[7]

Washington wrote twelve books. In this collection, we united three books by Washington including Washington's most known book, *Up from Slavery*, which is his autobiography first published in 1901, and a small fourth one. The other books are *The Negro Problem*, a 1903 collection of essays by prominent black American writers, *The Future of the American Negro*, originally published in 1899, and a short text about the history of slavery (originally *The Story of Slavery*), published in 1913, which was included as an appendix.

THE NEGRO PROBLEM

Booker T. Washington, et al.

CONTENTS

Industrial Education for the Negro

By BOOKER T. WASHINGTON

Principal of Tuskegee Institute

The necessity for the race's learning the difference between being worked and working. He would not confine the Negro to industrial life, but believes that the very best service which any one can render to what is called the "higher education" is to teach the present generation to work and save. This will create the wealth from which alone can come leisure and the opportunity for higher education.

One of the most fundamental and far-reaching deeds that has been accomplished during the last quarter of a century has been that by which the Negro has been helped to find himself and to learn the secrets of civilization--to learn that there are a few simple, cardinal principles upon which a race must start its upward course, unless it would fail, and its last estate be worse than its first.

It has been necessary for the Negro to learn the difference between being worked and working--to learn that being worked meant degradation, while working means civilization; that all forms of labor are honorable, and all forms of idleness disgraceful. It has been necessary for him to learn that all races that have got upon their feet have done so largely by laying an economic foundation, and, in general, by beginning in a proper cultivation and ownership of the soil.

Forty years ago my race emerged from slavery into freedom. If, in too many cases, the Negro race began development at the wrong end, it was largely because neither white nor black properly understood the case. Nor is it any wonder that this was so, for never before in the history of the world had just such a problem been presented as that of the two races at the coming of freedom in this country.

For two hundred and fifty years, I believe the way for the redemption of the Negro was being prepared through industrial development. Through all those years the Southern white man did business with the Negro in a way that no one else has done business with him. In most cases if a Southern white man wanted a house built he consulted a Negro mechanic about the plan and about the actual building of the structure. If he wanted a suit of clothes made he went to a Negro tailor, and for shoes he went to a shoemaker of the same race. In a

[13]

certain way every slave plantation in the South was an industrial school. On these plantations young colored men and women were constantly being trained not only as farmers but as carpenters, blacksmiths, wheelwrights, brick masons, engineers, cooks, laundresses, sewing women and housekeepers.

I do not mean in any way to apologize for the curse of slavery, which was a curse to both races, but in what I say about industrial training in slavery I am simply stating facts. This training was crude, and was given for selfish purposes. It did not answer the highest ends, because there was an absence of mental training in connection with the training of the hand. To a large degree, though, this business contact with the Southern white man, and the industrial training on the plantations, left the Negro at the close of the war in possession of nearly all the common and skilled labor in the South. The industries that gave the South its power, prominence and wealth prior to the Civil War were mainly the raising of cotton, sugar cane, rice and tobacco. Before the way could be prepared for the proper growing and marketing of these crops forests had to be cleared, houses to be built, public roads and railroads constructed. In all these works the Negro did most of the heavy work. In the planting, cultivating and marketing of the crops not only was the Negro the chief dependence, but in the manufacture of tobacco he became a skilled and proficient workman, and in this, up to the present time, in the South, holds the lead in the large tobacco manufactories.

In most of the industries, though, what happened? For nearly twenty years after the war, except in a few instances, the value of the industrial training given by the plantations was overlooked. Negro men and women were educated in literature, in mathematics and in the sciences, with little thought of what had been taking place during the preceding two hundred and fifty years, except, perhaps, as something to be escaped, to be got as far away from as possible. As a generation began to pass, those who had been trained as mechanics in slavery began to disappear by death, and gradually it began to be realized that there were few to take their places. There were young men educated in foreign tongues, but few in carpentry or in mechanical or architectural drawing. Many were trained in Latin, but few as engineers and blacksmiths. Too many were taken from the farm and educated, but educated in everything but farming. For this reason they had no interest in farming and did not return to it. And yet eighty-five per cent. of the Negro population of the Southern states lives and for a considerable time will continue to live in the country districts. The charge is often brought against the members of my race--and too often justly, I confess--that they are found leaving the country districts and flocking into the great cities where temptations are more frequent and harder to resist, and where the Negro people too often become demoralized. Think, though, how frequently it is the case that from the first day that a pupil begins to go to school his books teach him much about the cities of the world and city life, and almost nothing about the country. How natural it is, then, that when he has the ordering of his life he wants to live it in the city.

Only a short time before his death the late Mr. C.P. Huntington, to whose memory a magnificent library has just been given by his widow to the Hampton Institute for Negroes, in Virginia, said in a public address some words which seem to me so wise that I want to quote them here:

"Our schools teach everybody a little of almost everything, but, in my opinion, they teach very few children just what they ought to know in order to make their way successfully in life. They do not put into their hands the tools they are best fitted to use, and hence so many failures. Many a mother and sister have worked and slaved, living upon scanty food, in order to give a son and brother a "liberal education," and in doing this have built up a barrier between the boy and the work he was fitted to do. Let me say to you that all honest work is honorable work. If the labor is manual, and seems common, you will have all the more chance to be thinking of other things, or of work that is higher and brings better pay, and to work out in your minds better and higher duties and responsibilities for yourselves, and for thinking of ways by which you can help others as well as yourselves, and bring them up to your own higher level."

Some years ago, when we decided to make tailoring a part of our training at the Tuskegee Institute, I was amazed to find that it was almost impossible to find in the whole country an educated colored man who could teach the making of clothing. We could find numbers of them who could teach astronomy, theology, Latin or grammar, but almost none who could instruct in the making of clothing, something that has to be used by every one of us every day in the year. How often have I been discouraged as I have gone through the South, and into the homes of the people of my race, and have found women who could converse intelligently upon abstruse subjects, and yet could not tell how to improve the condition of the poorly cooked and still more poorly served bread and meat which they and their families were eating three times a day. It is discouraging to find a girl who can tell you the geographical location of any country on the globe and who does not know where to place the dishes upon a common dinner table. It is discouraging to find a woman who knows much about theoretical chemistry, and who cannot properly wash and iron a shirt.

In what I say here I would not by any means have it understood that I would limit or circumscribe the mental development of the Negro-student. No race can be lifted until its mind is awakened and strengthened. By the side of industrial training should always go mental and moral training, but the pushing of mere abstract knowledge into the head means little. We want more than the mere performance of mental gymnastics. Our knowledge must be harnessed to the things of real life. I would encourage the Negro to secure all the mental strength, all the mental culture--whether gleaned from science, mathematics, history, language or literature that his circumstances will allow, but I believe most earnestly that for years to come the education of the people of my race should be so directed that the greatest proportion of the mental strength of the masses will be brought to bear upon the every-day practical things of life, upon something that is needed to be done, and something which they will be permitted to do in the community in which they reside. And just the same with the professional class which the race needs and must have, I would say give the men and women of that class, too, the training which will best fit them to perform in the most successful manner the service which the race demands.

I would not confine the race to industrial life, not even to agriculture, for example, although I believe that by far the greater part of the Negro race is best off in the country districts and must and should continue to live there, but I would teach the race that in industry the foundation must be laid--that the very best service which any one can render to what is called the higher education is to teach the present generation to provide a material or industrial foundation. On such a foundation as this will grow habits of thrift, a love of work, economy, ownership of property, bank accounts. Out of it in the future will grow practical education, professional education, positions of public responsibility. Out of it will grow moral and religious strength. Out of it will grow wealth from which alone can come leisure and the opportunity for the enjoyment of literature and the fine arts.

In the words of the late beloved Frederick Douglass: "Every blow of the sledge hammer wielded by a sable arm is a powerful blow in support of our cause. Every colored mechanic is by virtue of circumstances an elevator of his race. Every house built by a black man is a strong tower against the allied hosts of prejudice. It is impossible for us to attach too much importance to this aspect of the subject. Without industrial development there can be no wealth; without wealth there can be no leisure; without leisure no opportunity for thoughtful reflection and the cultivation of the higher arts."

I would set no limits to the attainments of the Negro in arts, in letters or statesmanship, but I believe the surest way to reach those ends is by laying the foundation in the little things of life that lie immediately about one's door. I plead for industrial education and development for the Negro not because I want to

[16]

cramp him, but because I want to free him. I want to see him enter the all-powerful business and commercial world.

It was such combined mental, moral and industrial education which the late General Armstrong set out to give at the Hampton Institute when he established that school thirty years ago. The Hampton Institute has continued along the lines laid down by its great founder, and now each year an increasing number of similar schools are being established in the South, for the people of both races.

Early in the history of the Tuskegee Institute we began to combine industrial training with mental and moral culture. Our first efforts were in the direction of agriculture, and we began teaching this with no appliances except one hoe and a blind mule. From this small beginning we have grown until now the Institute owns two thousand acres of land, eight hundred of which are cultivated each year by the young men of the school. We began teaching wheelwrighting and blacksmithing in a small way to the men, and laundry work, cooking and sewing and housekeeping to the young women. The fourteen hundred and over young men and women who attended the school during the last school year received instruction--in addition to academic and religious training--in thirty-three trades and industries, including carpentry, blacksmithing, printing, wheelwrighting harnessmaking, painting, machinery, founding, shoemaking, brickmasonry and brickmaking, plastering, sawmilling, tinsmithing, tailoring, mechanical and architectural drawing, electrical and steam engineering, canning, sewing, dressmaking, millinery, cooking, laundering, housekeeping, mattress making, basketry, nursing, agriculture, dairying and stock raising, horticulture.

Not only do the students receive instruction in these trades, but they do actual work, by means of which more than half of them pay some part or all of their expenses while remaining at the school. Of the sixty buildings belonging to the school all but four were almost wholly erected by the students as a part of their industrial education. Even the bricks which go into the walls are made by students in the school's brick yard, in which, last year, they manufactured two million bricks.

When we first began this work at Tuskegee, and the idea got spread among the people of my race that the students who came to the Tuskegee school were to be taught industries in connection with their academic studies, were, in other words, to be taught to work, I received a great many verbal messages and letters from parents informing me that they wanted their children taught books, but not how to work. This protest went on for three or four years, but I am glad to be able to say now that our people have very generally been educated to a point where they see their own needs and conditions so clearly that it has been several years since we have had a single protest from parents against the teaching of industries, and there is now a positive enthusiasm for it. In fact, public sentiment among the students at Tuskegee is now so strong for industrial training that it would hardly permit a student to remain on the grounds who was unwilling to labor.

It seems to me that too often mere book education leaves the Negro young man or woman in a weak position. For example, I have seen a Negro girl taught by her mother to help her in doing laundry work at home. Later, when this same girl was graduated from the public schools or a high school and returned home she finds herself educated out of sympathy with laundry work, and yet not able to find anything to do which seems in keeping with the cost and character of her education. Under these circumstances we cannot be surprised if she does not fulfill the expectations made for her. What should have been done for her, it seems to me, was to give her along with her academic education thorough training in the latest and best methods of laundry work, so that she could have put so much skill and intelligence into it that the work would have been lifted out from the plane of drudgery[2]. The home which she would then have been able to found by the results of her work would have enabled her to help her children to take a still more responsible position in life.

Almost from the first Tuskegee has kept in mind--and this I think should be the policy of all industrial schools--fitting students for occupations which would be open to them in their home communities. Some years ago we noted the fact that there was beginning to be a demand in the South for men to operate dairies in a skillful, modern manner. We opened a dairy department in connection with the school, where a number of young men could have instruction in the latest and most scientific methods of dairy work. At present we have calls--mainly from Southern white men--for twice as many dairymen as we are able to supply. What is equally satisfactory, the reports which come to us indicate that our young men are giving the highest satisfaction and are fast changing and improving the dairy product in the communities into which they go. I use the dairy here as an example. What I have said of this is equally true of many of the other industries which we teach. Aside from the economic value of this work I cannot but believe, and my observation confirms me in my belief, that as we continue to place Negro men and women of intelligence, religion, modesty, conscience and skill in every community in the South, who will prove

---

[2] In the original, this was 'drudggery'.

by actual results their value to the community, I cannot but believe, I say, that this will constitute a solution to many of the present political and social difficulties.

Many seem to think that industrial education is meant to make the Negro work as he worked in the days of slavery. This is far from my conception of industrial education. If this training is worth anything to the Negro, it consists in teaching him how not to work, but how to make the forces of nature--air, steam, water, horse-power and electricity--work for him. If it has any value it is in lifting labor up out of toil and drudgery into the plane of the dignified and the beautiful. The Negro in the South works and works hard; but too often his ignorance and lack of skill causes him to do his work in the most costly and shiftless manner, and this keeps him near the bottom of the ladder in the economic world.

I have not emphasized particularly in these pages the great need of training the Negro in agriculture, but I believe that this branch of industrial education does need very great emphasis. In this connection I want to quote some words which Mr. Edgar Gardner Murphy, of Montgomery, Alabama, has recently written upon this subject:

"We must incorporate into our public school system a larger recognition of the practical and industrial elements in educational training. Ours is an agricultural population. The school must be brought more closely to the soil. The teaching of history, for example, is all very well, but nobody can really know anything of history unless he has been taught to see things grow--has so seen things not only with the outward eye, but with the eyes of his intelligence and conscience. The actual things of the present are more important, however, than the institutions of the past. Even to young children can be shown the simpler conditions and processes of growth--how corn is put into the ground--how cotton and potatoes should be planted--how to choose the soil best adapted to a particular plant, how to improve that soil, how to care for the plant while it grows, how to get the most value out of it, how to use the elements of waste for the fertilization of other crops; how, through the alternation of crops, the land may be made to increase the annual value of its products--these things, upon their elementary side are absolutely vital to the worth and success of hundreds of thousands of these people of the Negro race, and yet our whole educational system has practically ignored them.

* * * * *

"Such work will mean not only an education in agriculture, but an education through agriculture and education, through natural symbols and practical forms, which will educate as deeply, as broadly and as truly as any other system which

[19]

the world has known. Such changes will bring far larger results than the mere improvement of our Negroes. They will give us an agricultural class, a class of tenants or small land owners, trained not away from the soil, but in relation to the soil and in intelligent dependence upon its resources."

I close, then, as I began, by saying that as a slave the Negro was worked, and that as a freeman he must learn to work. There is still doubt in many quarters as to the ability of the Negro unguided, unsupported, to hew his own path and put into visible, tangible, indisputable form, products and signs of civilization. This doubt cannot be much affected by abstract arguments, no matter how delicately and convincingly woven together. Patiently, quietly, doggedly, persistently, through summer and winter, sunshine and shadow, by self-sacrifice, by foresight, by honesty and industry, we must re-enforce argument with results. One farm bought, one house built, one home sweetly and intelligently kept, one man who is the largest tax payer or has the largest bank account, one school or church maintained, one factory running successfully, one truck garden profitably cultivated, one patient cured by a Negro doctor, one sermon well preached, one office well filled, one life cleanly lived--these will tell more in our favor than all the abstract eloquence that can be summoned to plead our cause. Our pathway must be up through the soil, up through swamps, up through forests, up through the streams, the rocks, up through commerce, education and religion!

The Talented Tenth

By PROF. W.E. BURGHARDT DuBOIS

A strong plea for the higher education of the Negro, which those who are interested in the future of the freedmen cannot afford to ignore. Prof. DuBois produces ample evidence to prove conclusively the truth of his statement that "to attempt to establish any sort of a system of common and industrial school training, without *first* providing for the higher training of the very best teachers, is simply throwing your money to the winds."

The Negro race, like all races, is going to be saved by its exceptional men. The problem of education, then, among Negroes must first of all deal with the Talented Tenth; it is the problem of developing the Best of this race that they may guide the Mass away from the contamination and death of the Worst, in their own and other races. Now the training of men is a difficult and intricate task. Its technique is a matter for educational experts, but its object is for the vision of seers. If we make money the object of man-training, we shall develop money-makers but not necessarily men; if we make technical skill the object of education, we may possess artisans but not, in nature, men. Men we shall have only as we make manhood the object of the work of the schools--intelligence, broad sympathy, knowledge of the world that was and is, and of the relation of men to it--this is the curriculum of that Higher Education which must underlie true life. On this foundation we may build bread winning, skill of hand and quickness of brain, with never a fear lest the child and man mistake the means of living for the object of life.

* * * * *

If this be true--and who can deny it--three tasks lay before me; first to show from the past that the Talented Tenth as they have risen among American Negroes have been worthy of leadership; secondly, to show how these men may be educated and developed; and thirdly, to show their relation to the Negro problem.

* * * * *

You misjudge us because you do not know us. From the very first it has been the educated and intelligent of the Negro people that have led and elevated the mass, and the sole obstacles that nullified and retarded their efforts were slavery and race prejudice; for what is slavery but the legalized survival of the unfit and the nullification of the work of natural internal leadership? Negro leadership, therefore, sought from the first to rid the race of this awful incubus that it might make way for natural selection and the survival of the fittest. In colonial days came Phillis Wheatley and Paul Cuffe striving against the bars of prejudice; and Benjamin Banneker, the almanac maker, voiced their longings when he said to Thomas Jefferson, "I freely and cheerfully acknowledge that I am of the African race, and in colour which is natural to them, of the deepest dye; and it is under a sense of the most profound gratitude to the Supreme Ruler of the Universe, that I now confess to you that I am not under that state of tyrannical thraldom and inhuman captivity to which too many of my brethren are doomed, but that I have abundantly tasted of the fruition of those blessings which proceed from that free and unequalled liberty with which you are favored, and which I hope you will willingly allow, you have mercifully received from the immediate hand of that Being from whom proceedeth every good and perfect gift.

"Suffer me to recall to your mind that time, in which the arms of the British crown were exerted with every powerful effort, in order to reduce you to a state of servitude; look back, I entreat you, on the variety of dangers to which you were exposed; reflect on that period in which every human aid appeared unavailable, and in which even hope and fortitude wore the aspect of inability to the conflict, and you cannot but be led to a serious and grateful sense of your miraculous and providential preservation, you cannot but acknowledge, that the present freedom and tranquility which you enjoy, you have mercifully received, and that a peculiar blessing of heaven.

"This, sir, was a time when you clearly saw into the injustice of a state of Slavery, and in which you had just apprehensions of the horrors of its condition. It was then that your abhorrence thereof was so excited, that you publicly held forth this true and invaluable doctrine, which is worthy to be recorded and remembered in all succeeding ages: 'We hold these truths to be self evident, that all men are created equal; that they are endowed with certain inalienable rights, and that among these are life, liberty and the pursuit of happiness.'"

Then came Dr. James Derham, who could tell even the learned Dr. Rush something of medicine, and Lemuel Haynes, to whom Middlebury College gave an honorary A.M. in 1804. These and others we may call the Revolutionary group of distinguished Negroes--they were persons of marked ability, leaders of a Talented Tenth, standing conspicuously among the best of their time. They strove by word and deed to save the color line from becoming the line between the bond and free, but all they could do was nullified by Eli Whitney and the Curse of Gold. So they passed into forgetfulness.

[22]

But their spirit did not wholly die; here and there in the early part of the century came other exceptional men. Some were natural sons of unnatural fathers and were given often a liberal training and thus a race of educated mulattoes sprang up to plead for black men's rights. There was Ira Aldridge, whom all Europe loved to honor; there was that Voice crying in the Wilderness, David Walker, and saying:

"I declare it does appear to me as though some nations think God is asleep, or that he made the Africans for nothing else but to dig their mines and work their farms, or they cannot believe history, sacred or profane. I ask every man who has a heart, and is blessed with the privilege of believing--Is not God a God of justice to all his creatures? Do you say he is? Then if he gives peace and tranquility to tyrants and permits them to keep our fathers, our mothers, ourselves and our children in eternal ignorance and wretchedness to support them and their families, would he be to us a God of Justice? I ask, O, ye Christians, who hold us and our children in the most abject ignorance and degradation that ever a people were afflicted with since the world began--I say if God gives you peace and tranquility, and suffers you thus to go on afflicting us, and our children, who have never given you the least provocation--would He be to us a God of Justice? If you will allow that we are men, who feel for each other, does not the blood of our fathers and of us, their children, cry aloud to the Lord of Sabaoth against you for the cruelties and murders with which you have and do continue to afflict us?"

This was the wild voice that first aroused Southern legislators in 1829 to the terrors of abolitionism.

In 1831 there met that first Negro convention in Philadelphia, at which the world gaped curiously but which bravely attacked the problems of race and slavery, crying out against persecution and declaring that "Laws as cruel in themselves as they were unconstitutional and unjust, have in many places been enacted against our poor, unfriended and unoffending brethren (without a shadow of provocation on our part), at whose bare recital the very savage draws himself up for fear of contagion--looks noble and prides himself because he bears not the name of Christian." Side by side this free Negro movement, and the movement for abolition, strove until they merged into one strong stream. Too little notice has been taken of the work which the Talented Tenth among Negroes took in the great abolition crusade. From the very day that a Philadelphia colored man became the first subscriber to Garrison's "Liberator," to the day when Negro soldiers made the Emancipation Proclamation possible, black leaders worked shoulder to shoulder with white men in a movement, the success of which would have been impossible without them. There was Purvis

[23]

and Remond, Pennington and Highland Garnett, Sojourner Truth and Alexander Crummel, and above all, Frederick Douglass--what would the abolition movement have been without them? They stood as living examples of the possibilities of the Negro race, their own hard experiences and well wrought culture said silently more than all the drawn periods of orators--they were the men who made American slavery impossible. As Maria Weston Chapman once said, from the school of anti-slavery agitation "a throng of authors, editors, lawyers, orators and accomplished gentlemen of color have taken their degree! It has equally implanted hopes and aspirations, noble thoughts, and sublime purposes, in the hearts of both races. It has prepared the white man for the freedom of the black man, and it has made the black man scorn the thought of enslavement, as does a white man, as far as its influence has extended. Strengthen that noble influence! Before its organization, the country only saw here and there in slavery some faithful Cudjoe or Dinah, whose strong natures blossomed even in bondage, like a fine plant beneath a heavy stone. Now, under the elevating and cherishing influence of the American Anti-slavery Society, the colored race, like the white, furnishes Corinthian capitals for the noblest temples."

Where were these black abolitionists trained? Some, like Frederick Douglass, were self-trained, but yet trained liberally; others, like Alexander Crummell and McCune Smith, graduated from famous foreign universities. Most of them rose up through the colored schools of New York and Philadelphia and Boston, taught by college-bred men like Russworm, of Dartmouth, and college-bred white men like Neau and Benezet.

After emancipation came a new group of educated and gifted leaders: Langston, Bruce and Elliot, Greener, Williams and Payne. Through political organization, historical and polemic writing and moral regeneration, these men strove to uplift their people. It is the fashion of to-day to sneer at them and to say that with freedom Negro leadership should have begun at the plow and not in the Senate--a foolish and mischievous lie; two hundred and fifty years that black serf toiled at the plow and yet that toiling was in vain till the Senate passed the war amendments; and two hundred and fifty years more the half-free serf of to-day may toil at his plow, but unless he have political rights and righteously guarded civic status, he will still remain the poverty-stricken and ignorant plaything of rascals, that he now is. This all sane men know even if they dare not say it.

And so we come to the present--a day of cowardice and vacillation, of strident wide-voiced wrong and faint hearted compromise; of double-faced dallying with Truth and Right. Who are to-day guiding the work of the Negro people? The

[24]

"exceptions" of course. And yet so sure as this Talented Tenth is pointed out, the blind worshippers of the Average cry out in alarm: "These are exceptions, look here at death, disease and crime--these are the happy rule." Of course they are the rule, because a silly nation made them the rule: Because for three long centuries this people lynched Negroes who dared to be brave, raped black women who dared to be virtuous, crushed dark-hued youth who dared to be ambitious, and encouraged and made to flourish servility and lewdness and apathy. But not even this was able to crush all manhood and chastity and aspiration from black folk. A saving remnant continually survives and persists, continually aspires, continually shows itself in thrift and ability and character. Exceptional it is to be sure, but this is its chiefest promise; it shows the capability of Negro blood, the promise of black men. Do Americans ever stop to reflect that there are in this land a million men of Negro blood, well-educated, owners of homes, against the honor of whose womanhood no breath was ever raised, whose men occupy positions of trust and usefulness, and who, judged by any standard, have reached the full measure of the best type of modern European culture? Is it fair, is it decent, is it Christian to ignore these facts of the Negro problem, to belittle such aspiration, to nullify such leadership and seek to crush these people back into the mass out of which by toil and travail, they and their fathers have raised themselves?

Can the masses of the Negro people be in any possible way more quickly raised than by the effort and example of this aristocracy of talent and character? Was there ever a nation on God's fair earth civilized from the bottom upward? Never; it is, ever was and ever will be from the top downward that culture filters. The Talented Tenth rises and pulls all that are worth the saving up to their vantage ground. This is the history of human progress; and the two historic mistakes which have hindered that progress were the thinking first that no more could ever rise save the few already risen; or second, that it would better the unrisen to pull the risen down.

How then shall the leaders of a struggling people be trained and the hands of the risen few strengthened? There can be but one answer: The best and most capable of their youth must be schooled in the colleges and universities of the land. We will not quarrel as to just what the university of the Negro should teach or how it should teach it--I willingly admit that each soul and each race-soul needs its own peculiar curriculum. But this is true: A university is a human invention for the transmission of knowledge and culture from generation to generation, through the training of quick minds and pure hearts, and for this work no other human invention will suffice, not even trade and industrial schools.

[25]

All men cannot go to college but some men must; every isolated group or nation must have its yeast, must have for the talented few centers of training where men are not so mystified and befuddled by the hard and necessary toil of earning a living, as to have no aims higher than their bellies, and no God greater than Gold. This is true training, and thus in the beginning were the favored sons of the freedmen trained. Out of the colleges of the North came, after the blood of war, Ware, Cravath, Chase, Andrews, Bumstead and Spence to build the foundations of knowledge and civilization in the black South. Where ought they to have begun to build? At the bottom, of course, quibbles the mole with his eyes in the earth. Aye! truly at the bottom, at the very bottom; at the bottom of knowledge, down in the very depths of knowledge there where the roots of justice strike into the lowest soil of Truth. And so they did begin; they founded colleges, and up from the colleges shot normal schools, and out from the normal schools went teachers, and around the normal teachers clustered other teachers to teach the public schools; the college trained in Greek and Latin and mathematics, 2,000 men; and these men trained full 50,000 others in morals and manners, and they in turn taught thrift and the alphabet to nine millions of men, who to-day hold $300,000,000 of property. It was a miracle--the most wonderful peace-battle of the 19th century, and yet to-day men smile at it, and in fine superiority tell us that it was all a strange mistake; that a proper way to found a system of education is first to gather the children and buy them spelling books and hoes; afterward men may look about for teachers, if haply they may find them; or again they would teach men Work, but as for Life--why, what has Work to do with Life, they ask vacantly.

Was the work of these college founders successful; did it stand the test of time? Did the college graduates, with all their fine theories of life, really live? Are they useful men helping to civilize and elevate their less fortunate fellows? Let us see. Omitting all institutions which have not actually graduated students from a college course, there are to-day in the United States thirty-four institutions giving something above high school training to Negroes and designed especially for this race.

Three of these were established in border States before the War; thirteen were planted by the Freedmen's Bureau in the years 1864-1869; nine were established between 1870 and 1880 by various church bodies; five were established after 1881 by Negro churches, and four are state institutions supported by United States' agricultural funds. In most cases the college departments are small adjuncts to high and common school work. As a matter of fact six institutions--Atlanta, Fisk, Howard, Shaw, Wilberforce and Leland, are the important Negro colleges so far as actual work and number of students are concerned. In all these institutions, seven hundred and fifty Negro college students are enrolled. In grade the best of these colleges are about a year behind the smaller New England colleges and a typical curriculum is that of Atlanta University. Here students from the grammar grades, after a three years' high school course, take a college course of 136 weeks. One-fourth of this time is given to Latin and Greek; one-fifth, to English and modern languages; one-sixth, to history and social science; one-seventh, to natural science; one-eighth to mathematics, and one-eighth to philosophy and pedagogy.

In addition to these students in the South, Negroes have attended Northern colleges for many years. As early as 1826 one was graduated from Bowdoin College, and from that time till to-day nearly every year has seen elsewhere, other such graduates. They have, of course, met much color prejudice. Fifty years ago very few colleges would admit them at all. Even to-day no Negro has ever been admitted to Princeton, and at some other leading institutions they are rather endured than encouraged. Oberlin was the great pioneer in the work of blotting out the color line in colleges, and has more Negro graduates by far than any other Northern college.

The total number of Negro college graduates up to 1899, (several of the graduates of that year not being reported), was as follows:

	Negro Colleges	White Colleges
Before '76	137	75
'75-80	143	22
'80-85	250	31
'85-90	413	43
'90-95	465	66
'96-99	475	88
Class Unknown	57	64
Total	1,914	390

Of these graduates 2,079 were men and 252 were women; 50 per cent. of Northern-born college men come South to work among the masses of their people, at a sacrifice which few people realize; nearly 90 per cent. of the Southern-born graduates instead of seeking that personal freedom and broader intellectual atmosphere which their training has led them, in some degree, to conceive, stay and labor and wait in the midst of their black neighbors and

[27]

relatives.

The most interesting question, and in many respects the crucial question, to be asked concerning college-bred Negroes, is: Do they earn a living? It has been intimated more than once that the higher training of Negroes has resulted in sending into the world of work, men who could find nothing to do suitable to their talents. Now and then there comes a rumor of a colored college man working at menial service, etc. Fortunately, returns as to occupations of college-bred Negroes, gathered by the Atlanta conference, are quite full--nearly sixty per cent. of the total number of graduates.

This enables us to reach fairly certain conclusions as to the occupations of all college-bred Negroes. Of 1,312 persons reported, there were:

Teachers	53.4%
Clergymen	16.8%
Physicians, etc.	6.3%
Students	5.6%
Lawyers	4.7%
In Govt. Service	4.0%
In Business	3.6%
Farmers and Artisans	2.7%
Editors, Secretaries and Clerks	2.4%
Miscellaneous	0.5%

Over half are teachers, a sixth are preachers, another sixth are students and professional men; over 6 per cent. are farmers, artisans and merchants, and 4 per cent. are in government service. In detail the occupations are as follows:

Occupations of College-Bred Men.

Teachers:

Presidents and Deans: 19

Teacher of Music: 7

Professors, Principals and Teachers: 675   Total 701

Clergymen:

    Bishop: 1

    Chaplains U.S. Army: 2

    Missionaries: 9

    Presiding Elders: 12

    Preachers: 197   Total 221

Physicians etc.:

    Doctors of Medicine: 76

    Druggists: 4

    Dentists: 3   Total 83

Students: 74

Lawyers: 62

Civil Service:

    U.S. Minister Plenipotentiary: 1

    U.S. Consul: 1

    U.S. Deputy Collector: 1

    U.S. Gauger: 1

    U.S. Postmasters: 2

    U.S. Clerks: 44

    State Civil Service: 2

    City Civil Service: 1   Total 53

Business Men:

    Merchants, etc.: 30

    Managers: 13

    Real Estate Dealers: 4   Total 47

Farmers: 26

Clerks and Secretaries:

    Secretary of National Societies: 7

    Clerks etc.: 15   Total 22

Artisans: 9

Editors: 9

Miscellaneous: 5

These figures illustrate vividly the function of the college-bred Negro. He is, as he ought to be, the group leader, the man who sets the ideals of the community where he lives, directs its thoughts and heads its social movements. It need hardly be argued that the Negro people need social leadership more than most groups; that they have no traditions to fall back upon, no long established customs, no strong family ties, no well defined social classes. All these things must be slowly and painfully evolved. The preacher was, even before the war, the group leader of the Negroes, and the church their greatest social institution. Naturally this preacher was ignorant and often immoral, and the problem of replacing the older type by better educated men has been a difficult one. Both by direct work and by direct influence on other preachers, and on congregations, the college-bred preacher has an opportunity for reformatory work and moral inspiration, the value of which cannot be overestimated.

It has, however, been in the furnishing of teachers that the Negro college has found its peculiar function. Few persons realize how vast a work, how mighty a revolution has been thus accomplished. To furnish five millions and more of ignorant people with teachers of their own race and blood, in one generation, was not only a very difficult undertaking, but a very important one, in that, it placed before the eyes of almost every Negro child an attainable ideal. It brought the masses of the blacks in contact with modern civilization, made black men the leaders of their communities and trainers of the new generation. In this work college-bred Negroes were first teachers, and then teachers of teachers. And here it is that the broad culture of college work has been of peculiar value. Knowledge of life and its wider meaning, has been the point of the Negro's deepest ignorance, and the sending out of teachers whose training has not been simply for bread winning, but also for human culture, has been of inestimable value in the training of these men.

In earlier years the two occupations of preacher and teacher were practically the only ones open to the black college graduate. Of later years a larger diversity of life among his people, has opened new avenues of employment. Nor have these college men been paupers and spendthrifts; 557 college-bred Negroes owned in 1899, $1,342,862.50 worth of real estate, (assessed value) or $2,411 per family. The real value of the total accumulations of the whole group is perhaps about $10,000,000, or $5,000 a piece. Pitiful, is it not, beside the fortunes of oil kings and steel trusts, but after all is the fortune of the millionaire the only stamp of true and successful living? Alas! it is, with many, and there's the rub.

The problem of training the Negro is to-day immensely complicated by the fact that the whole question of the efficiency and appropriateness of our present systems of education, for any kind of child, is a matter of active debate, in which final settlement seems still afar off. Consequently it often happens that persons arguing for or against certain systems of education for Negroes, have these controversies in mind and miss the real question at issue. The main question, so far as the Southern Negro is concerned, is: What under the present circumstance, must a system of education do in order to raise the Negro as quickly as possible in the scale of civilization? The answer to this question seems to me clear: It must strengthen the Negro's character, increase his knowledge and teach him to earn a living. Now it goes without saying, that it is hard to do all these things simultaneously or suddenly, and that at the same time it will not do to give all the attention to one and neglect the others; we could give black boys trades, but that alone will not civilize a race of ex-slaves; we might simply increase their knowledge of the world, but this would not necessarily make them wish to use this knowledge honestly; we might seek to strengthen character and purpose, but to what end if this people have nothing to eat or to wear? A system of education is not one thing, nor does it have a single definite object, nor is it a mere matter of schools. Education is that whole system of human training within and without the school house walls, which molds and develops men. If then we start out to train an ignorant and unskilled people with a heritage of bad habits, our system of training must set before itself two great aims--the one dealing with knowledge and character, the other part seeking to give the child the technical knowledge necessary for him to earn a living under the present circumstances. These objects are accomplished in part by the opening of the common schools on the one, and of the industrial schools on the other. But only in part, for there must also be trained those who are to teach these schools--men and women of knowledge and culture and technical skill who understand modern civilization, and have the training and aptitude to impart it to the children under them. There must be teachers, and teachers of teachers, and to attempt to establish any sort of a system of common and industrial school training, without *first* (and I say *first* advisedly) without *first* providing for the higher training of the very best teachers, is simply throwing your money to the winds. School houses do not teach themselves--piles of brick and mortar and machinery do not send out *men*. It is the trained, living human soul, cultivated and strengthened by long study and thought, that breathes the real breath of life into boys and girls and makes them human, whether they be black or white, Greek, Russian or American. Nothing, in these latter days, has so dampened the faith of thinking Negroes in recent educational movements, as the fact that such movements have been accompanied by ridicule and denouncement and decrying of those very institutions of higher training which made the Negro public school possible, and make Negro industrial schools thinkable. It was Fisk, Atlanta, Howard and Straight, those colleges born of the faith and sacrifice of the abolitionists, that placed in the black schools of the South the 30,000 teachers and more, which some, who depreciate the work of these higher schools, are using to teach their own new experiments. If Hampton, Tuskegee and the hundred other industrial schools prove in the future to be as successful as they deserve to be, then their success in training black artisans for the South, will be due primarily to the white colleges of the North and the black colleges of the South, which trained the teachers who to-day conduct these institutions. There was a time when the American people believed pretty devoutly that a log of wood with a boy at one end and Mark Hopkins at the other, represented the highest ideal of human training. But in these eager days it would seem that we have changed all that and think it necessary to add a couple of saw-mills and a hammer to this outfit, and, at a pinch, to dispense with the services of Mark Hopkins.

I would not deny, or for a moment seem to deny, the paramount necessity of teaching the Negro to work, and to work steadily and skillfully; or seem to depreciate in the slightest degree the important part industrial schools must play in the accomplishment of these ends, but I *do* say, and insist upon it, that it is industrialism drunk with its vision of success, to imagine that its own work can be accomplished without providing for the training of broadly cultured men and women to teach its own teachers, and to teach the teachers of the public schools.

But I have already said that human education is not simply a matter of schools; it is much more a matter of family and group life--the training of one's home, of one's daily companions, of one's social class. Now the black boy of the South moves in a black world--a world with its own leaders, its own thoughts, its own ideals. In this world he gets by far the larger part of his life training, and through the eyes of this dark world he peers into the veiled world beyond. Who guides and determines the education which he receives in his world? His teachers here are the group-leaders of the Negro people--the physicians and clergymen, the trained fathers and mothers, the influential and forceful men about him of all kinds; here it is, if at all, that the culture of the surrounding world trickles through and is handed on by the graduates of the higher schools. Can such culture training of group leaders be neglected? Can we afford to ignore it? Do you think that if the leaders of thought among Negroes are not trained and educated thinkers, that they will have no leaders? On the contrary a hundred half-trained demagogues will still hold the places they so largely occupy now, and hundreds of vociferous busy-bodies will multiply. You have no choice; either you must help furnish this race from within its own ranks with thoughtful men of trained leadership, or you must suffer the evil consequences of a headless misguided rabble.

I am an earnest advocate of manual training and trade teaching for black boys, and for white boys, too. I believe that next to the founding of Negro colleges the most valuable addition to Negro education since the war, has been industrial training for black boys. Nevertheless, I insist that the object of all true education is not to make men carpenters, it is to make carpenters men; there are two means of making the carpenter a man, each equally important: the first is to give the group and community in which he works, liberally trained teachers and leaders to teach him and his family what life means; the second is to give him sufficient intelligence and technical skill to make him an efficient workman; the first object demands the Negro college and college-bred men--not a quantity of such colleges, but a few of excellent quality; not too many college-bred men, but enough to leaven the lump, to inspire the masses, to raise the Talented Tenth to leadership; the second object demands a good system of common schools, well-taught, conveniently located and properly equipped.

The Sixth Atlanta Conference truly said in 1901:

"We call the attention of the Nation to the fact that less than one million of the three million Negro children of school age, are at present regularly attending school, and these attend a session which lasts only a few months.

"We are to-day deliberately rearing millions of our citizens in ignorance, and at the same time limiting the rights of citizenship by educational qualifications. This is unjust. Half the black youth of the land have no opportunities open to them for learning to read, write and cipher. In the discussion as to the proper training of Negro children after they leave the public schools, we have forgotten that they are not yet decently provided with public schools.

"Propositions are beginning to be made in the South to reduce the already meagre school facilities of Negroes. We congratulate the South on resisting, as much as it has, this pressure, and on the many millions it has spent on Negro education. But it is only fair to point out that Negro taxes and the Negroes' share of the income from indirect taxes and endowments have fully repaid this expenditure, so that the Negro public school system has not in all probability cost the white taxpayers a single cent since the war.

"This is not fair. Negro schools should be a public burden, since they are a public benefit. The Negro has a right to demand good common school training at the hands of the States and the Nation since by their fault he is not in position to pay for this himself."

What is the chief need for the building up of the Negro public school in the South? The Negro race in the South needs teachers to-day above all else. This is the concurrent testimony of all who know the situation. For the supply of this great demand two things are needed--institutions of higher education and money for school houses and salaries. It is usually assumed that a hundred or more institutions for Negro training are to-day turning out so many teachers and college-bred men that the race is threatened with an over-supply. This is sheer nonsense. There are to-day less than 3,000 living Negro college graduates in the United States, and less than 1,000 Negroes in college. Moreover, in the 164 schools for Negroes, 95 per cent. of their students are doing elementary and secondary work, work which should be done in the public schools. Over half the remaining 2,157 students are taking high school studies. The mass of so-called "normal" schools for the Negro, are simply doing elementary common school work, or, at most, high school work, with a little instruction in methods. The Negro colleges and the post-graduate courses at other institutions are the only

[34]

agencies for the broader and more careful training of teachers. The work of these institutions is hampered for lack of funds. It is getting increasingly difficult to get funds for training teachers in the best modern methods, and yet all over the South, from State Superintendents, county officials, city boards and school principals comes the wail, "We need TEACHERS!" and teachers must be trained. As the fairest minded of all white Southerners, Atticus G. Haygood, once said: "The defects of colored teachers are so great as to create an urgent necessity for training better ones. Their excellencies and their successes are sufficient to justify the best hopes of success in the effort, and to vindicate the judgment of those who make large investments of money and service, to give to colored students opportunity for thoroughly preparing themselves for the work of teaching children of their people."

The truth of this has been strikingly shown in the marked improvement of white teachers in the South. Twenty years ago the rank and file of white public school teachers were not as good as the Negro teachers. But they, by scholarships and good salaries, have been encouraged to thorough normal and collegiate preparation, while the Negro teachers have been discouraged by starvation wages and the idea that any training will do for a black teacher. If carpenters are needed it is well and good to train men as carpenters. But to train men as carpenters, and then set them to teaching is wasteful and criminal; and to train men as teachers and then refuse them living wages, unless they become carpenters, is rank nonsense.

The United States Commissioner of Education says in his report for 1900: "For comparison between the white and colored enrollment in secondary and higher education, I have added together the enrollment in high schools and secondary schools, with the attendance on colleges and universities, not being sure of the actual grade of work done in the colleges and universities. The work done in the secondary schools is reported in such detail in this office, that there can be no doubt of its grade."

He then makes the following comparisons of persons in every million enrolled in secondary and higher education:

	Whole Country	Negroes
1880	4,362	1,289
1900	10,743	2,061

And he concludes: "While the number in colored high schools and colleges had increased somewhat faster than the population, it had not kept pace with the average of the whole country, for it had fallen from 30 per cent. to 24 per cent. of the average quota. Of all colored pupils, one (1) in one hundred was engaged in secondary and higher work, and that ratio has continued substantially for the past twenty years. If the ratio of colored population in secondary and higher education is to be equal to the average for the whole country, it must be increased to five times its present average." And if this be true of the secondary and higher education, it is safe to say that the Negro has not one-tenth his quota in college studies. How baseless, therefore, is the charge of too much training! We need Negro teachers for the Negro common schools, and we need first-class normal schools and colleges to train them. This is the work of higher Negro education and it must be done.

Further than this, after being provided with group leaders of civilization, and a foundation of intelligence in the public schools, the carpenter, in order to be a man, needs technical skill. This calls for trade schools. Now trade schools are not nearly such simple things as people once thought. The original idea was that the "Industrial" school was to furnish education, practically free, to those willing to work for it; it was to "do" things--i.e.: become a center of productive industry, it was to be partially, if not wholly, self-supporting, and it was to teach trades. Admirable as were some of the ideas underlying this scheme, the whole thing simply would not work in practice; it was found that if you were to use time and material to teach trades thoroughly, you could not at the same time keep the industries on a commercial basis and make them pay. Many schools started out to do this on a large scale and went into virtual bankruptcy. Moreover, it was found also that it was possible to teach a boy a trade mechanically, without giving him the full educative benefit of the process, and, viceversa, that there was a distinctive educative value in teaching a boy to use his hands and eyes in carrying out certain physical processes, even though he did not actually learn a trade. It has happened, therefore, in the last decade, that a noticeable change has come over the industrial schools. In the first place the idea of commercially remunerative industry in a school is being pushed rapidly to the back-ground. There are still schools with shops and farms that bring an income, and schools that use student labor partially for the erection of their buildings and the furnishing of equipment. It is coming to be seen, however, in the education of the Negro, as clearly as it has been seen in the education of the youths the world over, that it is the *boy* and not the material product, that is the true object of education. Consequently the object of the industrial school came to be the thorough training of boys regardless of the cost of the training, so long as it was

[36]

thoroughly well done.

Even at this point, however, the difficulties were not surmounted. In the first place modern industry has taken great strides since the war, and the teaching of trades is no longer a simple matter. Machinery and long processes of work have greatly changed the work of the carpenter, the ironworker and the shoemaker. A really efficient workman must be to-day an intelligent man who has had good technical training in addition to thorough common school, and perhaps even higher training. To meet this situation the industrial schools began a further development; they established distinct Trade Schools for the thorough training of better class artisans, and at the same time they sought to preserve for the purposes of general education, such of the simpler processes of elementary trade learning as were best suited therefor. In this differentiation of the Trade School and manual training, the best of the industrial schools simply followed the plain trend of the present educational epoch. A prominent educator tells us that, in Sweden, "In the beginning the economic conception was generally adopted, and everywhere manual training was looked upon as a means of preparing the children of the common people to earn their living. But gradually it came to be recognized that manual training has a more elevated purpose, and one, indeed, more useful in the deeper meaning of the term. It came to be considered as an educative process for the complete moral, physical and intellectual development of the child."

Thus, again, in the manning of trade schools and manual training schools we are thrown back upon the higher training as its source and chief support. There was a time when any aged and wornout carpenter could teach in a trade school. But not so to-day. Indeed the demand for college-bred men by a school like Tuskegee, ought to make Mr. Booker T. Washington the firmest friend of higher training. Here he has as helpers the son of a Negro senator, trained in Greek and the humanities, and graduated at Harvard; the son of a Negro congressman and lawyer, trained in Latin and mathematics, and graduated at Oberlin; he has as his wife, a woman who read Virgil and Homer in the same class room with me; he has as college chaplain, a classical graduate of Atlanta University; as teacher of science, a graduate of Fisk; as teacher of history, a graduate of Smith,--indeed some thirty of his chief teachers are college graduates, and instead of studying French grammars in the midst of weeds, or buying pianos for dirty cabins, they are at Mr. Washington's right hand helping him in a noble work. And yet one of the effects of Mr. Washington's propaganda has been to throw doubt upon the expediency of such training for Negroes, as these persons have had.

* * * * *

[37]

Men of America, the problem is plain before you. Here is a race transplanted through the criminal foolishness of your fathers. Whether you like it or not the millions are here, and here they will remain. If you do not lift them up, they will pull you down. Education and work are the levers to uplift a people. Work alone will not do it unless inspired by the right ideals and guided by intelligence. Education must not simply teach work--it must teach Life. The Talented Tenth of the Negro race must be made leaders of thought and missionaries of culture among their people. No others can do this work and Negro colleges must train men for it. The Negro race, like all other races, is going to be saved by its exceptional men.

The Disfranchisement of the Negro

By CHARLES W. CHESNUTT

In this paper the author presents a straightforward statement of facts concerning the disfranchisement of the Negro in the Southern States. Mr. Chesnutt, who is too well known as a writer to need any introduction to an American audience, puts the case for the Negro to the American people very plainly, and spares neither the North nor the South.

The right of American citizens of African descent, commonly called Negroes, to vote upon the same terms as other citizens of the United States, is plainly declared and firmly fixed by the Constitution. No such person is called upon to present reasons why he should possess this right: that question is foreclosed by the Constitution. The object of the elective franchise is to give representation. So long as the Constitution retains its present form, any State Constitution, or statute, which seeks, by juggling the ballot, to deny the colored race fair representation, is a clear violation of the fundamental law of the land, and a corresponding injustice to those thus deprived of this right.

For thirty-five years this has been the law. As long as it was measurably respected, the colored people made rapid strides in education, wealth, character and self-respect. This the census proves, all statements to the contrary notwithstanding. A generation has grown to manhood and womanhood under the great, inspiring freedom conferred by the Constitution and protected by the right of suffrage--protected in large degree by the mere naked right, even when its exercise was hindered or denied by unlawful means. They have developed, in every Southern community, good citizens, who, if sustained and encouraged by just laws and liberal institutions, would greatly augment their number with the passing years, and soon wipe out the reproach of ignorance, unthrift, low morals and social inefficiency, thrown at them indiscriminately and therefore unjustly, and made the excuse for the equally undiscriminating contempt of their persons and their rights. They have reduced their illiteracy nearly 50 per cent. Excluded from the institutions of higher learning in their own States, their young men hold their own, and occasionally carry away honors, in the universities of the North. They have accumulated three hundred million dollars worth of real and personal property. Individuals among them have acquired substantial wealth, and several have attained to something like national distinction in art, letters and educational leadership. They are numerously represented in the learned professions. Heavily handicapped, they have made such rapid progress that the suspicion is justified that their advancement, rather than any stagnation or retrogression, is the true secret of the virulent Southern hostility to their rights, which has so influenced Northern opinion that it stands mute, and leaves the colored people, upon whom the North conferred liberty, to the tender mercies of those who have always denied their fitness for it.

It may be said, in passing, that the word "Negro," where used in this paper, is used solely for convenience. By the census of 1890 there were 1,000,000 colored people in the country who were half, or more than half, white, and logically there must be, as in fact there are, so many who share the white blood in some degree, as to justify the assertion that the race problem in the United States concerns the welfare and the status of a mixed race. Their rights are not one whit the more sacred because of this fact; but in an argument where injustice is sought to be excused because of fundamental differences of race, it is well enough to bear in mind that the race whose rights and liberties are endangered all over this country by disfranchisement at the South, are the colored people who live in the United States to-day, and not the low-browed, man-eating savage whom the Southern white likes to set upon a block and contrast with Shakespeare and Newton and Washington and Lincoln.

Despite and in defiance of the Federal Constitution, to-day in the six Southern States of Mississippi, Louisiana, Alabama, North Carolina, South Carolina and Virginia, containing an aggregate colored population of about 6,000,000, these have been, to all intents and purposes, denied, so far as the States can effect it, the right to vote. This disfranchisement is accomplished by various methods, devised with much transparent ingenuity, the effort being in each instance to violate the spirit of the Federal Constitution by disfranchising the Negro, while seeming to respect its letter by avoiding the mention of race or color.

These restrictions fall into three groups. The first comprises a property qualification--the ownership of $300 worth or more of real or personal property (Alabama, Louisiana, Virginia and South Carolina); the payment of a poll tax (Mississippi, North Carolina, Virginia); an educational qualification--the ability to read and write (Alabama, Louisiana, North Carolina). Thus far, those who believe in a restricted suffrage everywhere, could perhaps find no reasonable fault with any one of these qualifications, applied either separately or together.

But the Negro has made such progress that these restrictions alone would perhaps not deprive him of effective representation. Hence the second group. This comprises an "understanding" clause--the applicant must be able "to read, or understand when read to him, any clause in the Constitution" (Mississippi), or

[40]

to read and explain, or to understand and explain when read to him, any section of the Constitution (Virginia); an employment qualification--the voter must be regularly employed in some lawful occupation (Alabama); a character qualification--the voter must be a person of good character and who "understands the duties and obligations of citizens under a republican (!) form of government" (Alabama).

The qualifications under the first group it will be seen, are capable of exact demonstration; those under the second group are left to the discretion and judgment of the registering officer--for in most instances these are all requirements for registration, which must precede voting.

But the first group, by its own force, and the second group, under imaginable conditions, might exclude not only the Negro vote, but a large part of the white vote. Hence, the third group, which comprises: a military service qualification--any man who went to war, willingly or unwillingly, in a good cause or a bad, is entitled to register (Ala., Va.); a prescriptive qualification, under which are included all male persons who were entitled to vote on January 1, 1867, at which date the Negro had not yet been given the right to vote; a hereditary qualification, (the so-called "grandfather" clause), whereby any son (Va.), or descendant (Ala.), of a soldier, and (N.C.) the descendant of any person who had the right to vote on January 1, 1867, inherits that right. If the voter wish to take advantage of these last provisions, which are in the nature of exceptions to a general rule, he must register within a stated time, whereupon he becomes a member of a privileged class of permanently enrolled voters not subject to any of the other restrictions.

It will be seen that these restrictions are variously combined in the different States, and it is apparent that if combined to their declared end, practically every Negro may, under color of law, be denied the right to vote, and practically every white man accorded that right. The effectiveness of these provisions to exclude the Negro vote is proved by the Alabama registration under the new State Constitution. Out of a total, by the census of 1900, of 181,471 Negro "males of voting age," less than 3,000 are registered; in Montgomery county alone, the seat of the State capital, where there are 7,000 Negro males of voting age, only 47 have been allowed to register, while in several counties not one single Negro is permitted to exercise the franchise.

These methods of disfranchisement have stood such tests as the United States Courts, including the Supreme Court, have thus far seen fit to apply, in such cases as have been before them for adjudication. These include a case based upon the "understanding" clause of the Mississippi Constitution, in which the Supreme Court held, in effect, that since there was no ambiguity in the language employed and the Negro was not directly named, the Court would not go behind the wording of the Constitution to find a meaning which discriminated against the colored voter; and the recent case of Jackson vs. Giles, brought by a colored citizen of Montgomery, Alabama, in which the Supreme Court confesses itself impotent to provide a remedy for what, by inference, it acknowledges *may* be a "great political wrong," carefully avoiding, however, to state that it is a wrong, although the vital prayer of the petition was for a decision upon this very point.

Now, what is the effect of this wholesale disfranchisement of colored men, upon their citizenship. The value of food to the human organism is not measured by the pains of an occasional surfeit, but by the effect of its entire deprivation. Whether a class of citizens should vote, even if not always wisely--what class does?--may best be determined by considering their condition when they are without the right to vote.

The colored people are left, in the States where they have been disfranchised, absolutely without representation, direct or indirect, in any law-making body, in any court of justice, in any branch of government--for the feeble remnant of voters left by law is so inconsiderable as to be without a shadow of power. Constituting one-eighth of the population of the whole country, two-fifths of the whole Southern people, and a majority in several States, they are not able, because disfranchised where most numerous, to send one representative to the Congress, which, by the decision in the Alabama case, is held by the Supreme Court to be the only body, outside of the State itself, competent to give relief from a great political wrong. By former decisions of the same tribunal, even Congress is impotent to protect their civil rights, the Fourteenth Amendment having long since, by the consent of the same Court, been in many respects as completely nullified as the Fifteenth Amendment is now sought to be. They have no direct representation in any Southern legislature, and no voice in determining the choice of white men who might be friendly to their rights. Nor are they able to influence the election of judges or other public officials, to whom are entrusted the protection of their lives, their liberties and their property. No judge is rendered careful, no sheriff diligent, for fear that he may offend a black constituency; the contrary is most lamentably true; day after day the catalogue of lynchings and anti-Negro riots upon every imaginable pretext, grows longer and more appalling. The country stands face to face with the revival of slavery; at the moment of this writing a federal grand jury in Alabama is uncovering a system of peonage established under cover of law.

[42]

Under the Southern program it is sought to exclude colored men from every grade of the public service; not only from the higher administrative functions, to which few of them would in any event, for a long time aspire, but from the lowest as well. A Negro may not be a constable or a policeman. He is subjected by law to many degrading discriminations. He is required to be separated from white people on railroads and street cars, and, by custom, debarred from inns and places of public entertainment. His equal right to a free public education is constantly threatened and is nowhere equitably recognized. In Georgia, as has been shown by Dr. DuBois, where the law provides for a pro rata distribution of the public school fund between the races, and where the colored school population is 48 per cent. of the total, the amount of the fund devoted to their schools is only 20 per cent. In New Orleans, with an immense colored population, many of whom are persons of means and culture, all colored public schools above the fifth grade have been abolished.

The Negro is subjected to taxation without representation, which the forefathers of this Republic made the basis of a bloody revolution.

Flushed with their local success, and encouraged by the timidity of the Courts and the indifference of public opinion, the Southern whites have carried their campaign into the national government, with an ominous degree of success. If they shall have their way, no Negro can fill any federal office, or occupy, in the public service, any position that is not menial. This is not an inference, but the openly, passionately avowed sentiment of the white South. The right to employment in the public service is an exceedingly valuable one, for which white men have struggled and fought. A vast army of men are employed in the administration of public affairs. Many avenues of employment are closed to colored men by popular prejudice. If their right to public employment is recognized, and the way to it open through the civil service, or the appointing power, or the suffrages of the people, it will prove, as it has already, a strong incentive to effort and a powerful lever for advancement. Its value to the Negro, like that of the right to vote, may be judged by the eagerness of the whites to deprive him of it.

Not only is the Negro taxed without representation in the States referred to, but he pays, through the tariff and internal revenue, a tax to a National government whose supreme judicial tribunal declares that it cannot, through the executive arm, enforce its own decrees, and, therefore, refuses to pass upon a question, squarely before it, involving a basic right of citizenship. For the decision of the Supreme Court in the Giles case, if it foreshadows the attitude which the Court will take upon other cases to the same general end which will soon come before it, is scarcely less than a reaffirmation of the Dred Scott

[43]

decision; it certainly amounts to this--that in spite of the Fifteenth Amendment, colored men in the United States have no political rights which the States are bound to respect. To say this much is to say that all the privileges and immunities which Negroes henceforth enjoy, must be by favor of the whites; they are not *rights*. The whites have so declared; they proclaim that the country is theirs, that the Negro should be thankful that he has so much, when so much more might be withheld from him. He stands upon a lower footing than any alien; he has no government to which he may look for protection.

Moreover, the white South sends to Congress, on a basis including the Negro population, a delegation nearly twice as large as it is justly entitled to, and one which may always safely be relied upon to oppose in Congress every measure which seeks to protect the equality, or to enlarge the rights of colored citizens. The grossness of this injustice is all the more apparent since the Supreme Court, in the Alabama case referred to, has declared the legislative and political department of the government to be the only power which can right a political wrong. Under this decision still further attacks upon the liberties of the citizen may be confidently expected. Armed with the Negro's sole weapon of defense, the white South stands ready to smite down his rights. The ballot was first given to the Negro to defend him against this very thing. He needs it now far more than then, and for even stronger reasons. The 9,000,000 free colored people of to-day have vastly more to defend than the 3,000,000 hapless blacks who had just emerged from slavery. If there be those who maintain that it was a mistake to give the Negro the ballot at the time and in the manner in which it was given, let them take to heart this reflection: that to deprive him of it to-day, or to so restrict it as to leave him utterly defenseless against the present relentless attitude of the South toward his rights, will prove to be a mistake so much greater than the first, as to be no less than a crime, from which not alone the Southern Negro must suffer, but for which the nation will as surely pay the penalty as it paid for the crime of slavery. Contempt for law is death to a republic, and this one has developed alarming symptoms of the disease.

And now, having thus robbed the Negro of every political and civil *right*, the white South, in palliation of its course, makes a great show of magnanimity in leaving him, as the sole remnant of what he acquired through the Civil War, a very inadequate public school education, which, by the present program, is to be directed mainly towards making him a better agricultural laborer. Even this is put forward as a favor, although the Negro's property is taxed to pay for it, and his labor as well. For it is a well settled principle of political economy, that land and machinery of themselves produce nothing, and that labor indirectly pays its fair proportion of the tax upon the public's wealth. The white South seems to stand to the Negro at present as one, who, having been reluctantly compelled to release another from bondage, sees him stumbling forward and upward, neglected by his friends and scarcely yet conscious of his own strength; seizes him, binds him, and having bereft him of speech, of sight and of manhood, "yokes him with the mule" and exclaims, with a show of virtue which ought to deceive no one: "Behold how good a friend I am of yours! Have I not left you a stomach and a pair of arms, and will I not generously permit you to work for me with the one, that you may thereby gain enough to fill the other? A brain you do not need. We will relieve you of any responsibility that might seem to demand such an organ."

The argument of peace-loving Northern white men and Negro opportunists that the political power of the Negro having long ago been suppressed by unlawful means, his right to vote is a mere paper right, of no real value, and therefore to be lightly yielded for the sake of a hypothetical harmony, is fatally short-sighted. It is precisely the attitude and essentially the argument which would have surrendered to the South in the sixties, and would have left this country to rot in slavery for another generation. White men do not thus argue concerning their own rights. They know too well the value of ideals. Southern white men see too clearly the latent power of these unexercised rights. If the political power of the Negro was a nullity because of his ignorance and lack of leadership, why were they not content to leave it so, with the pleasing assurance that if it ever became effective, it would be because the Negroes had grown fit for its exercise? On the contrary, they have not rested until the possibility of its revival was apparently headed off by new State Constitutions. Nor are they satisfied with this. There is no doubt that an effort will be made to secure the repeal of the Fifteenth Amendment, and thus forestall the development of the wealthy and educated Negro, whom the South seems to anticipate as a greater menace than the ignorant ex-slave. However improbable this repeal may seem, it is not a subject to be lightly dismissed; for it is within the power of the white people of the nation to do whatever they wish in the premises--they did it once; they can do it again. The Negro and his friends should see to it that the white majority shall never wish to do anything to his hurt. There still stands, before the Negro-hating whites of the South, the specter of a Supreme Court which will interpret the Constitution to mean what it says, and what those who enacted it meant, and what the nation, which ratified it, understood, and which will find power, in a nation which goes beyond seas to administer the affairs of distant peoples, to enforce its own fundamental laws; the specter, too, of an aroused public opinion which will compel Congress and the Courts to preserve the liberties of the Republic, which are the liberties of the people. To wilfully neglect the suffrage, to hold it lightly, is to tamper with a sacred right; to yield it for anything else whatever is simply suicidal. Dropping the element of race, disfranchisement is no more than to say to the poor and poorly taught, that they must relinquish the right to defend themselves against oppression until they shall have become rich and learned, in competition with those already thus favored and possessing the ballot in addition. This is not the philosophy of history. The growth of liberty has been the constant struggle of the poor against the privileged classes; and the goal of that struggle has ever been the equality of all men before the law. The Negro who would yield this right, deserves to be a slave; he has the servile spirit. The rich and the educated can, by virtue of their influence, command many votes; can find other means of protection; the poor man has but one, he should guard it as a sacred treasure. Long ago, by fair treatment, the white leaders of the South might have bound the Negro to themselves with hoops of steel. They have not chosen to take this course, but by assuming from the beginning an attitude hostile to his rights, have never gained his confidence, and now seek by foul means to destroy where they have never sought by fair means to control.

I have spoken of the effect of disfranchisement upon the colored race; it is to the race as a whole, that the argument of the problem is generally directed. But the unit of society in a republic is the individual, and not the race, the failure to recognize this fact being the fundamental error which has beclouded the whole discussion. The effect of disfranchisement upon the individual is scarcely less disastrous. I do not speak of the moral effect of injustice upon those who suffer from it; I refer rather to the practical consequences which may be appreciated by any mind. No country is free in which the way upward is not open for every man to try, and for every properly qualified man to attain whatever of good the community life may offer. Such a condition does not exist, at the South, even in theory, for any man of color. In no career can such a man compete with white men upon equal terms. He must not only meet the prejudice of the individual, not only the united prejudice of the white community; but lest some one should wish to treat him fairly, he is met at every turn with some legal prohibition which says, "Thou shalt not," or "Thus far shalt thou go and no farther." But the Negro race is viable; it adapts itself readily to circumstances; and being thus adaptable, there is always the temptation to

"Crook the pregnant hinges of the knee, Where thrift may follow fawning."

He who can most skilfully balance himself upon the advancing or receding wave of white opinion concerning his race, is surest of such measure of prosperity as is permitted to men of dark skins. There are Negro teachers in the South--the privilege of teaching in their own schools is the one respectable

[46]

branch of the public service still left open to them--who, for a grudging appropriation from a Southern legislature, will decry their own race, approve their own degradation, and laud their oppressors. Deprived of the right to vote, and, therefore, of any power to demand what is their due, they feel impelled to buy the tolerance of the whites at any sacrifice. If to live is the first duty of man, as perhaps it is the first instinct, then those who thus stoop to conquer may be right. But is it needful to stoop so low, and if so, where lies the ultimate responsibility for this abasement?

I shall say nothing about the moral effect of disfranchisement upon the white people, or upon the State itself. What slavery made of the Southern whites is a matter of history. The abolition of slavery gave the South an opportunity to emerge from barbarism. Present conditions indicate that the spirit which dominated slavery still curses the fair section over which that institution spread its blight.

And now, is the situation remediless? If not so, where lies the remedy? First let us take up those remedies suggested by the men who approve of disfranchisement, though they may sometimes deplore the method, or regret the necessity.

Time, we are told, heals all diseases, rights all wrongs, and is the only cure for this one. It is a cowardly argument. These people are entitled to their rights to-day, while they are yet alive to enjoy them; and it is poor statesmanship and worse morals to nurse a present evil and thrust it forward upon a future generation for correction. The nation can no more honestly do this than it could thrust back upon a past generation the responsibility for slavery. It had to meet that responsibility; it ought to meet this one.

Education has been put forward as the great corrective--preferably industrial education. The intellect of the whites is to be educated to the point where they will so appreciate the blessings of liberty and equality, as of their own motion to enlarge and defend the Negro's rights. The Negroes, on the other hand, are to be so trained as to make them, not equal with the whites in any way--God save the mark! this would be unthinkable!--but so useful to the community that the whites will protect them rather than to lose their valuable services. Some few enthusiasts go so far as to maintain that by virtue of education the Negro will, in time, become strong enough to protect himself against any aggression of the whites; this, it may be said, is a strictly Northern view.

It is not quite clearly apparent how education alone, in the ordinary meaning of the word, is to solve, in any appreciable time, the problem of the relations of Southern white and black people. The need of education of all kinds for both

[47]

races is wofully apparent. But men and nations have been free without being learned, and there have been educated slaves. Liberty has been known to languish where culture had reached a very high development. Nations do not first become rich and learned and then free, but the lesson of history has been that they first become free and then rich and learned, and oftentimes fall back into slavery again because of too great wealth, and the resulting luxury and carelessness of civic virtues. The process of education has been going on rapidly in the Southern States since the Civil War, and yet, if we take superficial indications, the rights of the Negroes are at a lower ebb than at any time during the thirty-five years of their freedom, and the race prejudice more intense and uncompromising. It is not apparent that educated Southerners are less rancorous than others in their speech concerning the Negro, or less hostile in their attitude toward his rights. It is their voice alone that we have heard in this discussion; and if, as they state, they are liberal in their views as compared with the more ignorant whites, then God save the Negro!

I was told, in so many words, two years ago, by the Superintendent of Public Schools of a Southern city that "there was no place in the modern world for the Negro, except under the ground." If gentlemen holding such opinions are to instruct the white youth of the South, would it be at all surprising if these, later on, should devote a portion of their leisure to the improvement of civilization by putting under the ground as many of this superfluous race as possible?

The sole excuse made in the South for the prevalent injustice to the Negro is the difference in race, and the inequalities and antipathies resulting therefrom. It has nowhere been declared as a part of the Southern program that the Negro, when educated, is to be given a fair representation in government or an equal opportunity in life; the contrary has been strenuously asserted; education can never make of him anything but a Negro, and, therefore, essentially inferior, and not to be safely trusted with any degree of power. A system of education which would tend to soften the asperities and lessen the inequalities between the races would be of inestimable value. An education which by a rigid separation of the races from the kindergarten to the university, fosters this racial antipathy, and is directed toward emphasizing the superiority of one class and the inferiority of another, might easily have disastrous, rather than beneficial results. It would render the oppressing class more powerful to injure, the oppressed quicker to perceive and keener to resent the injury, without proportionate power of defense. The same assimilative education which is given at the North to all children alike, whereby native and foreign, black and white, are taught side by side in every grade of instruction, and are compelled by the exigencies of discipline to keep their prejudices in abeyance, and are given the opportunity to learn and appreciate one another's good qualities, and to establish friendly relations which may exist throughout life, is absent from the Southern system of education, both of the past and as proposed for the future. Education is in a broad sense a remedy for all social ills; but the disease we have to deal with now is not only constitutional but acute. A wise physician does not simply give a tonic for a diseased limb, or a high fever; the patient might be dead before the constitutional remedy could become effective. The evils of slavery, its injury to whites and blacks, and to the body politic, was clearly perceived and acknowledged by the educated leaders of the South as far back as the Revolutionary War and the Constitutional Convention, and yet they made no effort to abolish it. Their remedy was the same--time, education, social and economic development;--and yet a bloody war was necessary to destroy slavery and put its spirit temporarily to sleep. When the South and its friends are ready to propose a system of education which will recognize and teach the equality of all men before the law, the potency of education alone to settle the race problem will be more clearly apparent.

At present even good Northern men, who wish to educate the Negroes, feel impelled to buy this privilege from the none too eager white South, by conceding away the civil and political rights of those whom they would benefit. They have, indeed, gone farther than the Southerners themselves in approving the disfranchisement of the colored race. Most Southern men, now that they have carried their point and disfranchised the Negro, are willing to admit, in the language of a recent number of the *Charleston Evening Post*, that "the attitude of the Southern white man toward the Negro is incompatible with the fundamental ideas of the republic." It remained for our Clevelands and Abbotts and Parkhursts to assure them that their unlawful course was right and justifiable, and for the most distinguished Negro leader to declare that "every revised Constitution throughout the Southern States has put a premium upon intelligence, ownership of property, thrift and character." So does every penitentiary sentence put a premium upon good conduct; but it is poor consolation to the one unjustly condemned, to be told that he may shorten his sentence somewhat by good behavior. Dr. Booker T. Washington, whose language is quoted above, has, by his eminent services in the cause of education, won deserved renown. If he has seemed, at times, to those jealous of the best things for their race, to decry the higher education, it can easily be borne in mind that his career is bound up in the success of an industrial school; hence any undue stress which he may put upon that branch of education may safely be ascribed to the natural zeal of the promoter, without detracting in any degree from the essential value of his teachings in favor of manual training,

[49]

thrift and character-building. But Mr. Washington's prominence as an educational leader, among a race whose prominent leaders are so few, has at times forced him, perhaps reluctantly, to express himself in regard to the political condition of his people, and here his utterances have not always been so wise nor so happy. He has declared himself in favor of a restricted suffrage, which at present means, for his own people, nothing less than complete loss of representation--indeed it is only in that connection that the question has been seriously mooted; and he has advised them to go slow in seeking to enforce their civil and political rights, which, in effect, means silent submission to injustice. Southern white men may applaud this advice as wise, because it fits in with their purposes; but Senator McEnery of Louisiana, in a recent article in the *Independent*, voices the Southern white opinion of such acquiescence when he says: "What other race would have submitted so many years to slavery without complaint? *What other race would have submitted so quietly to disfranchisement?* These facts stamp his (the Negro's) inferiority to the white race." The time to philosophize about the good there is in evil, is not while its correction is still possible, but, if at all, after all hope of correction is past. Until then it calls for nothing but rigorous condemnation. To try to read any good thing into these fraudulent Southern constitutions, or to accept them as an accomplished fact, is to condone a crime against one's race. Those who commit crime should bear the odium. It is not a pleasing spectacle to see the robbed applaud the robber. Silence were better.

It has become fashionable to question the wisdom of the Fifteenth Amendment. I believe it to have been an act of the highest statesmanship, based upon the fundamental idea of this Republic, entirely justified by conditions; experimental in its nature, perhaps, as every new thing must be, but just in principle; a choice between methods, of which it seemed to the great statesmen of that epoch the wisest and the best, and essentially the most just, bearing in mind the interests of the freedmen and the Nation, as well as the feelings of the Southern whites; never fairly tried, and therefore, not yet to be justly condemned. Not one of those who condemn it, has been able, even in the light of subsequent events, to suggest a better method by which the liberty and civil rights of the freedmen and their descendants could have been protected. Its abandonment, as I have shown, leaves this liberty and these rights frankly without any guaranteed protection. All the education which philanthropy or the State could offer as a *substitute* for equality of rights, would be a poor exchange; there is no defensible reason why they should not go hand in hand, each encouraging and strengthening the other. The education which one can demand as a right is likely to do more good than the education for which one

[50]

must sue as a favor.

The chief argument against Negro suffrage, the insistently proclaimed argument, worn threadbare in Congress, on the platform, in the pulpit, in the press, in poetry, in fiction, in impassioned rhetoric, is the reconstruction period. And yet the evils of that period were due far more to the venality and indifference of white men than to the incapacity of black voters. The revised Southern Constitutions adopted under reconstruction reveal a higher statesmanship than any which preceded or have followed them, and prove that the freed voters could as easily have been led into the paths of civic righteousness as into those of misgovernment. Certain it is that under reconstruction the civil and political rights of all men were more secure in those States than they have ever been since. We will hear less of the evils of reconstruction, now that the bugaboo has served its purpose by disfranchising the Negro, it will be laid aside for a time while the nation discusses the political corruption of great cities; the scandalous conditions in Rhode Island; the evils attending reconstruction in the Philippines, and the scandals in the postoffice department--for none of which, by the way, is the Negro charged with any responsibility, and for none of which is the restriction of the suffrage a remedy seriously proposed. Rhode Island is indeed the only Northern State which has a property qualification for the franchise!

There are three tribunals to which the colored people may justly appeal for the protection of their rights: the United States Courts, Congress and public opinion. At present all three seem mainly indifferent to any question of human rights under the Constitution. Indeed, Congress and the Courts merely follow public opinion, seldom lead it. Congress never enacts a measure which is believed to oppose public opinion;--your Congressman keeps his ear to the ground. The high, serene atmosphere of the Courts is not impervious to its voice; they rarely enforce a law contrary to public opinion, even the Supreme Court being able, as Charles Sumner once put it, to find a reason for every decision it may wish to render; or, as experience has shown, a method to evade any question which it cannot decently decide in accordance with public opinion. The art of straddling is not confined to the political arena. The Southern situation has been well described by a colored editor in Richmond: "When we seek relief at the hands of Congress, we are informed that our plea involves a legal question, and we are referred to the Courts. When we appeal to the Courts, we are gravely told that the question is a political one, and that we must go to Congress. When Congress enacts remedial legislation, our enemies take it to the Supreme Court, which promptly declares it unconstitutional." The Negro might chase his rights round and round this circle until the end of time, without finding any relief.

Yet the Constitution is clear and unequivocal in its terms, and no Supreme Court can indefinitely continue to construe it as meaning anything but what it says. This Court should be bombarded with suits until it makes some definite pronouncement, one way or the other, on the broad question of the constitutionality of the disfranchising Constitutions of the Southern States. The Negro and his friends will then have a clean-cut issue to take to the forum of public opinion, and a distinct ground upon which to demand legislation for the enforcement of the Federal Constitution. The case from Alabama was carried to the Supreme Court expressly to determine the constitutionality of the Alabama Constitution. The Court declared itself without jurisdiction, and in the same breath went into the merits of the case far enough to deny relief, without passing upon the real issue. Had it said, as it might with absolute justice and perfect propriety, that the Alabama Constitution is a bold and impudent violation of the Fifteenth Amendment, the purpose of the lawsuit would have been accomplished and a righteous cause vastly strengthened.

But public opinion cannot remain permanently indifferent to so vital a question. The agitation is already on. It is at present largely academic, but is slowly and resistlessly, forcing itself into politics, which is the medium through which republics settle such questions. It cannot much longer be contemptuously or indifferently elbowed aside. The South itself seems bent upon forcing the question to an issue, as, by its arrogant assumptions, it brought on the Civil War. From that section, too, there come now and then, side by side with tales of Southern outrage, excusing voices, which at the same time are accusing voices; which admit that the white South is dealing with the Negro unjustly and unwisely; that the Golden Rule has been forgotten; that the interests of white men alone have been taken into account, and that their true interests as well are being sacrificed. There is a silent white South, uneasy in conscience, darkened in counsel, groping for the light, and willing to do the right. They are as yet a feeble folk, their voices scarcely audible above the clamor of the mob. May their convictions ripen into wisdom, and may their numbers and their courage increase! If the class of Southern white men of whom Judge Jones of Alabama, is so noble a representative, are supported and encouraged by a righteous public opinion at the North, they may, in time, become the dominant white South, and we may then look for wisdom and justice in the place where, so far as the Negro is concerned, they now seem well-nigh strangers. But even these gentlemen will do well to bear in mind that so long as they discriminate in any way against the Negro's equality of right, so long do they set class against class and open the door to every sort of discrimination. There can be no middle

[52]

ground between justice and injustice, between the citizen and the serf.

It is not likely that the North, upon the sober second thought, will permit the dearly-bought results of the Civil War to be nullified by any change in the Constitution. As long as the Fifteenth Amendment stands, the *rights* of colored citizens are ultimately secure. There were would-be despots in England after the granting of Magna Charta; but it outlived them all, and the liberties of the English people are secure. There was slavery in this land after the Declaration of Independence, yet the faces of those who love liberty have ever turned to that immortal document. So will the Constitution and its principles outlive the prejudices which would seek to overthrow it.

What colored men of the South can do to secure their citizenship to-day, or in the immediate future, is not very clear. Their utterances on political questions, unless they be to concede away the political rights of their race, or to soothe the consciences of white men by suggesting that the problem is insoluble except by some slow remedial process which will become effectual only in the distant future, are received with scant respect--could scarcely, indeed, be otherwise received, without a voting constituency to back them up,--and must be cautiously made, lest they meet an actively hostile reception. But there are many colored men at the North, where their civil and political rights in the main are respected. There every honest man has a vote, which he may freely cast, and which is reasonably sure to be fairly counted. When this race develops a sufficient power of combination, under adequate leadership,--and there are signs already that this time is near at hand,--the Northern vote can be wielded irresistibly for the defense of the rights of their Southern brethren.

In the meantime the Northern colored men have the right of free speech, and they should never cease to demand their rights, to clamor for them, to guard them jealously, and insistently to invoke law and public sentiment to maintain them. He who would be free must learn to protect his freedom. Eternal vigilance is the price of liberty. He who would be respected must respect himself. The best friend of the Negro is he who would rather see, within the borders of this republic one million free citizens of that race, equal before the law, than ten million cringing serfs existing by a contemptuous sufferance. A race that is willing to survive upon any other terms is scarcely worthy of consideration.

The direct remedy for the disfranchisement of the Negro lies through political action. One scarcely sees the philosophy of distinguishing between a civil and a political right. But the Supreme Court has recognized this distinction and has designated Congress as the power to right a political wrong. The Fifteenth Amendment gives Congress power to enforce its provisions. The power would seem to be inherent in government itself; but anticipating that the enforcement of the Amendment might involve difficulty, they made the superorogatory declaration. Moreover, they went further, and passed laws by which they provided for such enforcement. These the Supreme Court has so far declared insufficient. It is for Congress to make more laws. It is for colored men and for white men who are not content to see the blood-bought results of the Civil War nullified, to urge and direct public opinion to the point where it will demand stringent legislation to enforce the Fourteenth and Fifteenth Amendments. This demand will rest in law, in morals and in true statesmanship; no difficulties attending it could be worse than the present ignoble attitude of the Nation toward its own laws and its own ideals--without courage to enforce them, without conscience to change them, the United States presents the spectacle of a Nation drifting aimlessly, so far as this vital, National problem is concerned, upon the sea of irresolution, toward the maelstrom of anarchy.

The right of Congress, under the Fourteenth Amendment, to reduce Southern representation can hardly be disputed. But Congress has a simpler and more direct method to accomplish the same end. It is the sole judge of the qualifications of its own members, and the sole judge of whether any member presenting his credentials has met those qualifications. It can refuse to seat any member who comes from a district where voters have been disfranchised: it can judge for itself whether this has been done, and there is no appeal from its decision.

If, when it has passed a law, any Court shall refuse to obey its behests, it can impeach the judges. If any president refuse to lend the executive arm of the government to the enforcement of the law, it can impeach the president. No such extreme measures are likely to be necessary for the enforcement of the Fourteenth and Fifteenth Amendments--and the Thirteenth, which is also threatened--but they are mentioned as showing that Congress is supreme; and Congress proceeds, the House directly, the Senate indirectly, from the people and is governed by public opinion. If the reduction of Southern representation were to be regarded in the light of a bargain by which the Fifteenth Amendment was surrendered, then it might prove fatal to liberty. If it be inflicted as a punishment and a warning, to be followed by more drastic measures if not sufficient, it would serve a useful purpose. The Fifteenth Amendment declares that the right to vote *shall not* be denied or abridged on account of color; and any measure adopted by Congress should look to that end. Only as the power to injure the Negro in Congress is reduced thereby, would a reduction of representation protect the Negro; without other measures it would still leave him in the hands of the Southern whites, who could safely be trusted to make him

[54]

pay for their humiliation.

Finally, there is, somewhere in the Universe a "Power that works for righteousness," and that leads men to do justice to one another. To this power, working upon the hearts and consciences of men, the Negro can always appeal. He has the right upon his side, and in the end the right will prevail. The Negro will, in time, attain to full manhood and citizenship throughout the United States. No better guaranty of this is needed than a comparison of his present with his past. Toward this he must do his part, as lies within his power and his opportunity. But it will be, after all, largely a white man's conflict, fought out in the forum of the public conscience. The Negro, though eager enough when opportunity offered, had comparatively little to do with the abolition of slavery, which was a vastly more formidable task than will be the enforcement of the Fifteenth Amendment.

The Negro and the Law

By WILFORD H. SMITH

The law and how it is dodged by enactments infringing upon the rights guaranteed to the freedmen by constitutional amendment. A powerful plea for justice for the Negro.

The colored people in the United States are indebted to the beneficent provisions of the 13th, 14th and 15th amendments to the Constitution of the United States, for the establishment of their freedom and citizenship, and it is to these mainly they must look for the maintenance of their liberty and the protection of their civil rights. These amendments followed close upon the Emancipation Proclamation issued January 1st, 1863, by President Lincoln, and his call for volunteers, which was answered by more than three hundred thousand negro soldiers, who, during three years of military service, helped the Union arms to victory at Appomattox. Standing in the shadow of the awful calamity and deep distress of the civil war, and grateful to God for peace and victory over the rebellion, the American people, who upheld the Union, rose to the sublime heights of doing justice to the former slaves, who had grown and multiplied with the country from the early settlement at Jamestown. It looked like an effort to pay them back for their years of faithfulness and unrequited toil, by not only making them free but placing them on equal footing with themselves in the fundamental law. Certainly, they intended at least, that they should have as many rights under the Constitution as are given to white naturalized citizens who come to this country from all the nations of Europe.

The 13th amendment provides that neither slavery nor involuntary servitude, except as a punishment for crime, whereof the party shall have been duly convicted, shall exist in the United States or any place subject to their jurisdiction.

The 14th amendment provides in section one, that all persons born or naturalized in the United States and subject to the jurisdiction thereof, are citizens of the United States, and of the State wherein they reside. No State shall make or enforce any law which shall abridge the privileges or immunities of citizens of the United States, nor shall any State deprive any person of life, liberty or property without due process of law, nor deny to any person within its jurisdiction the equal protection of the law.

The 15th amendment provides that the right of citizens of the United States to

[56]

vote shall not be denied or abridged by the United States, or by any State on account of race, color, or previous condition of servitude.

Chief Justice Waite, in the case of the United States vs. Cruikshank, 92nd U.S. 542, said:--

"The 14th amendment prohibits a State from denying to any person within its jurisdiction the equal protection of the law. The equality of the rights of citizens is a principle of republicanism. Every Republican government is in duty bound to protect all its citizens in the enjoyment of this principle if within its power."

The same Chief Justice, in the case of the United States vs. Reese, 92nd U.S. 214, said:

"The 15th amendment does not confer the right of suffrage upon anyone. It prevents the States or the United States from giving preference in this particular to one citizen of the United States over another, on account of race, color or previous condition of servitude. Before its adoption this could be done. It was as much within the power of a State to exclude citizens of the United States from voting on account of race and color, as it was on account of age, property or education. Now it is not."

Notwithstanding the manifest meaning of equality of citizenship contained in the constitutional amendments, it was found necessary to reinforce them by a civil rights law, enacted by the Congress of the United States, March 1st, 1875, entitled, "An Act To Protect All Citizens In Their Civil and Legal Rights." Its preamble and first section are as follows:--Preamble: "Whereas, it is essential to just government we recognize the equality of all men before the law, and hold that it is the duty of government in its dealings with the people to mete out equal and exact justice to all, of whatever nativity, race, color or persuasion, religious or political, and it being the appropriate object of legislation to enact great fundamental principles into law, therefore,

"Be it enacted that all persons within the jurisdiction of the United States shall be entitled to the full and equal enjoyment of the accommodations, advantages, facilities and privileges of inns, public conveyances on land or water, theatres and other places of public amusement, subject only to the conditions and limitations established by law, and applicable alike to citizens of every race and color, regardless to any previous condition of servitude."

The Supreme Court of the United States has held this salutary law unconstitutional and void as applied to the States, but binding in the District of Columbia, and the Territories over which the government of the United States has control.--Civil Rights cases 109 U.S. 63. Since the Supreme Court's ruling, many Northern and Western States have enacted similar civil rights laws. Equality of citizenship in the United States suffered a severe blow when the civil rights bill was struck down by the Supreme Court. The colored people looked upon the decision as unsound, and prompted by race prejudice. It was clear that the amendments to the Constitution were adopted to secure not only their freedom, but their equal civil rights, and by ratifying the amendments the several States conceded to the Federal government the power and authority of maintaining not alone their freedom, but their equal civil rights in the United States as well.

The Federal Supreme Court put a narrow interpretation on the Constitution, rather than a liberal one in favor of equal rights; in marked contrast to a recent decision of the Appellate Division of the Supreme Court of New York in a civil rights case arising under the statute of New York, Burks vs. Bosso, 81 N.Y. Supp, 384. The New York Supreme Court held this language: "The liberation of the slaves, and the suppression of the rebellion, was supplemented by the amendments to the national Constitution according to the colored people their civil rights and investing them with citizenship. The amendments indicated a clear purpose to secure equal rights to the black people with the white race. The legislative intent must control, and that may be gathered from circumstances inducing the act. Where that intent has been unvaryingly manifested in one direction, and that in the prohibition of any discrimination against a large class of citizens, the courts should not hesitate to keep apace with legislative purpose. We must remember that the slightest trace of African blood places a man under the ban of belonging to that race. However respectable and whatever he may be, he is ostracized socially, and when the policy of the law is against extending the prohibition of his civil rights, a liberal, rather than a narrow interpretation should be given to enactments evidencing the intent to eliminate race discrimination, as far as that can be accomplished by legislative intervention."

The statutory enactments and recent Constitutions of most of the former slave-holding States, show that they have never looked with favor upon the amendments to the national Constitution. They rather regard them as war measures designed by the North to humiliate and punish the people of those States lately in rebellion. While in the main they accept the 13th amendment and concede that the negro should have personal freedom, they have never been altogether in harmony with the spirit and purposes of the 14th and 15th amendments. There seems to be a distinct and positive fear on the part of the South that if the negro is given a man's chance, and is accorded equal civil rights with white men on the juries, on common carriers, and in public places, that it will in some way lead to his social equality. This fallacious argument is persisted in, notwithstanding the well-known fact, that although the Jews are the leaders in the wealth and commerce of the South, their civil equality has never, except in rare instances, led to any social intermingling with the Southern whites.

Holding these views the Southern people in 1875, found means to overcome the Republican majorities in all the re-constructed States, and practically drove the negroes out of the law-making bodies of all those States. So that, now in all the Southern States, so far as can be ascertained, there is not one negro sitting as a representative in any of the law-making bodies. The next step was to deny them representation on the grand and petit juries in the State courts, through Jury Commissioners, who excluded them from the panels.

To be taxed without representation is a serious injustice in a republic whose foundations are laid upon the principle of "no taxation without representation." But serious as this phase of the case must appear, infinitely more serious is the case when we consider the fact that they are likewise excluded from the grand and petit juries in all the State courts, with the fewest and rarest exceptions. The courts sit in judgment upon their lives and liberties, and dispose of their dearest earthly possessions. They are not entitled to life, liberty or property if the courts should decide they are not, and yet in this all-important tribunal they are denied all voice, except as parties and witnesses, and here and there a negro lawyer is permitted to appear. One vote on the grand jury might prevent an indictment, and save disgrace and the risk of public trial; while one vote on the petit jury might save a life or a term of imprisonment, for an innocent person pursued and persecuted by powerful enemies.

With no voice in the making of the laws, which they are bound to obey, nor in their administration by the courts, thus tied and helpless, the negroes were proscribed by a system of legal enactments intended to wholly nullify the letter and spirit of the war amendments to the national organic law. This crusade was begun by enacting a system of Jim-Crow car laws in all the Southern States, so that now the Jim-Crow cars run from the Gulf of Mexico into the national capital. They are called, "Separate Car Laws," providing for separate but equal accommodations for whites and negroes. Though fair on their face, they are everywhere known to discriminate against the colored people in their administration, and were intended to humiliate and degrade them.

Setting apart separate places for negroes on public carriers, is just as repugnant to the spirit and intent of the national Constitution, as would be a law compelling all Jews or all Roman Catholics to occupy compartments specially

[59]

set apart for them on account of their religion. If these statutes were not especially aimed at the negro, an arrangement of different fares, such as first, second and third classes, would have been far more just and preferable, and would have enabled the refined and exclusive of both races to avoid the presence of the coarse and vicious, by selecting the more expensive fare. Still these laws have been upheld by the Federal Supreme Court, and pronounced not in conflict with the amendments to the Constitution of the United States.

City ordinances providing for separate street cars for white and colored passengers, are in force in Atlanta, New Orleans, and in nearly all the cities of the South. In all the principal cities of Alabama, a certain portion of the street cars is set apart and marked for negroes. The conductors are clothed with the authority of determining to what race the passenger belongs, and may arrest persons refusing to obey his orders. It is often a very difficult task to determine to what race some passengers belong, there being so many dark-white persons that might be mistaken for negroes, and persons known as negroes who are as fair as any white person.

In the State of Georgia, a negro cannot purchase a berth in a sleeping car, under any circumstances, no matter where his destination, owing to the following statute enacted December 20th, 1899: "Sleeping car companies, and all railroads operating sleeping cars in this State, shall separate the white and colored races, and shall not permit them to occupy the same compartment; provided, that nothing in this act shall be construed to compel sleeping car companies or railroads operating sleeping cars, to carry persons of color in sleeping or parlor cars; provided also, that this act shall not apply to colored nurses or servants travelling with their employers." The violation of this statute is a misdemeanor.

Article 45, section 639 of the statutes of Georgia, 1895, makes it a misdemeanor to keep or confine white and colored convicts together, or to chain them together going to and from work. There is also a statute in Georgia requiring that a separate tax list be kept in every county, of the property of white and colored persons. Both races generally approve the laws prohibiting inter-marriages between white and colored persons, which seem to be uniform throughout the Southern States.

Florida seems to have gone a step further than the rest, and by sections 2612 and 2613, Revised Statutes, 1892, it is made a misdemeanor for a white man and a colored woman, and vice versa, to sleep under the same roof at night, occupying the same room. Florida is entitled to credit, however, for a statute making marriages between white and colored persons prior to 1866, where they continue to live together, valid and binding to all intents and purposes.

In addition to this forced separation of the races by law, "from the cradle to the grave," there is yet a sadder and more deplorable separation, in the almost universal disposition to leave the negroes wholly and severely to themselves in their home life and religious life, by the white Christian people of the South, distinctly manifesting no concern in their moral and religious development.

In Georgia and the Carolinas, and all the Gulf States (except Texas, where the farm labor is mostly white) the negroes on the farms are held by a system of laws which prevents them from leaving the plantations, and enables the landlord to punish them by fine and imprisonment for any alleged breach of contract. In the administration of these laws they are virtually made slaves to the landlord, as long as they are in debt, and it is wholly in the power of the landlord to forever keep them in debt.

By section 355, of the Criminal Code of South Carolina, 1902, it is made a misdemeanor to violate a contract to work and labor on a farm, subject to a fine of not less than five dollars, and more than one hundred dollars, or imprisonment for not less than ten days, or more than thirty. It is also made a misdemeanor to employ any farm laborer while under contract with another, or to persuade or entice a farm laborer to leave his employer.

The Georgia laws are a little stronger in this respect than the laws of the other States. By section 121, of the Code of Georgia, 1895, it is provided, "that if any person shall, by offering higher wages, or in any other way entice, persuade or decoy, or attempt to entice, persuade or decoy any farm laborer from his employer, he shall be guilty of a misdemeanor." Again, by act of December 17th, 1901, the Georgia Legislature passed a law making it an offense to rent land, or furnish land to a farm laborer, after he has contracted with another landlord, without first obtaining the consent of the first landlord.

The presence of large numbers of negroes in the towns and cities of the South and North can be accounted for by such laws as the above, administered by ignorant country magistrates, in nearly all cases the pliant tools of the landlords.

The boldest and most open violation of the negro's rights under the Federal Constitution, was the enactment of the grand-father clauses, and understanding clauses in the new Constitutions of Louisiana, Alabama, the Carolinas, and Virginia, which have had the effect to deprive the great body of them of the right to vote in those States, for no other reason than their race and color. Although thus depriving him of his vote, and all voice in the State governments at the

[61]

South, in all of them his property is taxed to pay pensions to Confederate soldiers, who fought to continue him in slavery. The fact is, the franchise had been practically taken from the negroes in the South since 1876, by admitted fraudulent methods and intimidation in elections, but it was not until late years that this nullification of the amendments was enacted into State Constitutions.

This brings me to the proposition that it is mainly in the enforcement, or the administration of the laws, however fair and equal they may appear on their face, that the constitutional rights of negroes to equal protection and treatment are denied, not only in the South but in many Northern States. There are noble exceptions, however, of high-toned honorable gentlemen on the bench as trial judges, and Supreme Court justices, in the South, who without regard to consequences have stood for fairness and justice to the negro in their courts.

With the population of the South distinctly divided into two classes, not the rich and poor, not the educated and ignorant, not the moral and immoral, but simply whites and blacks, all negroes being generally regarded as inferior and not entitled to the same rights as any white person, it is bound to be a difficult matter to obtain fair and just results, when there is any sort of conflict between the races. The negro realizes this, and knows that he is at an immense disadvantage when he is forced to litigate with a white man in civil matters, and much more so when he is charged with a crime by a white person.

The juries in the South almost always reject the testimony of any number of negroes if given in opposition to that of a white witness, and this is true in many instances, no matter how unreasonable or inconsistent the testimony of the white witness may be. Jurors in the South have been heard to admit that they would be socially ostracized if they brought in a verdict upon colored testimony alone, in opposition to white testimony.

Perhaps it can be best explained how the negro fares in the courts of the South by giving a few cases showing how justice is administered to him:

A negro boy was brought to the bar for trial before a police magistrate, in a Southern capital city, charged with assault and battery on a white boy about the same age, but a little larger. The testimony showed that the white boy had beat the negro on several previous occasions as he passed on his way to school, and each time the negro showed no disposition to fight. On the morning of the charge he attacked the negro and attempted to cut him with a knife, because the negro's mother had reported to the white boy's mother the previous assaults, and asked her to chastise him. The colored boy in trying to keep from being cut was compelled to fight, and got the advantage and threw the white boy down and blacked his eyes. The magistrate on this evidence fined the

[62]

negro twenty-five dollars. The mother of the negro having once been a servant for the magistrate, found courage to rise, and said: "Jedge, yo Honer, can I speak?" The magistrate replied, "Yes, go on." She said, "Well, Jedge, my boy is ben tellin' me about dis white boy meddlin' him on his way to school, but I would not let my boy fight, 'cause I 'tole him he couldn't git no jestice in law. But he had no other way to go to school 'ceptin' gwine dat way; and den jedge, dis white chile is bigger an my chile and jumped on him fust with a knife for nothin', befo' my boy tetched him. Jedge I am a po' woman, and washes fur a livin', and ain't got nobody to help me, and can't raise all dat money. I think dat white boy's mammy ought to pay half of dis fine." By this time her voice had become stifled by her tears. The judge turned to the mother of the white boy and said, "Madam, are you willing to pay half of this fine?" She answered, "Yes, Your Honor." And the judge changed the order to a fine of $12.50 each, against both boys.

A celebrated case in point reported in the books is, George Maury vs. The State of Miss., 68 Miss. 605. I reproduce the court's statement of the case:--"This is an appeal from the Circuit Court of Kemper County. Appellant was convicted of murder and sentenced to imprisonment for life. He appears in this court without counsel. The facts are briefly these: One, Nicholson, a white man, accompanied by his little son seven years old, was driving an ox team along a public road; he had occasion to stop and the oxen were driven by his son; defendant, a negro, also in an ox wagon, was going along the road in an opposite direction, and met Nicholson's wagon in charge of the little boy. It was after dark, and when the wagons met, according to the testimony of Nicholson, the defendant insultingly demanded of the boy to give the way, and cursed and abused him. Nicholson, hearing the colloquy, hurried to the scene and a fight ensued between him and Maury, in which the latter got the advantage, inflicting severe blows upon Nicholson. This occurred on Thursday, and on the following Sunday night, Nicholson, in company with eleven or twelve of his friends, rode to the farm of Maury, and after sending several of their number to ascertain if he was at home, rode rapidly into his yard and called for him. Not finding him, they proceeded to search the premises, and found several colored men shut up in the smoke house, the door of which some of the searching party had broken open. Maury, the accused, was not found there, and about that time some one called out, "Here is George." Some of the party then started in the direction of the cotton house from which the voice proceeded, when a volley was fired from it, and two of the searching party were killed, one of whom was the son of the former owner of the defendant, and the other a brother-in-law of Nicholson. The members of the raiding party testified that their purpose in going to the home of the defendant was merely to arrest him. It was, however, shown that Nicholson, immediately after the fight on Thursday, informed Cobb, and Cobb between Thursday and Sunday night collected the men who joined in the raid. No affidavit for the arrest of Maury had been made, and none of the party had any warrant, or made any announcement to the defendant or his family, of the object of their visit. The accused who testified in his own behalf, denied that he was at home at the time of the shooting, and says he fled before the raiding party arrived. He also contradicted Nicholson in his account of the difficulty with him, and denies that he spoke harshly to the child." Chief Justice Campbell, in delivering the opinion of the court said, "It is inconceivable that the crime of murder is predicable of the facts disclosed by the evidence in this case. The time and place and circumstances of the killing forbid any such conclusion as a verdict of guilty of murder." The judgment of the trial court was reversed.

This same Chief Justice, in the case of Monroe vs. Mississippi, 71 Miss. 201, where a negro was convicted of rape, makes use of the following brave and noble language, reversing the case on the ground of the insufficiency of the evidence: "We might greatly lighten our labors by deferring in all cases to the verdict approved by the presiding judge as to the facts, but our duty is to administer justice without respect of persons, and do equal right to the poor and the rich. Hence the disposition, which we are not ashamed to confess we have, to guard jealously the rights of the poor and friendless and despised, and to be astute as far as we properly may, against injustice, whether proceeding from wilfulness or indifference."

The country has produced no abler jurist, nor the South no greater man than Ex-Chief Justice Campbell of Mississippi. If the counsel of such men as he and Chief Justice Garret of the Court of Civil Appeals of Texas, could obtain in the South, there would be no problem between the races. All would be contented because justice would be administered to the whites and blacks alike.

In the administration of the suffrage sections under the new Constitutions of the South by the partisan boards of registrars, the same discrimination against negroes was practiced. Their methods are of more or less interest. The plan was to exclude all negroes from the electorate without excluding a single white man. Under the Alabama Constitution, a soldier in the Civil War, either on the Federal or Confederate side, is entitled to qualification. When a negro goes up to register as a soldier he is asked for his discharge. When he presents it he is asked, "How do we know that you are the man whose name is written in this discharge? Bring us two white men whom we know and who will swear that you have not found this paper, and that they know that you were a soldier in the company and regiment in which you claim to have been." This, of course, could

[64]

not be done, and the ex-soldier who risked his life for the Union is denied the right to vote.

The same Constitution provides that if not a soldier or the legal descendant of one, an elector must be of good character and understand the duties and obligations of citizenship under a Republican form of government. When a negro claims qualifications under the good character and understanding clauses he is put through an examination similar to the following:

"What is a republican form of government?

"What is a limited monarchy?

"What islands did the United States come into possession of by the Spanish-American War?

"What is the difference between Jeffersonian Democracy and Calhoun principles, as compared to the Monroe Doctrine?

"If the Nicaragua Canal is cut, what will be the effect if the Pacific Ocean is two feet higher than the Atlantic?" Should these questions be answered satisfactorily, the negro must still produce two white men known to the registrars to testify to his good character. A remarkable exception in the treatment of negroes by the registrars of Dallas county, Alabama, is shown in the following account taken from the Montgomery Advertizer:--

"An old negro barber by the name of Edward E. Harris, stepped in before the registrars, hat in hand, humble and polite, with a kindly smile on his face. He respectfully asked to be registered. He signed the application and waited a few minutes until the registrars had disposed of some other matters, and being impressed with his respectful bearing, some member of the board commenced to ask a few questions. The old man told his story in a straight forward manner. He said: "Gentlemen, I am getting to be a pretty old man. I was born here in the South, and I followed my young master through all of the campaigns in Virginia, when Mas' Bob Lee made it so warm for the Yankees. But our luck left us at Gettysburg. The Yankees got around in our rear there, and I got a bullet in the back of my head, and one in my leg before I got out of that scrape. But I was not hurt much, and my greatest anxiety was about my young master, Mr. John Holly, who was a member of the Bur Rifles, 18th Mississippi. He was a private and enlisted at Jackson, Miss.

"He could not be found the first day; I looked all among the dead on the battle field for him and he was not there. Next day I got a permit to go through the hospitals, and I looked into the face of every soldier closely, in the hope of

[65]

finding my young master. After many hours of searching I found him, but he was dangerously wounded. I stayed by his side, wounded as I was, for three long weeks, but he gradually grew worse and then he died. I went out with the body and saw it buried as decently as I could, and then I went back to Jackson and told the young mistress how brave he was in battle, how good he was to me, and told her all the words he had sent her, as he lay there on that rude cot in the hospital. That is my record as a Confederate soldier, and if you gentlemen care to give me a certificate of registration, I would be much obliged to you." It is needless to say that old Ed. Harris got his certificate.

It is insisted upon by the leaders of public opinion at the South, that negroes should not be given equal political and civil rights with white men, defined by law and enforceable by the courts; but that they should be content to strive to deserve the good wishes and friendly feeling of the whites, and if the South is let alone, they will see to it that negroes get becoming treatment.

While there is a large number of the high-toned, chivalrous element of the old master class yet living, who would stand by the negro and not permit him to be wronged if they could prevent it, yet they are powerless to control the great mass of the poor whites who are most bitter in their prejudices against the negro. They should also bear in mind that the old master class is rapidly passing way, and that there is constantly an influx of foreigners to the South, and in less than fifty years the Italians, or some other foreign nationality, may be the ruling class in all the Southern States; and the negro, deprived of all political and civil rights by the Constitution and laws, would be wholly at the mercy of a people without sympathy for him.

In order to show the fallacy and the wrong and injustice of this doctrine, and how helplessly exposed it leaves the negro to the prejudices of the poor whites, I relate a tragedy in the life of a friend of mine, who was well known and respected in the town of Rayville, Louisiana.

Sewall Smith, for many years ran the leading barber shop for whites in the town of Rayville, and was well-liked and respected by the leading white men of the entire parish. At the suggestion of his customers he bought Louisiana state lands while they were cheap, before the railroad was put through between Vicksburg and Shreveport; and as the road passed near his lands he was thereby made a rich man, as wealth goes in those parts. His good fortune, however, did not swell his head and he remained the same to his friends. He became so useful in his parish that there was never a public gathering of the leading white business men that he was not invited to it, and he was always on the delegations to all the levee or river conventions sent from his parish. He

[66]

was chosen to such places by white men exclusively; and in his own town he was as safe from wrong or injury, on account of his race or color, as any white man.

After the trains began to run through Rayville, on the Shreveport road, he had occasion to visit the town of Ruston, in another parish some miles in the interior, and as he got off at the depot, a barefoot, poor white boy asked to carry his satchel. Smith was a fine looking mulatto, dressed well, and could have easily been taken for a white man, and the boy might not have known at the time he was a negro. When he arrived at his stopping place he gave the boy such a large coin that he asked permission to take his satchel back to the train on the following day when he was to return. The next day the boy came for the satchel, and they had nearly reached the depot about train time, when they passed a saloon where a crowd of poor whites sat on boxes whittling sticks. The sight of a negro having a white boy carrying his satchel quite enraged them, and after cursing and abusing Smith and the boy, they undertook to kick and assault Smith. Smith defended himself. The result was a shooting affair, in which Smith shot two or three of them and was himself shot. The train rolled up while the fight was in progress, and without inquiring the cause or asking any questions whatever, fully a hundred white men jumped off the train and riddled Smith with bullets. That was the end of it. Nobody was indicted or even arrested for killing an insolent "nigger" that did not keep his place. That is the way the affair was regarded in Ruston. Of course, the people of Rayville very much regretted it, but they could not do anything, and could not afford to defend the rights of a negro against white men under such circumstances, and the matter dropped.

I have preferred not to mention the numerous ways and many instances in which the rights of negroes are denied in public places, and on the common carriers in the South, under circumstances very humiliating and degrading. Nor have I cared to refer to the barbarous and inhuman prison systems of the South, that are worse than anything the imagination can conceive in a civilized and Christian land, as shown by reports of legislative committees.

If the negro can secure a fair and impartial trial in the courts, and can be secure in his life and liberty and property, so as not to be deprived of them except by due process of law, and can have a voice in the making and administration of the laws, he shall have gone a great way in the South. It is to be hoped that public opinion can be awakened to this extent, and that it may assist him to attain that end.

[67]

The Characteristics of the Negro People

By H.T. KEALING

A frank statement of the virtues and failings of the race, indicating very clearly the evils which must be overcome, and the good which must be developed, if success is really to attend the effort to uplift them.

The characteristics of the Negro are of two kinds--the inborn and the inbred. As they reveal themselves to us, this distinction may not be seen, but it exists. Inborn qualities are ineradicable; they belong to the blood; they constitute individuality; they are independent, or nearly so, of time and habitat. Inbred qualities are acquired, and are the result of experience. They may be overcome by a reversal of the process which created them. The fundamental, or inborn, characteristics of the Negro may be found in the African, as well as the American, Negro; but the inbred characteristics of the latter belong to the American life alone.

There is but one human nature, made up of constituent elements the same in all men, and racial or national differences arise from the predominance of one or another element in this or that race. It is a question of proportion. The Negro is not a Caucasian, not a Chinese, not an Indian; though no psychological quality in the one is absent from the other. The same moral sense, called conscience; the same love of harmony in color or in sound; the same pleasure in acquiring knowledge; the same love of truth in word, or of fitness in relation; the same love of respect and approbation; the same vengeful or benevolent feelings; the same appetites, belong to all, but in varying proportions. They form the indicia to a people's mission, and are our best guides to God's purpose in creating us. They constitute the material to be worked on in educating a race, and suggest in every case where the stress of civilization or education should be applied in order to follow the lines of least resistance.

But there are also certain manifestations, the result of training or neglect, which are not inborn. As they are inculcable, so they are eradicable; and it is only by a loose terminology that we apply the term characteristics to them without distinction between them and the inherent traits. In considering the characteristics of the Negro people, therefore, we must not confuse the constitutional with the removable. Studied with sympathy and at first hand, the black man of America will be seen to possess certain predominant idiosyncrasies of which the following form a fair catalogue:

[68]

He is intensely religious. True religion is based upon a belief in the supernatural, upon faith and feeling. A people deeply superstitious are apt to be deeply religious, for both rest upon a belief in a spiritual world. Superstition differs from religion in being the untrained and unenlightened gropings of the human soul after the mysteries of the higher life; while the latter, more or less enlightened, "feels after God, if haply," it may find Him. The Negro gives abundant evidence of both phases. The absolute inability of the master, in the days of slavery, while successfully vetoing all other kinds of convocation, to stop the Negro's church meetings, as well as the almost phenomenal influence and growth of his churches since; and his constant referring of every event, adverse or favorable, to the personal ministrations of the Creator, are things unique and persistent. And the master class reposed more faith in their slaves' religion ofttimes than they did in their own. Doubtless much of the reverential feeling that pervades the American home to-day, above that of all other nations, is the result of the Negro mammy's devotion and loyalty to God.

He is imaginative. This is not evinced so much in creative directions as in poetical, musical, combinatory, inventional and what, if coupled with learning, we call literary imagination. Negro eloquence is proverbial. The crudest sermon of the most unlettered slave abounded in tropes and glowing tongue pictures of apocalyptic visions all his own; and, indeed, the poetic quality of his mind is seen in all his natural efforts when the self-consciousness of education does not stand guard. The staid religious muse of Phillis Wheatley and the rollicking, somewhat jibing, verse of Dunbar show it equally, unpremeditated and spontaneous.

I have heard by the hour some ordinary old uneducated Negro tell those inimitable animal stories, brought to literary existence in "Uncle Remus," with such quaint humor, delicious conceit and masterly delineation of plot, character and incident that nothing but the conventional rating of Aesop's Fables could put them in the same class. Then, there are more Negro inventors than the world supposes. This faculty is impossible without a well-ordered imagination held in leash by a good memory and large perception.

He is affectionate and without vindictiveness. He does not nurse even great wrongs. Mercurial as he is, often furiously angry and frequently in murderous mood, he comes nearer not letting the sun go down upon his anger than any other man I know. Like Brutus, he may be compared to the flint which,

"Much enforced, shows a hasty spark, And straight is cold again."

His affection is not less towards the Caucasian than to his own race. It is not saying too much to remark that the soul of the Negro yearns for the white man's

[69]

good will and respect; and the old ties of love that subsisted in so many instances in the days of slavery still survive where the ex-slave still lives. The touching case of a Negro Bishop who returned to the State in which he had been a slave, and rode twenty miles to see and alleviate the financial distress of his former master is an exception to numerous other similar cases only in the prominence of the Negro concerned. I know of another case of a man whose tongue seems dipped in hyssop when he begins to tell of the wrongs of his race, and who will not allow anyone to say in his presence that any good came out of slavery, even incidentally; yet he supports the widowed and aged wife of his former master. And, surely, if these two instances are not sufficient to establish the general proposition, none will gainsay the patience, vigilance, loyalty and helpfulness of the Negro slave during the Civil War, and of his good old wife who nursed white children at her breast at a time when all ties save those of affection were ruptured, and when no protection but devoted hearts watched over the "great house," whose head and master was at the front, fighting to perpetuate slavery. Was it stupidity on the Negro's part? Not at all. He was well informed as to the occurrences of the times. A freemasonry kept him posted as well as the whites were themselves on the course of the war and the issue of each battle. Was it fear that kept him at the old home? Not that, either. Many thousands *did* cross the line to freedom; many other thousands (200,000) fought in the ranks for freedom, but none of them--those who went and those who stayed--those who fought and those who worked,--betrayed a trust, outraged a female, or rebelled against a duty. It was love, the natural wellings of affectionate natures.

He has great endurance, both dispositional and physical. So true is the first that his patience has been the marvel of the world; and, indeed, many, regarding this trait manifested in such an unusual degree, doubted the Negro's courage, till the splendid record of the '60's and the equal, but more recent, record of the '90's, wrote forbearance as the real explanation of an endurance seemingly so at variance with manly spirit.

Of his physical powers, his whole record as a laborer at killing tasks in the most trying climate in America speaks so eloquently that nothing but the statistics of cotton, corn, rice, sugar, railroad ties and felled forests can add to the praise of this burden-bearer of the nation. The census tables here are more romantic and thrilling than figures of rhetoric.

He is courageous. His page in the war record of this country is without blot or blemish. His commanders unite in pronouncing him admirable for courage in the field, commendable for obedience in camp. That he should exhibit such excellent fighting qualities as a soldier, and yet exercise the forbearance that

[70]

characterizes him as a citizen, is remarkable.

He is cheerful. His ivories are as famous as his songs. That the South is "sunny" is largely due to the brightness his rollicking laugh and unfailing good nature bring to it. Though the mudsill of the labor world, he whistles as he hoes, and no dark broodings or whispered conspirings mar the cheerful acceptance of the load he bears. Against the rubber bumper of his good cheer things that have crushed and maddened others rebound without damage. When one hears the quaint jubilee songs, set to minor cadence, he might suppose them the expressions of a melancholy people. They are not to be so interpreted. Rather are they the expression of an experience, not a nature. Like the subdued voice of a caged bird, these songs are the coinage of an occasion, and not the free note of nature. The slave sang of griefs he was not allowed to discuss, hence his songs. This cheerfulness has enabled the Negro to live and increase under circumstances which, in all other instances, have decimated, if not exterminated, inferior peoples. His plasticity to moulding forces and his resiliency against crushing ones come from a Thalian philosophy, unconscious and unstudied, that extracts Epicurean delights from funeral meats.

The above traits are inborn and fundamental, belonging to the race everywhere, in Africa as well as America. Strict correctness requires, however, that attention be called to the fact that there are tribal differences among African Negroes that amount almost to the national variations of Europe; and these are reflected in American Negroes, who are the descendants of these different tribes. There is as much difference between the Mandingo and the Hottentot, both black, as between the Italian and the German, both white; or between the Bushman and the Zulu, both black, as between the Russian and the Englishman, both white. Scientific exactness, therefore, would require a closer analysis of racial characteristics than an article of this length could give; but, speaking in a large way, it may be said that in whatever outward conformity may come to the race in America by reason of training or contact, these traits will lie at the base, the very warp and woof of his soul texture.

If, now, we turn to consider his inbred traits, those the result of experience, conditions and environments, we find that they exist mainly as deficiencies and deformities. These have been superimposed upon the native soul endowment. Slavery has been called the Negro's great schoolmaster, because it took him a savage and released him civilized; took him a heathen and released him a Christian; took him an idler and released him a laborer. Undoubtedly it did these things superficially, but one great defect is to be charged against this school--it did not teach him the meaning of home, purity and providence. To do this is the burden of freedom.

[71]

The emancipated Negro struggles up to-day against many obstacles, the entailment of a brutal slavery. Leaving out of consideration the many who have already emerged, let us apply our thoughts to the great body of submerged people in the congested districts of city and country who present a real problem, and who must be helped to higher things. We note some of the heritages under which they stagger up into full development:

Shiftlessness. He had no need to devise and plan in bondage. There was no need for an enterprising spirit; consequently, he is lacking in leadership and self-reliance. He is inclined to stay in ruts, and applies himself listlessly to a task, feeling that the directive agency should come from without.

Incontinence. It is not to the point to say that others are, too. Undoubtedly, example has as much to do with this laxity as neglect. We simply record the fact. A slave's value was increased by his prolificacy. Begetting children for the auction block could hardly sanctify family ties. It was not nearly so necessary for a slave to know his father as his owner. Added to the promiscuity encouraged and often forced among this class, was the dreadful license which cast lustful Caucasian eyes upon "likely" Negro women.

Indolence. Most men are, especially in a warm climate: but the Negro acquired more than the natural share, because to him as a bondman laziness was great gain, for he had no pecuniary interest in his own labor. Hence, holidays were more to be desired than whole labor days, and he learned to do as little as he might, be excused as often as he could, and hail Saturday as the oasis in a desert week. He hails it yet. The labor efficiency of the Negro has greatly increased since the emancipation, for self-interest is a factor now. In 1865, each Negro produced two-thirds of a bale of cotton; now he produces an average of one whole bale to the man. But there is still woful waste of productive energy. A calculation showing the comparative productive capacity, man for man, between the Northern[3] and Southern laborer would be very interesting.

Improvidence and Extravagance. He will drop the most important job to go on an excursion or parade with his lodge. He spends large sums on expensive clothing and luxuries, while going without things necessary to a real home. He will cheerfully eat fat bacon and "pone" corn-bread all the week[4] in order to indulge in unlimited soda-water, melon and fish at the end. In the cities he is

---

[3] In the original, this was 'Northen'.

[4] In the original, this was 'weeek'.

oftener seen dealing with the pawn-broker than the banker. His house, when furnished at all, is better furnished that that of a white man of equal earning power, but it is on the installment plan. He is loath to buy a house, because he has no taste for responsibility nor faith in himself to manage large concerns; but organs, pianos, clocks, sewing-machines and parlor suits, on time, have no terrors for him. This is because he has been accustomed to think in small numbers. He does not regard the Scotchman's "mickle," because he does not stop to consider that the end is a "muckle." He has amassed, at full valuation, nearly a billion dollars' worth of property, despite this, but this is about one-half of what proper providence would have shown.

Untidiness. Travel through the South and you will be struck with the general misfit and dilapidated appearance of things. Palings are missing from the fences, gates sag on single hinges, houses are unpainted, window panes are broken, yards unkempt and the appearance of a squalor greater than the real is seen on every side. The inside of the house meets the suggestions of the outside. This is a projection of the slave's "quarters" into freedom. The cabin of the slave was, at best, a place to eat and sleep in; there was no thought of the esthetic in such places. A quilt on a plank was a luxury to the tired farm-hand, and paint was nothing to the poor, sun-scorched fellow who sought the house for shade rather than beauty. Habits of personal cleanliness were not inculcated, and even now it is the exception to find a modern bath-room in a Southern home.

Dishonesty. This is the logic, if not the training, of slavery. It is easy for the unrequited toiler in another's field to justify reprisal; hence there arose among the Negroes an amended Commandment which added to "Thou shalt not steal" the clause, "except thou be stolen from." It was no great fault, then, according to this code, to purloin a pig, a sheep, a chicken, or a few potatoes from a master who took all from the slave.

Untruthfulness. This is seen more in innocent and childish exaggeration than in vicious distortion. It is the vice of untutored minds to run to gossip and make miracles of the matter-of-fact. The Negro also tells falsehoods from excess of good nature. He promises to do a piece of work on a certain day, because it is so much easier and pleasanter to say Yes, and stay away, than it is to say No.

Business Unreliability. He does not meet a promise in the way and at the time promised. Not being accustomed to business, he has small conception of the place the promise has in the business world. It is only recently he has begun to

[73]

deal with banks. He, who has no credit, sees[5] no loss of it in a protested note, especially if he intends to pay it some time. That chain which links one man's obligation to another man's solvency he has not considered. He is really as good and safe a debt-payer when he owes a white man as the latter can have, but the methods of the modern bank, placing a time limit on debts, is his detestation. He much prefers the *laissez-faire* of the Southern plantation store.

Lack of Initiative. It was the policy of slavery to crush out the combining instinct, and it was well done; for, outside of churches and secret societies, the Negro has done little to increase the social efficiency which can combine many men into an organic whole, subject to the corporate will and direction. He has, however, made some hopeful beginnings.

Suspicion of his own race. He was taught to watch other Negroes and tell all that they did. This was slavery's native detective force to discover incipient insurrection. Each slave learned to distrust his fellow. And added to this is the knowledge one Negro has that no other has had half sufficient experience in business to be a wise counsellor, or a safe steward of another man's funds. Almost all Negroes who have acquired wealth have entrusted its management to white men.

Ignorance. The causes of his ignorance all know. That he has thrown off one-half of it in forty years is a wonderful showing; but a great incubus remains in the other half, and it demands the nation's attention. What the census calls literacy is often very shallow. The cause of this shallowness lies, in part, in the poor character and short duration of Southern schools; in the poverty that snatches the child from school prematurely to work for bread; in the multitude of mushroom colleges and get-smart-quick universities scattered over the South, and in the glamour of a professional education that entices poorly prepared students into special work.

Add to this, too, the commercialism of the age which regards each day in school as a day out of the market. Boys and girls by scores learn the mechanical parts of type-writing and stenography without the basal culture which gives these callings their greatest efficiency. They copy a manuscript, Chinese-like, mistakes and all; they take you phonetically in sense as well as sound, having no reserve to draw upon to interpret a learned allusion or unusual phrase. Thus while prejudice makes it hard to secure a place, auto-deficiency loses many a one that is secured.

---

[5] In the original, this was 'seees'.

We have discussed the leading characteristics of the Negro, his inborn excellencies and inbred defects, candidly and as they are to be seen in the great mass whose place determines the status of the race as a whole. It would, however, be to small purpose if we did not ask what can be done to develop the innate good and correct the bad in a race so puissant and numerous? This mass is not inert; it has great reactionary force, modifying and influencing all about it. The Negro's excellences have entered into American character and life already; so have his weaknesses. He has brought cheer, love, emotion and religion in saving measure to the land. He has given it wealth by his brawn and liberty by his blood. His self-respect, even in abasement, has kept him struggling upward; his confidence in his own future has infected his friends and kept him from nursing despondency or planning anarchy. But he has laid, and does lay, burdens upon the land, too: his ignorance, his low average of morality, his low standards of home, his lack of enterprise, his lack of self-reliance--these must be cured.

Evidently, he is to be "solved" by educational processes. Everyone of his inborn traits must be respected and developed to proper proportion. Excesses and excrescences must not be carelessly dealt with, for they mark the fertility of a soil that raises rank weeds because no gardener has tilled it. His religion must become "ethics touched with feeling"--not a paroxysm, but a principle. His imagination must be given a rudder to guide its sails; and the first fruits of its proper exercise, as seen in a Dunbar, a Chesnutt, a Coleridge-Taylor and a Tanner, must be pedestaled along the Appian Way over which others are to march. His affection must be met with larger love; his patience rewarded with privilege; his courage called to defend the rights of others rather than redress his own wrongs. Thus shall he supplement from within the best efforts of good men without.

To cure the evils entailed upon him by an unhappy past, he must be educated to work with skill, with self-direction, in combination and unremittingly. Industrial education with constant application, is the slogan of his rise from racial pauperism to productive manliness. Not that exceptional minds should not have exceptional opportunities (and they already exist); but that the great majority of awkward and unskilled ones, who must work somehow, somewhere, all the time, shall have their opportunities for training in industrial schools near them and with courses consonant with the lives they are to lead. Let the ninety and nine who must work, either with trained or fumbling hands, have a chance. Train the Negro to accept and carry responsibility by putting it upon him. Train him, more than any schools are now doing, in morals--to speak the truth, to keep a promise, to touch only his own property, to trust the trustworthy among

[75]

his own race, to risk something in business, to strike out in new lines of endeavor, to buy houses and make homes, to regard beauty as well as utility, to save rather than display. In short, let us subordinate mere knowledge to the work of invigorating the will, energizing productive effort and clarifying moral vision. Let us make safe men rather than vociferous mountebanks; let us put deftness in daily labor above sleight-of-hand tricks, and common sense, well trained, above classical smatterings, which awe the multitude but butter no parsnips.

If we do this, America will have enriched her blood, ennobled her record and shown the world how to deal with its Dark Races without reproach.

Representative American Negroes

By PAUL LAURENCE DUNBAR

An enumeration of some of the noteworthy American Negroes of to-day and yesterday, with some account of their lives and their work. In this paper Mr. Dunbar has turned out his largest and most successful picture of the colored people. It is a noble canvas crowded with heroic figures.

In considering who and what are representative Negroes there are circumstances which compel one to question what is a representative man of the colored race. Some men are born great, some achieve greatness and others lived during the reconstruction period. To have achieved something for the betterment of his race rather than for the aggrandizement of himself, seems to be a man's best title to be called representative. The street corner politician, who through questionable methods or even through skillful manipulation, succeeds in securing the janitorship of the Court House, may be written up in the local papers as "representative," but is he?

I have in mind a young man in Baltimore, Bernard Taylor by name, who to me is more truly representative of the race than half of the "Judges," "Colonels," "Doctors" and "Honorables" whose stock cuts burden the pages of our negro journals week after week. I have said that he is young. Beyond that he is quiet and unobtrusive; but quiet as he is, the worth of his work can be somewhat estimated when it is known that he has set the standard for young men in a city that has the largest colored population in the world.

It is not that as an individual he has ridden to success one enterprise after another. It is not that he has shown capabilities far beyond his years, nor yet that his personal energy will not let him stop at one triumph. The importance of him lies in the fact that his influence upon his fellows is all for good, and in a large community of young Negroes the worth of this cannot be over-estimated. He has taught them that striving is worth while, and by the very force of his example of industry and perseverance, he stands out from the mass. He does not tell how to do things, he does them. Nothing has contributed more to his success than his alertness, and nothing has been more closely followed by his observers, and yet I sometimes wonder when looking at him, how old he must be, how world weary, before the race turns from its worship of the political janitor and says of him, "this is one of our representative men."

This, however, is a matter of values and neither the negro himself, his friends,

[77]

his enemies, his lauders, nor his critics has grown quite certain in appraising these. The rabid agitator who goes about the land preaching the independence and glory of his race, and by his very mouthings retarding both, the saintly missionary, whose only mission is like that of "Pooh Bah," to be insulted; the man of the cloth who thunders against the sins of the world and from whom honest women draw away their skirts, the man who talks temperance and tipples high-balls--these are not representative, and whatever their station in life, they should be rated at their proper value, for there is a difference between attainment and achievement.

Under the pure light of reason, the ignorant carpet bagger judge is a person and not a personality. The illiterate and inefficient black man, whom circumstance put into Congress, was "a representative" but was not representative. So the peculiar conditions of the days immediately after the war have made it necessary to draw fine distinctions.

When Robert Smalls, a slave, piloted the Confederate ship Planter out of Charleston Harbor under the very guns of the men who were employing him, who owned him, his body, his soul, and the husk of his allegiance, and brought it over to the Union, it is a question which forty years has not settled as to whether he was a hero or a felon, a patriot or a traitor. So much has been said of the old Negro's fidelity to his masters that something different might have been expected of him. But take the singular conditions: the first faint streaks of a long delayed dawn had just begun to illumine the sky and this black pilot with his face turned toward the East had no eye for the darkness behind him. He had no time to analyze his position, the right or wrong of it. He had no opportunity to question whether it was loyalty to a union in which he aspired to citizenship, or disloyalty to his masters of the despised confederacy. It was not a time to argue, it was a time to do; and with rare power of decision, skill of action and with indomitable courage, he steered the good ship Planter past Fort Johnson, past Fort Sumter, past Morris Island, out where the flag, the flag of his hopes and fears floated over the federal fleet. And Robert Smalls had done something, something that made him loved and hated, praised and maligned, revered and despised, but something that made him representative of the best that there is in sturdy Negro manhood.

It may seem a far cry from Robert Smalls, the pilot of the Planter, to Booker T. Washington, Principal of the Institute at Tuskegee, Alabama. But much the same traits of character have made the success of the two men; the knowledge of what to do, the courage to do it, and the following out of a single purpose. They are both pilots, and the waters through which their helms have swung have been equally stormy. The methods of both have been questioned; but

[78]

singularly neither one has stopped to question himself, but has gone straight on to his goal over the barriers of criticism, malice and distrust. The secret of Mr. Washington's power is organization, and organization after all is only a concentration of force. This concentration only expresses his own personality, in which every trait and quality tend toward one definite end. They say of this man that he is a man of one idea, but that one is a great one and he has merely concentrated all his powers upon it; in other words he has organized himself and gone forth to gather in whatever about him was essential.

Pilot he is, steadfast and unafraid, strong in his own belief,--yes strong enough to make others believe in him. Without doubt or skepticism, himself he has confounded the skeptics.

Less statesmanlike than Douglass, less scholarly than DuBois, less eloquent than the late J.C. Price, he is yet the foremost figure in Negro national life. He is a great educator and a great man, and though one may not always agree with him, one must always respect him. The race has produced no more adroit diplomatist than he. The statement is broad but there is no better proof of it than the fact that while he is our most astute politician, he has succeeded in convincing both himself and the country that he is not in politics. He has none of the qualities of the curb-stone politician. He is bigger, broader, better, and the highest compliment that could be paid him is that through all his ups and downs, with all he has seen of humanity, he has kept his faith and his ideals. While Mr. Washington stands pre-eminent in his race there are other names that must be mentioned with him as co-workers in the education of the world, names that for lack of time can be only mentioned and passed.

W.H. Council, of Normal, Alabama, has been doing at his school a good and great work along the same lines as Tuskegee. R.R. Wright, of the State College of Georgia, "We'se a-risin' Wright," he is called, and by his own life and work for his people he has made true the boyish prophecy which in the old days inspired Whittier's poem. Three decades ago this was his message from the lowly South, "Tell 'em we'se a-risin'," and by thought, by word, by deed, he has been "Tellin' em so" ever since. The old Southern school has melted into the misty shades of an unregretted past. A new generation, new issues, new conditions, have replaced the old, but the boy who sent that message from the heart of the Southland to the North's heart of hearts has risen, and a martyred President did not blush to call him friend.

So much of the Negro's time has been given to the making of teachers that it is difficult to stop when one has begun enumerating some of those who have stood out more than usually forceful. For my part, there are two more whom I cannot pass over. Kelly Miller, of Howard University, Washington, D.C., is another instructor far above the average. He is a mathematician and a thinker. The world has long been convinced of what the colored man could do in music and in oratory, but it has always been skeptical, when he is to be considered as a student of any exact science. Miller, in his own person, has settled all that. He finished at Johns Hopkins where they will remember him. He is not only a teacher but an author who writes with authority upon his chosen themes, whether he is always known as a Negro writer or not. He is endowed with an accurate, analytical mind, and the most engaging blackness, for which some of us thank God, because there can be no argument as to the source of his mental powers.

Now of the other, William E.B. DuBois, what shall be said? Educator and author, political economist and poet, an Eastern man against a Southern back-ground, he looms up strong, vivid and in bold relief. I say looms advisedly, because, intellectually, there is something so distinctively big about the man. Since the death of the aged Dr. Crummell, we have had no such ripe and finished scholar. Dr. DuBois, Harvard gave him to us, and there he received his Ph.D., impresses one as having reduced all life and all literature to a perfect system. There is about him a fascinating calm of certain power, whether as a searcher after economic facts, under the wing of the University of Pennsylvania, or defying the "powers that be" in a Negro college or leading his pupils along the way of light, one always feels in him this same sense of conscious, restrained, but assured force.

Some years ago in the course of his researches, he took occasion to tell his own people some plain hard truths, and oh, what a howl of protest and denunciation went up from their assembled throats, but it never once disturbed his magnificent calm. He believed what he had said, and not for a single moment did he think of abandoning his position.

He goes at truth as a hard-riding old English squire would take a difficult fence. Let the ditch be beyond if it will.

Dr. DuBois would be the first to disclaim the name of poet but everything outside of his statistical work convicts him. The rhythm of his style, his fancy, his imagery, all bid him bide with those whose souls go singing by a golden way. He has written a number of notable pamphlets and books, the latest of which is "The Soul of the Black Folk," an invaluable contribution to the discussion of the race problem by a man who knows whereof he speaks.

Dr. DuBois is at Atlanta University and has had every opportunity to observe all the phases of America's great question, and I wish I might write at length of

[80]

his books.

It may be urged that too much time has already been taken up with the educational side of the Negro, but the reasonableness of this must become apparent when one remembers that for the last forty years the most helpful men of the race have come from the ranks of its teachers, and few of those who have finally done any big thing, but have at some time or other held the scepter of authority in a school. They may have changed later and grown, indeed they must have done so, but the fact remains that their poise, their discipline, the impulse for their growth came largely from their work in the school room.

There is perhaps no more notable example of this phase of Negro life than the Hon. Richard Theodore Greener, our present Consul at Vladivostok. He was, I believe, the first of our race to graduate from Harvard and he has always been regarded as one of the most scholarly men who, through the touch of Negro blood, belongs to us. He has been historian, journalist and lecturer, but back of all this he was a teacher; and for years after his graduation he was a distinguished professor at the most famous of all the old Negro colleges. This institution is now a thing of the past, but the men who knew it in its palmy days speak of it still with longing and regret. It is claimed, and from the names and qualities of the men, not without justice, that no school for the higher education of the black man has furnished a finer curriculum or possessed a better equipped or more efficient faculty. Among these, Richard T. Greener was a bright, particular star.

After the passing of the school, Mr. Greener turned to other activities. His highest characteristics were a fearless patience and a hope that buoyed him up through days of doubt and disappointment. Author and editor he was, but he was not satisfied with these. Beyond their scope were higher things that beckoned him. Politics, or perhaps better, political science, allured him, and he applied himself to a course that brought him into intimate contact with the leaders of his country, white and black. A man of wide information, great knowledge and close grasp of events he made himself invaluable to his party and then with his usual patience awaited his reward.

The story of how he came to his own cannot be told without just a shade of bitterness darkening the smile that one must give to it all. The cause for which he had worked triumphed. The men for whom he had striven gained their goal and now, Greener must be recognized, but--

Vladivostok, your dictionary will tell you, is a sea-port in the maritime Province of Siberia, situated on the Golden Horn of Peter the Great. It will tell you also that it is the chief Russian naval station on the Pacific. It is an out of the way place and one who has not the world-circling desire would rather hesitate before setting out thither. It was to this post that Mr. Greener was appointed.

"Exile," his friends did not hesitate to say. "Why didn't the Government make it a sentence instead of veiling it in the guise of an appointment?" asked others sarcastically.

"Will he go?" That was the general question that rose and fell, whispered and thundered about the new appointee, and in the midst of it all, silent and dignified, he kept his council. The next thing Washington knew he was gone. There was a gasp of astonishment and then things settled back into their former state of monotony and Greener was forgotten.

But in the eastern sky, darkness began to arise, the warning flash of danger swept across the heavens, the thunder drum of war began to roll. For a moment the world listened in breathless suspense, the suspense of horror. Louder and louder rose the thunder peal until it drowned every other sound in the ears of the nation, every other sound save the cries and wails of dying women and the shrieks of tortured children. Then France, England, Germany, Japan and America marshalled their forces and swept eastward to save and to avenge. The story of the Boxer uprising has been told, but little has been said of how Vladivostok, "A sea-port in the maritime Province of Siberia," became one of the most important points of communication with the outside world, and its Consul came frequently to be heard from by the State Department. And so Greener after years of patience and toil had come to his own. If the government had wished to get him out of the way, it had reckoned without China.

A new order of things has come into Negro-American politics and this man has become a part of it. It matters not that he began his work under the old regime. So did Judge Gibbs, a man eighty years of age, but he, too, has kept abreast of the times, and although the reminiscences in his delightful autobiography take one back to the hazy days when the land was young and politics a more strenuous thing than it is even now, when there was anarchy in Louisiana and civil war in Arkansas, when one shot first and questioned afterward; yet because his mind is still active, because he has changed his methods with the changing time, because his influence over young men is greatly potent still; he is, in the race, perhaps, the best representative of what the old has brought to the new.

Beside him strong, forceful, commanding, stands the figure of George H. White, whose farewell speech before the Fifty-sixth Congress, when through the disfranchisement of Negroes he was defeated for re-election, stirred the country and fired the hearts of his brothers. He has won his place through

[82]

honesty, bravery and aggressiveness. He has given something to the nation that the nation needed, and with such men as Pinchback, Lynch, Terrell and others of like ilk, acting in concert, it is but a matter of time when his worth shall induce a repentant people, with a justice builded upon the foundation of its old prejudice, to ask the Negro back to take a hand in the affairs of state.

Add to all this the facts that the Negro has his representatives in the commercial world: McCoy and Granville T. Woods, inventors; in the agricultural world with J.H. Groves, the potato king of Kansas, who last year shipped from his own railway siding seventy-two thousand five hundred bushels of potatoes alone; in the military, with Capt. Charles A. Young, a West Pointer, now stationed at the Presidio; that in medicine, he possesses in Daniel H. Williams, of Chicago, one of the really great surgeons of the country; that Edward H. Morris, a black man, is one of the most brilliant lawyers at the brilliant Cook County bar; that in every walk of life he has men and women who stand for something definite and concrete, and it seems to me that there can be little doubt that the race problem will gradually solve itself.

I have spoken of "men and women," and indeed the women must not be forgotten, for to them the men look for much of the inspiration and impulse that drives them forward to success. Mrs. Mary Church Terrell upon the platform speaking for Negro womanhood and Miss Sarah Brown, her direct opposite, a little woman sitting up in her aerie above a noisy New York street, stand for the very best that there is in our mothers, wives and sisters. The one fully in the public eye, with learning and eloquence, telling the hopes and fears of her kind; the other in suffering and retirement, with her knowledge of the human heart and her gentleness inspiring all who meet her to better and nobler lives. They are both doing their work bravely and grandly. But when the unitiate ask who is "la Petite Reine," we think of the quiet little woman in a New York fifth floor back and are silent.

She is a patron of all our literature and art and we have both. Whether it is a new song by Will Marion Cook or a new book by DuBois or Chestnut, than whom no one has ever told the life of the Negro more accurately and convincingly, she knows it and has a kindly word of praise or encouragement.

In looking over the field for such an article as this, one just begins to realize how many Negroes are representative of something, and now it seems that in closing no better names could be chosen than those of the two Tanners.

From time immemorial, Religion and Art have gone together, but it remained for us to place them in the persons of these two men, in the relation of father and son. Bishop Benj. Tucker Tanner, of the A.M.E. Church, is not only a theologian and a priest, he is a dignified, polished man of the higher world and a poet. He has succeeded because he was prepared for success. As to his writings, he will, perhaps, think most highly of "His Apology For African Methodism;" but some of us, while respecting this, will turn from it to the poems and hymns that have sung themselves out of his gentle heart.

Is it any wonder that his son, Henry O. Tanner, is a poet with the brush or that the French Government has found it out? From the father must have come the man's artistic impulse, and he carried it on and on to a golden fruition. In the Luxembourg gallery hangs his picture, "The Raising of Lazarus." At the Academy of Fine Arts, Philadelphia, I saw his "Annunciation," both a long way from his "Banjo Lesson," and thinking of him I began to wonder whether, in spite of all the industrial tumult, it were not in the field of art, music and literature that the Negro was to make his highest contribution to American civilization. But this is merely a question which time will answer.

All these of whom I have spoken are men who have striven and achieved and the reasons underlying their success are the same that account for the advancement of men of any other race: preparation, perseverance, bravery, patience, honesty and the power to seize the opportunity.

It is a little dark still, but there are warnings of the day and somewhere out of the darkness a bird is singing to the Dawn.

The Negro's Place in American Life at the Present Day

BY T. THOMAS FORTUNE

Considering the two hundred and forty-five years of his slavery and the comparatively short time he has enjoyed the opportunities of freedom, his place in American life at the present day is creditable to him and promising for the future.

There can be no healthy growth in the life of a race or a nation without a self-reliant spirit animating the whole body; if it amounts to optimism, devoid of egotism and vanity, so much the better. This spirit necessarily carries with it intense pride of race, or of nation, as the case may be, and ramifies the whole mass, inspiring and shaping its thought and effort, however humble or exalted these may be,--as it takes "all sorts and conditions of men" to make up a social order, instinct with the ambition and the activity which work for "high thinking and right living," of which modern evolution in all directions is the most powerful illustration in history. If pride of ancestry can, happily, be added to pride of race and nation, and these are re-enforced by self-reliance, courage and correct moral living, the possible success of such people may be accepted, without equivocation, as a foregone conclusion. I have found all of these requirements so finely blended in the life and character of no people as that of the Japanese, who are just now emerging from "the double night of ages" into the vivifying sunlight of modern progress.

What is the Negro's place in American life at the present day?

The answer depends entirely upon the point of view. Unfortunately for the Afro-American people, they have no pride of ancestry; in the main, few of them can trace their parentage back four generations; and the "daughter of an hundred earls" of whom there are probably many, is unconscious of her descent, and would profit nothing by it if this were not true. The blood of all the ethnic types that go to make up American citizenship flows in the veins of the Afro-American people, so that of the ten million of them in this country, accounted for by the Federal census, not more than four million are of pure negroid descent, while some four million of them, not accounted for by the Federal census, have escaped into the ranks of the white race, and are re-enforced very largely by such escapements every year. The vitiation of blood has operated irresistibly to weaken that pride of ancestry, which is the foundation-stone of pride of race; so that the Afro-American people have been held together rather by the segregation decreed by law and public opinion than by ties of consanguinity since their manumission and enfranchisement. It is not because they are poor and ignorant and oppressed, as a mass, that there is no such sympathy of thought and unity of effort among them as among Irishmen and Jews the world over, but because the vitiation of blood, beyond the honorable restrictions of law, has destroyed, in large measure, that pride of ancestry upon which pride of race must be builded. In no other logical way can we account for the failure of the Afro-American people to stand together, as other oppressed races do, and have done, for the righting of wrongs against them authorized by the laws of the several states, if not by the Federal Constitution, and sanctioned or tolerated by public opinion. In nothing has this radical defect been more noticeable since the War of the Rebellion than in the uniform failure of the people to sustain such civic organizations as exist and have existed, to test in the courts of law and in the forum of public opinion the validity of organic laws of States intended to deprive them of the civil and political rights guaranteed to them by the Federal Constitution. The two such organizations of this character which have appealed to them are the National Afro-American League, organized in Chicago, in 1890, and the National Afro-American Council, organized in Rochester, New York, out of the League, in 1898. The latter organization still exists, the strongest of its kind, but it has never commanded the sympathy and support of the masses of the people, nor is there, or has there been, substantial agreement and concert of effort among the thoughtful men of the race along these lines. They have been restrained by selfish, personal and petty motives, while the constitutional rights which vitalize their citizenship have been "denied or abridged" by legislation of certain of the States and by public opinion, even as Nero fiddled while Rome burned. If they had been actuated by a strong pride of ancestry and of race, if they had felt that injury to one was injury to all, if they had hung together instead of hanging separately, their place in the civil and political life of the Republic to-day would not be that, largely, of pariahs, with none so poor as to do them honor, but that of equality of right under the law enjoyed by all other alien ethnic forces in our citizenship. They who will not help themselves are usually not helped by others. They who make a loud noise and courageously contend for what is theirs, usually enjoy the respect and confidence of their fellows and get, in the end, what belongs to them, or a reasonable modification of it.

As a consequence of inability to unite in thought and effort for the conservation of their civil and political rights, the Afro-American Negroes and colored people have lost, by fundamental enactments of the old slave-holding

States, all of the civil and political rights guaranteed them by the Federal Constitution, in the full enjoyment of which they were from the adoption of the War Amendments up to 1876-7, when they were sacrificed by their Republican allies of the North and West, in the alienation of their State governments, in order to save the Presidency to Mr. Rutherford B. Hayes of Ohio. Their reverses in this matter in the old slave-holding States, coupled with a vast mass of class legislation, modelled on the slave code, have affected the Afro-American people in their civil and political rights in all of the States of the Republic, especially as far as public opinion is concerned. This was inevitable, and follows in every instance in history where a race element of the citizenship is set aside by law or public opinion as separate and distinct from its fellows, with a fixed status or caste.

It will take the Afro-American people fully a century to recover what they lost of civil and political equality under the law in the Southern States, as a result of the re-actionary and bloody movement begun in the Reconstruction period by the Southern whites, and culminating in 1877,--the excesses of the Reconstruction governments, about which so much is said to the discredit of the Negro, being chargeable to the weakness and corruption of Northern carpet-baggers, who were the master and responsible spirits of the time and the situation, rather than to the weakness, the ignorance and venality of their Negro dupes, who, very naturally, followed where they led, as any other grateful people would have done. For, were not these same Northern carpet-baggers the direct representatives of the Government and the Army which crushed the slave power and broke the shackles of the slave? Even so. The Northern carpet-baggers planned and got the plunder, and have it; the Negro got the credit and the odium, and have them yet. It often happens that way in history, that the innocent dupes are made to suffer for the misdeeds and crimes of the guilty.

The recovery of civil and political rights under the Constitution, as "denied or abridged" by the constitutions of the States, more especially those of the old slave holding ones, will be a slow and tedious process, and will come to the individual rather than to the race, as the reward of character and thrift; because, for reasons already stated, it will hardly be possible in the future, as it has not been in the past, to unify the mass of the Afro-American people, in thought and conduct, for a proper contention in the courts and at the ballot-box and in the education of public opinion, to accomplish this purpose. Perhaps there is no other instance in history where everything depended so largely upon the individual, and so little upon the mass of his race, for that development in the religious and civic virtues which makes more surely for an honorable status in

[87]

any citizenship than constitutions or legislative enactments built upon them.

But even from this point of view, I am disposed to believe that the Negro's civil and political rights are more firmly fixed in law and public opinion than was true at the close of the Reconstruction period, when everything relating to him was unsettled and confused, based in legislative guarantees, subject to approval or disapproval of the dominant public opinion of the several States, and that he will gradually work out his own salvation under the Constitution,--such as Charles Sumner, Thaddeus Stevens, Benjamin F. Butler, Frederick Douglass, and their co-workers, hoped and labored that he might enjoy. He has lost nothing under the fundamental law; such of these restrictions, as apply to him by the law of certain of the States, necessarily apply to white men in like circumstances of ignorance and poverty, and can be overcome, in time, by assiduous courtship of the schoolmaster and the bank cashier. The extent to which the individual members of the race are overcoming the restrictions made a bar to their enjoyment of civil and political rights under the Constitution is gratifying to those who wish the race well and who look beyond the present into the future: while it is disturbing the dreams of those who spend most of their time and thought in abortive efforts to "keep the 'nigger' in his place"--as if any man or race could have a place in the world's thought and effort which he did not make for himself! In our grand Republic, at least, it has been so often demonstrated as to become proverbial, that the door of opportunity shall be closed to no man, and that he shall be allowed to have that place in our national life which he makes for himself. So it is with the Negro now, as an individual. Will it be so with him in the future as a race? To answer that we shall first have to determine that he has a race.

However he may be lacking in pride of ancestry and race, no one can accuse the Negro of lack of pride of Nation and State, and even of county. Indeed, his pride in the Republic and his devotion to it are among the most pathetic phases of his pathetic history, from Jamestown, in 1620, to San Juan Hill, in 1898. He has given everything to the Republic,--his labor and blood and prayers. What has the Republic given him, but blows and rebuffs and criminal ingratitude! And he stands now, ready and eager, to give the Republic all that he has. What does the Republic stand ready and eager to give him? Let the answer come out of the mouth of the future.

It is a fair conclusion that the Negro has a firmer and more assured civil and political status in American life to-day than at the close of the Reconstruction period, paradoxical as this may appear to many, despite the adverse legislation of the old slave-holding States, and the tolerant favor shown such legislation by the Federal Supreme Court, in such opinions as it has delivered, from time to

[88]

time, upon the subject, since the adoption of the War amendments to the Federal Constitution. Technically, the Negro stands upon equality with all other citizens under this large body of special and class legislation; but, as a matter of fact, it is so framed that the greatest inequality prevails, and was intended to prevail, in the administration of it by the several States chiefly concerned. As long as such legislation by the States specifies, on the face of it, that it shall operate upon all citizens equally, however unequally and unjustly the legislation may be interpreted and administered by the local courts, the Federal Supreme Court has held, time and again, that no hardship was worked, and, if so, that the aggrieved had his recourse in appeal to the higher courts of the State of which he is a citizen,--a recourse at this time precisely like that of carrying coal to New Castle.

Under the circumstances, there is no alternative for the Negro citizen but to work out his salvation under the Constitution, as other citizens have done and are doing. It will be a long and tedious process before the equitable adjustment has been attained, but that does not much matter, as full and fair enjoyment of civil and political rights requires much time and patience and hard labor in any given situation, where two races come together in the same governmental environment; such as is the case of the Negro in America, the Irishman in Ireland, and the Jew everywhere in Europe. It is just as well, perhaps, that the Negro will have to work out his salvation under the Constitution as an individual rather than as a race, as the Jew has done it in Great Britain and as the Irishman will have to do it under the same Empire, as it is and has been the tendency of our law and precedent to subordinate race elements and to exalt the individual citizens as indivisible "parts of one stupendous whole." When this has been accomplished by the law in the case of the Negro, as in the case of other alien ethnic elements of the citizenship, it will be more gradually, but assuredly, accomplished by society at large, the indestructible foundation of which was laid by the reckless and brutal prostitution of black women by white men in the days of slavery, from which a vast army of mulattoes were produced, who have been and are, gradually, by honorable marriage among themselves, changing the alleged "race characteristics and tendencies" of the Negro people. A race element, it is safe and fair to conclude, incapable, like that of the North American Indian, of such a process of elimination and assimilation, will always be a thorn in the flesh of the Republic, in which there is, admittedly, no place for the integrality and growth of a distinct race type. The Afro-American people, for reasons that I have stated, are even now very far from being such a distinct race type, and without further admixture of white and black blood, will continue to be less so to the end of the chapter. It seems to me

[89]

that this view of the matter has not received the consideration that it deserves at the hands of those who set themselves up as past grand masters in the business of "solving the race problem," and in accurately defining "The Negro's Place in American Life at the Present Day." The negroid type and the Afro-American type are two very distinct types, and the sociologist who confounds them, as is very generally done, is bound to confuse his subject and his audience.

It is a debatable question as to whether the Negro's present industrial position is better or worse than it was, say, at the close of the Reconstruction period. As a mass, I am inclined to the opinion that it is worse, as the laws of the States where he is congregated most numerously are so framed as to favor the employer in every instance, and he does not scruple to get all out of the industrial slave that he can; which is, in the main, vastly more than the slave master got, as the latter was at the expense of housing, feeding, clothing and providing medical service for his chattel, while the former is relieved of this expense and trouble. Prof. W.E.B. DuBois, of Atlanta University, who has made a critical study of the rural Negro of the Southern States, sums up the industrial phase of the matter in the following ("The Souls of Black Folk," pp. 39-40):

"For this much all men know: Despite compromise, war and struggle, the Negro is not free. In the backwoods of the Gulf States, for miles and miles, he may not leave the plantation of his birth; in well-nigh the whole rural South the black farmers are peons, bound by law and custom to an economic slavery, from which the only escape is death or the penitentiary. In the most cultured sections and cities of the South the Negroes are a segregated servile caste, with restricted rights and privileges. Before the courts, both in law and custom, they stand on a different and peculiar basis. Taxation without representation is the rule of their political life. And the result of all this is, and in nature must have been, lawlessness and crime."

It is a dark and gloomy picture, the substitution of industrial for chattel slavery, with none of the legal and selfish restraints upon the employer which surrounded and actuated the master. And this is true of the entire mass of the Afro-American laborers of the Southern States. Out of the mass have arisen a large number of individuals who own and till their own lands. This element is very largely recruited every year, and to this source must we look for the gradual undermining of the industrial slavery of the mass of the people. Here, too, we have a long and tedious process of evolution, but it is nothing new in the history of races circumstanced as the Afro-American people are. That the Negro is destined, however, to be the landlord and master agriculturist of the Southern States is a probability sustained by all the facts in the situation; not

[90]

the least of which being the tendency of the poor white class and small farmers to abandon agricultural pursuits for those of the factory and the mine, from which the Negro laborer is excluded, partially in the mine and wholly in the factory. The development of mine and factory industries in the Southern States in the past two decades has been one of the most remarkable in industrial history.

In the skilled trades, at the close of the War of the Rebellion, most of the work was done by Negroes educated as artisans in the hard school of slavery, but there has been a steady decline in the number of such laborers, not because of lack of skill, but because trade unionism has gradually taken possession of such employments in the South, and will not allow the Negro to work alongside of the white man. And this is the rule of the trade unions in all parts of the country. It is to be hoped that there may be a gradual broadening of the views of white laborers in this vital matter and a change of attitude by the trade unions that they dominate. Can we reasonably expect this? As matters now stand, it is the individual Negro artisan, often a master contractor, who can work at his trade and give employment to his fellows. Fortunately, there are a great many of these in all parts of the Southern States, and their number is increasing every year, as the result of the rapid growth and high favor of industrial schools, where the trades are taught. A very great deal should be expected from this source, as a Negro contractor stands very nearly on as good footing as a white one in the bidding, when he has established a reputation for reliability. The facts obtained in every Southern city bear out this view of the matter. The individual black man has a fighting chance for success in the skilled trades; and, as he succeeds, will draw the skilled mass after him. The proper solution of the skilled labor problem is strictly within the power of the individual Negro. I believe that he is solving it, and that he will ultimately solve it.

It is, however, in the marvellous building up of a legal, comfortable and happy home life, where none whatever existed at the close of the War of the Rebellion; in the no less stupendous development of the church life, with large and puissant organizations that command the respect and admiration of mankind, and owning splendid church property valued at millions of dollars; in the quenchless thirst of the mass of the people for useful knowledge, displayed at the close of the War of the Rebellion, and abating nothing of its intense keenness since, with the remarkable reduction in the illiteracy of the mass of the people, as is eloquently disclosed by the census reports--it is in these results that no cause for complaint or discouragement can be found. The whole race here stands on improved ground over that it occupied at the close of the War of the Rebellion; albeit, even here, the individual has outstripped the mass of the race, as it was but natural that he should and always will. But, while this is true and gratifying to all those that hope the Afro-American people well, it is also true, and equally gratifying that, as far as the mass is concerned, the home life, the church and the school house have come into the life of the people, in some sort, everywhere, giving the whole race a character and a standing in the estimation of mankind which it did not have at the close of the war, and presaging, logically, unless all signs fail, a development along high and honorable lines in the future; the results from which, I predict, at the end of the ensuing half century, builded upon the foundation already laid, being such as to confound the prophets of evil, who never cease to doubt and shake their heads, asking: "Can any good thing come out of Nazareth?" We have the answer already in the social and home life of the people, which is so vast an improvement over the conditions and the heritage of slavery as to stagger the understanding of those who are informed on the subject, or will take the trouble to inform themselves.

If we have much loose moral living, it is not sanctioned by the mass, wedlock being the rule, and not the exception; if we have a vast volume of illiteracy, we have reduced it by forty per cent. since the war, and the school houses are all full of children eager to learn, and the schools of higher and industrial training cannot accommodate all those who knock at their doors for admission; if we have more than our share of criminality, we have also churches in every hamlet and city, to which a vast majority of the people belong, and which are insistently pointing "the way, the light and the truth" to higher and nobler living.

Mindful, therefore, of the Negro's two hundred and forty-five years of slave education and unrequited toil, and of his thirty years of partial freedom and less than partial opportunity, who shall say that his place in American life at the present day is not all that should be reasonably expected of him, that it is not creditable to him, and that it is not a sufficient augury for better and nobler and higher thinking, striving and building in the future? Social growth is the slowest of all growth. If there be signs of growth, then, there is reasonable hope for a healthy maturity. There are plenty of such signs, and he who runs may read them, if he will.

UP FROM SLAVERY

An Autobiography

Booker T. Washington

This volume is dedicated to my wife Margaret James Washington and to my brother John H. Washington, whose patience, fidelity, and hard work have gone far to make the work at Tuskegee successful.

CONTENTS

PREFACE

This volume is the outgrowth of a series of articles, dealing with incidents in my life, which were published consecutively in the Outlook. While they were appearing in that magazine I was constantly surprised at the number of requests which came to me from all parts of the country, asking that the articles be permanently preserved in book form. I am most grateful to the Outlook for permission to gratify these requests.

I have tried to tell a simple, straightforward story, with no attempt at embellishment. My regret is that what I have attempted to do has been done so imperfectly. The greater part of my time and strength is required for the executive work connected with the Tuskegee Normal and Industrial Institute, and in securing the money necessary for the support of the institution. Much of what I have said has been written on board trains, or at hotels or railroad stations while I have been waiting for trains, or during the moments that I could spare from my work while at Tuskegee. Without the painstaking and generous assistance of Mr. Max Bennett Thrasher I could not have succeeded in any satisfactory degree.

INTRODUCTION

The details of Mr. Washington's early life, as frankly set down in "Up from Slavery," do not give quite a whole view of his education. He had the training that a coloured youth receives at Hampton, which, indeed, the autobiography does explain. But the reader does not get his intellectual pedigree, for Mr. Washington himself, perhaps, does not as clearly understand it as another man might. The truth is he had a training during the most impressionable period of his life that was very extraordinary, such a training as few men of his generation have had. To see its full meaning one must start in the Hawaiian Islands half a century or more ago.* There Samuel Armstrong, a youth of missionary parents, earned enough money to pay his expenses at an American college. Equipped with this small sum and the earnestness that the undertaking implied, he came to Williams College when Dr. Mark Hopkins was president. Williams College had many good things for youth in that day, as it has in this, but the greatest was the strong personality of its famous president. Every student does not profit by a great teacher; but perhaps no young man ever came under the influence of Dr. Hopkins, whose whole nature was so ripe for profit by such an experience as young Armstrong. He lived in the family of President Hopkins, and thus had a training that was wholly out of the common; and this training had much to do with the development of his own strong character, whose originality and force we are only beginning to appreciate.

* For this interesting view of Mr. Washington's education, I am indebted to Robert C. Ogden, Esq., Chairman of the Board of Trustees of Hampton Institute and the intimate friend of General Armstrong during the whole period of his educational work.

In turn, Samuel Armstrong, the founder of Hampton Institute, took up his work as a trainer of youth. He had very raw material, and doubtless most of his pupils failed to get the greatest lessons from him; but, as he had been a peculiarly receptive pupil of Dr. Hopkins, so Booker Washington became a peculiarly receptive pupil of his. To the formation of Mr. Washington's character, then, went the missionary zeal of New England, influenced by one of the strongest personalities in modern education, and the wide-reaching moral earnestness of General Armstrong himself These influences are easily recognizable in Mr. Washington to-day by men who knew Dr. Hopkins and General Armstrong.

I got the cue to Mr. Washington's character from a very simple incident many years ago. I had never seen him, and I knew little about him, except that he was

[97]

the head of a school at Tuskegee, Alabama. I had occasion to write to him, and I addressed him as "The Rev. Booker T. Washington." In his reply there was no mention of my addressing him as a clergyman. But when I had occasion to write to him again, and persisted in making him a preacher, his second letter brought a postscript: "I have no claim to 'Rev.'" I knew most of the coloured men who at that time had become prominent as leaders of their race, but I had not then known one who was neither a politician nor a preacher; and I had not heard of the head of an important coloured school who was not a preacher. "A new kind of man in the coloured world," I said to myself--"a new kind of man surely if he looks upon his task as an economic one instead of a theological one." I wrote him an apology for mistaking him for a preacher.

The first time that I went to Tuskegee I was asked to make an address to the school on Sunday evening. I sat upon the platform of the large chapel and looked forth on a thousand coloured faces, and the choir of a hundred or more behind me sang a familiar religious melody, and the whole company joined in the chorus with unction. I was the only white man under the roof, and the scene and the songs made an impression on me that I shall never forget. Mr. Washington arose and asked them to sing one after another of the old melodies that I had heard all my life; but I had never before heard them sung by a thousand voices nor by the voices of educated Negroes. I had associated them with the Negro of the past, not with the Negro who was struggling upward. They brought to my mind the plantation, the cabin, the slave, not the freedman in quest of education. But on the plantation and in the cabin they had never been sung as these thousand students sang them. I saw again all the old plantations that I had ever seen; the whole history of the Negro ran through my mind; and the inexpressible pathos of his life found expression in these songs as I had never before felt it.

And the future? These were the ambitious youths of the race, at work with an earnestness that put to shame the conventional student life of most educational institutions. Another song rolled up along the rafters. And as soon as silence came, I found myself in front of this extraordinary mass of faces, thinking not of them, but of that long and unhappy chapter in our country's history which followed the one great structural mistake of the Fathers of the Republic; thinking of the one continuous great problem that generations of statesmen had wrangled over, and a million men fought about, and that had so dwarfed the mass of English men in the Southern States as to hold them back a hundred years behind their fellows in every other part of the world--in England, in Australia, and in the Northern and Western States; I was thinking of this dark shadow that had oppressed every large-minded statesman from Jefferson to

Lincoln. These thousand young men and women about me were victims of it. I, too, was an innocent victim of it. The whole Republic was a victim of that fundamental error of importing Africa into America. I held firmly to the first article of my faith that the Republic must stand fast by the principle of a fair ballot; but I recalled the wretched mess that Reconstruction had made of it; I recalled the low level of public life in all the "black" States. Every effort of philanthropy seemed to have miscarried, every effort at correcting abuses seemed of doubtful value, and the race friction seemed to become severer. Here was the century-old problem in all its pathos seated singing before me. Who were the more to be pitied--these innocent victims of an ancient wrong, or I and men like me, who had inherited the problem? I had long ago thrown aside illusions and theories, and was willing to meet the facts face to face, and to do whatever in God's name a man might do towards saving the next generation from such a burden. But I felt the weight of twenty well-nigh hopeless years of thought and reading and observation; for the old difficulties remained and new ones had sprung up. Then I saw clearly that the way out of a century of blunders had been made by this man who stood beside me and was introducing me to this audience. Before me was the material he had used. All about me was the indisputable evidence that he had found the natural line of development. He had shown the way. Time and patience and encouragement and work would do the rest.

It was then more clearly than ever before that I understood the patriotic significance of Mr. Washington's work. It is this conception of it and of him that I have ever since carried with me. It is on this that his claim to our gratitude rests.

To teach the Negro to read, whether English, or Greek, or Hebrew, butters no parsnips. To make the Negro work, that is what his master did in one way and hunger has done in another; yet both these left Southern life where they found it. But to teach the Negro to do skilful work, as men of all the races that have risen have worked,--responsible work, which IS education and character; and most of all when Negroes so teach Negroes to do this that they will teach others with a missionary zeal that puts all ordinary philanthropic efforts to shame,--this is to change the whole economic basis of life and the whole character of a people.

The plan itself is not a new one. It was worked out at Hampton Institute, but it was done at Hampton by white men. The plan had, in fact, been many times theoretically laid down by thoughtful students of Southern life. Handicrafts were taught in the days of slavery on most well-managed plantations. But Tuskegee is, nevertheless, a brand-new chapter in the history of the Negro, and in the history of the knottiest problem we have ever faced. It not only makes "a carpenter of a man; it makes a man of a carpenter." In one sense, therefore, it is of greater value than any other institution for the training of men and women that we have, from Cambridge to Palo Alto. It is almost the only one of which it may be said that it points the way to a new epoch in a large area of our national life.

To work out the plan on paper, or at a distance--that is one thing. For a white man to work it out--that too, is an easy thing. For a coloured man to work it out in the South, where, in its constructive period, he was necessarily misunderstood by his own people as well as by the whites, and where he had to adjust it at every step to the strained race relations--that is so very different and more difficult a thing that the man who did it put the country under lasting obligations to him.

It was not and is not a mere educational task. Anybody could teach boys trades and give them an elementary education. Such tasks have been done since the beginning of civilization. But this task had to be done with the rawest of raw material, done within the civilization of the dominant race, and so done as not to run across race lines and social lines that are the strongest forces in the community. It had to be done for the benefit of the whole community. It had to be done, moreover, without local help, in the face of the direst poverty, done by begging, and done in spite of the ignorance of one race and the prejudice of the other.

No man living had a harder task, and a task that called for more wisdom to do it right. The true measure of Mr. Washington's success is, then, not his teaching the pupils of Tuskegee, nor even gaining the support of philanthropic persons at a distance, but this--that every Southern white man of character and of wisdom has been won to a cordial recognition of the value of the work, even men who held and still hold to the conviction that a mere book education for the Southern blacks under present conditions is a positive evil. This is a demonstration of the efficiency of the Hampton-Tuskegee idea that stands like the demonstration of the value of democratic institutions themselves--a demonstration made so clear in spite of the greatest odds that it is no longer open to argument.

Consider the change that has come in twenty years in the discussion of the Negro problem. Two or three decades ago social philosophers and statisticians and well-meaning philanthropists were still talking and writing about the deportation of the Negroes, or about their settlement within some restricted area, or about their settling in all parts of the Union, or about their decline through their neglect of their children, or about their rapid multiplication till they should expel the whites from the South--of every sort of nonsense under

[100]

heaven. All this has given place to the simple plan of an indefinite extension among the neglected classes of both races of the Hampton-Tuskegee system of training. The "problem" in one sense has disappeared. The future will have for the South swift or slow development of its masses and of its soil in proportion to the swift or slow development of this kind of training. This change of view is a true measure of Mr. Washington's work.

The literature of the Negro in America is colossal, from political oratory through abolitionism to "Uncle Tom's Cabin" and "Cotton is King"--a vast mass of books which many men have read to the waste of good years (and I among them); but the only books that I have read a second time or ever care again to read in the whole list (most of them by tiresome and unbalanced "reformers") are "Uncle Remus" and "Up from Slavery"; for these are the great literature of the subject. One has all the best of the past, the other foreshadows a better future; and the men who wrote them are the only men who have written of the subject with that perfect frankness and perfect knowledge and perfect poise whose other name is genius.

Mr. Washington has won a world-wide fame at an early age. His story of his own life already has the distinction of translation into more languages, I think, than any other American book; and I suppose that he has as large a personal acquaintance among men of influence as any private citizen now living.

His own teaching at Tuskegee is unique. He lectures to his advanced students on the art of right living, not out of text-books, but straight out of life. Then he sends them into the country to visit Negro families. Such a student will come back with a minute report of the way in which the family that he has seen lives, what their earnings are, what they do well and what they do ill; and he will explain how they might live better. He constructs a definite plan for the betterment of that particular family out of the resources that they have. Such a student, if he be bright, will profit more by an experience like this than he could profit by all the books on sociology and economics that ever were written. I talked with a boy at Tuskegee who had made such a study as this, and I could not keep from contrasting his knowledge and enthusiasm with what I heard in a class room at a Negro university in one of the Southern cities, which is conducted on the idea that a college course will save the soul. Here the class was reciting a lesson from an abstruse text-book on economics, reciting it by rote, with so obvious a failure to assimilate it that the waste of labour was pitiful.

I asked Mr. Washington years ago what he regarded as the most important result of his work, and he replied:

"I do not know which to put first, the effect of Tuskegee's work on the Negro, or the effect on the attitude of the white man to the Negro."

The race divergence under the system of miseducation was fast getting wider. Under the influence of the Hampton-Tuskegee idea the races are coming into a closer sympathy and into an honourable and helpful relation. As the Negro becomes economically independent, he becomes a responsible part of the Southern life; and the whites so recognize him. And this must be so from the nature of things. There is nothing artificial about it. It is development in a perfectly natural way. And the Southern whites not only so recognize it, but they are imitating it in the teaching of the neglected masses of their own race. It has thus come about that the school is taking a more direct and helpful hold on life in the South than anywhere else in the country. Education is not a thing apart from life--not a "system," nor a philosophy; it is direct teaching how to live and how to work.

To say that Mr. Washington has won the gratitude of all thoughtful Southern white men, is to say that he has worked with the highest practical wisdom at a large constructive task; for no plan for the up-building of the freedman could succeed that ran counter to Southern opinion. To win the support of Southern opinion and to shape it was a necessary part of the task; and in this he has so well succeeded that the South has a sincere and high regard for him. He once said to me that he recalled the day, and remembered it thankfully, when he grew large enough to regard a Southern white man as he regarded a Northern one. It is well for our common country that the day is come when he and his work are regarded as highly in the South as in any other part of the Union. I think that no man of our generation has a more noteworthy achievement to his credit than this; and it is an achievement of moral earnestness of the strong character of a man who has done a great national service.

Walter H. Page.

CHAPTER 1
A SLAVE AMONG SLAVES

I was born a slave on a plantation in Franklin County, Virginia. I am not quite sure of the exact place or exact date of my birth, but at any rate I suspect I must have been born somewhere and at some time. As nearly as I have been able to learn, I was born near a cross-roads post-office called Hale's Ford, and the year was 1858 or 1859. I do not know the month or the day. The earliest impressions I can now recall are of the plantation and the slave quarters--the latter being the part of the plantation where the slaves had their cabins.

My life had its beginning in the midst of the most miserable, desolate, and discouraging surroundings. This was so, however, not because my owners were especially cruel, for they were not, as compared with many others. I was born in a typical log cabin, about fourteen by sixteen feet square. In this cabin I lived with my mother and a brother and sister till after the Civil War, when we were all declared free.

Of my ancestry I know almost nothing. In the slave quarters, and even later, I heard whispered conversations among the coloured people of the tortures which the slaves, including, no doubt, my ancestors on my mother's side, suffered in the middle passage of the slave ship while being conveyed from Africa to America. I have been unsuccessful in securing any information that would throw any accurate light upon the history of my family beyond my mother. She, I remember, had a half-brother and a half-sister. In the days of slavery not very much attention was given to family history and family records--that is, black family records. My mother, I suppose, attracted the attention of a purchaser who was afterward my owner and hers. Her addition to the slave family attracted about as much attention as the purchase of a new horse or cow. Of my father I know even less than of my mother. I do not even know his name. I have heard reports to the effect that he was a white man who lived on one of the near-by plantations. Whoever he was, I never heard of his taking the least interest in me or providing in any way for my rearing. But I do not find especial fault with him. He was simply another unfortunate victim of the institution which the Nation unhappily had engrafted upon it at that time.

The cabin was not only our living-place, but was also used as the kitchen for the plantation. My mother was the plantation cook. The cabin was without glass windows; it had only openings in the side which let in the light, and also the cold, chilly air of winter. There was a door to the cabin--that is, something that was called a door--but the uncertain hinges by which it was hung, and the large cracks in it, to say nothing of the fact that it was too small, made the room a very uncomfortable one. In addition to these openings there was, in the lower right-hand corner of the room, the "cat-hole," --a contrivance which almost every mansion or cabin in Virginia possessed during the ante-bellum period. The "cat-hole" was a square opening, about seven by eight inches, provided for the purpose of letting the cat pass in and out of the house at will during the night. In the case of our particular cabin I could never understand the necessity for this convenience, since there were at least a half-dozen other places in the cabin that would have accommodated the cats. There was no wooden floor in our cabin, the naked earth being used as a floor. In the centre of the earthen floor there was a large, deep opening covered with boards, which was used as a place in which to store sweet potatoes during the winter. An impression of this potato-hole is very distinctly engraved upon my memory, because I recall that during the process of putting the potatoes in or taking them out I would often come into possession of one or two, which I roasted and thoroughly enjoyed. There was no cooking-stove on our plantation, and all the cooking for the whites and slaves my mother had to do over an open fireplace, mostly in pots and "skillets." While the poorly built cabin caused us to suffer with cold in the winter, the heat from the open fireplace in summer was equally trying.

The early years of my life, which were spent in the little cabin, were not very different from those of thousands of other slaves. My mother, of course, had little time in which to give attention to the training of her children during the day. She snatched a few moments for our care in the early morning before her work began, and at night after the day's work was done. One of my earliest recollections is that of my mother cooking a chicken late at night, and awakening her children for the purpose of feeding them. How or where she got it I do not know. I presume, however, it was procured from our owner's farm. Some people may call this theft. If such a thing were to happen now, I should condemn it as theft myself. But taking place at the time it did, and for the reason that it did, no one could ever make me believe that my mother was guilty of thieving. She was simply a victim of the system of slavery. I cannot remember having slept in a bed until after our family was declared free by the Emancipation Proclamation. Three children--John, my older brother, Amanda, my sister, and myself--had a pallet on the dirt floor, or, to be more correct, we slept in and on a bundle of filthy rags laid upon the dirt floor.

I was asked not long ago to tell something about the sports and pastimes that

[104]

I engaged in during my youth. Until that question was asked it had never occurred to me that there was no period of my life that was devoted to play. From the time that I can remember anything, almost every day of my life had been occupied in some kind of labour; though I think I would now be a more useful man if I had had time for sports. During the period that I spent in slavery I was not large enough to be of much service, still I was occupied most of the time in cleaning the yards, carrying water to the men in the fields, or going to the mill to which I used to take the corn, once a week, to be ground. The mill was about three miles from the plantation. This work I always dreaded. The heavy bag of corn would be thrown across the back of the horse, and the corn divided about evenly on each side; but in some way, almost without exception, on these trips, the corn would so shift as to become unbalanced and would fall off the horse, and often I would fall with it. As I was not strong enough to reload the corn upon the horse, I would have to wait, sometimes for many hours, till a chance passer-by came along who would help me out of my trouble. The hours while waiting for some one were usually spent in crying. The time consumed in this way made me late in reaching the mill, and by the time I got my corn ground and reached home it would be far into the night. The road was a lonely one, and often led through dense forests. I was always frightened. The woods were said to be full of soldiers who had deserted from the army, and I had been told that the first thing a deserter did to a Negro boy when he found him alone was to cut off his ears. Besides, when I was late in getting home I knew I would always get a severe scolding or a flogging.

I had no schooling whatever while I was a slave, though I remember on several occasions I went as far as the schoolhouse door with one of my young mistresses to carry her books. The picture of several dozen boys and girls in a schoolroom engaged in study made a deep impression upon me, and I had the feeling that to get into a schoolhouse and study in this way would be about the same as getting into paradise.

So far as I can now recall, the first knowledge that I got of the fact that we were slaves, and that freedom of the slaves was being discussed, was early one morning before day, when I was awakened by my mother kneeling over her children and fervently praying that Lincoln and his armies might be successful, and that one day she and her children might be free. In this connection I have never been able to understand how the slaves throughout the South, completely ignorant as were the masses so far as books or newspapers were concerned, were able to keep themselves so accurately and completely informed about the great National questions that were agitating the country. From the time that Garrison, Lovejoy, and others began to agitate for freedom, the slaves throughout the South kept in close touch with the progress of the movement. Though I was a mere child during the preparation for the Civil War and during the war itself, I now recall the many late-at-night whispered discussions that I heard my mother and the other slaves on the plantation indulge in. These discussions showed that they understood the situation, and that they kept themselves informed of events by what was termed the "grape-vine" telegraph.

During the campaign when Lincoln was first a candidate for the Presidency, the slaves on our far-off plantation, miles from any railroad or large city or daily newspaper, knew what the issues involved were. When war was begun between the North and the South, every slave on our plantation felt and knew that, though other issues were discussed, the primal one was that of slavery. Even the most ignorant members of my race on the remote plantations felt in their hearts, with a certainty that admitted of no doubt, that the freedom of the slaves would be the one great result of the war, if the northern armies conquered. Every success of the Federal armies and every defeat of the Confederate forces was watched with the keenest and most intense interest. Often the slaves got knowledge of the results of great battles before the white people received it. This news was usually gotten from the coloured man who was sent to the post-office for the mail. In our case the post-office was about three miles from the plantation, and the mail came once or twice a week. The man who was sent to the office would linger about the place long enough to get the drift of the conversation from the group of white people who naturally congregated there, after receiving their mail, to discuss the latest news. The mail-carrier on his way back to our master's house would as naturally retail the news that he had secured among the slaves, and in this way they often heard of important events before the white people at the "big house," as the master's house was called.

I cannot remember a single instance during my childhood or early boyhood when our entire family sat down to the table together, and God's blessing was asked, and the family ate a meal in a civilized manner. On the plantation in Virginia, and even later, meals were gotten by the children very much as dumb animals get theirs. It was a piece of bread here and a scrap of meat there. It was a cup of milk at one time and some potatoes at another. Sometimes a portion of our family would eat out of the skillet or pot, while some one else would eat from a tin plate held on the knees, and often using nothing but the hands with which to hold the food. When I had grown to sufficient size, I was required to go to the "big house" at meal-times to fan the flies from the table by means of a large set of paper fans operated by a pulley. Naturally much of the

[106]

conversation of the white people turned upon the subject of freedom and the war, and I absorbed a good deal of it. I remember that at one time I saw two of my young mistresses and some lady visitors eating ginger-cakes, in the yard. At that time those cakes seemed to me to be absolutely the most tempting and desirable things that I had ever seen; and I then and there resolved that, if I ever got free, the height of my ambition would be reached if I could get to the point where I could secure and eat ginger-cakes in the way that I saw those ladies doing.

Of course as the war was prolonged the white people, in many cases, often found it difficult to secure food for themselves. I think the slaves felt the deprivation less than the whites, because the usual diet for slaves was corn bread and pork, and these could be raised on the plantation; but coffee, tea, sugar, and other articles which the whites had been accustomed to use could not be raised on the plantation, and the conditions brought about by the war frequently made it impossible to secure these things. The whites were often in great straits. Parched corn was used for coffee, and a kind of black molasses was used instead of sugar. Many times nothing was used to sweeten the so-called tea and coffee.

The first pair of shoes that I recall wearing were wooden ones. They had rough leather on the top, but the bottoms, which were about an inch thick, were of wood. When I walked they made a fearful noise, and besides this they were very inconvenient, since there was no yielding to the natural pressure of the foot. In wearing them one presented and exceedingly awkward appearance. The most trying ordeal that I was forced to endure as a slave boy, however, was the wearing of a flax shirt. In the portion of Virginia where I lived it was common to use flax as part of the clothing for the slaves. That part of the flax from which our clothing was made was largely the refuse, which of course was the cheapest and roughest part. I can scarcely imagine any torture, except, perhaps, the pulling of a tooth, that is equal to that caused by putting on a new flax shirt for the first time. It is almost equal to the feeling that one would experience if he had a dozen or more chestnut burrs, or a hundred small pin-points, in contact with his flesh. Even to this day I can recall accurately the tortures that I underwent when putting on one of these garments. The fact that my flesh was soft and tender added to the pain. But I had no choice. I had to wear the flax shirt or none; and had it been left to me to choose, I should have chosen to wear no covering. In connection with the flax shirt, my brother John, who is several years older than I am, performed one of the most generous acts that I ever heard of one slave relative doing for another. On several occasions when I was being forced to wear a new flax shirt, he generously agreed to put it on in my stead and wear it for several days, till it was "broken in." Until I had grown to be quite a youth this single garment was all that I wore.

One may get the idea, from what I have said, that there was bitter feeling toward the white people on the part of my race, because of the fact that most of the white population was away fighting in a war which would result in keeping the Negro in slavery if the South was successful. In the case of the slaves on our place this was not true, and it was not true of any large portion of the slave population in the South where the Negro was treated with anything like decency. During the Civil War one of my young masters was killed, and two were severely wounded. I recall the feeling of sorrow which existed among the slaves when they heard of the death of "Mars' Billy." It was no sham sorrow, but real. Some of the slaves had nursed "Mars' Billy"; others had played with him when he was a child. "Mars' Billy" had begged for mercy in the case of others when the overseer or master was thrashing them. The sorrow in the slave quarter was only second to that in the "big house." When the two young masters were brought home wounded, the sympathy of the slaves was shown in many ways. They were just as anxious to assist in the nursing as the family relatives of the wounded. Some of the slaves would even beg for the privilege of sitting up at night to nurse their wounded masters. This tenderness and sympathy on the part of those held in bondage was a result of their kindly and generous nature. In order to defend and protect the women and children who were left on the plantations when the white males went to war, the slaves would have laid down their lives. The slave who was selected to sleep in the "big house" during the absence of the males was considered to have the place of honour. Any one attempting to harm "young Mistress" or "old Mistress" during the night would have had to cross the dead body of the slave to do so. I do not know how many have noticed it, but I think that it will be found to be true that there are few instances, either in slavery or freedom, in which a member of my race has been known to betray a specific trust.

As a rule, not only did the members of my race entertain no feelings of bitterness against the whites before and during the war, but there are many instances of Negroes tenderly carrying for their former masters and mistresses who for some reason have become poor and dependent since the war. I know of instances where the former masters of slaves have for years been supplied with money by their former slaves to keep them from suffering. I have known of still other cases in which the former slaves have assisted in the education of the descendants of their former owners. I know of a case on a large plantation in the South in which a young white man, the son of the former owner of the estate, has become so reduced in purse and self-control by reason of drink that he is a pitiable creature; and yet, notwithstanding the poverty of the coloured people themselves on this plantation, they have for years supplied this young white man with the necessities of life. One sends him a little coffee or sugar, another a little meat, and so on. Nothing that the coloured people possess is too good for the son of "old Mars' Tom," who will perhaps never be permitted to suffer while any remain on the place who knew directly or indirectly of "old Mars' Tom."

I have said that there are few instances of a member of my race betraying a specific trust. One of the best illustrations of this which I know of is in the case of an ex-slave from Virginia whom I met not long ago in a little town in the state of Ohio. I found that this man had made a contract with his master, two or three years previous to the Emancipation Proclamation, to the effect that the slave was to be permitted to buy himself, by paying so much per year for his body; and while he was paying for himself, he was to be permitted to labour where and for whom he pleased. Finding that he could secure better wages in Ohio, he went there. When freedom came, he was still in debt to his master some three hundred dollars. Notwithstanding that the Emancipation Proclamation freed him from any obligation to his master, this black man walked the greater portion of the distance back to where his old master lived in Virginia, and placed the last dollar, with interest, in his hands. In talking to me about this, the man told me that he knew that he did not have to pay the debt, but that he had given his word to the master, and his word he had never broken. He felt that he could not enjoy his freedom till he had fulfilled his promise.

From some things that I have said one may get the idea that some of the slaves did not want freedom. This is not true. I have never seen one who did not want to be free, or one who would return to slavery.

I pity from the bottom of my heart any nation or body of people that is so unfortunate as to get entangled in the net of slavery. I have long since ceased to cherish any spirit of bitterness against the Southern white people on account of the enslavement of my race. No one section of our country was wholly responsible for its introduction, and, besides, it was recognized and protected for years by the General Government. Having once got its tentacles fastened on to the economic and social life of the Republic, it was no easy matter for the country to relieve itself of the institution. Then, when we rid ourselves of prejudice, or racial feeling, and look facts in the face, we must acknowledge that, notwithstanding the cruelty and moral wrong of slavery, the ten million Negroes inhabiting this country, who themselves or whose ancestors went through the school of American slavery, are in a stronger and more hopeful condition, materially, intellectually, morally, and religiously, than is true of an equal number of black people in any other portion of the globe. This is so to such an extend that Negroes in this country, who themselves or whose forefathers went through the school of slavery, are constantly returning to Africa as missionaries to enlighten those who remained in the fatherland. This I say, not to justify slavery--on the other hand, I condemn it as an institution, as we all know that in America it was established for selfish and financial reasons, and not from a missionary motive--but to call attention to a fact, and to show how Providence so often uses men and institutions to accomplish a purpose. When persons ask me in these days how, in the midst of what sometimes seem hopelessly discouraging conditions, I can have such faith in the future of my race in this country, I remind them of the wilderness through which and out of which, a good Providence has already led us.

Ever since I have been old enough to think for myself, I have entertained the idea that, notwithstanding the cruel wrongs inflicted upon us, the black man got nearly as much out of slavery as the white man did. The hurtful influences of the institution were not by any means confined to the Negro. This was fully illustrated by the life upon our own plantation. The whole machinery of slavery was so constructed as to cause labour, as a rule, to be looked upon as a badge of degradation, of inferiority. Hence labour was something that both races on the slave plantation sought to escape. The slave system on our place, in a large measure, took the spirit of self-reliance and self-help out of the white people. My old master had many boys and girls, but not one, so far as I know, ever mastered a single trade or special line of productive industry. The girls were not taught to cook, sew, or to take care of the house. All of this was left to the slaves. The slaves, of course, had little personal interest in the life of the plantation, and their ignorance prevented them from learning how to do things in the most improved and thorough manner. As a result of the system, fences were out of repair, gates were hanging half off the hinges, doors creaked, window-panes were out, plastering had fallen but was not replaced, weeds grew in the yard. As a rule, there was food for whites and blacks, but inside the house, and on the dining-room table, there was wanting that delicacy and refinement of touch and finish which can make a home the most convenient, comfortable, and attractive place in the world. Withal there was a waste of food and other materials which was sad. When freedom came, the slaves were almost as well fitted to begin life anew as the master, except in the matter of book-learning and ownership of property. The slave owner and his sons had mastered no special industry. They unconsciously had imbibed the feeling that manual labour was not the proper thing for them. On the other hand, the slaves, in many cases, had mastered some handicraft, and none were ashamed, and few unwilling, to labour.

Finally the war closed, and the day of freedom came. It was a momentous and eventful day to all upon our plantation. We had been expecting it. Freedom was in the air, and had been for months. Deserting soldiers returning to their homes were to be seen every day. Others who had been discharged, or whose regiments had been paroled, were constantly passing near our place. The "grape-vine telegraph" was kept busy night and day. The news and mutterings of great events were swiftly carried from one plantation to another. In the fear of "Yankee" invasions, the silverware and other valuables were taken from the "big house," buried in the woods, and guarded by trusted slaves. Woe be to any one who would have attempted to disturb the buried treasure. The slaves would give the Yankee soldiers food, drink, clothing--anything but that which had been specifically intrusted to their care and honour. As the great day drew nearer, there was more singing in the slave quarters than usual. It was bolder, had more ring, and lasted later into the night. Most of the verses of the plantation songs had some reference to freedom. True, they had sung those same verses before, but they had been careful to explain that the "freedom" in these songs referred to the next world, and had no connection with life in this world. Now they gradually threw off the mask, and were not afraid to let it be known that the "freedom" in their songs meant freedom of the body in this world. The night before the eventful day, word was sent to the slave quarters to the effect that something unusual was going to take place at the "big house" the next morning. There was little, if any, sleep that night. All as excitement and expectancy. Early the next morning word was sent to all the slaves, old and young, to gather at the house. In company with my mother, brother, and sister, and a large number of other slaves, I went to the master's house. All of our master's family were either standing or seated on the veranda of the house, where they could see what was to take place and hear what was said. There was a feeling of deep interest, or perhaps sadness, on their faces, but not bitterness. As I now recall the impression they made upon me, they did not at the moment seem to be sad because of the loss of property, but rather because of parting with those whom they had reared and who were in many ways very close to them. The most distinct thing that I now recall in connection with the scene was that some man who seemed to be a stranger (a United States officer, I presume) made a little speech and then read a rather long paper--the Emancipation Proclamation, I think. After the reading we were told that we were all free, and could go when and where we pleased. My mother, who was standing by my side, leaned over and kissed her children, while tears of joy ran down her cheeks. She explained to us what it all meant, that this was the day for which she had been so long

[111]

praying, but fearing that she would never live to see.

For some minutes there was great rejoicing, and thanksgiving, and wild scenes of ecstasy. But there was no feeling of bitterness. In fact, there was pity among the slaves for our former owners. The wild rejoicing on the part of the emancipated coloured people lasted but for a brief period, for I noticed that by the time they returned to their cabins there was a change in their feelings. The great responsibility of being free, of having charge of themselves, of having to think and plan for themselves and their children, seemed to take possession of them. It was very much like suddenly turning a youth of ten or twelve years out into the world to provide for himself. In a few hours the great questions with which the Anglo-Saxon race had been grappling for centuries had been thrown upon these people to be solved. These were the questions of a home, a living, the rearing of children, education, citizenship, and the establishment and support of churches. Was it any wonder that within a few hours the wild rejoicing ceased and a feeling of deep gloom seemed to pervade the slave quarters? To some it seemed that, now that they were in actual possession of it, freedom was a more serious thing than they had expected to find it. Some of the slaves were seventy or eighty years old; their best days were gone. They had no strength with which to earn a living in a strange place and among strange people, even if they had been sure where to find a new place of abode. To this class the problem seemed especially hard. Besides, deep down in their hearts there was a strange and peculiar attachment to "old Marster" and "old Missus," and to their children, which they found it hard to think of breaking off. With these they had spent in some cases nearly a half-century, and it was no light thing to think of parting. Gradually, one by one, stealthily at first, the older slaves began to wander from the slave quarters back to the "big house" to have a whispered conversation with their former owners as to the future.

CHAPTER 2
BOYHOOD DAYS

After the coming of freedom there were two points upon which practically all the people on our place were agreed, and I found that this was generally true throughout the South: that they must change their names, and that they must leave the old plantation for at least a few days or weeks in order that they might really feel sure that they were free.

In some way a feeling got among the coloured people that it was far from proper for them to bear the surname of their former owners, and a great many of them took other surnames. This was one of the first signs of freedom. When they were slaves, a coloured person was simply called "John" or "Susan." There was seldom occasion for more than the use of the one name. If "John" or "Susan" belonged to a white man by the name of "Hatcher," sometimes he was called "John Hatcher," or as often "Hatcher's John." But there was a feeling that "John Hatcher" or "Hatcher's John" was not the proper title by which to denote a freeman; and so in many cases "John Hatcher" was changed to "John S. Lincoln" or "John S. Sherman," the initial "S" standing for no name, it being simply a part of what the coloured man proudly called his "entitles."

As I have stated, most of the coloured people left the old plantation for a short while at least, so as to be sure, it seemed, that they could leave and try their freedom on to see how it felt. After they had remained away for a while, many of the older slaves, especially, returned to their old homes and made some kind of contract with their former owners by which they remained on the estate.

My mother's husband, who was the stepfather of my brother John and myself, did not belong to the same owners as did my mother. In fact, he seldom came to our plantation. I remember seeing his there perhaps once a year, that being about Christmas time. In some way, during the war, by running away and following the Federal soldiers, it seems, he found his way into the new state of West Virginia. As soon as freedom was declared, he sent for my mother to come to the Kanawha Valley, in West Virginia. At that time a journey from Virginia over the mountains to West Virginia was rather a tedious and in some cases a painful undertaking. What little clothing and few household goods we had were placed in a cart, but the children walked the greater portion of the distance, which was several hundred miles.

[113]

I do not think any of us ever had been very far from the plantation, and the taking of a long journey into another state was quite an event. The parting from our former owners and the members of our own race on the plantation was a serious occasion. From the time of our parting till their death we kept up a correspondence with the older members of the family, and in later years we have kept in touch with those who were the younger members. We were several weeks making the trip, and most of the time we slept in the open air and did our cooking over a log fire out-of-doors. One night I recall that we camped near an abandoned log cabin, and my mother decided to build a fire in that for cooking, and afterward to make a "pallet" on the floor for our sleeping. Just as the fire had gotten well started a large black snake fully a yard and a half long dropped down the chimney and ran out on the floor. Of course we at once abandoned that cabin. Finally we reached our destination--a little town called Malden, which is about five miles from Charleston, the present capital of the state.

At that time salt-mining was the great industry in that part of West Virginia, and the little town of Malden was right in the midst of the salt-furnaces. My stepfather had already secured a job at a salt-furnace, and he had also secured a little cabin for us to live in. Our new house was no better than the one we had left on the old plantation in Virginia. In fact, in one respect it was worse. Notwithstanding the poor condition of our plantation cabin, we were at all times sure of pure air. Our new home was in the midst of a cluster of cabins crowded closely together, and as there were no sanitary regulations, the filth about the cabins was often intolerable. Some of our neighbours were coloured people, and some were the poorest and most ignorant and degraded white people. It was a motley mixture. Drinking, gambling, quarrels, fights, and shockingly immoral practices were frequent. All who lived in the little town were in one way or another connected with the salt business. Though I was a mere child, my stepfather put me and my brother at work in one of the furnaces. Often I began work as early as four o'clock in the morning.

The first thing I ever learned in the way of book knowledge was while working in this salt-furnace. Each salt-packer had his barrels marked with a certain number. The number allotted to my stepfather was "18." At the close of the day's work the boss of the packers would come around and put "18" on each of our barrels, and I soon learned to recognize that figure wherever I saw it, and after a while got to the point where I could make that figure, though I knew nothing about any other figures or letters.

From the time that I can remember having any thoughts about anything, I recall that I had an intense longing to learn to read. I determined, when quite a small child, that, if I accomplished nothing else in life, I would in some way get enough education to enable me to read common books and newspapers. Soon after we got settled in some manner in our new cabin in West Virginia, I induced my mother to get hold of a book for me. How or where she got it I do not know, but in some way she procured an old copy of Webster's "blue-back" spelling-book, which contained the alphabet, followed by such meaningless words as "ab," "ba," "ca," "da." I began at once to devour this book, and I think that it was the first one I ever had in my hands. I had learned from somebody that the way to begin to read was to learn the alphabet, so I tried in all the ways I could think of to learn it,--all of course without a teacher, for I could find no one to teach me. At that time there was not a single member of my race anywhere near us who could read, and I was too timid to approach any of the white people. In some way, within a few weeks, I mastered the greater portion of the alphabet. In all my efforts to learn to read my mother shared fully my ambition, and sympathized with me and aided me in every way that she could. Though she was totally ignorant, she had high ambitions for her children, and a large fund of good, hard, common sense, which seemed to enable her to meet and master every situation. If I have done anything in life worth attention, I feel sure that I inherited the disposition from my mother.

In the midst of my struggles and longing for an education, a young coloured boy who had learned to read in the state of Ohio came to Malden. As soon as the coloured people found out that he could read, a newspaper was secured, and at the close of nearly every day's work this young man would be surrounded by a group of men and women who were anxious to hear him read the news contained in the papers. How I used to envy this man! He seemed to me to be the one young man in all the world who ought to be satisfied with his attainments.

About this time the question of having some kind of a school opened for the coloured children in the village began to be discussed by members of the race. As it would be the first school for Negro children that had ever been opened in that part of Virginia, it was, of course, to be a great event, and the discussion excited the wildest interest. The most perplexing question was where to find a teacher. The young man from Ohio who had learned to read the papers was considered, but his age was against him. In the midst of the discussion about a teacher, another young coloured man from Ohio, who had been a soldier, in some way found his way into town. It was soon learned that he possessed considerable education, and he was engaged by the coloured people to teach their first school. As yet no free schools had been started for coloured people in that section, hence each family agreed to pay a certain amount per month, with the understanding that the teacher was to "board 'round"--that is, spend a day with each family. This was not bad for the teacher, for each family tried to provide the very best on the day the teacher was to be its guest. I recall that I looked forward with an anxious appetite to the "teacher's day" at our little cabin.

This experience of a whole race beginning to go to school for the first time, presents one of the most interesting studies that has ever occurred in connection with the development of any race. Few people who were not right in the midst of the scenes can form any exact idea of the intense desire which the people of my race showed for an education. As I have stated, it was a whole race trying to go to school. Few were too young, and none too old, to make the attempt to learn. As fast as any kind of teachers could be secured, not only were day-schools filled, but night-schools as well. The great ambition of the older people was to try to learn to read the Bible before they died. With this end in view men and women who were fifty or seventy-five years old would often be found in the night-school. Some day-schools were formed soon after freedom, but the principal book studied in the Sunday-school was the spelling-book. Day-school, night-school, Sunday-school, were always crowded, and often many had to be turned away for want of room.

The opening of the school in the Kanawha Valley, however, brought to me one of the keenest disappointments that I ever experienced. I had been working in a salt-furnace for several months, and my stepfather had discovered that I had a financial value, and so, when the school opened, he decided that he could not spare me from my work. This decision seemed to cloud my every ambition. The disappointment was made all the more severe by reason of the fact that my place of work was where I could see the happy children passing to and from school mornings and afternoons. Despite this disappointment, however, I determined that I would learn something, anyway. I applied myself with greater earnestness than ever to the mastering of what was in the "blue-back" speller.

My mother sympathized with me in my disappointment, and sought to comfort me in all the ways she could, and to help me find a way to learn. After a while I succeeded in making arrangements with the teacher to give me some lessons at night, after the day's work was done. These night lessons were so welcome that I think I learned more at night than the other children did during the day. My own experiences in the night-school gave me faith in the night-school idea, with which, in after years, I had to do both at Hampton and Tuskegee. But my boyish heart was still set upon going to the day-school, and I let no opportunity slip to push my case. Finally I won, and was permitted to go to the school in the day for a few months, with the understanding that I was to rise early in the morning

[116]

and work in the furnace till nine o'clock, and return immediately after school closed in the afternoon for at least two more hours of work.

The schoolhouse was some distance from the furnace, and as I had to work till nine o'clock, and the school opened at nine, I found myself in a difficulty. School would always be begun before I reached it, and sometimes my class had recited. To get around this difficulty I yielded to a temptation for which most people, I suppose, will condemn me; but since it is a fact, I might as well state it. I have great faith in the power and influence of facts. It is seldom that anything is permanently gained by holding back a fact. There was a large clock in a little office in the furnace. This clock, of course, all the hundred or more workmen depended upon to regulate their hours of beginning and ending the day's work. I got the idea that the way for me to reach school on time was to move the clock hands from half-past eight up to the nine o'clock mark. This I found myself doing morning after morning, till the furnace "boss" discovered that something was wrong, and locked the clock in a case. I did not mean to inconvenience anybody. I simply meant to reach that schoolhouse in time.

When, however, I found myself at the school for the first time, I also found myself confronted with two other difficulties. In the first place, I found that all the other children wore hats or caps on their heads, and I had neither hat nor cap. In fact, I do not remember that up to the time of going to school I had ever worn any kind of covering upon my head, nor do I recall that either I or anybody else had even thought anything about the need of covering for my head. But, of course, when I saw how all the other boys were dressed, I began to feel quite uncomfortable. As usual, I put the case before my mother, and she explained to me that she had no money with which to buy a "store hat," which was a rather new institution at that time among the members of my race and was considered quite the thing for young and old to own, but that she would find a way to help me out of the difficulty. She accordingly got two pieces of "homespun" (jeans) and sewed them together, and I was soon the proud possessor of my first cap.

The lesson that my mother taught me in this has always remained with me, and I have tried as best as I could to teach it to others. I have always felt proud, whenever I think of the incident, that my mother had strength of character enough not to be led into the temptation of seeming to be that which she was not--of trying to impress my schoolmates and others with the fact that she was able to buy me a "store hat" when she was not. I have always felt proud that she refused to go into debt for that which she did not have the money to pay for. Since that time I have owned many kinds of caps and hats, but never one of which I have felt so proud as of the cap made of the two pieces of cloth sewed together by my mother. I have noted the fact, but without satisfaction, I need not add, that several of the boys who began their careers with "store hats" and who were my schoolmates and used to join in the sport that was made of me because I had only a "homespun" cap, have ended their careers in the penitentiary, while others are not able now to buy any kind of hat.

My second difficulty was with regard to my name, or rather A name. From the time when I could remember anything, I had been called simply "Booker." Before going to school it had never occurred to me that it was needful or appropriate to have an additional name. When I heard the schoolroll called, I noticed that all of the children had at least two names, and some of them indulged in what seemed to me the extravagance of having three. I was in deep perplexity, because I knew that the teacher would demand of me at least two names, and I had only one. By the time the occasion came for the enrolling of my name, an idea occurred to me which I thought would make me equal to the situation; and so, when the teacher asked me what my full name was, I calmly told him "Booker Washington," as if I had been called by that name all my life; and by that name I have since been known. Later in my life I found that my mother had given me the name of "Booker Taliaferro" soon after I was born, but in some way that part of my name seemed to disappear and for a long while was forgotten, but as soon as I found out about it I revived it, and made my full name "Booker Taliaferro Washington." I think there are not many men in our country who have had the privilege of naming themselves in the way that I have.

More than once I have tried to picture myself in the position of a boy or man with an honoured and distinguished ancestry which I could trace back through a period of hundreds of years, and who had not only inherited a name, but fortune and a proud family homestead; and yet I have sometimes had the feeling that if I had inherited these, and had been a member of a more popular race, I should have been inclined to yield to the temptation of depending upon my ancestry and my colour to do that for me which I should do for myself. Years ago I resolved that because I had no ancestry myself I would leave a record of which my children would be proud, and which might encourage them to still higher effort.

The world should not pass judgment upon the Negro, and especially the Negro youth, too quickly or too harshly. The Negro boy has obstacles, discouragements, and temptations to battle with that are little know to those not situated as he is. When a white boy undertakes a task, it is taken for granted that he will succeed. On the other hand, people are usually surprised if the Negro boy does not fail. In a word, the Negro youth starts out with the presumption against him.

[118]

The influence of ancestry, however, is important in helping forward any individual or race, if too much reliance is not placed upon it. Those who constantly direct attention to the Negro youth's moral weaknesses, and compare his advancement with that of white youths, do not consider the influence of the memories which cling about the old family homesteads. I have no idea, as I have stated elsewhere, who my grandmother was. I have, or have had, uncles and aunts and cousins, but I have no knowledge as to where most of them are. My case will illustrate that of hundreds of thousands of black people in every part of our country. The very fact that the white boy is conscious that, if he fails in life, he will disgrace the whole family record, extending back through many generations, is of tremendous value in helping him to resist temptations. The fact that the individual has behind and surrounding him proud family history and connection serves as a stimulus to help him to overcome obstacles when striving for success.

The time that I was permitted to attend school during the day was short, and my attendance was irregular. It was not long before I had to stop attending day-school altogether, and devote all of my time again to work. I resorted to the night-school again. In fact, the greater part of the education I secured in my boyhood was gathered through the night-school after my day's work was done. I had difficulty often in securing a satisfactory teacher. Sometimes, after I had secured some one to teach me at night, I would find, much to my disappointment, that the teacher knew but little more than I did. Often I would have to walk several miles at night in order to recite my night-school lessons. There was never a time in my youth, no matter how dark and discouraging the days might be, when one resolve did not continually remain with me, and that was a determination to secure an education at any cost.

Soon after we moved to West Virginia, my mother adopted into our family, notwithstanding our poverty, an orphan boy, to whom afterward we gave the name of James B. Washington. He has ever since remained a member of the family.

After I had worked in the salt-furnace for some time, work was secured for me in a coal-mine which was operated mainly for the purpose of securing fuel for the salt-furnace. Work in the coal-mine I always dreaded. One reason for this was that any one who worked in a coal-mine was always unclean, at least while at work, and it was a very hard job to get one's skin clean after the day's work was over. Then it was fully a mile from the opening of the coal-mine to the face of the coal, and all, of course, was in the blackest darkness. I do not believe that one ever experiences anywhere else such darkness as he does in a coal-mine. The mine was divided into a large number of different "rooms" or departments, and, as I never was able to learn the location of all these "rooms," I many times found myself lost in the mine. To add to the horror of being lost, sometimes my light would go out, and then, if I did not happen to have a match, I would wander about in the darkness until by chance I found some one to give me a light. The work was not only hard, but it was dangerous. There was always the danger of being blown to pieces by a premature explosion of powder, or of being crushed by falling slate. Accidents from one or the other of these causes were frequently occurring, and this kept me in constant fear. Many children of the tenderest years were compelled then, as is now true I fear, in most coal-mining districts, to spend a large part of their lives in these coal-mines, with little opportunity to get an education; and, what is worse, I have often noted that, as a rule, young boys who begin life in a coal-mine are often physically and mentally dwarfed. They soon lose ambition to do anything else than to continue as a coal-miner.

In those days, and later as a young man, I used to try to picture in my imagination the feelings and ambitions of a white boy with absolutely no limit placed upon his aspirations and activities. I used to envy the white boy who had no obstacles placed in the way of his becoming a Congressman, Governor, Bishop, or President by reason of the accident of his birth or race. I used to picture the way that I would act under such circumstances; how I would begin at the bottom and keep rising until I reached the highest round of success.

In later years, I confess that I do not envy the white boy as I once did. I have learned that success is to be measured not so much by the position that one has reached in life as by the obstacles which he has overcome while trying to succeed. Looked at from this standpoint, I almost reached the conclusion that often the Negro boy's birth and connection with an unpopular race is an advantage, so far as real life is concerned. With few exceptions, the Negro youth must work harder and must perform his tasks even better than a white youth in order to secure recognition. But out of the hard and unusual struggle through which he is compelled to pass, he gets a strength, a confidence, that one misses whose pathway is comparatively smooth by reason of birth and race.

From any point of view, I had rather be what I am, a member of the Negro race, than be able to claim membership with the most favoured of any other race. I have always been made sad when I have heard members of any race claiming rights or privileges, or certain badges of distinction, on the ground simply that they were members of this or that race, regardless of their own individual worth or attainments. I have been made to feel sad for such persons because I am conscious of the fact that mere connection with what is known as a superior race will not permanently carry an individual forward unless he has individual worth, and mere connection with what is regarded as an inferior race will not finally hold an individual back if he possesses intrinsic, individual merit. Every persecuted individual and race should get much consolation out of the great human law, which is universal and eternal, that merit, no matter under what skin found, is, in the long run, recognized and rewarded. This I have said here, not to call attention to myself as an individual, but to the race to which I am proud to belong.

CHAPTER 3
THE STRUGGLE FOR AN EDUCATION

One day, while at work in the coal-mine, I happened to overhear two miners talking about a great school for coloured people somewhere in Virginia. This was the first time that I had ever heard anything about any kind of school or college that was more pretentious than the little coloured school in our town.

In the darkness of the mine I noiselessly crept as close as I could to the two men who were talking. I heard one tell the other that not only was the school established for the members of any race, but the opportunities that it provided by which poor but worthy students could work out all or a part of the cost of a board, and at the same time be taught some trade or industry.

As they went on describing the school, it seemed to me that it must be the greatest place on earth, and not even Heaven presented more attractions for me at that time than did the Hampton Normal and Agricultural Institute in Virginia, about which these men were talking. I resolved at once to go to that school, although I had no idea where it was, or how many miles away, or how I was going to reach it; I remembered only that I was on fire constantly with one ambition, and that was to go to Hampton. This thought was with me day and night.

After hearing of the Hampton Institute, I continued to work for a few months longer in the coal-mine. While at work there, I heard of a vacant position in the household of General Lewis Ruffner, the owner of the salt-furnace and coal-mine. Mrs. Viola Ruffner, the wife of General Ruffner, was a "Yankee" woman from Vermont. Mrs. Ruffner had a reputation all through the vicinity for being very strict with her servants, and especially with the boys who tried to serve her. Few of them remained with her more than two or three weeks. They all left with the same excuse: she was too strict. I decided, however, that I would rather try Mrs. Ruffner's house than remain in the coal-mine, and so my mother applied to her for the vacant position. I was hired at a salary of $5 per month.

I had heard so much about Mrs. Ruffner's severity that I was almost afraid to see her, and trembled when I went into her presence. I had not lived with her many weeks, however, before I began to understand her. I soon began to learn that, first of all, she wanted everything kept clean about her, that she wanted things done promptly and systematically, and that at the bottom of everything she wanted absolute honesty and frankness. Nothing must be sloven or slipshod; every door, every fence, must be kept in repair.

I cannot now recall how long I lived with Mrs. Ruffner before going to Hampton, but I think it must have been a year and a half. At any rate, I here repeat what I have said more than once before, that the lessons that I learned in the home of Mrs. Ruffner were as valuable to me as any education I have ever gotten anywhere else. Even to this day I never see bits of paper scattered around a house or in the street that I do not want to pick them up at once. I never see a filthy yard that I do not want to clean it, a paling off of a fence that I do not want to put it on, an unpainted or unwhitewashed house that I do not want to pain or whitewash it, or a button off one's clothes, or a grease-spot on them or on a floor, that I do not want to call attention to it.

From fearing Mrs. Ruffner I soon learned to look upon her as one of my best friends. When she found that she could trust me she did so implicitly. During the one or two winters that I was with her she gave me an opportunity to go to school for an hour in the day during a portion of the winter months, but most of my studying was done at night, sometimes alone, sometimes under some one whom I could hire to teach me. Mrs. Ruffner always encouraged and sympathized with me in all my efforts to get an education. It was while living with her that I began to get together my first library. I secured a dry-goods box, knocked out one side of it, put some shelves in it, and began putting into it every kind of book that I could get my hands upon, and called it my "library."

Notwithstanding my success at Mrs. Ruffner's I did not give up the idea of going to the Hampton Institute. In the fall of 1872 I determined to make an effort to get there, although, as I have stated, I had no definite idea of the direction in which Hampton was, or of what it would cost to go there. I do not think that any one thoroughly sympathized with me in my ambition to go to Hampton unless it was my mother, and she was troubled with a grave fear that I was starting out on a "wild-goose chase." At any rate, I got only a half-hearted consent from her that I might start. The small amount of money that I had earned had been consumed by my stepfather and the remainder of the family, with the exception of a very few dollars, and so I had very little with which to buy clothes and pay my travelling expenses. My brother John helped me all that he could, but of course that was not a great deal, for his work was in the coal-mine, where he did not earn much, and most of what he did earn went in the direction of paying the household expenses.

[123]

Perhaps the thing that touched and pleased me most in connection with my starting for Hampton was the interest that many of the older coloured people took in the matter. They had spent the best days of their lives in slavery, and hardly expected to live to see the time when they would see a member of their race leave home to attend a boarding-school. Some of these older people would give me a nickel, others a quarter, or a handkerchief.

Finally the great day came, and I started for Hampton. I had only a small, cheap satchel that contained a few articles of clothing I could get. My mother at the time was rather weak and broken in health. I hardly expected to see her again, and thus our parting was all the more sad. She, however, was very brave through it all. At that time there were no through trains connecting that part of West Virginia with eastern Virginia. Trains ran only a portion of the way, and the remainder of the distance was travelled by stage-coaches.

The distance from Malden to Hampton is about five hundred miles. I had not been away from home many hours before it began to grow painfully evident that I did not have enough money to pay my fair to Hampton. One experience I shall long remember. I had been travelling over the mountains most of the afternoon in an old-fashion stage-coach, when, late in the evening, the coach stopped for the night at a common, unpainted house called a hotel. All the other passengers except myself were whites. In my ignorance I supposed that the little hotel existed for the purpose of accommodating the passengers who travelled on the stage-coach. The difference that the colour of one's skin would make I had not thought anything about. After all the other passengers had been shown rooms and were getting ready for supper, I shyly presented myself before the man at the desk. It is true I had practically no money in my pocket with which to pay for bed or food, but I had hoped in some way to beg my way into the good graces of the landlord, for at that season in the mountains of Virginia the weather was cold, and I wanted to get indoors for the night. Without asking as to whether I had any money, the man at the desk firmly refused to even consider the matter of providing me with food or lodging. This was my first experience in finding out what the colour of my skin meant. In some way I managed to keep warm by walking about, and so got through the night. My whole soul was so bent upon reaching Hampton that I did not have time to cherish any bitterness toward the hotel-keeper.

By walking, begging rides both in wagons and in the cars, in some way, after a number of days, I reached the city of Richmond, Virginia, about eighty-two miles from Hampton. When I reached there, tired, hungry, and dirty, it was late in the night. I had never been in a large city, and this rather added to my misery. When I reached Richmond, I was completely out of money. I had not a single acquaintance in the place, and, being unused to city ways, I did not know where to go. I applied at several places for lodging, but they all wanted money, and that was what I did not have. Knowing nothing else better to do, I walked the streets. In doing this I passed by many a food-stands where fried chicken and half-moon apple pies were piled high and made to present a most tempting appearance. At that time it seemed to me that I would have promised all that I expected to possess in the future to have gotten hold of one of those chicken legs or one of those pies. But I could not get either of these, nor anything else to eat.

I must have walked the streets till after midnight. At last I became so exhausted that I could walk no longer. I was tired, I was hungry, I was everything but discouraged. Just about the time when I reached extreme physical exhaustion, I came upon a portion of a street where the board sidewalk was considerably elevated. I waited for a few minutes, till I was sure that no passers-by could see me, and then crept under the sidewalk and lay for the night upon the ground, with my satchel of clothing for a pillow. Nearly all night I could hear the tramp of feet over my head. The next morning I found myself somewhat refreshed, but I was extremely hungry, because it had been a long time since I had had sufficient food. As soon as it became light enough for me to see my surroundings I noticed that I was near a large ship, and that this ship seemed to be unloading a cargo of pig iron. I went at once to the vessel and asked the captain to permit me to help unload the vessel in order to get money for food. The captain, a white man, who seemed to be kind-hearted, consented. I worked long enough to earn money for my breakfast, and it seems to me, as I remember it now, to have been about the best breakfast that I have ever eaten.

My work pleased the captain so well that he told me if I desired I could continue working for a small amount per day. This I was very glad to do. I continued working on this vessel for a number of days. After buying food with the small wages I received there was not much left to add on the amount I must get to pay my way to Hampton. In order to economize in every way possible, so as to be sure to reach Hampton in a reasonable time, I continued to sleep under the same sidewalk that gave me shelter the first night I was in Richmond. Many years after that the coloured citizens of Richmond very kindly tendered me a reception at which there must have been two thousand people present. This reception was held not far from the spot where I slept the first night I spent in the city, and I must confess that my mind was more upon the sidewalk that first gave me shelter than upon the recognition, agreeable and cordial as it was.

When I had saved what I considered enough money with which to reach Hampton, I thanked the captain of the vessel for his kindness, and started

[125]

again. Without any unusual occurrence I reached Hampton, with a surplus of exactly fifty cents with which to begin my education. To me it had been a long, eventful journey; but the first sight of the large, three-story, brick school building seemed to have rewarded me for all that I had undergone in order to reach the place. If the people who gave the money to provide that building could appreciate the influence the sight of it had upon me, as well as upon thousands of other youths, they would feel all the more encouraged to make such gifts. It seemed to me to be the largest and most beautiful building I had ever seen. The sight of it seemed to give me new life. I felt that a new kind of existence had now begun--that life would now have a new meaning. I felt that I had reached the promised land, and I resolved to let no obstacle prevent me from putting forth the highest effort to fit myself to accomplish the most good in the world.

As soon as possible after reaching the grounds of the Hampton Institute, I presented myself before the head teacher for an assignment to a class. Having been so long without proper food, a bath, and a change of clothing, I did not, of course, make a very favourable impression upon her, and I could see at once that there were doubts in her mind about the wisdom of admitting me as a student. I felt that I could hardly blame her if she got the idea that I was a worthless loafer or tramp. For some time she did not refuse to admit me, neither did she decide in my favour, and I continued to linger about her, and to impress her in all the ways I could with my worthiness. In the meantime I saw her admitting other students, and that added greatly to my discomfort, for I felt, deep down in my heart, that I could do as well as they, if I could only get a chance to show what was in me.

After some hours had passed, the head teacher said to me: "The adjoining recitation-room needs sweeping. Take the broom and sweep it."

It occurred to me at once that here was my chance. Never did I receive an order with more delight. I knew that I could sweep, for Mrs. Ruffner had thoroughly taught me how to do that when I lived with her.

I swept the recitation-room three times. Then I got a dusting-cloth and dusted it four times. All the woodwork around the walls, every bench, table, and desk, I went over four times with my dusting-cloth. Besides, every piece of furniture had been moved and every closet and corner in the room had been thoroughly cleaned. I had the feeling that in a large measure my future dependent upon the impression I made upon the teacher in the cleaning of that room. When I was through, I reported to the head teacher. She was a "Yankee" woman who knew just where to look for dirt. She went into the room and inspected the floor and closets; then she took her handkerchief and rubbed it on the woodwork about the walls, and over the table and benches. When she was unable to find one bit of dirt on the floor, or a particle of dust on any of the furniture, she quietly remarked, "I guess you will do to enter this institution."

I was one of the happiest souls on Earth. The sweeping of that room was my college examination, and never did any youth pass an examination for entrance into Harvard or Yale that gave him more genuine satisfaction. I have passed several examinations since then, but I have always felt that this was the best one I ever passed.

I have spoken of my own experience in entering the Hampton Institute. Perhaps few, if any, had anything like the same experience that I had, but about the same period there were hundreds who found their way to Hampton and other institutions after experiencing something of the same difficulties that I went through. The young men and women were determined to secure an education at any cost.

The sweeping of the recitation-room in the manner that I did it seems to have paved the way for me to get through Hampton. Miss Mary F. Mackie, the head teacher, offered me a position as janitor. This, of course, I gladly accepted, because it was a place where I could work out nearly all the cost of my board. The work was hard and taxing but I stuck to it. I had a large number of rooms to care for, and had to work late into the night, while at the same time I had to rise by four o'clock in the morning, in order to build the fires and have a little time in which to prepare my lessons. In all my career at Hampton, and ever since I have been out in the world, Miss Mary F. Mackie, the head teacher to whom I have referred, proved one of my strongest and most helpful friends. Her advice and encouragement were always helpful in strengthening to me in the darkest hour.

I have spoken of the impression that was made upon me by the buildings and general appearance of the Hampton Institute, but I have not spoken of that which made the greatest and most lasting impression on me, and that was a great man--the noblest, rarest human being that it has ever been my privilege to meet. I refer to the late General Samuel C. Armstrong.

It has been my fortune to meet personally many of what are called great characters, both in Europe and America, but I do not hesitate to say that I never met any man who, in my estimation, was the equal of General Armstrong. Fresh from the degrading influences of the slave plantation and the coal-mines, it was a rare privilege for me to be permitted to come into direct contact with such a character as General Armstrong. I shall always remember that the first time I went into his presence he made the impression upon me of being a perfect man: I was made to feel that there was something about him that was superhuman. It was my privilege to know the General personally from the time I entered Hampton till he died, and the more I saw of him the greater he grew in my estimation. One might have removed from Hampton all the buildings, class-rooms, teachers, and industries, and given the men and women there the opportunity of coming into daily contact with General Armstrong, and that alone would have been a liberal education. The older I grow, the more I am convinced that there is no education which one can get from books and costly apparatus that is equal to that which can be gotten from contact with great men and women. Instead of studying books so constantly, how I wish that our schools and colleges might learn to study men and things!

General Armstrong spent two of the last six months of his life in my home at Tuskegee. At that time he was paralyzed to the extent that he had lost control of his body and voice in a very large degree. Notwithstanding his affliction, he worked almost constantly night and day for the cause to which he had given his life. I never saw a man who so completely lost sight of himself. I do not believe he ever had a selfish thought. He was just as happy in trying to assist some other institution in the South as he was when working for Hampton. Although he fought the Southern white man in the Civil War, I never heard him utter a bitter word against him afterward. On the other hand, he was constantly seeking to find ways by which he could be of service to the Southern whites.

It would be difficult to describe the hold that he had upon the students at Hampton, or the faith they had in him. In fact, he was worshipped by his students. It never occurred to me that General Armstrong could fail in anything that he undertook. There is almost no request that he could have made that would not have been complied with. When he was a guest at my home in Alabama, and was so badly paralyzed that he had to be wheeled about in an invalid's chair, I recall that one of the General's former students had occasion to push his chair up a long, steep hill that taxed his strength to the utmost. When the top of the hill was reached, the former pupil, with a glow of happiness on his face, exclaimed, "I am so glad that I have been permitted to do something that was real hard for the General before he dies!" While I was a student at Hampton, the dormitories became so crowded that it was impossible to find room for all who wanted to be admitted. In order to help remedy the difficulty, the General conceived the plan of putting up tents to be used as rooms. As soon as it became known that General Armstrong would be pleased if some of the older students would live in the tents during the winter, nearly every student in school volunteered to go.

I was one of the volunteers. The winter that we spent in those tents was an intensely cold one, and we suffered severely--how much I am sure General Armstrong never knew, because we made no complaints. It was enough for us to know that we were pleasing General Armstrong, and that we were making it possible for an additional number of students to secure an education. More than once, during a cold night, when a stiff gale would be blowing, our tend was lifted bodily, and we would find ourselves in the open air. The General would usually pay a visit to the tents early in the morning, and his earnest, cheerful, encouraging voice would dispel any feeling of despondency.

I have spoken of my admiration for General Armstrong, and yet he was but a type of that Christlike body of men and women who went into the Negro schools at the close of the war by the hundreds to assist in lifting up my race. The history of the world fails to show a higher, purer, and more unselfish class of men and women than those who found their way into those Negro schools.

Life at Hampton was a constant revelation to me; was constantly taking me into a new world. The matter of having meals at regular hours, of eating on a tablecloth, using a napkin, the use of the bath-tub and of the tooth-brush, as well as the use of sheets upon the bed, were all new to me.

I sometimes feel that almost the most valuable lesson I got at the Hampton Institute was in the use and value of the bath. I learned there for the first time some of its value, not only in keeping the body healthy, but in inspiring self-respect and promoting virtue. In all my travels in the South and elsewhere since leaving Hampton I have always in some way sought my daily bath. To get it sometimes when I have been the guest of my own people in a single-roomed cabin has not always been easy to do, except by slipping away to some stream in the woods. I have always tried to teach my people that some provision for bathing should be a part of every house.

For some time, while a student at Hampton, I possessed but a single pair of socks, but when I had worn these till they became soiled, I would wash them at night and hang them by the fire to dry, so that I might wear them again the next morning.

The charge for my board at Hampton was ten dollars per month. I was expected to pay a part of this in cash and to work out the remainder. To meet this cash payment, as I have stated, I had just fifty cents when I reached the institution. Aside from a very few dollars that my brother John was able to send me once in a while, I had no money with which to pay my board. I was determined from the first to make my work as janitor so valuable that my services would be indispensable. This I succeeded in doing to such an extent

[129]

that I was soon informed that I would be allowed the full cost of my board in return for my work. The cost of tuition was seventy dollars a year. This, of course, was wholly beyond my ability to provide. If I had been compelled to pay the seventy dollars for tuition, in addition to providing for my board, I would have been compelled to leave the Hampton school. General Armstrong, however, very kindly got Mr. S. Griffitts Morgan, of New Bedford, Mass., to defray the cost of my tuition during the whole time that I was at Hampton. After I finished the course at Hampton and had entered upon my lifework at Tuskegee, I had the pleasure of visiting Mr. Morgan several times.

After having been for a while at Hampton, I found myself in difficulty because I did not have books and clothing. Usually, however, I got around the trouble about books by borrowing from those who were more fortunate than myself. As to clothes, when I reached Hampton I had practically nothing. Everything that I possessed was in a small hand satchel. My anxiety about clothing was increased because of the fact that General Armstrong made a personal inspection of the young men in ranks, to see that their clothes were clean. Shoes had to be polished, there must be no buttons off the clothing, and no grease-spots. To wear one suit of clothes continually, while at work and in the schoolroom, and at the same time keep it clean, was rather a hard problem for me to solve. In some way I managed to get on till the teachers learned that I was in earnest and meant to succeed, and then some of them were kind enough to see that I was partly supplied with second-hand clothing that had been sent in barrels from the North. These barrels proved a blessing to hundreds of poor but deserving students. Without them I question whether I should ever have gotten through Hampton.

When I first went to Hampton I do not recall that I had ever slept in a bed that had two sheets on it. In those days there were not many buildings there, and room was very precious. There were seven other boys in the same room with me; most of them, however, students who had been there for some time. The sheets were quite a puzzle to me. The first night I slept under both of them, and the second night I slept on top of them; but by watching the other boys I learned my lesson in this, and have been trying to follow it ever since and to teach it to others.

I was among the youngest of the students who were in Hampton at the time. Most of the students were men and women--some as old as forty years of ago. As I now recall the scene of my first year, I do not believe that one often has the opportunity of coming into contact with three or four hundred men and women who were so tremendously in earnest as these men and women were. Every hour was occupied in study or work. Nearly all had had enough actual contact with the world to teach them the need of education. Many of the older ones were, of course, too old to master the text-books very thoroughly, and it was often sad to watch their struggles; but they made up in earnest much of what they lacked in books. Many of them were as poor as I was, and, besides having to wrestle with their books, they had to struggle with a poverty which prevented their having the necessities of life. Many of them had aged parents who were dependent upon them, and some of them were men who had wives whose support in some way they had to provide for.

The great and prevailing idea that seemed to take possession of every one was to prepare himself to lift up the people at his home. No one seemed to think of himself. And the officers and teachers, what a rare set of human beings they were! They worked for the students night and day, in seasons and out of season. They seemed happy only when they were helping the students in some manner. Whenever it is written--and I hope it will be--the part that the Yankee teachers played in the education of the Negroes immediately after the war will make one of the most thrilling parts of the history off this country. The time is not far distant when the whole South will appreciate this service in a way that it has not yet been able to do.

CHAPTER 4
HELPING OTHERS

At the end of my first year at Hampton I was confronted with another difficulty. Most of the students went home to spend their vacation. I had no money with which to go home, but I had to go somewhere. In those days very few students were permitted to remain at the school during vacation. It made me feel very sad and homesick to see the other students preparing to leave and starting for home. I not only had no money with which to go home, but I had none with which to go anywhere.

In some way, however, I had gotten hold of an extra, second-hand coat which I thought was a pretty valuable coat. This I decided to sell, in order to get a little money for travelling expenses. I had a good deal of boyish pride, and I tried to hide, as far as I could, from the other students the fact that I had no money and nowhere to go. I made it known to a few people in the town of Hampton that I had this coat to sell, and, after a good deal of persuading, one coloured man promised to come to my room to look the coat over and consider the matter of buying it. This cheered my drooping spirits considerably. Early the next morning my prospective customer appeared. After looking the garment over carefully, he asked me how much I wanted for it. I told him I thought it was worth three dollars. He seemed to agree with me as to price, but remarked in the most matter-of-fact way: "I tell you what I will do; I will take the coat, and will pay you five cents, cash down, and pay you the rest of the money just as soon as I can get it." It is not hard to imagine what my feelings were at the time.

With this disappointment I gave up all hope of getting out of the town of Hampton for my vacation work. I wanted very much to go where I might secure work that would at least pay me enough to purchase some much-needed clothing and other necessities. In a few days practically all the students and teachers had left for their homes, and this served to depress my spirits even more.

After trying for several days in and near the town of Hampton, I finally secured work in a restaurant at Fortress Monroe. The wages, however, were very little more than my board. At night, and between meals, I found considerable time for study and reading; and in this direction I improved myself very much during the summer.

When I left school at the end of my first year, I owed the institution sixteen dollars that I had not been able to work out. It was my greatest ambition during the summer to save money enough with which to pay this debt. I felt that this was a debt of honour, and that I could hardly bring myself to the point of even trying to enter school again till it was paid. I economized in every way that I could think of--did my own washing, and went without necessary garments--but still I found my summer vacation ending and I did not have the sixteen dollars.

One day, during the last week of my stay in the restaurant, I found under one of the tables a crisp, new ten-dollar bill. I could hardly contain myself, I was so happy. As it was not my place of business I felt it to be the proper thing to show the money to the proprietor. This I did. He seemed as glad as I was, but he coolly explained to me that, as it was his place of business, he had a right to keep the money, and he proceeded to do so. This, I confess, was another pretty hard blow to me. I will not say that I became discouraged, for as I now look back over my life I do not recall that I ever became discouraged over anything that I set out to accomplish. I have begun everything with the idea that I could succeed, and I never had much patience with the multitudes of people who are always ready to explain why one cannot succeed. I determined to face the situation just as it was. At the end of the week I went to the treasurer of the Hampton Institute, General J.F.B. Marshall, and told him frankly my condition. To my gratification he told me that I could reenter the institution, and that he would trust me to pay the debt when I could. During the second year I continued to work as a janitor.

The education that I received at Hampton out of the text-books was but a small part of what I learned there. One of the things that impressed itself upon me deeply, the second year, was the unselfishness of the teachers. It was hard for me to understand how any individuals could bring themselves to the point where they could be so happy in working for others. Before the end of the year, I think I began learning that those who are happiest are those who do the most for others. This lesson I have tried to carry with me ever since.

I also learned a valuable lesson at Hampton by coming into contact with the best breeds of live stock and fowls. No student, I think, who has had the opportunity of doing this could go out into the world and content himself with the poorest grades.

Perhaps the most valuable thing that I got out of my second year was an understanding of the use and value of the Bible. Miss Nathalie Lord, one of the teachers, from Portland, Me., taught me how to use and love the Bible. Before this I had never cared a great deal about it, but now I learned to love to read the

Bible, not only for the spiritual help which it gives, but on account of it as literature. The lessons taught me in this respect took such a hold upon me that at the present time, when I am at home, no matter how busy I am, I always make it a rule to read a chapter or a portion of a chapter in the morning, before beginning the work of the day.

Whatever ability I may have as a public speaker I owe in a measure to Miss Lord. When she found out that I had some inclination in this direction, she gave me private lessons in the matter of breathing, emphasis, and articulation. Simply to be able to talk in public for the sake of talking has never had the least attraction to me. In fact, I consider that there is nothing so empty and unsatisfactory as mere abstract public speaking; but from my early childhood I have had a desire to do something to make the world better, and then to be able to speak to the world about that thing.

The debating societies at Hampton were a constant source of delight to me. These were held on Saturday evening; and during my whole life at Hampton I do not recall that I missed a single meeting. I not only attended the weekly debating society, but was instrumental in organizing an additional society. I noticed that between the time when supper was over and the time to begin evening study there were about twenty minutes which the young men usually spent in idle gossip. About twenty of us formed a society for the purpose of utilizing this time in debate or in practice in public speaking. Few persons ever derived more happiness or benefit from the use of twenty minutes of time than we did in this way.

At the end of my second year at Hampton, by the help of some money sent me by my mother and brother John, supplemented by a small gift from one of the teachers at Hampton, I was enabled to return to my home in Malden, West Virginia, to spend my vacation. When I reached home I found that the salt-furnaces were not running, and that the coal-mine was not being operated on account of the miners being out on "strike." This was something which, it seemed, usually occurred whenever the men got two or three months ahead in their savings. During the strike, of course, they spent all that they had saved, and would often return to work in debt at the same wages, or would move to another mine at considerable expense. In either case, my observations convinced me that the miners were worse off at the end of the strike. Before the days of strikes in that section of the country, I knew miners who had considerable money in the bank, but as soon as the professional labour agitators got control, the savings of even the more thrifty ones began disappearing.

[134]

My mother and the other members of my family were, of course, much rejoiced to see me and to note the improvement that I had made during my two years' absence. The rejoicing on the part of all classes of the coloured people, and especially the older ones, over my return, was almost pathetic. I had to pay a visit to each family and take a meal with each, and at each place tell the story of my experiences at Hampton. In addition to this I had to speak before the church and Sunday-school, and at various other places. The thing that I was most in search of, though, work, I could not find. There was no work on account of the strike. I spent nearly the whole of the first month of my vacation in an effort to find something to do by which I could earn money to pay my way back to Hampton and save a little money to use after reaching there.

Toward the end of the first month, I went to place a considerable distance from my home, to try to find employment. I did not succeed, and it was night before I got started on my return. When I had gotten within a mile or so of my home I was so completely tired out that I could not walk any farther, and I went into an old, abandoned house to spend the remainder of the night. About three o'clock in the morning my brother John found me asleep in this house, and broke to me, as gently as he could, the sad news that our dear mother had died during the night.

This seemed to me the saddest and blankest moment in my life. For several years my mother had not been in good health, but I had no idea, when I parted from her the previous day, that I should never see her alive again. Besides that, I had always had an intense desire to be with her when she did pass away. One of the chief ambitions which spurred me on at Hampton was that I might be able to get to be in a position in which I could better make my mother comfortable and happy. She had so often expressed the wish that she might be permitted to live to see her children educated and started out in the world.

In a very short time after the death of my mother our little home was in confusion. My sister Amanda, although she tried to do the best she could, was too young to know anything about keeping house, and my stepfather was not able to hire a housekeeper. Sometimes we had food cooked for us, and sometimes we did not. I remember that more than once a can of tomatoes and some crackers constituted a meal. Our clothing went uncared for, and everything about our home was soon in a tumble-down condition. It seems to me that this was the most dismal period of my life.

My good friend, Mrs. Ruffner, to whom I have already referred, always made me welcome at her home, and assisted me in many ways during this trying period. Before the end of the vacation she gave me some work, and this, together with work in a coal-mine at some distance from my home, enabled me to earn a little money.

At one time it looked as if I would have to give up the idea of returning to Hampton, but my heart was so set on returning that I determined not to give up going back without a struggle. I was very anxious to secure some clothes for the winter, but in this I was disappointed, except for a few garments which my brother John secured for me. Notwithstanding my need of money and clothing, I was very happy in the fact that I had secured enough money to pay my travelling expenses back to Hampton. Once there, I knew that I could make myself so useful as a janitor that I could in some way get through the school year.

Three weeks before the time for the opening of the term at Hampton, I was pleasantly surprised to receive a letter from my good friend Miss Mary F. Mackie, the lady principal, asking me to return to Hampton two weeks before the opening of the school, in order that I might assist her in cleaning the buildings and getting things in order for the new school year. This was just the opportunity I wanted. It gave me a chance to secure a credit in the treasurer's office. I started for Hampton at once.

During these two weeks I was taught a lesson which I shall never forget. Miss Mackie was a member of one of the oldest and most cultured families of the North, and yet for two weeks she worked by my side cleaning windows, dusting rooms, putting beds in order, and what not. She felt that things would not be in condition for the opening of school unless every window-pane was perfectly clean, and she took the greatest satisfaction in helping to clean them herself. The work which I have described she did every year that I was at Hampton.

It was hard for me at this time to understand how a woman of her education and social standing could take such delight in performing such service, in order to assist in the elevation of an unfortunate race. Ever since then I have had no patience with any school for my race in the South which did not teach its students the dignity of labour.

During my last year at Hampton every minute of my time that was not occupied with my duties as janitor was devoted to hard study. I was determined, if possible, to make such a record in my class as would cause me to be placed on the "honour roll" of Commencement speakers. This I was successful in doing. It was June of 1875 when I finished the regular course of study at Hampton. The greatest benefits that I got out of my at the Hampton Institute, perhaps, may be classified under two heads:--

[136]

First was contact with a great man, General S.C. Armstrong, who, I repeat, was, in my opinion, the rarest, strongest, and most beautiful character that it has ever been my privilege to meet.

Second, at Hampton, for the first time, I learned what education was expected to do for an individual. Before going there I had a good deal of the then rather prevalent idea among our people that to secure an education meant to have a good, easy time, free from all necessity for manual labour. At Hampton I not only learned that it was not a disgrace to labour, but learned to love labour, not alone for its financial value, but for labour's own sake and for the independence and self-reliance which the ability to do something which the world wants done brings. At that institution I got my first taste of what it meant to live a life of unselfishness, my first knowledge of the fact that the happiest individuals are those who do the most to make others useful and happy.

I was completely out of money when I graduated. In company with our other Hampton students, I secured a place as a table waiter in a summer hotel in Connecticut, and managed to borrow enough money with which to get there. I had not been in this hotel long before I found out that I knew practically nothing about waiting on a hotel table. The head waiter, however, supposed that I was an accomplished waiter. He soon gave me charge of the table at which their sat four or five wealthy and rather aristocratic people. My ignorance of how to wait upon them was so apparent that they scolded me in such a severe manner that I became frightened and left their table, leaving them sitting there without food. As a result of this I was reduced from the position of waiter to that of a dish-carrier.

But I determined to learn the business of waiting, and did so within a few weeks and was restored to my former position. I have had the satisfaction of being a guest in this hotel several times since I was a waiter there.

At the close of the hotel season I returned to my former home in Malden, and was elected to teach the coloured school at that place. This was the beginning of one of the happiest periods of my life. I now felt that I had the opportunity to help the people of my home town to a higher life. I felt from the first that mere book education was not all that the young people of that town needed. I began my work at eight o'clock in the morning, and, as a rule, it did not end until ten o'clock at night. In addition to the usual routine of teaching, I taught the pupils to comb their hair, and to keep their hands and faces clean, as well as their clothing. I gave special attention to teaching them the proper use of the tooth-brush and the bath. In all my teaching I have watched carefully the influence of the tooth-brush, and I am convinced that there are few single

[137]

agencies of civilization that are more far-reaching.

There were so many of the older boys and girls in the town, as well as men and women, who had to work in the daytime and still were craving an opportunity for an education, that I soon opened a night-school. From the first, this was crowded every night, being about as large as the school that I taught in the day. The efforts of some of the men and women, who in many cases were over fifty years of age, to learn, were in some cases very pathetic.

My day and night school work was not all that I undertook. I established a small reading-room and a debating society. On Sundays I taught two Sunday-schools, one in the town of Malden in the afternoon, and the other in the morning at a place three miles distant from Malden. In addition to this, I gave private lessons to several young men whom I was fitting to send to the Hampton Institute. Without regard to pay and with little thought of it, I taught any one who wanted to learn anything that I could teach him. I was supremely happy in the opportunity of being able to assist somebody else. I did receive, however, a small salary from the public fund, for my work as a public-school teacher.

During the time that I was a student at Hampton my older brother, John, not only assisted me all that he could, but worked all of the time in the coal-mines in order to support the family. He willingly neglected his own education that he might help me. It was my earnest wish to help him to prepare to enter Hampton, and to save money to assist him in his expenses there. Both of these objects I was successful in accomplishing. In three years my brother finished the course at Hampton, and he is now holding the important position of Superintendent of Industries at Tuskegee. When he returned from Hampton, we both combined our efforts and savings to send our adopted brother, James, through the Hampton Institute. This we succeeded in doing, and he is now the postmaster at the Tuskegee Institute. The year 1877, which was my second year of teaching in Malden, I spent very much as I did the first.

It was while my home was at Malden that what was known as the "Ku Klux Klan" was in the height of its activity. The "Ku Klux" were bands of men who had joined themselves together for the purpose of regulating the conduct of the coloured people, especially with the object of preventing the members of the race from exercising any influence in politics. They corresponded somewhat to the "patrollers" of whom I used to hear a great deal during the days of slavery, when I was a small boy. The "patrollers" were bands of white men--usually young men--who were organized largely for the purpose of regulating the conduct of the slaves at night in such matters as preventing the slaves from

[138]

going from one plantation to another without passes, and for preventing them from holding any kind of meetings without permission and without the presence at these meetings of at least one white man.

Like the "patrollers" the "Ku Klux" operated almost wholly at night. They were, however, more cruel than the "patrollers." Their objects, in the main, were to crush out the political aspirations of the Negroes, but they did not confine themselves to this, because schoolhouses as well as churches were burned by them, and many innocent persons were made to suffer. During this period not a few coloured people lost their lives.

As a young man, the acts of these lawless bands made a great impression upon me. I saw one open battle take place at Malden between some of the coloured and white people. There must have been not far from a hundred persons engaged on each side; many on both sides were seriously injured, among them General Lewis Ruffner, the husband of my friend Mrs. Viola Ruffner. General Ruffner tried to defend the coloured people, and for this he was knocked down and so seriously wounded that he never completely recovered. It seemed to me as I watched this struggle between members of the two races, that there was no hope for our people in this country. The "Ku Klux" period was, I think, the darkest part of the Reconstruction days.

I have referred to this unpleasant part of the history of the South simply for the purpose of calling attention to the great change that has taken place since the days of the "Ku Klux." To-day there are no such organizations in the South, and the fact that such ever existed is almost forgotten by both races. There are few places in the South now where public sentiment would permit such organizations to exist.

CHAPTER 5
THE RECONSTRUCTION PERIOD

The years from 1867 to 1878 I think may be called the period of Reconstruction. This included the time that I spent as a student at Hampton and as a teacher in West Virginia. During the whole of the Reconstruction period two ideas were constantly agitating in the minds of the coloured people, or, at least, in the minds of a large part of the race. One of these was the craze for Greek and Latin learning, and the other was a desire to hold office.

It could not have been expected that a people who had spent generations in slavery, and before that generations in the darkest heathenism, could at first form any proper conception of what an education meant. In every part of the South, during the Reconstruction period, schools, both day and night, were filled to overflowing with people of all ages and conditions, some being as far along in age as sixty and seventy years. The ambition to secure an education was most praiseworthy and encouraging. The idea, however, was too prevalent that, as soon as one secured a little education, in some unexplainable way he would be free from most of the hardships of the world, and, at any rate, could live without manual labour. There was a further feeling that a knowledge, however little, of the Greek and Latin languages would make one a very superior human being, something bordering almost on the supernatural. I remember that the first coloured man whom I saw who knew something about foreign languages impressed me at the time as being a man of all others to be envied.

Naturally, most of our people who received some little education became teachers or preachers. While among those two classes there were many capable, earnest, godly men and women, still a large proportion took up teaching or preaching as an easy way to make a living. Many became teachers who could do little more than write their names. I remember there came into our neighbourhood one of this class, who was in search of a school to teach, and the question arose while he was there as to the shape of the earth and how he could teach the children concerning the subject. He explained his position in the matter by saying that he was prepared to teach that the earth was either flat or round, according to the preference of a majority of his patrons.

The ministry was the profession that suffered most--and still suffers, though

[140]

there has been great improvement--on account of not only ignorant but in many cases immoral men who claimed that they were "called to preach." In the earlier days of freedom almost every coloured man who learned to read would receive "a call to preach" within a few days after he began reading. At my home in West Virginia the process of being called to the ministry was a very interesting one. Usually the "call" came when the individual was sitting in church. Without warning the one called would fall upon the floor as if struck by a bullet, and would lie there for hours, speechless and motionless. Then the news would spread all through the neighborhood that this individual had received a "call." If he were inclined to resist the summons, he would fall or be made to fall a second or third time. In the end he always yielded to the call. While I wanted an education badly, I confess that in my youth I had a fear that when I had learned to read and write very well I would receive one of these "calls"; but, for some reason, my call never came.

When we add the number of wholly ignorant men who preached or "exhorted" to that of those who possessed something of an education, it can be seen at a glance that the supply of ministers was large. In fact, some time ago I knew a certain church that had a total membership of about two hundred, and eighteen of that number were ministers. But, I repeat, in many communities in the South the character of the ministry is being improved, and I believe that within the next two or three decades a very large proportion of the unworthy ones will have disappeared. The "calls" to preach, I am glad to say, are not nearly so numerous now as they were formerly, and the calls to some industrial occupation are growing more numerous. The improvement that has taken place in the character of the teachers is even more marked than in the case of the ministers.

During the whole of the Reconstruction period our people throughout the South looked to the Federal Government for everything, very much as a child looks to its mother. This was not unnatural. The central government gave them freedom, and the whole Nation had been enriched for more than two centuries by the labour of the Negro. Even as a youth, and later in manhood, I had the feeling that it was cruelly wrong in the central government, at the beginning of our freedom, to fail to make some provision for the general education of our people in addition to what the states might do, so that the people would be the better prepared for the duties of citizenship.

It is easy to find fault, to remark what might have been done, and perhaps, after all, and under all the circumstances, those in charge of the conduct of affairs did the only thing that could be done at the time. Still, as I look back now over the entire period of our freedom, I cannot help feeling that it would have

[141]

been wiser if some plan could have been put in operation which would have made the possession of a certain amount of education or property, or both, a test for the exercise of the franchise, and a way provided by which this test should be made to apply honestly and squarely to both the white and black races.

Though I was but little more than a youth during the period of Reconstruction, I had the feeling that mistakes were being made, and that things could not remain in the condition that they were in then very long. I felt that the Reconstruction policy, so far as it related to my race, was in a large measure on a false foundation, was artificial and forced. In many cases it seemed to me that the ignorance of my race was being used as a tool with which to help white men into office, and that there was an element in the North which wanted to punish the Southern white men by forcing the Negro into positions over the heads of the Southern whites. I felt that the Negro would be the one to suffer for this in the end. Besides, the general political agitation drew the attention of our people away from the more fundamental matters of perfecting themselves in the industries at their doors and in securing property.

The temptations to enter political life were so alluring that I came very near yielding to them at one time, but I was kept from doing so by the feeling that I would be helping in a more substantial way by assisting in the laying of the foundation of the race through a generous education of the hand, head, and heart. I saw coloured men who were members of the state legislatures, and county officers, who, in some cases, could not read or write, and whose morals were as weak as their education. Not long ago, when passing through the streets of a certain city in the South, I heard some brick-masons calling out, from the top of a two-story brick building on which they were working, for the "Governor" to "hurry up and bring up some more bricks." Several times I heard the command, "Hurry up, Governor!" "Hurry up, Governor!" My curiosity was aroused to such an extent that I made inquiry as to who the "Governor" was, and soon found that he was a coloured man who at one time had held the position of Lieutenant-Governor of his state.

But not all the coloured people who were in office during Reconstruction were unworthy of their positions, by any means. Some of them, like the late Senator B.K. Bruce, Governor Pinchback, and many others, were strong, upright, useful men. Neither were all the class designated as carpetbaggers dishonourable men. Some of them, like ex-Governor Bullock, of Georgia, were men of high character and usefulness.

Of course the coloured people, so largely without education, and wholly

[142]

without experience in government, made tremendous mistakes, just as many people similarly situated would have done. Many of the Southern whites have a feeling that, if the Negro is permitted to exercise his political rights now to any degree, the mistakes of the Reconstruction period will repeat themselves. I do not think this would be true, because the Negro is a much stronger and wiser man than he was thirty-five years ago, and he is fast learning the lesson that he cannot afford to act in a manner that will alienate his Southern white neighbours from him. More and more I am convinced that the final solution of the political end of our race problem will be for each state that finds it necessary to change the law bearing upon the franchise to make the law apply with absolute honesty, and without opportunity for double dealing or evasion, to both races alike. Any other course my daily observation in the South convinces me, will be unjust to the Negro, unjust to the white man, and unfair to the rest of the state in the Union, and will be, like slavery, a sin that at some time we shall have to pay for.

In the fall of 1878, after having taught school in Malden for two years, and after I had succeeded in preparing several of the young men and women, besides my two brothers, to enter the Hampton Institute, I decided to spend some months in study at Washington, D.C. I remained there for eight months. I derived a great deal of benefit from the studies which I pursued, and I came into contact with some strong men and women. At the institution I attended there was no industrial training given to the students, and I had an opportunity of comparing the influence of an institution with no industrial training with that of one like the Hampton Institute, that emphasizes the industries. At this school I found the students, in most cases, had more money, were better dressed, wore the latest style of all manner of clothing, and in some cases were more brilliant mentally. At Hampton it was a standing rule that, while the institution would be responsible for securing some one to pay the tuition for the students, the men and women themselves must provide for their own board, books, clothing, and room wholly by work, or partly by work and partly in cash. At the institution at which I now was, I found that a large portion of the students by some means had their personal expenses paid for them. At Hampton the student was constantly making the effort through the industries to help himself, and that very effort was of immense value in character-building. The students at the other school seemed to be less self-dependent. They seemed to give more attention to mere outward appearances. In a word, they did not appear to me to be beginning at the bottom, on a real, solid foundation, to the extent that they were at Hampton. They knew more about Latin and Greek when they left school, but they seemed to know less about life and its conditions as they would meet it at their homes. Having lived for a number of years in the midst of comfortable surroundings, they were not as much inclined as the Hampton students to go into the country districts of the South, where there was little of comfort, to take up work for our people, and they were more inclined to yield to the temptation to become hotel waiters and Pullman-car porters as their life-work.

During the time I was a student at Washington the city was crowded with coloured people, many of whom had recently come from the South. A large proportion of these people had been drawn to Washington because they felt that they could lead a life of ease there. Others had secured minor government positions, and still another large class was there in the hope of securing Federal positions. A number of coloured men--some of them very strong and brilliant--were in the House of Representatives at that time, and one, the Hon. B.K. Bruce, was in the Senate. All this tended to make Washington an attractive place for members of the coloured race. Then, too, they knew that at all times they could have the protection of the law in the District of Columbia. The public schools in Washington for coloured people were better then than they were elsewhere. I took great interest in studying the life of our people there closely at that time. I found that while among them there was a large element of substantial, worthy citizens, there was also a superficiality about the life of a large class that greatly alarmed me. I saw young coloured men who were not earning more than four dollars a week spend two dollars or more for a buggy on Sunday to ride up and down Pennsylvania Avenue in, in order that they might try to convince the world that they were worth thousands. I saw other young men who received seventy-five or one hundred dollars per month from the Government, who were in debt at the end of every month. I saw men who but a few months previous were members of Congress, then without employment and in poverty. Among a large class there seemed to be a dependence upon the Government for every conceivable thing. The members of this class had little ambition to create a position for themselves, but wanted the Federal officials to create one for them. How many times I wished them, and have often wished since, that by some power of magic I might remove the great bulk of these people into the county districts and plant them upon the soil, upon the solid and never deceptive foundation of Mother Nature, where all nations and races that have ever succeeded have gotten their start,--a start that at first may be slow and toilsome, but one that nevertheless is real.

In Washington I saw girls whose mothers were earning their living by laundrying. These girls were taught by their mothers, in rather a crude way it is true, the industry of laundrying. Later, these girls entered the public schools and remained there perhaps six or eight years. When the public school course was

[144]

finally finished, they wanted more costly dresses, more costly hats and shoes. In a word, while their wants have been increased, their ability to supply their wants had not been increased in the same degree. On the other hand, their six or eight years of book education had weaned them away from the occupation of their mothers. The result of this was in too many cases that the girls went to the bad. I often thought how much wiser it would have been to give these girls the same amount of maternal training--and I favour any kind of training, whether in the languages or mathematics, that gives strength and culture to the mind --but at the same time to give them the most thorough training in the latest and best methods of laundrying and other kindred occupations.

CHAPTER 6

BLACK RACE AND RED RACE

During the year that I spent in Washington, and for some little time before this, there had been considerable agitation in the state of West Virginia over the question of moving the capital of the state from Wheeling to some other central point. As a result of this, the Legislature designated three cities to be voted upon by the citizens of the state as the permanent seat of government. Among these cities was Charleston, only five miles from Malden, my home. At the close of my school year in Washington I was very pleasantly surprised to receive, from a committee of three white people in Charleston, an invitation to canvass the state in the interests of that city. This invitation I accepted, and spent nearly three months in speaking in various parts of the state. Charleston was successful in winning the prize, and is now the permanent seat of government.

The reputation that I made as a speaker during this campaign induced a number of persons to make an earnest effort to get me to enter political life, but I refused, still believing that I could find other service which would prove of more permanent value to my race. Even then I had a strong feeling that what our people most needed was to get a foundation in education, industry, and property, and for this I felt that they could better afford to strive than for political preferment. As for my individual self, it appeared to me to be reasonably certain that I could succeed in political life, but I had a feeling that it would be a rather selfish kind of success--individual success at the cost of failing to do my duty in assisting in laying a foundation for the masses.

At this period in the progress of our race a very large proportion of the young men who went to school or to college did so with the expressed determination to prepare themselves to be great lawyers, or Congressmen, and many of the women planned to become music teachers; but I had a reasonably fixed idea, even at that early period in my life, that there was a need for something to be done to prepare the way for successful lawyers, Congressmen, and music teachers.

I felt that the conditions were a good deal like those of an old coloured man, during the days of slavery, who wanted to learn how to play on the guitar. In his desire to take guitar lessons he applied to one of his young masters to teach him, but the young man, not having much faith in the ability of the slave to master the guitar at his age, sought to discourage him by telling him: "Uncle Jake, I will give you guitar lessons; but, Jake, I will have to charge you three dollars for the first lesson, two dollars for the second lesson, and one dollar for the third lesson. But I will charge you only twenty-five cents for the last lesson."

Uncle Jake answered: "All right, boss, I hires you on dem terms. But, boss! I wants yer to be sure an' give me dat las' lesson first."

Soon after my work in connection with the removal of the capital was finished, I received an invitation which gave me great joy and which at the same time was a very pleasant surprise. This was a letter from General Armstrong, inviting me to return to Hampton at the next Commencement to deliver what was called the "post-graduate address." This was an honour which I had not dreamed of receiving. With much care I prepared the best address that I was capable of. I chose for my subject "The Force That Wins."

As I returned to Hampton for the purpose of delivering this address, I went over much of the same ground--now, however, covered entirely by railroad--that I had traversed nearly six years before, when I first sought entrance into Hampton Institute as a student. Now I was able to ride the whole distance in the train. I was constantly contrasting this with my first journey to Hampton. I think I may say, without seeming egotism, that it is seldom that five years have wrought such a change in the life and aspirations of an individual.

At Hampton I received a warm welcome from teachers and students. I found that during my absence from Hampton the institute each year had been getting closer to the real needs and conditions of our people; that the industrial reaching, as well as that of the academic department, had greatly improved. The plan of the school was not modelled after that of any other institution then in existence, but every improvement was made under the magnificent leadership of General Armstrong solely with the view of meeting and helping the needs of our people as they presented themselves at the time. Too often, it seems to me, in missionary and educational work among underdeveloped races, people yield to the temptation of doing that which was done a hundred years before, or is being done in other communities a thousand miles away. The temptation often is to run each individual through a certain educational mould, regardless of the condition of the subject or the end to be accomplished. This was not so at Hampton Institute.

The address which I delivered on Commencement Day seems to have pleased every one, and many kind and encouraging words were spoken to me regarding it. Soon after my return to my home in West Virginia, where I had planned to continue teaching, I was again surprised to receive a letter from

General Armstrong, asking me to return to Hampton partly as a teacher and partly to pursue some supplementary studies. This was in the summer of 1879. Soon after I began my first teaching in West Virginia I had picked out four of the brightest and most promising of my pupils, in addition to my two brothers, to whom I have already referred, and had given them special attention, with the view of having them go to Hampton. They had gone there, and in each case the teachers had found them so well prepared that they entered advanced classes. This fact, it seems, led to my being called back to Hampton as a teacher. One of the young men that I sent to Hampton in this way is now Dr. Samuel E. Courtney, a successful physician in Boston, and a member of the School Board of that city.

About this time the experiment was being tried for the first time, by General Armstrong, of education Indians at Hampton. Few people then had any confidence in the ability of the Indians to receive education and to profit by it. General Armstrong was anxious to try the experiment systematically on a large scale. He secured from the reservations in the Western states over one hundred wild and for the most part perfectly ignorant Indians, the greater proportion of whom were young men. The special work which the General desired me to do was be a sort of "house father" to the Indian young men--that is, I was to live in the building with them and have the charge of their discipline, clothing, rooms, and so on. This was a very tempting offer, but I had become so much absorbed in my work in West Virginia that I dreaded to give it up. However, I tore myself away from it. I did not know how to refuse to perform any service that General Armstrong desired of me.

On going to Hampton, I took up my residence in a building with about seventy-five Indian youths. I was the only person in the building who was not a member of their race. At first I had a good deal of doubt about my ability to succeed. I knew that the average Indian felt himself above the white man, and, of course, he felt himself far above the Negro, largely on account of the fact of the Negro having submitted to slavery--a thing which the Indian would never do. The Indians, in the Indian Territory, owned a large number of slaves during the days of slavery. Aside from this, there was a general feeling that the attempt to education and civilize the red men at Hampton would be a failure. All this made me proceed very cautiously, for I felt keenly the great responsibility. But I was determined to succeed. It was not long before I had the complete confidence of the Indians, and not only this, but I think I am safe in saying that I had their love and respect. I found that they were about like any other human beings; that they responded to kind treatment and resented ill-treatment. They were continually planning to do something that would add to my happiness and

[148]

comfort. The things that they disliked most, I think, were to have their long hair cut, to give up wearing their blankets, and to cease smoking; but no white American ever thinks that any other race is wholly civilized until he wears the white man's clothes, eats the white man's food, speaks the white man's language, and professes the white man's religion.

When the difficulty of learning the English language was subtracted, I found that in the matter of learning trades and in mastering academic studies there was little difference between the coloured and Indian students. It was a constant delight to me to note the interest which the coloured students took in trying to help the Indians in every way possible. There were a few of the coloured students who felt that the Indians ought not to be admitted to Hampton, but these were in the minority. Whenever they were asked to do so, the Negro students gladly took the Indians as room-mates, in order that they might teach them to speak English and to acquire civilized habits.

I have often wondered if there was a white institution in this country whose students would have welcomed the incoming of more than a hundred companions of another race in the cordial way that these black students at Hampton welcomed the red ones. How often I have wanted to say to white students that they lift themselves up in proportion as they help to lift others, and the more unfortunate the race, and the lower in the scale of civilization, the more does one raise one's self by giving the assistance.

This reminds me of a conversation which I once had with the Hon. Frederick Douglass. At one time Mr. Douglass was travelling in the state of Pennsylvania, and was forced, on account of his colour, to ride in the baggage-car, in spite of the fact that he had paid the same price for his passage that the other passengers had paid. When some of the white passengers went into the baggage-car to console Mr. Douglass, and one of them said to him: "I am sorry, Mr. Douglass, that you have been degraded in this manner," Mr. Douglass straightened himself up on the box upon which he was sitting, and replied: "They cannot degrade Frederick Douglass. The soul that is within me no man can degrade. I am not the one that is being degraded on account of this treatment, but those who are inflicting it upon me."

In one part of the country, where the law demands the separation of the races on the railroad trains, I saw at one time a rather amusing instance which showed how difficult it sometimes is to know where the black begins and the white ends.

There was a man who was well known in his community as a Negro, but who was so white that even an expert would have hard work to classify him as a black man. This man was riding in the part of the train set aside for the coloured passengers. When the train conductor reached him, he showed at once that he was perplexed. If the man was a Negro, the conductor did not want to send him to the white people's coach; at the same time, if he was a white man, the conductor did not want to insult him by asking him if he was a Negro. The official looked him over carefully, examining his hair, eyes, nose, and hands, but still seemed puzzled. Finally, to solve the difficulty, he stooped over and peeped at the man's feet. When I saw the conductor examining the feet of the man in question, I said to myself, "That will settle it;" and so it did, for the trainman promptly decided that the passenger was a Negro, and let him remain where he was. I congratulated myself that my race was fortunate in not losing one of its members.

My experience has been that the time to test a true gentleman is to observe him when he is in contact with individuals of a race that is less fortunate than his own. This is illustrated in no better way than by observing the conduct of the old-school type of Southern gentleman when he is in contact with his former slaves or their descendants.

An example of what I mean is shown in a story told of George Washington, who, meeting a coloured man in the road once, who politely lifted his hat, lifted his own in return. Some of his white friends who saw the incident criticised Washington for his action. In reply to their criticism George Washington said: "Do you suppose that I am going to permit a poor, ignorant, coloured man to be more polite than I am?"

While I was in charge of the Indian boys at Hampton, I had one or two experiences which illustrate the curious workings of caste in America. One of the Indian boys was taken ill, and it became my duty to take him to Washington, deliver him over to the Secretary of the Interior, and get a receipt for him, in order that he might be returned to his Western reservation. At that time I was rather ignorant of the ways of the world. During my journey to Washington, on a steamboat, when the bell rang for dinner, I was careful to wait and not enter the dining room until after the greater part of the passengers had finished their meal. Then, with my charge, I went to the dining saloon. The man in charge politely informed me that the Indian could be served, but that I could not. I never could understand how he knew just where to draw the colour line, since the Indian and I were of about the same complexion. The steward, however, seemed to be an expert in this manner. I had been directed by the authorities at Hampton to stop at a certain hotel in Washington with my charge, but when I went to this hotel the clerk stated that he would be glad to receive the Indian into the house, but said that he could not accommodate me.

An illustration of something of this same feeling came under my observation afterward. I happened to find myself in a town in which so much excitement and indignation were being expressed that it seemed likely for a time that there would be a lynching. The occasion of the trouble was that a dark-skinned man had stopped at the local hotel. Investigation, however, developed the fact that this individual was a citizen of Morocco, and that while travelling in this country he spoke the English language. As soon as it was learned that he was not an American Negro, all the signs of indignation disappeared. The man who was the innocent cause of the excitement, though, found it prudent after that not to speak English.

At the end of my first year with the Indians there came another opening for me at Hampton, which, as I look back over my life now, seems to have come providentially, to help to prepare me for my work at Tuskegee later. General Armstrong had found out that there was quite a number of young coloured men and women who were intensely in earnest in wishing to get an education, but who were prevented from entering Hampton Institute because they were too poor to be able to pay any portion of the cost of their board, or even to supply themselves with books. He conceived the idea of starting a night-school in connection with the Institute, into which a limited number of the most promising of these young men and women would be received, on condition that they were to work for ten hours during the day, and attend school for two hours at night. They were to be paid something above the cost of their board for their work. The greater part of their earnings was to be reserved in the school's treasury as a fund to be drawn on to pay their board when they had become students in the day-school, after they had spent one or two years in the night-school. In this way they would obtain a start in their books and a knowledge of some trade or industry, in addition to the other far-reaching benefits of the institution.

General Armstrong asked me to take charge of the night-school, and I did so. At the beginning of this school there were about twelve strong, earnest men and women who entered the class. During the day the greater part of the young men worked in the school's sawmill, and the young men worked in the laundry. The work was not easy in either place, but in all my teaching I never taught pupils who gave me much genuine satisfaction as these did. They were good students, and mastered their work thoroughly. They were so much in earnest that only the ringing of the retiring-bell would make them stop studying, and often they would urge me to continue the lessons after the usual hour for going to bed had come.

These students showed so much earnestness, both in their hard work during the day, as well as in their application to their studies at night, that I gave them

[151]

the name of "The Plucky Class"--a name which soon grew popular and spread throughout the institution. After a student had been in the night-school long enough to prove what was in him, I gave him a printed certificate which read something like this:--

"This is to certify that James Smith is a member of The Plucky Class of the Hampton Institute, and is in good and regular standing."

The students prized these certificates highly, and they added greatly to the popularity of the night-school. Within a few weeks this department had grown to such an extent that there were about twenty-five students in attendance. I have followed the course of many of these twenty-five men and women ever since then, and they are now holding important and useful positions in nearly every part of the South. The night-school at Hampton, which started with only twelve students, now numbers between three and four hundred, and is one of the permanent and most important features of the institution.

CHAPTER 7

EARLY DAYS AT TUSKEGEE

During the time that I had charge of the Indians and the night-school at Hampton, I pursued some studies myself, under the direction of the instructors there. One of these instructors was the Rev. Dr. H.B. Frissell, the present Principal of the Hampton Institute, General Armstrong's successor.

In May, 1881, near the close of my first year in teaching the night-school, in a way that I had not dared expect, the opportunity opened for me to begin my life-work. One night in the chapel, after the usual chapel exercises were over, General Armstrong referred to the fact that he had received a letter from some gentlemen in Alabama asking him to recommend some one to take charge of what was to be a normal school for the coloured people in the little town of Tuskegee in that state. These gentlemen seemed to take it for granted that no coloured man suitable for the position could be secured, and they were expecting the General to recommend a white man for the place. The next day General Armstrong sent for me to come to his office, and, much to my surprise, asked me if I thought I could fill the position in Alabama. I told him that I would be willing to try. Accordingly, he wrote to the people who had applied to him for the information, that he did not know of any white man to suggest, but if they would be willing to take a coloured man, he had one whom he could recommend. In this letter he gave them my name.

Several days passed before anything more was heard about the matter. Some time afterward, one Sunday evening during the chapel exercises, a messenger came in and handed the general a telegram. At the end of the exercises he read the telegram to the school. In substance, these were its words: "Booker T. Washington will suit us. Send him at once."

There was a great deal of joy expressed among the students and teachers, and I received very hearty congratulations. I began to get ready at once to go to Tuskegee. I went by way of my old home in West Virginia, where I remained for several days, after which I proceeded to Tuskegee. I found Tuskegee to be a town of about two thousand inhabitants, nearly one-half of whom were coloured. It was in what was known as the Black Belt of the South. In the county in which Tuskegee is situated the coloured people outnumbered the whites by about three to one. In some of the adjoining and near-by counties the proportion was not far from six coloured persons to one white.

I have often been asked to define the term "Black Belt." So far as I can learn, the term was first used to designated a part of the country which was distinguished by the colour of the soil. The part of the country possessing this thick, dark, and naturally rich soil was, of course, the part of the South where the slaves were most profitable, and consequently they were taken there in the largest numbers. Later, and especially since the war, the term seems to be used wholly in a political sense--that is, to designate the counties where the black people outnumber the white.

Before going to Tuskegee I had expected to find there a building and all the necessary apparatus ready for me to begin teaching. To my disappointment, I found nothing of the kind. I did find, though, that which no costly building and apparatus can supply,--hundreds of hungry, earnest souls who wanted to secure knowledge.

Tuskegee seemed an ideal place for the school. It was in the midst of the great bulk of the Negro population, and was rather secluded, being five miles from the main line of railroad, with which it was connected by a short line. During the days of slavery, and since, the town had been a centre for the education of the white people. This was an added advantage, for the reason that I found the white people possessing a degree of culture and education that is not surpassed by many localities. While the coloured people were ignorant, they had not, as a rule, degraded and weakened their bodies by vices such as are common to the lower class of people in the large cities. In general, I found the relations between the two races pleasant. For example, the largest, and I think at that time the only hardware store in the town was owned and operated jointly by a coloured man and a white man. This copartnership continued until the death of the white partner.

I found that about a year previous to my going to Tuskegee some of the coloured people who had heard something of the work of education being done at Hampton had applied to the state Legislature, through their representatives, for a small appropriation to be used in starting a normal school in Tuskegee. This request the Legislature had complied with to the extent of granting an annual appropriation of two thousand dollars. I soon learned, however, that this money could be used only for the payment of the salaries of the instructors, and that there was no provision for securing land, buildings, or apparatus. The task before me did not seem a very encouraging one. It seemed much like making bricks without straw. The coloured people were overjoyed, and were constantly offering their services in any way in which they could be of assistance in getting

[154]

the school started.

My first task was to find a place in which to open the school. After looking the town over with some care, the most suitable place that could be secured seemed to be a rather dilapidated shanty near the coloured Methodist church, together with the church itself as a sort of assembly-room. Both the church and the shanty were in about as bad condition as was possible. I recall that during the first months of school that I taught in this building it was in such poor repair that, whenever it rained, one of the older students would very kindly leave his lessons and hold an umbrella over me while I heard the recitations of the others. I remember, also, that on more than one occasion my landlady held an umbrella over me while I ate breakfast.

At the time I went to Alabama the coloured people were taking considerable interest in politics, and they were very anxious that I should become one of them politically, in every respect. They seemed to have a little distrust of strangers in this regard. I recall that one man, who seemed to have been designated by the others to look after my political destiny, came to me on several occasions and said, with a good deal of earnestness: "We wants you to be sure to vote jes' like we votes. We can't read de newspapers very much, but we knows how to vote, an' we wants you to vote jes' like we votes." He added: "We watches de white man, and we keeps watching de white man till we finds out which way de white man's gwine to vote; an' when we finds out which way de white man's gwine to vote, den we votes 'xactly de other way. Den we knows we's right."

I am glad to add, however, that at the present time the disposition to vote against the white man merely because he is white is largely disappearing, and the race is learning to vote from principle, for what the voter considers to be for the best interests of both races.

I reached Tuskegee, as I have said, early in June, 1881. The first month I spent in finding accommodations for the school, and in travelling through Alabama, examining into the actual life of the people, especially in the court districts, and in getting the school advertised among the glass of people that I wanted to have attend it. The most of my travelling was done over the country roads, with a mule and a cart or a mule and a buggy wagon for conveyance. I ate and slept with the people, in their little cabins. I saw their farms, their schools, their churches. Since, in the case of the most of these visits, there had been no notice given in advance that a stranger was expected, I had the advantage of seeing the real, everyday life of the people.

In the plantation districts I found that, as a rule, the whole family slept in one room, and that in addition to the immediate family there sometimes were relatives, or others not related to the family, who slept in the same room. On more than one occasion I went outside the house to get ready for bed, or to wait until the family had gone to bed. They usually contrived some kind of a place for me to sleep, either on the floor or in a special part of another's bed. Rarely was there any place provided in the cabin where one could bathe even the face and hands, but usually some provision was made for this outside the house, in the yard.

The common diet of the people was fat pork and corn bread. At times I have eaten in cabins where they had only corn bread and "black-eye peas" cooked in plain water. The people seemed to have no other idea than to live on this fat meat and corn bread,--the meat, and the meal of which the bread was made, having been bought at a high price at a store in town, notwithstanding the face that the land all about the cabin homes could easily have been made to produce nearly every kind of garden vegetable that is raised anywhere in the country. Their one object seemed to be to plant nothing but cotton; and in many cases cotton was planted up to the very door of the cabin.

In these cabin homes I often found sewing-machines which had been bought, or were being bought, on instalments, frequently at a cost of as much as sixty dollars, or showy clocks for which the occupants of the cabins had paid twelve or fourteen dollars. I remember that on one occasion when I went into one of these cabins for dinner, when I sat down to the table for a meal with the four members of the family, I noticed that, while there were five of us at the table, there was but one fork for the five of us to use. Naturally there was an awkward pause on my part. In the opposite corner of that same cabin was an organ for which the people told me they were paying sixty dollars in monthly instalments. One fork, and a sixty-dollar organ!

In most cases the sewing-machine was not used, the clocks were so worthless that they did not keep correct time--and if they had, in nine cases out of ten there would have been no one in the family who could have told the time of day--while the organ, of course, was rarely used for want of a person who could play upon it.

In the case to which I have referred, where the family sat down to the table for the meal at which I was their guest, I could see plainly that this was an awkward and unusual proceeding, and was done in my honour. In most cases, when the family got up in the morning, for example, the wife would put a piece of meat in a frying-pan and put a lump of dough in a "skillet," as they called it. These utensils would be placed on the fire, and in ten or fifteen minutes breakfast would be ready. Frequently the husband would take his bread and meat in his hand and start for the field, eating as he walked. The mother would sit down in a corner and eat her breakfast, perhaps from a plate and perhaps directly from the "skillet" or frying-pan, while the children would eat their portion of the bread and meat while running about the yard. At certain seasons of the year, when meat was scarce, it was rarely that the children who were not old enough or strong enough to work in the fields would have the luxury of meat.

The breakfast over, and with practically no attention given to the house, the whole family would, as a general thing, proceed to the cotton-field. Every child that was large enough to carry a hoe was put to work, and the baby--for usually there was at least one baby--would be laid down at the end of the cotton row, so that its mother could give it a certain amount of attention when she had finished chopping her row. The noon meal and the supper were taken in much the same way as the breakfast.

All the days of the family would be spent after much this same routine, except Saturday and Sunday. On Saturday the whole family would spent at least half a day, and often a whole day, in town. The idea in going to town was, I suppose, to do shopping, but all the shopping that the whole family had money for could have been attended to in ten minutes by one person. Still, the whole family remained in town for most of the day, spending the greater part of the time in standing on the streets, the women, too often, sitting about somewhere smoking or dipping snuff. Sunday was usually spent in going to some big meeting. With few exceptions, I found that the crops were mortgaged in the counties where I went, and that the most of the coloured farmers were in debt. The state had not been able to build schoolhouses in the country districts, and, as a rule, the schools were taught in churches or in log cabins. More than once, while on my journeys, I found that there was no provision made in the house used for school purposes for heating the building during the winter, and consequently a fire had to be built in the yard, and teacher and pupils passed in and out of the house as they got cold or warm. With few exceptions, I found the teachers in these country schools to be miserably poor in preparation for their work, and poor in moral character. The schools were in session from three to five months. There was practically no apparatus in the schoolhouses, except that occasionally there was a rough blackboard. I recall that one day I went into a schoolhouse--or rather into an abandoned log cabin that was being used as a schoolhouse--and found five pupils who were studying a lesson from one book. Two of these, on the front seat, were using the book between them; behind these were two others peeping over the shoulders of the first two, and behind the four was a fifth little fellow who was peeping over the shoulders of all four.

[157]

What I have said concerning the character of the schoolhouses and teachers will also apply quite accurately as a description of the church buildings and the ministers.

I met some very interesting characters during my travels. As illustrating the peculiar mental processes of the country people, I remember that I asked one coloured man, who was about sixty years old, to tell me something of his history. He said that he had been born in Virginia, and sold into Alabama in 1845. I asked him how many were sold at the same time. He said, "There were five of us; myself and brother and three mules."

In giving all these descriptions of what I saw during my mouth of travel in the country around Tuskegee, I wish my readers to keep in mind the fact that there were many encouraging exceptions to the conditions which I have described. I have stated in such plain words what I saw, mainly for the reason that later I want to emphasize the encouraging changes that have taken place in the community, not wholly by the work of the Tuskegee school, but by that of other institutions as well.

CHAPTER 8

TEACHING SCHOOL IN A STABLE AND A HEN-HOUSE

I confess that what I saw during my month of travel and investigation left me with a very heavy heart. The work to be done in order to lift these people up seemed almost beyond accomplishing. I was only one person, and it seemed to me that the little effort which I could put forth could go such a short distance toward bringing about results. I wondered if I could accomplish anything, and if it were worth while for me to try.

Of one thing I felt more strongly convinced than ever, after spending this month in seeing the actual life of the coloured people, and that was that, in order to lift them up, something must be done more than merely to imitate New England education as it then existed. I saw more clearly than ever the wisdom of the system which General Armstrong had inaugurated at Hampton. To take the children of such people as I had been among for a month, and each day give them a few hours of mere book education, I felt would be almost a waste of time.

After consultation with the citizens of Tuskegee, I set July 4, 1881, as the day for the opening of the school in the little shanty and church which had been secured for its accommodation. The white people, as well as the coloured, were greatly interested in the starting of the new school, and the opening day was looked forward to with much earnest discussion. There were not a few white people in the vicinity of Tuskegee who looked with some disfavour upon the project. They questioned its value to the coloured people, and had a fear that it might result in bringing about trouble between the races. Some had the feeling that in proportion as the Negro received education, in the same proportion would his value decrease as an economic factor in the state. These people feared the result of education would be that the Negroes would leave the farms, and that it would be difficult to secure them for domestic service.

The white people who questioned the wisdom of starting this new school had in their minds pictures of what was called an educated Negro, with a high hat, imitation gold eye-glasses, a showy walking-stick, kid gloves, fancy boots, and what not--in a word, a man who was determined to live by his wits. It was difficult for these people to see how education would produce any other kind of a coloured man.

In the midst of all the difficulties which I encountered in getting the little school started, and since then through a period of nineteen years, there are two men among all the many friends of the school in Tuskegee upon whom I have depended constantly for advice and guidance; and the success of the undertaking is largely due to these men, from whom I have never sought anything in vain. I mention them simply as types. One is a white man and an ex-slaveholder, Mr. George W. Campbell; the other is a black man and an ex-slave, Mr. Lewis Adams. These were the men who wrote to General Armstrong for a teacher.

Mr. Campbell is a merchant and banker, and had had little experience in dealing with matters pertaining to education. Mr. Adams was a mechanic, and had learned the trades of shoemaking, harness-making, and tinsmithing during the days of slavery. He had never been to school a day in his life, but in some way he had learned to read and write while a slave. From the first, these two men saw clearly what my plan of education was, sympathized with me, and supported me in every effort. In the days which were darkest financially for the school, Mr. Campbell was never appealed to when he was not willing to extend all the aid in his power. I do not know two men, one an ex-slaveholder, one an ex-slave, whose advice and judgment I would feel more like following in everything which concerns the life and development of the school at Tuskegee than those of these two men.

I have always felt that Mr. Adams, in a large degree, derived his unusual power of mind from the training given his hands in the process of mastering well three trades during the days of slavery. If one goes to-day into any Southern town, and asks for the leading and most reliable coloured man in the community, I believe that in five cases out of ten he will be directed to a Negro who learned a trade during the days of slavery.

On the morning that the school opened, thirty students reported for admission. I was the only teacher. The students were about equally divided between the sexes. Most of them lived in Macon County, the county in which Tuskegee is situated, and of which it is the county-seat. A great many more students wanted to enter the school, but it had been decided to receive only those who were above fifteen years of age, and who had previously received some education. The greater part of the thirty were public-school teachers, and some of them were nearly forty years of age. With the teachers came some of their former pupils, and when they were examined it was amusing to note that

[160]

in several cases the pupil entered a higher class than did his former teacher. It was also interesting to note how many big books some of them had studied, and how many high-sounding subjects some of them claimed to have mastered. The bigger the book and the longer the name of the subject, the prouder they felt of their accomplishment. Some had studied Latin, and one or two Greek. This they thought entitled them to special distinction.

In fact, one of the saddest things I saw during the month of travel which I have described was a young man, who had attended some high school, sitting down in a one-room cabin, with grease on his clothing, filth all around him, and weeds in the yard and garden, engaged in studying a French grammar.

The students who came first seemed to be fond of memorizing long and complicated "rules" in grammar and mathematics, but had little thought or knowledge of applying these rules to their everyday affairs of their life. One subject which they liked to talk about, and tell me that they had mastered, in arithmetic, was "banking and discount," but I soon found out that neither they nor almost any one in the neighbourhood in which they had lived had ever had a bank account. In registering the names of the students, I found that almost every one of them had one or more middle initials. When I asked what the "J" stood for, in the name of John J. Jones, it was explained to me that this was a part of his "entitles." Most of the students wanted to get an education because they thought it would enable them to earn more money as school-teachers.

Notwithstanding what I have said about them in these respects, I have never seen a more earnest and willing company of young men and women than these students were. They were all willing to learn the right thing as soon as it was shown them what was right. I was determined to start them off on a solid and thorough foundation, so far as their books were concerned. I soon learned that most of them had the merest smattering of the high-sounding things that they had studied. While they could locate the Desert of Sahara or the capital of China on an artificial globe, I found out that the girls could not locate the proper places for the knives and forks on an actual dinner-table, or the places on which the bread and meat should be set.

I had to summon a good deal of courage to take a student who had been studying cube root and "banking and discount," and explain to him that the wisest thing for him to do first was thoroughly master the multiplication table.

The number of pupils increased each week, until by the end of the first month there were nearly fifty. Many of them, however, said that, as they could remain only for two or three months, they wanted to enter a high class and get a diploma the first year if possible.

[161]

At the end of the first six weeks a new and rare face entered the school as a co-teacher. This was Miss Olivia A. Davidson, who later became my wife. Miss Davidson was born in Ohio, and received her preparatory education in the public schools of that state. When little more than a girl, she heard of the need of teachers in the South. She went to the state of Mississippi and began teaching there. Later she taught in the city of Memphis. While teaching in Mississippi, one of her pupils became ill with smallpox. Every one in the community was so frightened that no one would nurse the boy. Miss Davidson closed her school and remained by the bedside of the boy night and day until he recovered. While she was at her Ohio home on her vacation, the worst epidemic of yellow fever broke out in Memphis, Tenn., that perhaps has ever occurred in the South. When she heard of this, she at once telegraphed the Mayor of Memphis, offering her services as a yellow-fever nurse, although she had never had the disease.

Miss Davidon's experience in the South showed her that the people needed something more than mere book-learning. She heard of the Hampton system of education, and decided that this was what she wanted in order to prepare herself for better work in the South. The attention of Mrs. Mary Hemenway, of Boston, was attracted to her rare ability. Through Mrs. Hemenway's kindness and generosity, Miss Davidson, after graduating at Hampton, received an opportunity to complete a two years' course of training at the Massachusetts State Normal School at Framingham.

Before she went to Framingham, some one suggested to Miss Davidson that, since she was so very light in colour, she might find it more comfortable not to be known as a coloured women in this school in Massachusetts. She at once replied that under no circumstances and for no considerations would she consent to deceive any one in regard to her racial identity.

Soon after her graduation from the Framingham institution, Miss Davidson came to Tuskegee, bringing into the school many valuable and fresh ideas as to the best methods of teaching, as well as a rare moral character and a life of unselfishness that I think has seldom been equalled. No single individual did more toward laying the foundations of the Tuskegee Institute so as to insure the successful work that has been done there than Olivia A. Davidson.

Miss Davidson and I began consulting as to the future of the school from the first. The students were making progress in learning books and in development their minds; but it became apparent at once that, if we were to make any permanent impression upon those who had come to us for training we must do something besides teach them mere books. The students had come from

[162]

homes where they had had no opportunities for lessons which would teach them how to care for their bodies. With few exceptions, the homes in Tuskegee in which the students boarded were but little improvement upon those from which they had come. We wanted to teach the students how to bathe; how to care for their teeth and clothing. We wanted to teach them what to eat, and how to eat it properly, and how to care for their rooms. Aside from this, we wanted to give them such a practical knowledge of some one industry, together with the spirit of industry, thrift, and economy, that they would be sure of knowing how to make a living after they had left us. We wanted to teach them to study actual things instead of mere books alone.

We found that the most of our students came from the country districts, where agriculture in some form or other was the main dependence of the people. We learned that about eighty-five per cent of the coloured people in the Gulf states depended upon agriculture for their living. Since this was true, we wanted to be careful not to education our students out of sympathy with agricultural life, so that they would be attracted from the country to the cities, and yield to the temptation of trying to live by their wits. We wanted to give them such an education as would fit a large proportion of them to be teachers, and at the same time cause them to return to the plantation districts and show the people there how to put new energy and new ideas into farming, as well as into the intellectual and moral and religious life of the people.

All these ideas and needs crowded themselves upon us with a seriousness that seemed well-night overwhelming. What were we to do? We had only the little old shanty and the abandoned church which the good coloured people of the town of Tuskegee had kindly loaned us for the accommodation of the classes. The number of students was increasing daily. The more we saw of them, and the more we travelled through the country districts, the more we saw that our efforts were reaching, to only a partial degree, the actual needs of the people whom we wanted to lift up through the medium of the students whom we should education and send out as leaders.

The more we talked with the students, who were then coming to us from several parts of the state, the more we found that the chief ambition among a large proportion of them was to get an education so that they would not have to work any longer with their hands.

This is illustrated by a story told of a coloured man in Alabama, who, one hot day in July, while he was at work in a cotton-field, suddenly stopped, and, looking toward the skies, said: "O Lawd, de cottom am so grassy, de work am so hard, and the sun am so hot dat I b'lieve dis darky am called to preach!"

About three months after the opening of the school, and at the time when we were in the greatest anxiety about our work, there came into market for sale an old and abandoned plantation which was situated about a mile from the town of Tuskegee. The mansion house--or "big house," as it would have been called--which had been occupied by the owners during slavery, had been burned. After making a careful examination of the place, it seemed to be just the location that we wanted in order to make our work effective and permanent.

But how were we to get it? The price asked for it was very little --only five hundred dollars--but we had no money, and we were strangers in the town and had no credit. The owner of the land agreed to let us occupy the place if we could make a payment of two hundred and fifty dollars down, with the understanding that the remaining two hundred and fifty dollars must be paid within a year. Although five hundred dollars was cheap for the land, it was a large sum when one did not have any part of it.

In the midst of the difficulty I summoned a great deal of courage and wrote to my friend General J.F.B. Marshall, the Treasurer of the Hampton Institute, putting the situation before him and beseeching him to lend me the two hundred and fifty dollars on my own personal responsibility. Within a few days a reply came to the effect that he had no authority to lend me the money belonging to the Hampton Institute, but that he would gladly lend me the amount needed from his own personal funds.

I confess that the securing of this money in this way was a great surprise to me, as well as a source of gratification. Up to that time I never had had in my possession so much money as one hundred dollars at a time, and the loan which I had asked General Marshall for seemed a tremendously large sum to me. The fact of my being responsible for the repaying of such a large amount of money weighed very heavily upon me.

I lost no time in getting ready to move the school on to the new farm. At the time we occupied the place there were standing upon it a cabin, formerly used as a dining room, an old kitchen, a stable, and an old hen-house. Within a few weeks we had all of these structures in use. The stable was repaired and used as a recitation-room, and very presently the hen-house was utilized for the same purpose.

I recall that one morning, when I told an old coloured man who lived near, and who sometimes helped me, that our school had grown so large that it would be necessary for us to use the hen-house for school purposes, and that I wanted him to help me give it a thorough cleaning out the next day, he replied, in the most earnest manner: "What you mean, boss? You sholy ain't gwine clean out de hen-house in de day-time?"

Nearly all the work of getting the new location ready for school purposes was done by the students after school was over in the afternoon. As soon as we got the cabins in condition to be used, I determined to clear up some land so that we could plant a crop. When I explained my plan to the young men, I noticed that they did not seem to take to it very kindly. It was hard for them to see the connection between clearing land and an education. Besides, many of them had been school-teachers, and they questioned whether or not clearing land would be in keeping with their dignity. In order to relieve them from any embarrassment, each afternoon after school I took my axe and led the way to the woods. When they saw that I was not afraid or ashamed to work, they began to assist with more enthusiasm. We kept at the work each afternoon, until we had cleared about twenty acres and had planted a crop.

In the meantime Miss Davidson was devising plans to repay the loan. Her first effort was made by holding festivals, or "suppers." She made a personal canvass among the white and coloured families in the town of Tuskegee, and got them to agree to give something, like a cake, a chicken, bread, or pies, that could be sold at the festival. Of course the coloured people were glad to give anything that they could spare, but I want to add that Miss Davidson did not apply to a single white family, so far as I now remember, that failed to donate something; and in many ways the white families showed their interested in the school.

Several of these festivals were held, and quite a little sum of money was raised. A canvass was also made among the people of both races for direct gifts of money, and most of those applied to gave small sums. It was often pathetic to note the gifts of the older coloured people, most of whom had spent their best days in slavery. Sometimes they would give five cents, sometimes twenty-five cents. Sometimes the contribution was a quilt, or a quantity of sugarcane. I recall one old coloured women who was about seventy years of age, who came to see me when we were raising money to pay for the farm. She hobbled into the room where I was, leaning on a cane. She was clad in rags; but they were clean. She said: "Mr. Washin'ton, God knows I spent de bes' days of my life in slavery. God knows I's ignorant an' poor; but," she added, "I knows what you an' Miss Davidson is tryin' to do. I knows you is tryin' to make better men an' better women for de coloured race. I ain't got no money, but I wants you to take dese six eggs, what I's been savin' up, an' I wants you to put dese six eggs into the eddication of dese boys an' gals."

Since the work at Tuskegee started, it has been my privilege to receive many

[165]

gifts for the benefit of the institution, but never any, I think, that touched me so deeply as this one.

CHAPTER 9
ANXIOUS DAYS AND SLEEPLESS NIGHTS

The coming of Christmas, that first year of our residence in Alabama, gave us an opportunity to get a farther insight into the real life of the people. The first thing that reminded us that Christmas had arrived was the "foreday" visits of scores of children rapping at our doors, asking for "Chris'mus gifts! Chris'mus gifts!" Between the hours of two o'clock and five o'clock in the morning I presume that we must have had a half-hundred such calls. This custom prevails throughout this portion of the South to-day.

During the days of slavery it was a custom quite generally observed throughout all the Southern states to give the coloured people a week of holiday at Christmas, or to allow the holiday to continue as long as the "yule log" lasted. The male members of the race, and often the female members, were expected to get drunk. We found that for a whole week the coloured people in and around Tuskegee dropped work the day before Christmas, and that it was difficult for any one to perform any service from the time they stopped work until after the New Year. Persons who at other times did not use strong drink thought it quite the proper thing to indulge in it rather freely during the Christmas week. There was a widespread hilarity, and a free use of guns, pistols, and gunpowder generally. The sacredness of the season seemed to have been almost wholly lost sight of.

During this first Christmas vacation I went some distance from the town to visit the people on one of the large plantations. In their poverty and ignorance it was pathetic to see their attempts to get joy out of the season that in most parts of the country is so sacred and so dear to the heart. In one cabin I notice that all that the five children had to remind them of the coming of Christ was a single bunch of firecrackers, which they had divided among them. In another cabin, where there were at least a half-dozen persons, they had only ten cents' worth of ginger-cakes, which had been bought in the store the day before. In another family they had only a few pieces of sugarcane. In still another cabin I found nothing but a new jug of cheap, mean whiskey, which the husband and wife were making free use of, notwithstanding the fact that the husband was one of the local ministers. In a few instances I found that the people had gotten hold of

[167]

some bright-coloured cards that had been designed for advertising purposes, and were making the most of these. In other homes some member of the family had bought a new pistol. In the majority of cases there was nothing to be seen in the cabin to remind one of the coming of the Saviour, except that the people had ceased work in the fields and were lounging about their homes. At night, during Christmas week, they usually had what they called a "frolic," in some cabin on the plantation. That meant a kind of rough dance, where there was likely to be a good deal of whiskey used, and where there might be some shooting or cutting with razors.

While I was making this Christmas visit I met an old coloured man who was one of the numerous local preachers, who tried to convince me, from the experience Adam had in the Garden of Eden, that God had cursed all labour, and that, therefore, it was a sin for any man to work. For that reason this man sought to do as little work as possible. He seemed at that time to be supremely happy, because he was living, as he expressed it, through one week that was free from sin.

In the school we made a special effort to teach our students the meaning of Christmas, and to give them lessons in its proper observance. In this we have been successful to a degree that makes me feel safe in saying that the season now has a new meaning, not only through all that immediate region, but, in a measure, wherever our graduates have gone.

At the present time one of the most satisfactory features of the Christmas and Thanksgiving season at Tuskegee is the unselfish and beautiful way in which our graduates and students spend their time in administering to the comfort and happiness of others, especially the unfortunate. Not long ago some of our young men spent a holiday in rebuilding a cabin for a helpless coloured women who was about seventy-five years old. At another time I remember that I made it known in chapel, one night, that a very poor student was suffering from cold, because he needed a coat. The next morning two coats were sent to my office for him.

I have referred to the disposition on the part of the white people in the town of Tuskegee and vicinity to help the school. From the first, I resolved to make the school a real part of the community in which it was located. I was determined that no one should have the feeling that it was a foreign institution, dropped down in the midst of the people, for which they had no responsibility and in which they had no interest. I noticed that the very fact that they had been asking to contribute toward the purchase of the land made them begin to feel as if it was going to be their school, to a large degree. I noted that just in proportion

[168]

as we made the white people feel that the institution was a part of the life of the community, and that, while we wanted to make friends in Boston, for example, we also wanted to make white friends in Tuskegee, and that we wanted to make the school of real service to all the people, their attitude toward the school became favourable.

Perhaps I might add right here, what I hope to demonstrate later, that, so far as I know, the Tuskegee school at the present time has no warmer and more enthusiastic friends anywhere than it has among the white citizens of Tuskegee and throughout the state of Alabama and the entire South. From the first, I have advised our people in the South to make friends in every straightforward, manly way with their next-door neighbour, whether he be a black man or a white man. I have also advised them, where no principle is at stake, to consult the interests of their local communities, and to advise with their friends in regard to their voting.

For several months the work of securing the money with which to pay for the farm went on without ceasing. At the end of three months enough was secured to repay the loan of two hundred and fifty dollars to General Marshall, and within two months more we had secured the entire five hundred dollars and had received a deed of the one hundred acres of land. This gave us a great deal of satisfaction. It was not only a source of satisfaction to secure a permanent location for the school, but it was equally satisfactory to know that the greater part of the money with which it was paid for had been gotten from the white and coloured people in the town of Tuskegee. The most of this money was obtained by holding festivals and concerts, and from small individual donations.

Our next effort was in the direction of increasing the cultivation of the land, so as to secure some return from it, and at the same time give the students training in agriculture. All the industries at Tuskegee have been started in natural and logical order, growing out of the needs of a community settlement. We began with farming, because we wanted something to eat.

Many of the students, also, were able to remain in school but a few weeks at a time, because they had so little money with which to pay their board. Thus another object which made it desirable to get an industrial system started was in order to make in available as a means of helping the students to earn money enough so that they might be able to remain in school during the nine months' session of the school year.

The first animal that the school came into possession of was an old blind horse given us by one of the white citizens of Tuskegee. Perhaps I may add here that at the present time the school owns over two hundred horses, colts,

[169]

mules, cows, calves, and oxen, and about seven hundred hogs and pigs, as well as a large number of sheep and goats.

The school was constantly growing in numbers, so much so that, after we had got the farm paid for, the cultivation of the land begun, and the old cabins which we had found on the place somewhat repaired, we turned our attention toward providing a large, substantial building. After having given a good deal of thought to the subject, we finally had the plans drawn for a building that was estimated to cost about six thousand dollars. This seemed to us a tremendous sum, but we knew that the school must go backward or forward, and that our work would mean little unless we could get hold of the students in their home life.

One incident which occurred about this time gave me a great deal of satisfaction as well as surprise. When it became known in the town that we were discussing the plans for a new, large building, a Southern white man who was operating a sawmill not far from Tuskegee came to me and said that he would gladly put all the lumber necessary to erect the building on the grounds, with no other guarantee for payment than my word that it would be paid for when we secured some money. I told the man frankly that at the time we did not have in our hands one dollar of the money needed. Notwithstanding this, he insisted on being allowed to put the lumber on the grounds. After we had secured some portion of the money we permitted him to do this.

Miss Davidson again began the work of securing in various ways small contributions for the new building from the white and coloured people in and near Tuskegee. I think I never saw a community of people so happy over anything as were the coloured people over the prospect of this new building. One day, when we were holding a meeting to secure funds for its erection, an old, ante-bellum coloured man came a distance of twelve miles and brought in his ox-cart a large hog. When the meeting was in progress, he rose in the midst of the company and said that he had no money which he could give, but he had raised two fine hogs, and that he had brought one of them as a contribution toward the expenses of the building. He closed his announcement by saying: "Any nigger that's got any love for his race, or any respect for himself, will bring a hog to the next meeting." Quite a number of men in the community also volunteered to give several days' work, each, toward the erection of the building.

After we had secured all the help that we could in Tuskegee, Miss Davidson decided to go North for the purpose of securing additional funds. For weeks she visited individuals and spoke in churches and before Sunday schools and other

[170]

organizations. She found this work quite trying, and often embarrassing. The school was not known, but she was not long in winning her way into the confidence of the best people in the North.

The first gift from any Northern person was received from a New York lady whom Miss Davidson met on the boat that was bringing her North. They fell into a conversation, and the Northern lady became so much interested in the effort being made at Tuskegee that before they parted Miss Davidson was handed a check for fifty dollars. For some time before our marriage, and also after it, Miss Davidson kept up the work of securing money in the North and in the South by interesting people by personal visits and through correspondence. At the same time she kept in close touch with the work at Tuskegee, as lady principal and classroom teacher. In addition to this, she worked among the older people in and near Tuskegee, and taught a Sunday school class in the town. She was never very strong, but never seemed happy unless she was giving all of her strength to the cause which she loved. Often, at night, after spending the day in going from door to door trying to interest persons in the work at Tuskegee, she would be so exhausted that she could not undress herself. A lady upon whom she called, in Boston, afterward told me that at one time when Miss Davidson called her to see and send up her card the lady was detained a little before she could see Miss Davidson, and when she entered the parlour she found Miss Davidson so exhausted that she had fallen asleep.

While putting up our first building, which was named Porter Hall, after Mr. A.H. Porter, of Brooklyn, N.Y., who gave a generous sum toward its erection, the need for money became acute. I had given one of our creditors a promise that upon a certain day he should be paid four hundred dollars. On the morning of that day we did not have a dollar. The mail arrived at the school at ten o'clock, and in this mail there was a check sent by Miss Davidson for exactly four hundred dollars. I could relate many instances of almost the same character. This four hundred dollars was given by two ladies in Boston. Two years later, when the work at Tuskegee had grown considerably, and when we were in the midst of a season when we were so much in need of money that the future looked doubtful and gloomy, the same two Boston ladies sent us six thousand dollars. Words cannot describe our surprise, or the encouragement that the gift brought to us. Perhaps I might add here that for fourteen years these same friends have sent us six thousand dollars a year.

As soon as the plans were drawn for the new building, the students began digging out the earth where the foundations were to be laid, working after the regular classes were over. They had not fully outgrown the idea that it was hardly the proper thing for them to use their hands, since they had come there, as one of them expressed it, "to be educated, and not to work." Gradually, though, I noted with satisfaction that a sentiment in favour of work was gaining ground. After a few weeks of hard work the foundations were ready, and a day was appointed for the laying of the corner-stone.

When it is considered that the laying of this corner-stone took place in the heart of the South, in the "Black Belt," in the centre of that part of our country that was most devoted to slavery; that at that time slavery had been abolished only about sixteen years; that only sixteen years before no Negro could be taught from books without the teacher receiving the condemnation of the law or of public sentiment--when all this is considered, the scene that was witnessed on that spring day at Tuskegee was a remarkable one. I believe there are few places in the world where it could have taken place.

The principal address was delivered by the Hon. Waddy Thompson, the Superintendent of Education for the county. About the corner-stone were gathered the teachers, the students, their parents and friends, the county officials--who were white--and all the leading white men in that vicinity, together with many of the black men and women whom the same white people but a few years before had held a title to as property. The members of both races were anxious to exercise the privilege of placing under the corner-stone some momento.

Before the building was completed we passed through some very trying seasons. More than once our hearts were made to bleed, as it were, because bills were falling due that we did not have the money to meet. Perhaps no one who has not gone through the experience, month after month, of trying to erect buildings and provide equipment for a school when no one knew where the money was to come from, can properly appreciate the difficulties under which we laboured. During the first years at Tuskegee I recall that night after night I would roll and toss on my bed, without sleep, because of the anxiety and uncertainty which we were in regarding money. I knew that, in a large degree, we were trying an experiment--that of testing whether or not it was possible for Negroes to build up and control the affairs of a large education institution. I knew that if we failed it would injure the whole race. I knew that the presumption was against us. I knew that in the case of white people beginning such an enterprise it would be taken for granted that they were going to succeed, but in our case I felt that people would be surprised if we succeeded. All this made a burden which pressed down on us, sometimes, it seemed, at the rate of a thousand pounds to the square inch.

In all our difficulties and anxieties, however, I never went to a white or a black

[172]

person in the town of Tuskegee for any assistance that was in their power to render, without being helped according to their means. More than a dozen times, when bills figuring up into the hundreds of dollars were falling due, I applied to the white men of Tuskegee for small loans, often borrowing small amounts from as many as a half-dozen persons, to meet our obligations. One thing I was determined to do from the first, and that was to keep the credit of the school high; and this, I think I can say without boasting, we have done all through these years.

I shall always remember a bit of advice given me by Mr. George W. Campbell, the white man to whom I have referred to as the one who induced General Armstrong to send me to Tuskegee. Soon after I entered upon the work Mr. Campbell said to me, in his fatherly way: "Washington, always remember that credit is capital."

At one time when we were in the greatest distress for money that we ever experienced, I placed the situation frankly before General Armstrong. Without hesitation he gave me his personal check for all the money which he had saved for his own use. This was not the only time that General Armstrong helped Tuskegee in this way. I do not think I have ever made this fact public before.

During the summer of 1882, at the end of the first year's work of the school, I was married to Miss Fannie N. Smith, of Malden, W. Va. We began keeping house in Tuskegee early in the fall. This made a home for our teachers, who now had been increase to four in number. My wife was also a graduate of the Hampton Institute. After earnest and constant work in the interests of the school, together with her housekeeping duties, my wife passed away in May, 1884. One child, Portia M. Washington, was born during our marriage.

From the first, my wife most earnestly devoted her thoughts and time to the work of the school, and was completely one with me in every interest and ambition. She passed away, however, before she had an opportunity of seeing what the school was designed to be.

CHAPTER 10

A HARDER TASK THAN MAKING BRICKS WITHOUT STRAW

From the very beginning, at Tuskegee, I was determined to have the students do not only the agricultural and domestic work, but to have them erect their own buildings. My plan was to have them, while performing this service, taught the latest and best methods of labour, so that the school would not only get the benefit of their efforts, but the students themselves would be taught to see not only utility in labour, but beauty and dignity; would be taught, in fact, how to lift labour up from mere drudgery and toil, and would learn to love work for its own sake. My plan was not to teach them to work in the old way, but to show them how to make the forces of nature--air, water, steam, electricity, horse-power--assist them in their labour.

At first many advised against the experiment of having the buildings erected by the labour of the students, but I was determined to stick to it. I told those who doubted the wisdom of the plan that I knew that our first buildings would not be so comfortable or so complete in their finish as buildings erected by the experienced hands of outside workmen, but that in the teaching of civilization, self-help, and self-reliance, the erection of buildings by the students themselves would more than compensate for any lack of comfort or fine finish.

I further told those who doubted the wisdom of this plan, that the majority of our students came to us in poverty, from the cabins of the cotton, sugar, and rice plantations of the South, and that while I knew it would please the students very much to place them at once in finely constructed buildings, I felt that it would be following out a more natural process of development to teach them how to construct their own buildings. Mistakes I knew would be made, but these mistakes would teach us valuable lessons for the future.

During the now nineteen years' existence of the Tuskegee school, the plan of having the buildings erected by student labour has been adhered to. In this time forty buildings, counting small and large, have been built, and all except four are almost wholly the product of student labour. As an additional result, hundreds of men are now scattered throughout the South who received their knowledge of mechanics while being taught how to erect these buildings. Skill and knowledge are now handed down from one set of students to another in this way, until at the present time a building of any description or size can be constructed wholly by our instructors and students, from the drawing of the plans to the putting in of the electric fixtures, without going off the grounds for a single workman.

Not a few times, when a new student has been led into the temptation of marring the looks of some building by leadpencil marks or by the cuts of a jack-knife, I have heard an old student remind him: "Don't do that. That is our building. I helped put it up."

In the early days of the school I think my most trying experience was in the matter of brickmaking. As soon as we got the farm work reasonably well started, we directed our next efforts toward the industry of making bricks. We needed these for use in connection with the erection of our own buildings; but there was also another reason for establishing this industry. There was no brickyard in the town, and in addition to our own needs there was a demand for bricks in the general market.

I had always sympathized with the "Children of Israel," in their task of "making bricks without straw," but ours was the task of making bricks with no money and no experience.

In the first place, the work was hard and dirty, and it was difficult to get the students to help. When it came to brickmaking, their distaste for manual labour in connection with book education became especially manifest. It was not a pleasant task for one to stand in the mud-pit for hours, with the mud up to his knees. More than one man became disgusted and left the school.

We tried several locations before we opened up a pit that furnished brick clay. I had always supposed that brickmaking was very simple, but I soon found out by bitter experience that it required special skill and knowledge, particularly in the burning of the bricks. After a good deal of effort we moulded about twenty-five thousand bricks, and put them into a kiln to be burned. This kiln turned out to be a failure, because it was not properly constructed or properly burned. We began at once, however, on a second kiln. This, for some reason, also proved a failure. The failure of this kiln made it still more difficult to get the students to take part in the work. Several of the teachers, however, who had been trained in the industries at Hampton, volunteered their services, and in some way we succeeded in getting a third kiln ready for burning. The burning of a kiln required about a week. Toward the latter part of the week, when it seemed as if we were going to have a good many thousand bricks in a few hours, in the middle of the night the kiln fell. For the third time we had failed.

[175]

The failure of this last kiln left me without a single dollar with which to make another experiment. Most of the teachers advised the abandoning of the effort to make bricks. In the midst of my troubles I thought of a watch which had come into my possession years before. I took the watch to the city of Montgomery, which was not far distant, and placed it in a pawn-shop. I secured cash upon it to the amount of fifteen dollars, with which to renew the brickmaking experiment. I returned to Tuskegee, and, with the help of the fifteen dollars, rallied our rather demoralized and discouraged forces and began a fourth attempt to make bricks. This time, I am glad to say, we were successful. Before I got hold of any money, the time-limit on my watch had expired, and I have never seen it since; but I have never regretted the loss of it.

Brickmaking has now become such an important industry at the school that last season our students manufactured twelve hundred thousand of first-class bricks, of a quality stable to be sold in any market. Aside from this, scores of young men have mastered the brickmaking trade--both the making of bricks by hand and by machinery--and are now engaged in this industry in many parts of the South.

The making of these bricks taught me an important lesson in regard to the relations of the two races in the South. Many white people who had had no contact with the school, and perhaps no sympathy with it, came to us to buy bricks because they found out that ours were good bricks. They discovered that we were supplying a real want in the community. The making of these bricks caused many of the white residents of the neighbourhood to begin to feel that the education of the Negro was not making him worthless, but that in educating our students we were adding something to the wealth and comfort of the community. As the people of the neighbourhood came to us to buy bricks, we got acquainted with them; they traded with us and we with them. Our business interests became intermingled. We had something which they wanted; they had something which we wanted. This, in a large measure, helped to lay the foundation for the pleasant relations that have continued to exist between us and the white people in that section, and which now extend throughout the South.

Wherever one of our brickmakers has gone in the South, we find that he has something to contribute to the well-being of the community into which he has gone; something that has made the community feel that, in a degree, it is indebted to him, and perhaps, to a certain extent, dependent upon him. In this way pleasant relations between the races have been simulated.

My experience is that there is something in human nature which always makes an individual recognize and reward merit, no matter under what colour of skin merit is found. I have found, too, that it is the visible, the tangible, that goes a long ways in softening prejudices. The actual sight of a first-class house that a Negro has built is ten times more potent than pages of discussion about a house that he ought to build, or perhaps could build.

The same principle of industrial education has been carried out in the building of our own wagons, carts, and buggies, from the first. We now own and use on our farm and about the school dozens of these vehicles, and every one of them has been built by the hands of the students. Aside from this, we help supply the local market with these vehicles. The supplying of them to the people in the community has had the same effect as the supplying of bricks, and the man who learns at Tuskegee to build and repair wagons and carts is regarded as a benefactor by both races in the community where he goes. The people with whom he lives and works are going to think twice before they part with such a man.

The individual who can do something that the world wants done will, in the end, make his way regardless of race. One man may go into a community prepared to supply the people there with an analysis of Greek sentences. The community may not at the time be prepared for, or feel the need of, Greek analysis, but it may feel its need of bricks and houses and wagons. If the man can supply the need for those, then, it will lead eventually to a demand for the first product, and with the demand will come the ability to appreciate it and to profit by it.

About the time that we succeeded in burning our first kiln of bricks we began facing in an emphasized form the objection of the students to being taught to work. By this time it had gotten to be pretty well advertised throughout the state that every student who came to Tuskegee, no matter what his financial ability might be, must learn some industry. Quite a number of letters came from parents protesting against their children engaging in labour while they were in the school. Other parents came to the school to protest in person. Most of the new students brought a written or a verbal request from their parents to the effect that they wanted their children taught nothing but books. The more books, the larger they were, and the longer the titles printed upon them, the better pleased the students and their parents seemed to be.

I gave little heed to these protests, except that I lost no opportunity to go into as many parts of the state as I could, for the purpose of speaking to the parents, and showing them the value of industrial education. Besides, I talked to the students constantly on the subject. Notwithstanding the unpopularity of industrial work, the school continued to increase in numbers to such an extent that by the middle of the second year there was an attendance of about one hundred and fifty, representing almost all parts of the state of Alabama, and including a few from other states.

In the summer of 1882 Miss Davidson and I both went North and engaged in the work of raising funds for the completion of our new building. On my way North I stopped in New York to try to get a letter of recommendation from an officer of a missionary organization who had become somewhat acquainted with me a few years previous. This man not only refused to give me the letter, but advised me most earnestly to go back home at once, and not make any attempt to get money, for he was quite sure that I would never get more than enough to pay my travelling expenses. I thanked him for his advice, and proceeded on my journey.

The first place I went to in the North, was Northampton, Mass., where I spent nearly a half-day in looking for a coloured family with whom I could board, never dreaming that any hotel would admit me. I was greatly surprised when I found that I would have no trouble in being accommodated at a hotel.

We were successful in getting money enough so that on Thanksgiving Day of that year we held our first service in the chapel of Porter Hall, although the building was not completed.

In looking about for some one to preach the Thanksgiving sermon, I found one of the rarest men that it has ever been my privilege to know. This was the Rev. Robert C. Bedford, a white man from Wisconsin, who was then pastor of a little coloured Congregational church in Montgomery, Ala. Before going to Montgomery to look for some one to preach this sermon I had never heard of Mr. Bedford. He had never heard of me. He gladly consented to come to Tuskegee and hold the Thanksgiving service. It was the first service of the kind that the coloured people there had ever observed, and what a deep interest they manifested in it! The sight of the new building made it a day of Thanksgiving for them never to be forgotten.

Mr. Bedford consented to become one of the trustees of the school, and in that capacity, and as a worker for it, he has been connected with it for eighteen years. During this time he has borne the school upon his heart night and day, and is never so happy as when he is performing some service, no matter how humble, for it. He completely obliterates himself in everything, and looks only for permission to serve where service is most disagreeable, and where others would not be attracted. In all my relations with him he has seemed to me to approach as nearly to the spirit of the Master as almost any man I ever met.

[178]

A little later there came into the service of the school another man, quite young at the time, and fresh from Hampton, without whose service the school never could have become what it is. This was Mr. Warren Logan, who now for seventeen years has been the treasurer of the Institute, and the acting principal during my absence. He has always shown a degree of unselfishness and an amount of business tact, coupled with a clear judgment, that has kept the school in good condition no matter how long I have been absent from it. During all the financial stress through which the school has passed, his patience and faith in our ultimate success have not left him.

As soon as our first building was near enough to completion so that we could occupy a portion of it--which was near the middle of the second year of the school--we opened a boarding department. Students had begun coming from quite a distance, and in such increasing numbers that we felt more and more that we were merely skimming over the surface, in that we were not getting hold of the students in their home life.

We had nothing but the students and their appetites with which to begin a boarding department. No provision had been made in the new building for a kitchen and dining room; but we discovered that by digging out a large amount of earth from under the building we could make a partially lighted basement room that could be used for a kitchen and dining room. Again I called on the students to volunteer for work, this time to assist in digging out the basement. This they did, and in a few weeks we had a place to cook and eat in, although it was very rough and uncomfortable. Any one seeing the place now would never believe that it was once used for a dining room.

The most serious problem, though, was to get the boarding department started off in running order, with nothing to do with in the way of furniture, and with no money with which to buy anything. The merchants in the town would let us have what food we wanted on credit. In fact, in those earlier years I was constantly embarrassed because people seemed to have more faith in me than I had in myself. It was pretty hard to cook, however, with stoves, and awkward to eat without dishes. At first the cooking was done out-of-doors, in the old-fashioned, primitive style, in pots and skillets placed over a fire. Some of the carpenters' benches that had been used in the construction of the building were utilized for tables. As for dishes, there were too few to make it worth while to spend time in describing them.

No one connected with the boarding department seemed to have any idea that meals must be served at certain fixed and regular hours, and this was a source of great worry. Everything was so out of joint and so inconvenient that I feel safe in saying that for the first two weeks something was wrong at every meal. Either the meat was not done or had been burnt, or the salt had been left out of the bread, or the tea had been forgotten.

Early one morning I was standing near the dining-room door listening to the complaints of the students. The complaints that morning were especially emphatic and numerous, because the whole breakfast had been a failure. One of the girls who had failed to get any breakfast came out and went to the well to draw some water to drink and take the place of the breakfast which she had not been able to get. When she reached the well, she found that the rope was broken and that she could get no water. She turned from the well and said, in the most discouraged tone, not knowing that I was where I could hear her, "We can't even get water to drink at this school." I think no one remark ever came so near discouraging me as that one.

At another time, when Mr. Bedford--whom I have already spoken of as one of our trustees, and a devoted friend of the institution--was visiting the school, he was given a bedroom immediately over the dining room. Early in the morning he was awakened by a rather animated discussion between two boys in the dining room below. The discussion was over the question as to whose turn it was to use the coffee-cup that morning. One boy won the case by proving that for three mornings he had not had an opportunity to use the cup at all.

But gradually, with patience and hard work, we brought order out of chaos, just as will be true of any problem if we stick to it with patience and wisdom and earnest effort.

As I look back now over that part of our struggle, I am glad to see that we had it. I am glad that we endured all those discomforts and inconveniences. I am glad that our students had to dig out the place for their kitchen and dining room. I am glad that our first boarding-place was in the dismal, ill-lighted, and damp basement. Had we started in a fine, attractive, convenient room, I fear we would have "lost our heads" and become "stuck up." It means a great deal, I think, to start off on a foundation which one has made for one's self.

When our old students return to Tuskegee now, as they often do, and go into our large, beautiful, well-ventilated, and well-lighted dining room, and see tempting, well-cooked food--largely grown by the students themselves--and see tables, neat tablecloths and napkins, and vases of flowers upon the tables, and hear singing birds, and note that each meal is served exactly upon the minute, with no disorder, and with almost no complaint coming from the hundreds that now fill our dining room, they, too, often say to me that they are glad that we started as we did, and built ourselves up year by year, by a slow and natural process of growth.

CHAPTER 11

MAKING THEIR BEDS BEFORE THEY COULD LIE ON THEM

A little later in the history of the school we had a visit from General J.F.B. Marshall, the Treasurer of the Hampton Institute, who had had faith enough to lend us the first two hundred and fifty dollars with which to make a payment down on the farm. He remained with us a week, and made a careful inspection of everything. He seemed well pleased with our progress, and wrote back interesting and encouraging reports to Hampton. A little later Miss Mary F. Mackie, the teacher who had given me the "sweeping" examination when I entered Hampton, came to see us, and still later General Armstrong himself came.

At the time of the visits of these Hampton friends the number of teachers at Tuskegee had increase considerably, and the most of the new teachers were graduates of the Hampton Institute. We gave our Hampton friends, especially General Armstrong, a cordial welcome. They were all surprised and pleased at the rapid progress that the school had made within so short a time. The coloured people from miles around came to the school to get a look at General Armstrong, about whom they had heard so much. The General was not only welcomed by the members of my own race, but by the Southern white people as well.

This first visit which General Armstrong made to Tuskegee gave me an opportunity to get an insight into his character such as I had not before had. I refer to his interest in the Southern white people. Before this I had had the thought that General Armstrong, having fought the Southern white man, rather cherished a feeling of bitterness toward the white South, and was interested in helping only the coloured man there. But this visit convinced me that I did not know the greatness and the generosity of the man. I soon learned, by his visits to the Southern white people, and from his conversations with them, that he was as anxious about the prosperity and the happiness of the white race as the black. He cherished no bitterness against the South, and was happy when an opportunity offered for manifesting his sympathy. In all my acquaintance with General Armstrong I never heard him speak, in public or in private, a single bitter word against the white man in the South. From his example in this respect

[182]

I learned the lesson that great men cultivate love, and that only little men cherish a spirit of hatred. I learned that assistance given to the weak makes the one who gives it strong; and that oppression of the unfortunate makes one weak.

It is now long ago that I learned this lesson from General Armstrong, and resolved that I would permit no man, no matter what his colour might be, to narrow and degrade my soul by making me hate him. With God's help, I believe that I have completely rid myself of any ill feeling toward the Southern white man for any wrong that he may have inflicted upon my race. I am made to feel just as happy now when I am rendering service to Southern white men as when the service is rendered to a member of my own race. I pity from the bottom of my heart any individual who is so unfortunate as to get into the habit of holding race prejudice.

The more I consider the subject, the more strongly I am convinced that the most harmful effect of the practice to which the people in certain sections of the South have felt themselves compelled to resort, in order to get rid of the force of the Negroes' ballot, is not wholly in the wrong done to the Negro, but in the permanent injury to the morals of the white man. The wrong to the Negro is temporary, but to the morals of the white man the injury is permanent. I have noted time and time again that when an individual perjures himself in order to break the force of the black man's ballot, he soon learns to practise dishonesty in other relations of life, not only where the Negro is concerned, but equally so where a white man is concerned. The white man who begins by cheating a Negro usually ends by cheating a white man. The white man who begins to break the law by lynching a Negro soon yields to the temptation to lynch a white man. All this, it seems to me, makes it important that the whole Nation lend a hand in trying to lift the burden of ignorance from the South.

Another thing that is becoming more apparent each year in the development of education in the South is the influence of General Armstrong's idea of education; and this not upon the blacks alone, but upon the whites also. At the present time there is almost no Southern state that is not putting forth efforts in the direction of securing industrial education for its white boys and girls, and in most cases it is easy to trace the history of these efforts back to General Armstrong.

Soon after the opening of our humble boarding department students began coming to us in still larger numbers. For weeks we not only had to contend with the difficulty of providing board, with no money, but also with that of providing sleeping accommodations. For this purpose we rented a number of cabins near

[183]

the school. These cabins were in a dilapidated condition, and during the winter months the students who occupied them necessarily suffered from the cold. We charge the students eight dollars a month--all they were able to pay--for their board. This included, besides board, room, fuel, and washing. We also gave the students credit on their board bills for all the work which they did for the school which was of any value to the institution. The cost of tuition, which was fifty dollars a year for each student, we had to secure then, as now, wherever we could.

This small charge in cash gave us no capital with which to start a boarding department. The weather during the second winter of our work was very cold. We were not able to provide enough bed-clothes to keep the students warm. In fact, for some time we were not able to provide, except in a few cases, bedsteads and mattresses of any kind. During the coldest nights I was so troubled about the discomfort of the students that I could not sleep myself. I recall that on several occasions I went in the middle of the night to the shanties occupied by the young men, for the purpose of confronting them. Often I found some of them sitting huddled around a fire, with the one blanket which we had been able to provide wrapped around them, trying in this way to keep warm. During the whole night some of them did not attempt to lie down. One morning, when the night previous had been unusually cold, I asked those of the students in the chapel who thought that they had been frostbitten during the night to raise their hands. Three hands went up. Notwithstanding these experiences, there was almost no complaining on the part of the students. They knew that we were doing the best that we could for them. They were happy in the privilege of being permitted to enjoy any kind of opportunity that would enable them to improve their condition. They were constantly asking what they might do to lighten the burdens of the teachers.

I have heard it stated more than once, both in the North and in the South, that coloured people would not obey and respect each other when one member of the race is placed in a position of authority over others. In regard to this general belief and these statements, I can say that during the nineteen years of my experience at Tuskegee I never, either by word or act, have been treated with disrespect by any student or officer connected with the institution. On the other hand, I am constantly embarrassed by the many acts of thoughtful kindness. The students do not seem to want to see me carry a large book or a satchel or any kind of a burden through the grounds. In such cases more than one always offers to relieve me. I almost never go out of my office when the rain is falling that some student does not come to my side with an umbrella and ask to be allowed to hold it over me.

[184]

While writing upon this subject, it is a pleasure for me to add that in all my contact with the white people of the South I have never received a single personal insult. The white people in and near Tuskegee, to an especial degree, seem to count it as a privilege to show me all the respect within their power, and often go out of their way to do this.

Not very long ago I was making a journey between Dallas (Texas) and Houston. In some way it became known in advance that I was on the train. At nearly every station at which the train stopped, numbers of white people, including in most cases of the officials of the town, came aboard and introduced themselves and thanked me heartily for the work that I was trying to do for the South.

On another occasion, when I was making a trip from Augusta, Georgia, to Atlanta, being rather tired from much travel, I road in a Pullman sleeper. When I went into the car, I found there two ladies from Boston whom I knew well. These good ladies were perfectly ignorant, it seems, of the customs of the South, and in the goodness of their hearts insisted that I take a seat with them in their section. After some hesitation I consented. I had been there but a few minutes when one of them, without my knowledge, ordered supper to be served for the three of us. This embarrassed me still further. The car was full of Southern white men, most of whom had their eyes on our party. When I found that supper had been ordered, I tried to contrive some excuse that would permit me to leave the section, but the ladies insisted that I must eat with them. I finally settled back in my seat with a sigh, and said to myself, "I am in for it now, sure."

To add further to the embarrassment of the situation, soon after the supper was placed on the table one of the ladies remembered that she had in her satchel a special kind of tea which she wished served, and as she said she felt quite sure the porter did not know how to brew it properly, she insisted upon getting up and preparing and serving it herself. At last the meal was over; and it seemed the longest one that I had ever eaten. When we were through, I decided to get myself out of the embarrassing situation and go to the smoking-room, where most of the men were by that time, to see how the land lay. In the meantime, however, it had become known in some way throughout the car who I was. When I went into the smoking-room I was never more surprised in my life than when each man, nearly every one of them a citizen of Georgia, came up and introduced himself to me and thanked me earnestly for the work that I was trying to do for the whole South. This was not flattery, because each one of these individuals knew that he had nothing to gain by trying to flatter me.

[185]

From the first I have sought to impress the students with the idea that Tuskegee is not my institution, or that of the officers, but that it is their institution, and that they have as much interest in it as any of the trustees or instructors. I have further sought to have them feel that I am at the institution as their friend and adviser, and not as their overseer. It has been my aim to have them speak with directness and frankness about anything that concerns the life of the school. Two or three times a year I ask the students to write me a letter criticising or making complaints or suggestions about anything connected with the institution. When this is not done, I have them meet me in the chapel for a heart-to-heart talk about the conduct of the school. There are no meetings with our students that I enjoy more than these, and none are more helpful to me in planning for the future. These meetings, it seems to me, enable me to get at the very heart of all that concerns the school. Few things help an individual more than to place responsibility upon him, and to let him know that you trust him. When I have read of labour troubles between employers and employees, I have often thought that many strikes and similar disturbances might be avoided if the employers would cultivate the habit of getting nearer to their employees, of consulting and advising with them, and letting them feel that the interests of the two are the same. Every individual responds to confidence, and this is not more true of any race than of the Negroes. Let them once understand that you are unselfishly interested in them, and you can lead them to any extent.

It was my aim from the first at Tuskegee to not only have the buildings erected by the students themselves, but to have them make their own furniture as far as was possible. I now marvel at the patience of the students while sleeping upon the floor while waiting for some kind of a bedstead to be constructed, or at their sleeping without any kind of a mattress while waiting for something that looked like a mattress to be made.

In the early days we had very few students who had been used to handling carpenters' tools, and the bedsteads made by the students then were very rough and very weak. Not unfrequently when I went into the students' rooms in the morning I would find at least two bedsteads lying about on the floor. The problem of providing mattresses was a difficult one to solve. We finally mastered this, however, by getting some cheap cloth and sewing pieces of this together as to make large bags. These bags we filled with the pine straw--or, as it is sometimes called, pine needles--which we secured from the forests near by. I am glad to say that the industry of mattress-making has grown steadily since then, and has been improved to such an extent that at the present time it is an important branch of the work which is taught systematically to a number of our girls, and that the mattresses that now come out of the mattress-shop at

[186]

Tuskegee are about as good as those bought in the average store. For some time after the opening of the boarding department we had no chairs in the students' bedrooms or in the dining rooms. Instead of chairs we used stools which the students constructed by nailing together three pieces of rough board. As a rule, the furniture in the students' rooms during the early days of the school consisted of a bed, some stools, and sometimes a rough table made by the students. The plan of having the students make the furniture is still followed, but the number of pieces in a room has been increased, and the workmanship has so improved that little fault can be found with the articles now. One thing that I have always insisted upon at Tuskegee is that everywhere there should be absolute cleanliness. Over and over again the students were reminded in those first years--and are reminded now--that people would excuse us for our poverty, for our lack of comforts and conveniences, but that they would not excuse us for dirt.

Another thing that has been insisted upon at the school is the use of the tooth-brush. "The gospel of the tooth-brush," as General Armstrong used to call it, is part of our creed at Tuskegee. No student is permitted to retain who does not keep and use a tooth-brush. Several times, in recent years, students have come to us who brought with them almost no other article except a tooth-brush. They had heard from the lips of other students about our insisting upon the use of this, and so, to make a good impression, they brought at least a tooth-brush with them. I remember that one morning, not long ago, I went with the lady principal on her usual morning tour of inspection of the girls' rooms. We found one room that contained three girls who had recently arrived at the school. When I asked them if they had tooth-brushes, one of the girls replied, pointing to a brush: "Yes, sir. That is our brush. We bought it together, yesterday." It did not take them long to learn a different lesson.

It has been interesting to note the effect that the use of the tooth-brush has had in bringing about a higher degree of civilization among the students. With few exceptions, I have noticed that, if we can get a student to the point where, when the first or second tooth-brush disappears, he of his own motion buys another, I have not been disappointed in the future of that individual. Absolute cleanliness of the body has been insisted upon from the first. The students have been taught to bathe as regularly as to take their meals. This lesson we began teaching before we had anything in the shape of a bath-house. Most of the students came from plantation districts, and often we had to teach them how to sleep at night; that is, whether between the two sheets--after we got to the point where we could provide them two sheets--or under both of them. Naturally I found it difficult to teach them to sleep between two sheets when we were able to supply but one. The importance of the use of the night-gown received the same attention.

For a long time one of the most difficult tasks was to teach the students that all the buttons were to be kept on their clothes, and that there must be no torn places or grease-spots. This lesson, I am pleased to be able to say, has been so thoroughly learned and so faithfully handed down from year to year by one set of students to another that often at the present time, when the students march out of the chapel in the evening and their dress is inspected, as it is every night, not one button is found to be missing.

CHAPTER 12
RAISING MONEY

When we opened our boarding department, we provided rooms in the attic of Porter Hall, our first building, for a number of girls. But the number of students, of both sexes, continued to increase. We could find rooms outside the school grounds for many of the young men, but the girls we did not care to expose in this way. Very soon the problem of providing more rooms for the girls, as well as a larger boarding department for all the students, grew serious. As a result, we finally decided to undertake the construction of a still larger building--a building that would contain rooms for the girls and boarding accommodations for all.

After having had a preliminary sketch of the needed building made, we found that it would cost about ten thousand dollars. We had no money whatever with which to begin; still we decided to give the needed building a name. We knew we could name it, even though we were in doubt about our ability to secure the means for its construction. We decided to call the proposed building Alabama Hall, in honour of the state in which we were labouring. Again Miss Davidson began making efforts to enlist the interest and help of the coloured and white people in and near Tuskegee. They responded willingly, in proportion to their means. The students, as in the case of our first building, Porter Hall, began digging out the dirt in order to allow the laying of the foundations.

When we seemed at the end of our resources, so far as securing money was concerned, something occurred which showed the greatness of General Armstrong--something which proved how far he was above the ordinary individual. When we were in the midst of great anxiety as to where and how we were to get funds for the new building, I received a telegram from General Armstrong asking me if I could spend a month travelling with him through the North, and asking me, if I could do so, to come to Hampton at once. Of course I accepted General Armstrong's invitation, and went to Hampton immediately. On arriving there I found that the General had decided to take a quartette of singers through the North, and hold meetings for a month in important cities, at which meetings he and I were to speak. Imagine my surprise when the General told me, further, that these meetings were to be held, not in the interests of Hampton, but in the interests of Tuskegee, and that the Hampton Institute was to be responsible for all the expenses.

Although he never told me so in so many words, I found that General Armstrong took this method of introducing me to the people of the North, as well as for the sake of securing some immediate funds to be used in the erection of Alabama Hall. A weak and narrow man would have reasoned that all the money which came to Tuskegee in this way would be just so much taken from the Hampton Institute; but none of these selfish or short-sighted feelings ever entered the breast of General Armstrong. He was too big to be little, too good to be mean. He knew that the people in the North who gave money gave it for the purpose of helping the whole cause of Negro civilization, and not merely for the advancement of any one school. The General knew, too, that the way to strengthen Hampton was to make it a centre of unselfish power in the working out of the whole Southern problem.

In regard to the addresses which I was to make in the North, I recall just one piece of advice which the General gave me. He said: "Give them an idea for every word." I think it would be hard to improve upon this advice; and it might be made to apply to all public speaking. From that time to the present I have always tried to keep his advice in mind.

Meetings were held in New York, Brooklyn, Boston, Philadelphia, and other large cities, and at all of these meetings General Armstrong pleased, together with myself, for help, not for Hampton, but for Tuskegee. At these meetings an especial effort was made to secure help for the building of Alabama Hall, as well as to introduce the school to the attention of the general public. In both these respects the meetings proved successful.

After that kindly introduction I began going North alone to secure funds. During the last fifteen years I have been compelled to spend a large proportion of my time away from the school, in an effort to secure money to provide for the growing needs of the institution. In my efforts to get funds I have had some experiences that may be of interest to my readers. Time and time again I have been asked, by people who are trying to secure money for philanthropic purposes, what rule or rules I followed to secure the interest and help of people who were able to contribute money to worthy objects. As far as the science of what is called begging can be reduced to rules, I would say that I have had but two rules. First, always to do my whole duty regarding making our work known to individuals and organizations; and, second, not to worry about the results. This second rule has been the hardest for me to live up to. When bills are on the eve of falling due, with not a dollar in hand with which to meet them, it is pretty difficult to learn not to worry, although I think I am learning more and more each year that all worry simply consumes, and to no purpose, just so much physical and mental strength that might otherwise be given to effective work. After considerable experience in coming into contact with wealthy and noted men, I have observed that those who have accomplished the greatest results are those who "keep under the body"; are those who never grow excited or lose self-control, but are always calm, self-possessed, patient, and polite. I think that President William McKinley is the best example of a man of this class that I have ever seen.

In order to be successful in any kind of undertaking, I think the main thing is for one to grow to the point where he completely forgets himself; that is, to lose himself in a great cause. In proportion as one loses himself in the way, in the same degree does he get the highest happiness out of his work.

My experience in getting money for Tuskegee has taught me to have no patience with those people who are always condemning the rich because they are rich, and because they do not give more to objects of charity. In the first place, those who are guilty of such sweeping criticisms do not know how many people would be made poor, and how much suffering would result, if wealthy people were to part all at once with any large proportion of their wealth in a way to disorganize and cripple great business enterprises. Then very few persons have any idea of the large number of applications for help that rich people are constantly being flooded with. I know wealthy people who receive as much as twenty calls a day for help. More than once when I have gone into the offices of rich men, I have found half a dozen persons waiting to see them, and all come for the same purpose, that of securing money. And all these calls in person, to say nothing of the applications received through the mails. Very few people have any idea of the amount of money given away by persons who never permit their names to be known. I have often heard persons condemned for not giving away money, who, to my own knowledge, were giving away thousands of dollars every year so quietly that the world knew nothing about it.

As an example of this, there are two ladies in New York, whose names rarely appear in print, but who, in a quiet way, have given us the means with which to erect three large and important buildings during the last eight years. Besides the gift of these buildings, they have made other generous donations to the school. And they not only help Tuskegee, but they are constantly seeking opportunities to help other worthy causes.

Although it has been my privilege to be the medium through which a good many hundred thousand dollars have been received for the work at Tuskegee, I have always avoided what the world calls "begging." I often tell people that I have never "begged" any money, and that I am not a "beggar." My experience and observation have convinced me that persistent asking outright for money from the rich does not, as a rule, secure help. I have usually proceeded on the principle that persons who possess sense enough to earn money have sense enough to know how to give it away, and that the mere making known of the facts regarding Tuskegee, and especially the facts regarding the work of the graduates, has been more effective than outright begging. I think that the presentation of facts, on a high, dignified plane, is all the begging that most rich people care for.

While the work of going from door to door and from office to office is hard, disagreeable, and costly in bodily strength, yet it has some compensations. Such work gives one a rare opportunity to study human nature. It also has its compensations in giving one an opportunity to meet some of the best people in the world--to be more correct, I think I should say the best people in the world. When one takes a broad survey of the country, he will find that the most useful and influential people in it are those who take the deepest interest in institutions that exist for the purpose of making the world better.

At one time, when I was in Boston, I called at the door of a rather wealthy lady, and was admitted to the vestibule and sent up my card. While I was waiting for an answer, her husband came in, and asked me in the most abrupt manner what I wanted. When I tried to explain the object of my call, he became still more ungentlemanly in his words and manner, and finally grew so excited that I left the house without waiting for a reply from the lady. A few blocks from that house I called to see a gentleman who received me in the most cordial manner. He wrote me his check for a generous sum, and then, before I had had an opportunity to thank him, said: "I am so grateful to you, Mr. Washington, for giving me the opportunity to help a good cause. It is a privilege to have a share in it. We in Boston are constantly indebted to you for doing our work." My experience in securing money convinces me that the first type of man is growing more rare all the time, and that the latter type is increasing; that is, that, more and more, rich people are coming to regard men and women who apply to them for help for worthy objects, not as beggars, but as agents for doing their work.

In the city of Boston I have rarely called upon an individual for funds that I have not been thanked for calling, usually before I could get an opportunity to thank the donor for the money. In that city the donors seem to feel, in a large degree, that an honour is being conferred upon them in their being permitted to give. Nowhere else have I met with, in so large a measure, this fine and Christlike spirit as in the city of Boston, although there are many notable instances of it outside that city. I repeat my belief that the world is growing in the direction of giving. I repeat that the main rule by which I have been guided in collecting money is to do my full duty in regard to giving people who have money an opportunity for help.

In the early years of the Tuskegee school I walked the streets or travelled country roads in the North for days and days without receiving a dollar. Often as it happened, when during the week I had been disappointed in not getting a cent from the very individuals from whom I most expected help, and when I was almost broken down and discouraged, that generous help has come from some one who I had had little idea would give at all.

I recall that on one occasion I obtained information that led me to believe that a gentleman who lived about two miles out in the country from Stamford, Conn., might become interest in our efforts at Tuskegee if our conditions and needs were presented to him. On an unusually cold and stormy day I walked the two miles to see him. After some difficulty I succeeded in securing an interview with him. He listened with some degree of interest to what I had to say, but did not give me anything. I could not help having the feeling that, in a measure, the three hours that I had spent in seeing him had been thrown away. Still, I had followed my usual rule of doing my duty. If I had not seen him, I should have felt unhappy over neglect of duty.

Two years after this visit a letter came to Tuskegee from this man, which read like this: "Enclosed I send you a New York draft for ten thousand dollars, to be used in furtherance of your work. I had placed this sum in my will for your school, but deem it wiser to give it to you while I live. I recall with pleasure your visit to me two years ago."

I can hardly imagine any occurrence which could have given me more genuine satisfaction than the receipt of this draft. It was by far the largest single donation which up to that time the school had ever received. It came at a time when an unusually long period had passed since we had received any money. We were in great distress because of lack of funds, and the nervous strain was tremendous. It is difficult for me to think of any situation that is more trying on the nerves than that of conducting a large institution, with heavy obligations to meet, without knowing where the money is to come from to meet these obligations from month to month.

In our case I felt a double responsibility, and this made the anxiety all the more intense. If the institution had been officered by white persons, and had failed, it would have injured the cause of Negro education; but I knew that the failure of our institution, officered by Negroes, would not only mean the loss of a

[193]

school, but would cause people, in a large degree, to lose faith in the ability of the entire race. The receipt of this draft for ten thousand dollars, under all these circumstances, partially lifted a burden that had been pressing down upon me for days.

From the beginning of our work to the present I have always had the feeling, and lose no opportunity to impress our teachers with the same idea, that the school will always be supported in proportion as the inside of the institution is kept clean and pure and wholesome.

The first time I ever saw the late Collis P. Huntington, the great railroad man, he gave me two dollars for our school. The last time I saw him, which was a few months before he died, he gave me fifty thousand dollars toward our endowment fund. Between these two gifts there were others of generous proportions which came every year from both Mr. and Mrs. Huntington.

Some people may say that it was Tuskegee's good luck that brought to us this gift of fifty thousand dollars. No, it was not luck. It was hard work. Nothing ever comes to me, that is worth having, except as the result of hard work. When Mr. Huntington gave me the first two dollars, I did not blame him for not giving me more, but made up my mind that I was going to convince him by tangible results that we were worthy of larger gifts. For a dozen years I made a strong effort to convince Mr. Huntington of the value of our work. I noted that just in proportion as the usefulness of the school grew, his donations increased. Never did I meet an individual who took a more kindly and sympathetic interest in our school than did Mr. Huntington. He not only gave money to us, but took time in which to advise me, as a father would a son, about the general conduct of the school.

More than once I have found myself in some pretty tight places while collecting money in the North. The following incident I have never related but once before, for the reason that I feared that people would not believe it. One morning I found myself in Providence, Rhode Island, without a cent of money with which to buy breakfast. In crossing the street to see a lady from whom I hoped to get some money, I found a bright new twenty-five-cent piece in the middle of the street track. I not only had this twenty-five cents for my breakfast, but within a few minutes I had a donation from the lady on whom I had started to call.

At one of our Commencements I was bold enough to invite the Rev. E. Winchester Donald, D.D., rector of Trinity Church, Boston, to preach the Commencement sermon. As we then had no room large enough to accommodate all who would be present, the place of meeting was under a large improvised arbour, built partly of brush and partly of rough boards. Soon after Dr. Donald had begun speaking, the rain came down in torrents, and he had to stop, while someone held an umbrella over him.

The boldness of what I had done never dawned upon me until I saw the picture made by the rector of Trinity Church standing before that large audience under an old umbrella, waiting for the rain to cease so that he could go on with his address.

It was not very long before the rain ceased and Dr. Donald finished his sermon; and an excellent sermon it was, too, in spite of the weather. After he had gone to his room, and had gotten the wet threads of his clothes dry, Dr. Donald ventured the remark that a large chapel at Tuskegee would not be out of place. The next day a letter came from two ladies who were then travelling in Italy, saying that they had decided to give us the money for such a chapel as we needed.

A short time ago we received twenty thousand dollars from Mr. Andrew Carnegie, to be used for the purpose of erecting a new library building. Our first library and reading-room were in a corner of a shanty, and the whole thing occupied a space about five by twelve feet. It required ten years of work before I was able to secure Mr. Carnegie's interest and help. The first time I saw him, ten years ago, he seemed to take but little interest in our school, but I was determined to show him that we were worthy of his help. After ten years of hard work I wrote him a letter reading as follows:

December 15, 1900.

Mr. Andrew Carnegie, 5 W. Fifty-first St., New York.

Dear Sir: Complying with the request which you made of me when I saw you at your residence a few days ago, I now submit in writing an appeal for a library building for our institution.

We have 1100 students, 86 officers and instructors, together with their families, and about 200 coloured people living near the school, all of whom would make use of the library building.

We have over 12,000 books, periodicals, etc., gifts from our friends, but we have no suitable place for them, and we have no suitable reading-room.

Our graduates go to work in every section of the South, and whatever knowledge might be obtained in the library would serve to assist in the elevation of the whole Negro race.

[195]

Such a building as we need could be erected for about $20,000. All of the work for the building, such as brickmaking, brick-masonry, carpentry, blacksmithing, etc., would be done by the students. The money which you would give would not only supply the building, but the erection of the building would give a large number of students an opportunity to learn the building trades, and the students would use the money paid to them to keep themselves in school. I do not believe that a similar amount of money often could be made go so far in uplifting a whole race.

If you wish further information, I shall be glad to furnish it.

Yours truly,

Booker T. Washington, Principal.

The next mail brought back the following reply: "I will be very glad to pay the bills for the library building as they are incurred, to the extent of twenty thousand dollars, and I am glad of this opportunity to show the interest I have in your noble work."

I have found that strict business methods go a long way in securing the interest of rich people. It has been my constant aim at Tuskegee to carry out, in our financial and other operations, such business methods as would be approved of by any New York banking house.

I have spoken of several large gifts to the school; but by far the greater proportion of the money that has built up the institution has come in the form of small donations from persons of moderate means. It is upon these small gifts, which carry with them the interest of hundreds of donors, that any philanthropic work must depend largely for its support. In my efforts to get money I have often been surprised at the patience and deep interest of the ministers, who are besieged on every hand and at all hours of the day for help. If no other consideration had convinced me of the value of the Christian life, the Christlike work which the Church of all denominations in America has done during the last thirty-five years for the elevation of the black man would have made me a Christian. In a large degree it has been the pennies, the nickels, and the dimes which have come from the Sunday-schools, the Christian Endeavour societies, and the missionary societies, as well as from the church proper, that have helped to elevate the Negro at so rapid a rate.

This speaking of small gifts reminds me to say that very few Tuskegee graduates fail to send us an annual contribution. These contributions range from twenty-five cents up to ten dollars.

Soon after beginning our third year's work we were surprised to receive money from three special sources, and up to the present time we have continued to receive help from them. First, the State Legislature of Alabama increased its annual appropriation from two thousand dollars to three thousand dollars; I might add that still later it increased this sum to four thousand five hundred dollars a year. The effort to secure this increase was led by the Hon. M.F. Foster, the member of the Legislature from Tuskegee. Second, we received one thousand dollars from the John F. Slater Fund. Our work seemed to please the trustees of this fund, as they soon began increasing their annual grant. This has been added to from time to time until at present we receive eleven thousand dollars annually from the Fund. The other help to which I have referred came in the shape of an allowance from the Peabody Fund. This was at first five hundred dollars, but it has since been increased to fifteen hundred dollars.

The effort to secure help from the Slater and Peabody Funds brought me into contact with two rare men--men who have had much to do in shaping the policy for the education of the Negro. I refer to the Hon. J.L.M. Curry, of Washington, who is the general agent for these two funds, and Mr. Morris K. Jessup, of New York. Dr. Curry is a native of the South, an ex-Confederate soldier, yet I do not believe there is any man in the country who is more deeply interest in the highest welfare of the Negro than Dr. Curry, or one who is more free from race prejudice. He enjoys the unique distinction of possessing to an equal degree of confidence of the black man and the Southern white man. I shall never forget the first time I met him. It was in Richmond, Va., where he was then living. I had heard much about him. When I first went into his presence, trembling because of my youth and inexperience, he took me by the hand so cordially, and spoke such encouraging words, and gave me such helpful advice regarding the proper course to pursue, that I came to know him then, as I have known him ever since, as a high example of one who is constantly and unselfishly at work for the betterment of humanity.

Mr. Morris K. Jessup, the treasurer of the Slater Fund, I refer to because I know of no man of wealth and large and complication business responsibilities who gives not only money but his time and thought to the subject of the proper method of elevating the Negro to the extent that is true of Mr. Jessup. It is very largely through this effort and influence that during the last few years the subject of industrial education has assumed the importance that it has, and been placed on its present footing.

CHAPTER 13
TWO THOUSAND MILES FOR A FIVE-MINUTE SPEECH

Soon after the opening of our boarding department, quite a number of students who evidently were worthy, but who were so poor that they did not have any money to pay even the small charges at the school, began applying for admission. This class was composed of both men and women. It was a great trial to refuse admission to these applicants, and in 1884 we established a night-school to accommodate a few of them.

The night-school was organized on a plan similar to the one which I had helped to establish at Hampton. At first it was composed of about a dozen students. They were admitted to the night-school only when they had no money with which to pay any part of their board in the regular day-school. It was further required that they must work for ten hours during the day at some trade or industry, and study academic branches for two hours during the evening. This was the requirement for the first one or two years of their stay. They were to be paid something above the cost of their board, with the understanding that all of their earnings, except a very small part, were to be reserved in the school's treasury, to be used for paying their board in the regular day-school after they had entered that department. The night-school, started in this manner, has grown until there are at present four hundred and fifty-seven students enrolled in it alone.

There could hardly be a more severe test of a student's worth than this branch of the Institute's worth. It is largely because it furnishes such a good opportunity to test the backbone of a student that I place such high value upon our night-school. Any one who is willing to work ten hours a day at the brick-yard, or in the laundry, through one or two years, in order that he or she may have the privilege of studying academic branches for two hours in the evening, has enough bottom to warrant being further educated.

After the student has left the night-school he enters the day-school, where he takes academic branches four days in a week, and works at his trade two days. Besides this he usually works at his trade during the three summer months. As a rule, after a student has succeeded in going through the night-school test, he finds a way to finish the regular course in industrial and academic training. No student, no matter how much money he may be able to command, is permitted to go through school without doing manual labour. In fact, the industrial work is now as popular as the academic branches. Some of the most successful men and women who have graduated from the institution obtained their start in the night-school.

While a great deal of stress is laid upon the industrial side of the work at Tuskegee, we do not neglect or overlook in any degree the religious and spiritual side. The school is strictly undenominational, but it is thoroughly Christian, and the spiritual training or the students is not neglected. Our preaching service, prayer-meetings, Sunday-school, Christian Endeavour Society, Young Men's Christian Association, and various missionary organizations, testify to this.

In 1885, Miss Olivia Davidson, to whom I have already referred as being largely responsible for the success of the school during its early history, and I were married. During our married life she continued to divide her time and strength between our home and the work for the school. She not only continued to work in the school at Tuskegee, but also kept up her habit of going North to secure funds. In 1889 she died, after four years of happy married life and eight years of hard and happy work for the school. She literally wore herself out in her never ceasing efforts in behalf of the work that she so dearly loved. During our married life there were born to us two bright, beautiful boys, Booker Taliaferro and Ernest Davidson. The older of these, Booker, has already mastered the brick-maker's trade at Tuskegee.

I have often been asked how I began the practice of public speaking. In answer I would say that I never planned to give any large part of my life to speaking in public. I have always had more of an ambition to DO things than merely to talk ABOUT doing them. It seems that when I went North with General Armstrong to speak at the series of public meetings to which I have referred, the President of the National Educational Association, the Hon. Thomas W. Bicknell, was present at one of those meetings and heard me speak. A few days afterward he sent me an invitation to deliver an address at the next meeting of the Educational Association. This meeting was to be held in Madison, Wis. I accepted the invitation. This was, in a sense, the beginning of my public-speaking career.

On the evening that I spoke before the Association there must have been not far from four thousand persons present. Without my knowing it, there were a large number of people present from Alabama, and some from the town of Tuskegee. These white people afterward frankly told me that they went to this meeting expecting to hear the South roundly abused, but were pleasantly surprised to find that there was no word of abuse in my address. On the contrary, the South was given credit for all the praiseworthy things that it had done. A white lady who was teacher in a college in Tuskegee wrote back to the local paper that she was gratified, as well as surprised, to note the credit which I gave the white people of Tuskegee for their help in getting the school started. This address at Madison was the first that I had delivered that in any large measure dealt with the general problem of the races. Those who heard it seemed to be pleased with what I said and with the general position that I took.

When I first came to Tuskegee, I determined that I would make it my home, that I would take as much pride in the right actions of the people of the town as any white man could do, and that I would, at the same time, deplore the wrong-doing of the people as much as any white man. I determined never to say anything in a public address in the North that I would not be willing to say in the South. I early learned that it is a hard matter to convert an individual by abusing him, and that this is more often accomplished by giving credit for all the praiseworthy actions performed than by calling attention alone to all the evil done.

While pursuing this policy I have not failed, at the proper time and in the proper manner, to call attention, in no uncertain terms, to the wrongs which any part of the South has been guilty of. I have found that there is a large element in the South that is quick to respond to straightforward, honest criticism of any wrong policy. As a rule, the place to criticise the South, when criticism is necessary, is in the South--not in Boston. A Boston man who came to Alabama to criticise Boston would not effect so much good, I think, as one who had his word of criticism to say in Boston.

In this address at Madison I took the ground that the policy to be pursued with references to the races was, by every honourable means, to bring them together and to encourage the cultivation of friendly relations, instead of doing that which would embitter. I further contended that, in relation to his vote, the Negro should more and more consider the interests of the community in which he lived, rather than seek alone to please some one who lived a thousand miles away from him and from his interests.

In this address I said that the whole future of the Negro rested largely upon the question as to whether or not he should make himself, through his skill, intelligence, and character, of such undeniable value to the community in which

[200]

he lived that the community could not dispense with his presence. I said that any individual who learned to do something better than anybody else--learned to do a common thing in an uncommon manner--had solved his problem, regardless of the colour of his skin, and that in proportion as the Negro learned to produce what other people wanted and must have, in the same proportion would he be respected.

I spoke of an instance where one of our graduates had produced two hundred and sixty-six bushels of sweet potatoes from an acre of ground, in a community where the average production had been only forty-nine bushels to the acre. He had been able to do this by reason of his knowledge of the chemistry of the soil and by his knowledge of improved methods of agriculture. The white farmers in the neighbourhood respected him, and came to him for ideas regarding the raising of sweet potatoes. These white farmers honoured and respected him because he, by his skill and knowledge, had added something to the wealth and the comfort of the community in which he lived. I explained that my theory of education for the Negro would not, for example, confine him for all time to farm life--to the production of the best and the most sweet potatoes--but that, if he succeeded in this line of industry, he could lay the foundations upon which his children and grand-children could grow to higher and more important things in life.

Such, in brief, were some of the views I advocated in this first address dealing with the broad question of the relations of the two races, and since that time I have not found any reason for changing my views on any important point.

In my early life I used to cherish a feeling of ill will toward any one who spoke in bitter terms against the Negro, or who advocated measures that tended to oppress the black man or take from him opportunities for growth in the most complete manner. Now, whenever I hear any one advocating measures that are meant to curtail the development of another, I pity the individual who would do this. I know that the one who makes this mistake does so because of his own lack of opportunity for the highest kind of growth. I pity him because I know that he is trying to stop the progress of the world, and because I know that in time the development and the ceaseless advance of humanity will make him ashamed of his weak and narrow position. One might as well try to stop the progress of a mighty railroad train by throwing his body across the track, as to try to stop the growth of the world in the direction of giving mankind more intelligence, more culture, more skill, more liberty, and in the direction of extending more sympathy and more brotherly kindness.

The address which I delivered at Madison, before the National Educational

Association, gave me a rather wide introduction in the North, and soon after that opportunities began offering themselves for me to address audiences there.

I was anxious, however, that the way might also be opened for me to speak directly to a representative Southern white audience. A partial opportunity of this kind, one that seemed to me might serve as an entering wedge, presented itself in 1893, when the international meeting of Christian Workers was held at Atlanta, Ga. When this invitation came to me, I had engagements in Boston that seemed to make it impossible for me to speak in Atlanta. Still, after looking over my list of dates and places carefully, I found that I could take a train from Boston that would get me into Atlanta about thirty minutes before my address was to be delivered, and that I could remain in that city before taking another train for Boston. My invitation to speak in Atlanta stipulated that I was to confine my address to five minutes. The question, then, was whether or not I could put enough into a five-minute address to make it worth while for me to make such a trip.

I knew that the audience would be largely composed of the most influential class of white men and women, and that it would be a rare opportunity for me to let them know what we were trying to do at Tuskegee, as well as to speak to them about the relations of the races. So I decided to make the trip. I spoke for five minutes to an audience of two thousand people, composed mostly of Southern and Northern whites. What I said seemed to be received with favour and enthusiasm. The Atlanta papers of the next day commented in friendly terms on my address, and a good deal was said about it in different parts of the country. I felt that I had in some degree accomplished my object--that of getting a hearing from the dominant class of the South.

The demands made upon me for public addresses continued to increase, coming in about equal numbers from my own people and from Northern whites. I gave as much time to these addresses as I could spare from the immediate work at Tuskegee. Most of the addresses in the North were made for the direct purpose of getting funds with which to support the school. Those delivered before the coloured people had for their main object the impressing upon them the importance of industrial and technical education in addition to academic and religious training.

I now come to that one of the incidents in my life which seems to have excited the greatest amount of interest, and which perhaps went further than anything else in giving me a reputation that in a sense might be called National. I refer to the address which I delivered at the opening of the Atlanta Cotton states and International Exposition, at Atlanta, Ga., September 18, 1895.

So much has been said and written about this incident, and so many questions have been asked me concerning the address, that perhaps I may be excused for taking up the matter with some detail. The five-minute address in Atlanta, which I came from Boston to deliver, was possibly the prime cause for an opportunity being given me to make the second address there. In the spring of 1895 I received a telegram from prominent citizens in Atlanta asking me to accompany a committee from that city to Washington for the purpose of appearing before a committee of Congress in the interest of securing Government help for the Exposition. The committee was composed of about twenty-five of the most prominent and most influential white men of Georgia. All the members of this committee were white men except Bishop Grant, Bishop Gaines, and myself. The Mayor and several other city and state officials spoke before the committee. They were followed by the two coloured bishops. My name was the last on the list of speakers. I had never before appeared before such a committee, nor had I ever delivered any address in the capital of the Nation. I had many misgivings as to what I ought to say, and as to the impression that my address would make. While I cannot recall in detail what I said, I remember that I tried to impress upon the committee, with all the earnestness and plainness of any language that I could command, that if Congress wanted to do something which would assist in ridding the South of the race question and making friends between the two races, it should, in every proper way, encourage the material and intellectual growth of both races. I said that the Atlanta Exposition would present an opportunity for both races to show what advance they had made since freedom, and would at the same time afford encouragement to them to make still greater progress.

I tried to emphasize the fact that while the Negro should not be deprived by unfair means of the franchise, political agitation alone would not save him, and that back of the ballot he must have property, industry, skill, economy, intelligence, and character, and that no race without these elements could permanently succeed. I said that in granting the appropriation Congress could do something that would prove to be of real and lasting value to both races, and that it was the first great opportunity of the kind that had been presented since the close of the Civil War.

I spoke for fifteen or twenty minutes, and was surprised at the close of my address to receive the hearty congratulations of the Georgia committee and of the members of Congress who were present. The Committee was unanimous in making a favourable report, and in a few days the bill passed Congress. With the passing of this bill the success of the Atlanta Exposition was assured.

Soon after this trip to Washington the directors of the Exposition decided that it would be a fitting recognition of the coloured race to erect a large and attractive building which should be devoted wholly to showing the progress of the Negro since freedom. It was further decided to have the building designed and erected wholly by Negro mechanics. This plan was carried out. In design, beauty, and general finish the Negro Building was equal to the others on the grounds.

After it was decided to have a separate Negro exhibit, the question arose as to who should take care of it. The officials of the Exposition were anxious that I should assume this responsibility, but I declined to do so, on the plea that the work at Tuskegee at that time demanded my time and strength. Largely at my suggestion, Mr. I. Garland Penn, of Lynchburg, Va., was selected to be at the head of the Negro department. I gave him all the aid that I could. The Negro exhibit, as a whole, was large and creditable. The two exhibits in this department which attracted the greatest amount of attention were those from the Hampton Institute and the Tuskegee Institute. The people who seemed to be the most surprised, as well as pleased, at what they saw in the Negro Building were the Southern white people.

As the day for the opening of the Exposition drew near, the Board of Directors began preparing the programme for the opening exercises. In the discussion from day to day of the various features of this programme, the question came up as to the advisability of putting a member of the Negro race on for one of the opening addresses, since the Negroes had been asked to take such a prominent part in the Exposition. It was argued, further, that such recognition would mark the good feeling prevailing between the two races. Of course there were those who were opposed to any such recognition of the rights of the Negro, but the Board of Directors, composed of men who represented the best and most progressive element in the South, had their way, and voted to invite a black man to speak on the opening day. The next thing was to decide upon the person who was thus to represent the Negro race. After the question had been canvassed for several days, the directors voted unanimously to ask me to deliver one of the opening-day addresses, and in a few days after that I received the official invitation.

The receiving of this invitation brought to me a sense of responsibility that it would be hard for any one not placed in my position to appreciate. What were my feelings when this invitation came to me? I remembered that I had been a slave; that my early years had been spent in the lowest depths of poverty and ignorance, and that I had had little opportunity to prepare me for such a responsibility as this. It was only a few years before that time that any white man in the audience might have claimed me as his slave; and it was easily possible that some of my former owners might be present to hear me speak.

I knew, too, that this was the first time in the entire history of the Negro that a member of my race had been asked to speak from the same platform with white Southern men and women on any important National occasion. I was asked now to speak to an audience composed of the wealth and culture of the white South, the representatives of my former masters. I knew, too, that while the greater part of my audience would be composed of Southern people, yet there would be present a large number of Northern whites, as well as a great many men and women of my own race.

I was determined to say nothing that I did not feel from the bottom of my heart to be true and right. When the invitation came to me, there was not one word of intimation as to what I should say or as to what I should omit. In this I felt that the Board of Directors had paid a tribute to me. They knew that by one sentence I could have blasted, in a large degree, the success of the Exposition. I was also painfully conscious of the fact that, while I must be true to my own race in my utterances, I had it in my power to make such an ill-timed address as would result in preventing any similar invitation being extended to a black man again for years to come. I was equally determined to be true to the North, as well as to the best element of the white South, in what I had to say.

The papers, North and South, had taken up the discussion of my coming speech, and as the time for it drew near this discussion became more and more widespread. Not a few of the Southern white papers were unfriendly to the idea of my speaking. From my own race I received many suggestions as to what I ought to say. I prepared myself as best I could for the address, but as the eighteenth of September drew nearer, the heavier my heart became, and the more I feared that my effort would prove a failure and a disappointment.

The invitation had come at a time when I was very busy with my school work, as it was the beginning of our school year. After preparing my address, I went through it, as I usually do with those utterances which I consider particularly important, with Mrs. Washington, and she approved of what I intended to say. On the sixteenth of September, the day before I was to start for Atlanta, so many of the Tuskegee teachers expressed a desire to hear my address that I consented to read it to them in a body. When I had done so, and had heard their criticisms and comments, I felt somewhat relieved, since they seemed to think well of what I had to say.

On the morning of September 17, together with Mrs. Washington and my three children, I started for Atlanta. I felt a good deal as I suppose a man feels when he is on his way to the gallows. In passing through the town of Tuskegee I met a white farmer who lived some distance out in the country. In a jesting manner this man said: "Washington, you have spoken before the Northern white people, the Negroes in the South, and to us country white people in the South; but Atlanta, to-morrow, you will have before you the Northern whites, the Southern whites, and the Negroes all together. I am afraid that you have got yourself in a tight place." This farmer diagnosed the situation correctly, but his frank words did not add anything to my comfort.

In the course of the journey from Tuskegee to Atlanta both coloured and white people came to the train to point me out, and discussed with perfect freedom, in my hearings, what was going to take place the next day. We were met by a committee in Atlanta. Almost the first thing that I heard when I got off the train in that city was an expression something like this, from an old coloured man near by: "Dat's de man of my race what's gwine to make a speech at de Exposition to-morrow. I'se sho' gwine to hear him."

Atlanta was literally packed, at the time, with people from all parts of the country, and with representatives of foreign governments, as well as with military and civic organizations. The afternoon papers had forecasts of the next day's proceedings in flaring headlines. All this tended to add to my burden. I did not sleep much that night. The next morning, before day, I went carefully over what I planned to say. I also kneeled down and asked God's blessing upon my effort. Right here, perhaps, I ought to add that I make it a rule never to go before an audience, on any occasion, without asking the blessing of God upon what I want to say.

I always make it a rule to make especial preparation for each separate address. No two audiences are exactly alike. It is my aim to reach and talk to the heart of each individual audience, taking it into my confidence very much as I would a person. When I am speaking to an audience, I care little for how what I am saying is going to sound in the newspapers, or to another audience, or to an individual. At the time, the audience before me absorbs all my sympathy, thought, and energy.

Early in the morning a committee called to escort me to my place in the procession which was to march to the Exposition grounds. In this procession were prominent coloured citizens in carriages, as well as several Negro military organizations. I noted that the Exposition officials seemed to go out of their way to see that all of the coloured people in the procession were properly placed and properly treated. The procession was about three hours in reaching the Exposition grounds, and during all of this time the sun was shining down upon

[206]

us disagreeably hot. When we reached the grounds, the heat, together with my nervous anxiety, made me feel as if I were about ready to collapse, and to feel that my address was not going to be a success. When I entered the audience-room, I found it packed with humanity from bottom to top, and there were thousands outside who could not get in.

The room was very large, and well suited to public speaking. When I entered the room, there were vigorous cheers from the coloured portion of the audience, and faint cheers from some of the white people. I had been told, while I had been in Atlanta, that while many white people were going to be present to hear me speak, simply out of curiosity, and that others who would be present would be in full sympathy with me, there was a still larger element of the audience which would consist of those who were going to be present for the purpose of hearing me make a fool of myself, or, at least, of hearing me say some foolish thing so that they could say to the officials who had invited me to speak, "I told you so!"

One of the trustees of the Tuskegee Institute, as well as my personal friend, Mr. William H. Baldwin, Jr. was at the time General Manager of the Southern Railroad, and happened to be in Atlanta on that day. He was so nervous about the kind of reception that I would have, and the effect that my speech would produce, that he could not persuade himself to go into the building, but walked back and forth in the grounds outside until the opening exercises were over.

CHAPTER 14
THE ATLANTA EXPOSITION ADDRESS

The Atlanta Exposition, at which I had been asked to make an address as a representative of the Negro race, as stated in the last chapter, was opened with a short address from Governor Bullock. After other interesting exercises, including an invocation from Bishop Nelson, of Georgia, a dedicatory ode by Albert Howell, Jr., and addresses by the President of the Exposition and Mrs. Joseph Thompson, the President of the Woman's Board, Governor Bullock introduce me with the words, "We have with us to-day a representative of Negro enterprise and Negro civilization."

When I arose to speak, there was considerable cheering, especially from the coloured people. As I remember it now, the thing that was uppermost in my mind was the desire to say something that would cement the friendship of the races and bring about hearty cooperation between them. So far as my outward surroundings were concerned, the only thing that I recall distinctly now is that when I got up, I saw thousands of eyes looking intently into my face. The following is the address which I delivered:--

Mr. President and Gentlemen of the Board of Directors and Citizens.

One-third of the population of the South is of the Negro race. No enterprise seeking the material, civil, or moral welfare of this section can disregard this element of our population and reach the highest success. I but convey to you, Mr. President and Directors, the sentiment of the masses of my race when I say that in no way have the value and manhood of the American Negro been more fittingly and generously recognized than by the managers of this magnificent Exposition at every stage of its progress. It is a recognition that will do more to cement the friendship of the two races than any occurrence since the dawn of our freedom.

Not only this, but the opportunity here afforded will awaken among us a new era of industrial progress. Ignorant and inexperienced, it is not strange that in the first years of our new life we began at the top instead of at the bottom; that a seat in Congress or the state legislature was more sought than real estate or industrial skill; that the political convention or stump speaking had more

[208]

attractions than starting a dairy farm or truck garden.

A ship lost at sea for many days suddenly sighted a friendly vessel. From the mast of the unfortunate vessel was seen a signal, "Water, water; we die of thirst!" The answer from the friendly vessel at once came back, "Cast down your bucket where you are." A second time the signal, "Water, water; send us water!" ran up from the distressed vessel, and was answered, "Cast down your bucket where you are." And a third and fourth signal for water was answered, "Cast down your bucket where you are." The captain of the distressed vessel, at last heading the injunction, cast down his bucket, and it came up full of fresh, sparkling water from the mouth of the Amazon River. To those of my race who depend on bettering their condition in a foreign land or who underestimate the importance of cultivating friendly relations with the Southern white man, who is their next-door neighbour, I would say: "Cast down your bucket where you are"--cast it down in making friends in every manly way of the people of all races by whom we are surrounded.

Cast it down in agriculture, mechanics, in commerce, in domestic service, and in the professions. And in this connection it is well to bear in mind that whatever other sins the South may be called to bear, when it comes to business, pure and simple, it is in the South that the Negro is given a man's chance in the commercial world, and in nothing is this Exposition more eloquent than in emphasizing this chance. Our greatest danger is that in the great leap from slavery to freedom we may overlook the fact that the masses of us are to live by the productions of our hands, and fail to keep in mind that we shall prosper in proportion as we learn to dignify and glorify common labour and put brains and skill into the common occupations of life; shall prosper in proportion as we learn to draw the line between the superficial and the substantial, the ornamental gewgaws of life and the useful. No race can prosper till it learns that there is as much dignity in tilling a field as in writing a poem. It is at the bottom of life we must begin, and not at the top. Nor should we permit our grievances to overshadow our opportunities.

To those of the white race who look to the incoming of those of foreign birth and strange tongue and habits of the prosperity of the South, were I permitted I would repeat what I say to my own race: "Cast down your bucket where you are." Cast it down among the eight millions of Negroes whose habits you know, whose fidelity and love you have tested in days when to have proved treacherous meant the ruin of your firesides. Cast down your bucket among these people who have, without strikes and labour wars, tilled your fields, cleared your forests, builded your railroads and cities, and brought forth treasures from the bowels of the earth, and helped make possible this magnificent representation of the progress of the South. Casting down your bucket among my people, helping and encouraging them as you are doing on these grounds, and to education of head, hand, and heart, you will find that they will buy your surplus land, make blossom the waste places in your fields, and run your factories. While doing this, you can be sure in the future, as in the past, that you and your families will be surrounded by the most patient, faithful, law-abiding, and unresentful people that the world has seen. As we have proved our loyalty to you in the past, nursing your children, watching by the sick-bed of your mothers and fathers, and often following them with tear-dimmed eyes to their graves, so in the future, in our humble way, we shall stand by you with a devotion that no foreigner can approach, ready to lay down our lives, if need be, in defence of yours, interlacing our industrial, commercial, civil, and religious life with yours in a way that shall make the interests of both races one. In all things that are purely social we can be as separate as the fingers, yet one as the hand in all things essential to mutual progress.

There is no defence or security for any of us except in the highest intelligence and development of all. If anywhere there are efforts tending to curtail the fullest growth of the Negro, let these efforts be turned into stimulating, encouraging, and making him the most useful and intelligent citizen. Effort or means so invested will pay a thousand per cent interest. These efforts will be twice blessed--"blessing him that gives and him that takes."

There is no escape through law of man or God from the inevitable:--

The laws of changeless justice bind Oppressor with oppressed; And close as sin and suffering joined We march to fate abreast.

Nearly sixteen millions of hands will aid you in pulling the load upward, or they will pull against you the load downward. We shall constitute one-third and more of the ignorance and crime of the South, or one-third its intelligence and progress; we shall contribute one-third to the business and industrial prosperity of the South, or we shall prove a veritable body of death, stagnating, depressing, retarding every effort to advance the body politic.

Gentlemen of the Exposition, as we present to you our humble effort at an exhibition of our progress, you must not expect overmuch. Starting thirty years ago with ownership here and there in a few quilts and pumpkins and chickens (gathered from miscellaneous sources), remember the path that has led from these to the inventions and production of agricultural implements, buggies, steam-engines, newspapers, books, statuary, carving, paintings, the management of drug-stores and banks, has not been trodden without contact with thorns and thistles. While we take pride in what we exhibit as a result of our independent efforts, we do not for a moment forget that our part in this exhibition would fall far short of your expectations but for the constant help that has come to our education life, not only from the Southern states, but especially from Northern philanthropists, who have made their gifts a constant stream of blessing and encouragement.

The wisest among my race understand that the agitation of questions of social equality is the extremest folly, and that progress in the enjoyment of all the privileges that will come to us must be the result of severe and constant struggle rather than of artificial forcing. No race that has anything to contribute to the markets of the world is long in any degree ostracized. It is important and right that all privileges of the law be ours, but it is vastly more important that we be prepared for the exercises of these privileges. The opportunity to earn a dollar in a factory just now is worth infinitely more than the opportunity to spend a dollar in an opera-house.

In conclusion, may I repeat that nothing in thirty years has given us more hope and encouragement, and drawn us so near to you of the white race, as this opportunity offered by the Exposition; and here bending, as it were, over the altar that represents the results of the struggles of your race and mine, both starting practically empty-handed three decades ago, I pledge that in your effort to work out the great and intricate problem which God has laid at the doors of the South, you shall have at all times the patient, sympathetic help of my race; only let this be constantly in mind, that, while from representations in these buildings of the product of field, of forest, of mine, of factory, letters, and art, much good will come, yet far above and beyond material benefits will be that higher good, that, let us pray God, will come, in a blotting out of sectional differences and racial animosities and suspicions, in a determination to administer absolute justice, in a willing obedience among all classes to the mandates of law. This, this, coupled with our material prosperity, will bring into our beloved South a new heaven and a new earth.

The first thing that I remember, after I had finished speaking, was that Governor Bullock rushed across the platform and took me by the hand, and that others did the same. I received so many and such hearty congratulations that I found it difficult to get out of the building. I did not appreciate to any degree, however, the impression which my address seemed to have made, until the next morning, when I went into the business part of the city. As soon as I was recognized, I was surprised to find myself pointed out and surrounded by a crowd of men who wished to shake hands with me. This was kept up on every street on to which I went, to an extent which embarrassed me so much that I went back to my boarding-place. The next morning I returned to Tuskegee. At the station in Atlanta, and at almost all of the stations at which the train stopped between that city and Tuskegee, I found a crowd of people anxious to shake hands with me.

The papers in all parts of the United States published the address in full, and for months afterward there were complimentary editorial references to it. Mr. Clark Howell, the editor of the Atlanta Constitution, telegraphed to a New York paper, among other words, the following, "I do not exaggerate when I say that Professor Booker T. Washington's address yesterday was one of the most notable speeches, both as to character and as to the warmth of its reception, ever delivered to a Southern audience. The address was a revelation. The whole speech is a platform upon which blacks and whites can stand with full justice to each other."

The Boston Transcript said editorially: "The speech of Booker T. Washington at the Atlanta Exposition, this week, seems to have dwarfed all the other proceedings and the Exposition itself. The sensation that it has caused in the press has never been equalled."

I very soon began receiving all kinds of propositions from lecture bureaus, and editors of magazines and papers, to take the lecture platform, and to write articles. One lecture bureau offered me fifty thousand dollars, or two hundred dollars a night and expenses, if I would place my services at its disposal for a given period. To all these communications I replied that my life-work was at Tuskegee; and that whenever I spoke it must be in the interests of Tuskegee school and my race, and that I would enter into no arrangements that seemed to place a mere commercial value upon my services.

Some days after its delivery I sent a copy of my address to the President of the United States, the Hon. Grover Cleveland. I received from him the following autograph reply:--

Gray Gables, Buzzard's Bay, Mass.,

October 6, 1895.

Booker T. Washington, Esq.:

My Dear Sir: I thank you for sending me a copy of your address delivered at the Atlanta Exposition.

I thank you with much enthusiasm for making the address. I have read it with intense interest, and I think the Exposition would be fully justified if it did not do more than furnish the opportunity for its delivery. Your words cannot fail to delight and encourage all who wish well for your race; and if our coloured fellow-citizens do not from your utterances gather new hope and form new determinations to gain every valuable advantage offered them by their citizenship, it will be strange indeed.

Yours very truly,

Grover Cleveland.

Later I met Mr. Cleveland, for the first time, when, as President, he visited the Atlanta Exposition. At the request of myself and others he consented to spend an hour in the Negro Building, for the purpose of inspecting the Negro exhibit and of giving the coloured people in attendance an opportunity to shake hands with him. As soon as I met Mr. Cleveland I became impressed with his simplicity, greatness, and rugged honesty. I have met him many times since then, both at public functions and at his private residence in Princeton, and the more I see of him the more I admire him. When he visited the Negro Building in Atlanta he seemed to give himself up wholly, for that hour, to the coloured people. He seemed to be as careful to shake hands with some old coloured "auntie" clad partially in rags, and to take as much pleasure in doing so, as if he were greeting some millionaire. Many of the coloured people took advantage of the occasion to get him to write his name in a book or on a slip of paper. He was as careful and patient in doing this as if he were putting his signature to some great state document.

Mr. Cleveland has not only shown his friendship for me in many personal ways, but has always consented to do anything I have asked of him for our school. This he has done, whether it was to make a personal donation or to use his influence in securing the donations of others. Judging from my personal acquaintance with Mr. Cleveland, I do not believe that he is conscious of possessing any colour prejudice. He is too great for that. In my contact with people I find that, as a rule, it is only the little, narrow people who live for themselves, who never read good books, who do not travel, who never open up their souls in a way to permit them to come into contact with other souls--with the great outside world. No man whose vision is bounded by colour can come into contact with what is highest and best in the world. In meeting men, in many places, I have found that the happiest people are those who do the most for others; the most miserable are those who do the least. I have also found that few things, if any, are capable of making one so blind and narrow as race prejudice. I often say to our students, in the course of my talks to them on Sunday evenings in the chapel, that the longer I live and the more experience I have of the world, the more I am convinced that, after all, the one thing that is most worth living for--and dying for, if need be--is the opportunity of making some one else more happy and more useful.

The coloured people and the coloured newspapers at first seemed to be greatly pleased with the character of my Atlanta address, as well as with its reception. But after the first burst of enthusiasm began to die away, and the coloured people began reading the speech in cold type, some of them seemed to feel that they had been hypnotized. They seemed to feel that I had been too liberal in my remarks toward the Southern whites, and that I had not spoken out strongly enough for what they termed the "rights" of my race. For a while there was a reaction, so far as a certain element of my own race was concerned, but later these reactionary ones seemed to have been won over to my way of believing and acting.

While speaking of changes in public sentiment, I recall that about ten years after the school at Tuskegee was established, I had an experience that I shall never forget. Dr. Lyman Abbott, then the pastor of Plymouth Church, and also editor of the Outlook (then the Christian Union), asked me to write a letter for his paper giving my opinion of the exact condition, mental and moral, of the coloured ministers in the South, as based upon my observations. I wrote the letter, giving the exact facts as I conceived them to be. The picture painted was a rather black one--or, since I am black, shall I say "white"? It could not be otherwise with a race but a few years out of slavery, a race which had not had time or opportunity to produce a competent ministry.

What I said soon reached every Negro minister in the country, I think, and the letters of condemnation which I received from them were not few. I think that for a year after the publication of this article every association and every conference or religious body of any kind, of my race, that met, did not fail before adjourning to pass a resolution condemning me, or calling upon me to retract or modify what I had said. Many of these organizations went so far in their resolutions as to advise parents to cease sending their children to Tuskegee. One association even appointed a "missionary" whose duty it was to warn the people against sending their children to Tuskegee. This missionary had a son in the school, and I noticed that, whatever the "missionary" might have said or done with regard to others, he was careful not to take his son away from the institution. Many of the coloured papers, especially those that were the organs of religious bodies, joined in the general chorus of condemnation or demands for retraction.

During the whole time of the excitement, and through all the criticism, I did not utter a word of explanation of retraction. I knew that I was right, and that time and the sober second thought of the people would vindicate me. It was not long before the bishops and other church leaders began to make careful investigation of the conditions of the ministry, and they found out that I was right. In fact, the oldest and most influential bishop in one branch of the Methodist Church said that my words were far too mild. Very soon public sentiment began making itself felt, in demanding a purifying of the ministry. While this is not yet complete by any means, I think I may say, without egotism, and I have been told by many of our most influential ministers, that my words had much to do with starting a demand for the placing of a higher type of men in the pulpit. I have had the satisfaction of having many who once condemned me thank me heartily for my frank words.

The change of the attitude of the Negro ministry, so far as regards myself, is so complete that at the present time I have no warmer friends among any class than I have among the clergymen. The improvement in the character and life of the Negro ministers is one of the most gratifying evidences of the progress of the race. My experience with them, as well as other events in my life, convince me that the thing to do, when one feels sure that he has said or done the right thing, and is condemned, is to stand still and keep quiet. If he is right, time will show it.

In the midst of the discussion which was going on concerning my Atlanta speech, I received the letter which I give below, from Dr. Gilman, the President of Johns Hopkins University, who had been made chairman of the judges of award in connection with the Atlanta Exposition:--

Johns Hopkins University, Baltimore,

President's Office, September 30, 1895.

Dear Mr. Washington: Would it be agreeable to you to be one of the Judges of Award in the Department of Education at Atlanta? If so, I shall be glad to place your name upon the list. A line by telegraph will be welcomed.

Yours very truly,

D.C. Gilman

I think I was even more surprised to receive this invitation than I had been to receive the invitation to speak at the opening of the Exposition. It was to be a part of my duty, as one of the jurors, to pass not only upon the exhibits of the coloured schools, but also upon those of the white schools. I accepted the position, and spent a month in Atlanta in performance of the duties which it entailed. The board of jurors was a large one, containing in all of sixty members. It was about equally divided between Southern white people and

Northern white people. Among them were college presidents, leading scientists and men of letters, and specialists in many subjects. When the group of jurors to which I was assigned met for organization, Mr. Thomas Nelson Page, who was one of the number, moved that I be made secretary of that division, and the motion was unanimously adopted. Nearly half of our division were Southern people. In performing my duties in the inspection of the exhibits of white schools I was in every case treated with respect, and at the close of our labours I parted from my associates with regret.

I am often asked to express myself more freely than I do upon the political condition and the political future of my race. These recollections of my experience in Atlanta give me the opportunity to do so briefly. My own belief is, although I have never before said so in so many words, that the time will come when the Negro in the South will be accorded all the political rights which his ability, character, and material possessions entitle him to. I think, though, that the opportunity to freely exercise such political rights will not come in any large degree through outside or artificial forcing, but will be accorded to the Negro by the Southern white people themselves, and that they will protect him in the exercise of those rights. Just as soon as the South gets over the old feeling that it is being forced by "foreigners," or "aliens," to do something which it does not want to do, I believe that the change in the direction that I have indicated is going to begin. In fact, there are indications that it is already beginning in a slight degree.

Let me illustrate my meaning. Suppose that some months before the opening of the Atlanta Exposition there had been a general demand from the press and public platform outside the South that a Negro be given a place on the opening programme, and that a Negro be placed upon the board of jurors of award. Would any such recognition of the race have taken place? I do not think so. The Atlanta officials went as far as they did because they felt it to be a pleasure, as well as a duty, to reward what they considered merit in the Negro race. Say what we will, there is something in human nature which we cannot blot out, which makes one man, in the end, recognize and reward merit in another, regardless of colour or race.

I believe it is the duty of the Negro--as the greater part of the race is already doing--to deport himself modestly in regard to political claims, depending upon the slow but sure influences that proceed from the possession of property, intelligence, and high character for the full recognition of his political rights. I think that the according of the full exercise of political rights is going to be a matter of natural, slow growth, not an over-night, gourd-vine affair. I do not believe that the Negro should cease voting, for a man cannot learn the exercise of self-government by ceasing to vote, any more than a boy can learn to swim by keeping out of the water, but I do believe that in his voting he should more and more be influenced by those of intelligence and character who are his next-door neighbours.

I know coloured men who, through the encouragement, help, and advice of Southern white people, have accumulated thousands of dollars' worth of property, but who, at the same time, would never think of going to those same persons for advice concerning the casting of their ballots. This, it seems to me, is unwise and unreasonable, and should cease. In saying this I do not mean that the Negro should truckle, or not vote from principle, for the instant he ceases to vote from principle he loses the confidence and respect of the Southern white man even.

I do not believe that any state should make a law that permits an ignorant and poverty-stricken white man to vote, and prevents a black man in the same condition from voting. Such a law is not only unjust, but it will react, as all unjust laws do, in time; for the effect of such a law is to encourage the Negro to secure education and property, and at the same time it encourages the white man to remain in ignorance and poverty. I believe that in time, through the operation of intelligence and friendly race relations, all cheating at the ballot-box in the South will cease. It will become apparent that the white man who begins by cheating a Negro out of his ballot soon learns to cheat a white man out of his, and that the man who does this ends his career of dishonesty by the theft of property or by some equally serious crime. In my opinion, the time will come when the South will encourage all of its citizens to vote. It will see that it pays better, from every standpoint, to have healthy, vigorous life than to have that political stagnation which always results when one-half of the population has no share and no interest in the Government.

As a rule, I believe in universal, free suffrage, but I believe that in the South we are confronted with peculiar conditions that justify the protection of the ballot in many of the states, for a while at least, either by an education test, a property test, or by both combined; but whatever tests are required, they should be made to apply with equal and exact justice to both races.

[217]

CHAPTER 15

THE SECRET OF SUCCESS IN PUBLIC SPEAKING

As to how my address at Atlanta was received by the audience in the Exposition building, I think I prefer to let Mr. James Creelman, the noted war correspondent, tell. Mr. Creelman was present, and telegraphed the following account to the New York World:--

Atlanta, September 18.

While President Cleveland was waiting at Gray Gables to-day, to send the electric spark that started the machinery of the Atlanta Exposition, a Negro Moses stood before a great audience of white people and delivered an oration that marks a new epoch in the history of the South; and a body of Negro troops marched in a procession with the citizen soldiery of Georgia and Louisiana. The whole city is thrilling to-night with a realization of the extraordinary significance of these two unprecedented events. Nothing has happened since Henry Grady's immortal speech before the New England society in New York that indicates so profoundly the spirit of the New South, except, perhaps, the opening of the Exposition itself.

When Professor Booker T. Washington, Principal of an industrial school for coloured people in Tuskegee, Ala. stood on the platform of the Auditorium, with the sun shining over the heads of his auditors into his eyes, and with his whole face lit up with the fire of prophecy, Clark Howell, the successor of Henry Grady, said to me, "That man's speech is the beginning of a moral revolution in America."

It is the first time that a Negro has made a speech in the South on any important occasion before an audience composed of white men and women. It electrified the audience, and the response was as if it had come from the throat of a whirlwind.

Mrs. Thompson had hardly taken her seat when all eyes were turned on a tall tawny Negro sitting in the front row of the platform. It was Professor Booker T. Washington, President of the Tuskegee (Alabama) Normal and Industrial Institute, who must rank from this time forth as the foremost man of his race in

America. Gilmore's Band played the "Star-Spangled Banner," and the audience cheered. The tune changed to "Dixie" and the audience roared with shrill "hi-yis." Again the music changed, this time to "Yankee Doodle," and the clamour lessened.

All this time the eyes of the thousands present looked straight at the Negro orator. A strange thing was to happen. A black man was to speak for his people, with none to interrupt him. As Professor Washington strode to the edge of the stage, the low, descending sun shot fiery rays through the windows into his face. A great shout greeted him. He turned his head to avoid the blinding light, and moved about the platform for relief. Then he turned his wonderful countenance to the sun without a blink of the eyelids, and began to talk.

There was a remarkable figure; tall, bony, straight as a Sioux chief, high forehead, straight nose, heavy jaws, and strong, determined mouth, with big white teeth, piercing eyes, and a commanding manner. The sinews stood out on his bronzed neck, and his muscular right arm swung high in the air, with a lead-pencil grasped in the clinched brown fist. His big feet were planted squarely, with the heels together and the toes turned out. His voice range out clear and true, and he paused impressively as he made each point. Within ten minutes the multitude was in an uproar of enthusiasm--handkerchiefs were waved, canes were flourished, hats were tossed in the air. The fairest women of Georgia stood up and cheered. It was as if the orator had bewitched them.

And when he held his dusky hand high above his head, with the fingers stretched wide apart, and said to the white people of the South on behalf of his race, "In all things that are purely social we can be as separate as the fingers, yet one as the hand in all things essential to mutual progress," the great wave of sound dashed itself against the walls, and the whole audience was on its feet in a delirium of applause, and I thought at that moment of the night when Henry Grady stood among the curling wreaths of tobacco-smoke in Delmonico's banquet-hall and said, "I am a Cavalier among Roundheads."

I have heard the great orators of many countries, but not even Gladstone himself could have pleased a cause with most consummate power than did this angular Negro, standing in a nimbus of sunshine, surrounded by the men who once fought to keep his race in bondage. The roar might swell ever so high, but the expression of his earnest face never changed.

A ragged, ebony giant, squatted on the floor in one of the aisles, watched the orator with burning eyes and tremulous face until the supreme burst of applause came, and then the tears ran down his face. Most of the Negroes in the audience were crying, perhaps without knowing just why.

[219]

At the close of the speech Governor Bullock rushed across the stage and seized the orator's hand. Another shout greeted this demonstration, and for a few minutes the two men stood facing each other, hand in hand.

So far as I could spare the time from the immediate work at Tuskegee, after my Atlanta address, I accepted some of the invitations to speak in public which came to me, especially those that would take me into territory where I thought it would pay to plead the cause of my race, but I always did this with the understanding that I was to be free to talk about my life-work and the needs of my people. I also had it understood that I was not to speak in the capacity of a professional lecturer, or for mere commercial gain.

In my efforts on the public platform I never have been able to understand why people come to hear me speak. This question I never can rid myself of. Time and time again, as I have stood in the street in front of a building and have seen men and women passing in large numbers into the audience room where I was to speak, I have felt ashamed that I should be the cause of people--as it seemed to me--wasting a valuable hour of their time. Some years ago I was to deliver an address before a literary society in Madison, Wis. An hour before the time set for me to speak, a fierce snow-storm began, and continued for several hours. I made up my mind that there would be no audience, and that I should not have to speak, but, as a matter of duty, I went to the church, and found it packed with people. The surprise gave me a shock that I did not recover from during the whole evening.

People often ask me if I feel nervous before speaking, or else they suggest that, since I speak often, they suppose that I get used to it. In answer to this question I have to say that I always suffer intensely from nervousness before speaking. More than once, just before I was to make an important address, this nervous strain has been so great that I have resolved never again to speak in public. I not only feel nervous before speaking, but after I have finished I usually feel a sense of regret, because it seems to me as if I had left out of my address the main thing and the best thing that I had meant to say.

There is a great compensation, though, for this preliminary nervous suffering, that comes to me after I have been speaking for about ten minutes, and have come to feel that I have really mastered my audience, and that we have gotten into full and complete sympathy with each other. It seems to me that there is rarely such a combination of mental and physical delight in any effort as that which comes to a public speaker when he feels that he has a great audience completely within his control. There is a thread of sympathy and oneness that connects a public speaker with his audience, that is just as strong as though it

[220]

was something tangible and visible. If in an audience of a thousand people there is one person who is not in sympathy with my views, or is inclined to be doubtful, cold, or critical, I can pick him out. When I have found him I usually go straight at him, and it is a great satisfaction to watch the process of his thawing out. I find that the most effective medicine for such individuals is administered at first in the form of a story, although I never tell an anecdote simply for the sake of telling one. That kind of thing, I think, is empty and hollow, and an audience soon finds it out.

I believe that one always does himself and his audience an injustice when he speaks merely for the sake of speaking. I do not believe that one should speak unless, deep down in his heart, he feels convinced that he has a message to deliver. When one feels, from the bottom of his feet to the top of his head, that he has something to say that is going to help some individual or some cause, then let him say it; and in delivering his message I do not believe that many of the artificial rules of elocution can, under such circumstances, help him very much. Although there are certain things, such as pauses, breathing, and pitch of voice, that are very important, none of these can take the place of soul in an address. When I have an address to deliver, I like to forget all about the rules for the proper use of the English language, and all about rhetoric and that sort of thing, and I like to make the audience forget all about these things, too.

Nothing tends to throw me off my balance so quickly, when I am speaking, as to have some one leave the room. To prevent this, I make up my mind, as a rule, that I will try to make my address so interesting, will try to state so many interesting facts one after another, that no one can leave. The average audience, I have come to believe, wants facts rather than generalities or sermonizing. Most people, I think, are able to draw proper conclusions if they are given the facts in an interesting form on which to base them.

As to the kind of audience that I like best to talk to, I would put at the top of the list an organization of strong, wide-awake, business men, such, for example, as is found in Boston, New York, Chicago, and Buffalo. I have found no other audience so quick to see a point, and so responsive. Within the last few years I have had the privilege of speaking before most of the leading organizations of this kind in the large cities of the United States. The best time to get hold of an organization of business men is after a good dinner, although I think that one of the worst instruments of torture that was ever invented is the custom which makes it necessary for a speaker to sit through a fourteen-course dinner, every minute of the time feeling sure that his speech is going to prove a dismal failure and disappointment.

[221]

I rarely take part in one of these long dinners that I do not wish that I could put myself back in the little cabin where I was a slave boy, and again go through the experience there--one that I shall never forget--of getting molasses to eat once a week from the "big house." Our usual diet on the plantation was corn bread and pork, but on Sunday morning my mother was permitted to bring down a little molasses from the "big house" for her three children, and when it was received how I did wish that every day was Sunday! I would get my tin plate and hold it up for the sweet morsel, but I would always shut my eyes while the molasses was being poured out into the plate, with the hope that when I opened them I would be surprised to see how much I had got. When I opened my eyes I would tip the plate in one direction and another, so as to make the molasses spread all over it, in the full belief that there would be more of it and that it would last longer if spread out in this way. So strong are my childish impressions of those Sunday morning feasts that it would be pretty hard for any one to convince me that there is not more molasses on a plate when it is spread all over the plate than when it occupies a little corner--if there is a corner in a plate. At any rate, I have never believed in "cornering" syrup. My share of the syrup was usually about two tablespoonfuls, and those two spoonfuls of molasses were much more enjoyable to me than is a fourteen-course dinner after which I am to speak.

Next to a company of business men, I prefer to speak to an audience of Southern people, of either race, together or taken separately. Their enthusiasm and responsiveness are a constant delight. The "amens" and "dat's de truf" that come spontaneously from the coloured individuals are calculated to spur any speaker on to his best efforts. I think that next in order of preference I would place a college audience. It has been my privilege to deliver addresses at many of our leading colleges including Harvard, Yale, Williams, Amherst, Fisk University, the University of Pennsylvania, Wellesley, the University of Michigan, Trinity College in North Carolina, and many others.

It has been a matter of deep interest to me to note the number of people who have come to shake hands with me after an address, who say that this is the first time they have ever called a Negro "Mister."

When speaking directly in the interests of the Tuskegee Institute, I usually arrange, some time in advance, a series of meetings in important centres. This takes me before churches, Sunday-schools, Christian Endeavour Societies, and men's and women's clubs. When doing this I sometimes speak before as many as four organizations in a single day.

Three years ago, at the suggestion of Mr. Morris K. Jessup, of New York, and

[222]

Dr. J.L.M. Curry, the general agent of the fund, the trustees of the John F. Slater Fund voted a sum of money to be used in paying the expenses of Mrs. Washington and myself while holding a series of meetings among the coloured people in the large centres of Negro population, especially in the large cities of the ex-slaveholding states. Each year during the last three years we have devoted some weeks to this work. The plan that we have followed has been for me to speak in the morning to the ministers, teachers, and professional men. In the afternoon Mrs. Washington would speak to the women alone, and in the evening I spoke to a large mass-meeting. In almost every case the meetings have been attended not only by the coloured people in large numbers, but by the white people. In Chattanooga, Tenn., for example, there was present at the mass-meeting an audience of not less than three thousand persons, and I was informed that eight hundred of these were white. I have done no work that I really enjoyed more than this, or that I think has accomplished more good.

These meetings have given Mrs. Washington and myself an opportunity to get first-hand, accurate information as to the real condition of the race, by seeing the people in their homes, their churches, their Sunday-schools, and their places of work, as well as in the prisons and dens of crime. These meetings also gave us an opportunity to see the relations that exist between the races. I never feel so hopeful about the race as I do after being engaged in a series of these meetings. I know that on such occasions there is much that comes to the surface that is superficial and deceptive, but I have had experience enough not to be deceived by mere signs and fleeting enthusiasms. I have taken pains to go to the bottom of things and get facts, in a cold, business-like manner.

I have seen the statement made lately, by one who claims to know what he is talking about, that, taking the whole Negro race into account, ninety per cent of the Negro women are not virtuous. There never was a baser falsehood uttered concerning a race, or a statement made that was less capable of being proved by actual facts.

No one can come into contact with the race for twenty years, as I have done in the heart of the South, without being convinced that the race is constantly making slow but sure progress materially, educationally, and morally. One might take up the life of the worst element in New York City, for example, and prove almost anything he wanted to prove concerning the white man, but all will agree that this is not a fair test.

Early in the year 1897 I received a letter inviting me to deliver an address at the dedication of the Robert Gould Shaw monument in Boston. I accepted the invitation. It is not necessary for me, I am sure, to explain who Robert Gould Shaw was, and what he did. The monument to his memory stands near the head of the Boston Common, facing the State House. It is counted to be the most perfect piece of art of the kind to be found in the country.

The exercises connected with the dedication were held in Music Hall, in Boston, and the great hall was packed from top to bottom with one of the most distinguished audiences that ever assembled in the city. Among those present were more persons representing the famous old anti-slavery element that it is likely will ever be brought together in the country again. The late Hon. Roger Wolcott, then Governor of Massachusetts, was the presiding officer, and on the platform with him were many other officials and hundreds of distinguished men. A report of the meeting which appeared in the Boston Transcript will describe it better than any words of mine could do:--

The core and kernel of yesterday's great noon meeting, in honour of the Brotherhood of Man, in Music Hall, was the superb address of the Negro President of Tuskegee. "Booker T. Washington received his Harvard A.M. last June, the first of his race," said Governor Wolcott, "to receive an honorary degree from the oldest university in the land, and this for the wise leadership of his people." When Mr. Washington rose in the flag-filled, enthusiasm-warmed, patriotic, and glowing atmosphere of Music Hall, people felt keenly that here was the civic justification of the old abolition spirit of Massachusetts; in his person the proof of her ancient and indomitable faith; in his strong through and rich oratory, the crown and glory of the old war days of suffering and strife. The scene was full of historic beauty and deep significance. "Cold" Boston was alive with the fire that is always hot in her heart for righteousness and truth. Rows and rows of people who are seldom seen at any public function, whole families of those who are certain to be out of town on a holiday, crowded the place to overflowing. The city was at her birthright fete in the persons of hundreds of her best citizens, men and women whose names and lives stand for the virtues that make for honourable civic pride.

Battle-music had filled the air. Ovation after ovation, applause warm and prolonged, had greeted the officers and friends of Colonel Shaw, the sculptor, St. Gaudens, the memorial Committee, the Governor and his staff, and the Negro soldiers of the Fifty-fourth Massachusetts as they came upon the platform or entered the hall. Colonel Henry Lee, of Governor Andrew's old staff, had made a noble, simple presentation speech for the committee, paying tribute to Mr. John M. Forbes, in whose stead he served. Governor Wolcott had made his short, memorable speech, saying, "Fort Wagner marked an epoch in the history of a race, and called it into manhood." Mayor Quincy had received the monument for the city of Boston. The story of Colonel Shaw and his black regiment had been told in gallant words, and then, after the singing of

Mine eyes have seen the glory Of the coming of the Lord,

Booker Washington arose. It was, of course, just the moment for him. The multitude, shaken out of its usual symphony-concert calm, quivered with an excitement that was not suppressed. A dozen times it had sprung to its feet to cheer and wave and hurrah, as one person. When this man of culture and voice and power, as well as a dark skin, began, and uttered the names of Stearns and of Andrew, feeling began to mount. You could see tears glisten in the eyes of soldiers and civilians. When the orator turned to the coloured soldiers on the platform, to the colour-bearer of Fort Wagner, who smilingly bore still the flag he had never lowered even when wounded, and said, "To you, to the scarred and scattered remnants of the Fifty-fourth, who, with empty sleeve and wanting leg, have honoured this occasion with your presence, to you, your commander is not dead. Though Boston erected no monument and history recorded no story, in you and in the loyal race which you represent, Robert Gould Shaw would have a monument which time could not wear away," then came the climax of the emotion of the day and the hour. It was Roger Wolcott, as well as the Governor of Massachusetts, the individual representative of the people's sympathy as well as the chief magistrate, who had sprung first to his feet and cried, "Three cheers to Booker T. Washington!"

Among those on the platform was Sergeant William H. Carney, of New Bedford, Mass., the brave coloured officer who was the colour-bearer at Fort Wagner and held the American flag. In spite of the fact that a large part of his regiment was killed, he escape, and exclaimed, after the battle was over, "The old flag never touched the ground."

This flag Sergeant Carney held in his hands as he sat on the platform, and when I turned to address the survivors of the coloured regiment who were present, and referred to Sergeant Carney, he rose, as if by instinct, and raised the flag. It has been my privilege to witness a good many satisfactory and rather sensational demonstrations in connection with some of my public addresses, but in dramatic effect I have never seen or experienced anything which equalled this. For a number of minutes the audience seemed to entirely lose control of itself.

In the general rejoicing throughout the country which followed the close of the Spanish-American war, peace celebrations were arranged in several of the large cities. I was asked by President William R. Harper, of the University of Chicago, who was chairman of the committee of invitations for the celebration to be held in the city of Chicago, to deliver one of the addresses at the celebration there. I accepted the invitation, and delivered two addresses there during the Jubilee week. The first of these, and the principal one, was given in the Auditorium, on the evening of Sunday, October 16. This was the largest audience that I have ever addressed, in any part of the country; and besides speaking in the main Auditorium, I also addressed, that same evening, two overflow audiences in other parts of the city.

It was said that there were sixteen thousand persons in the Auditorium, and it seemed to me as if there were as many more on the outside trying to get in. It was impossible for any one to get near the entrance without the aid of a policeman. President William McKinley attended this meeting, as did also the members of his Cabinet, many foreign ministers, and a large number of army and navy officers, many of whom had distinguished themselves in the war which had just closed. The speakers, besides myself, on Sunday evening, were Rabbi Emil G. Hirsch, Father Thomas P. Hodnett, and Dr. John H. Barrows.

The Chicago Times-Herald, in describing the meeting, said of my address:--

He pictured the Negro choosing slavery rather than extinction; recalled Crispus Attucks shedding his blood at the beginning of the American Revolution, that white Americans might be free, while black Americans remained in slavery; rehearsed the conduct of the Negroes with Jackson at New Orleans; drew a vivid and pathetic picture of the Southern slaves protecting and supporting the families of their masters while the latter were fighting to perpetuate black slavery; recounted the bravery of coloured troops at Port Hudson and Forts Wagner and Pillow, and praised the heroism of the black regiments that stormed El Caney and Santiago to give freedom to the enslaved people of Cuba, forgetting, for the time being, the unjust discrimination that law and custom make against them in their own country.

In all of these things, the speaker declared, his race had chosen the better part. And then he made his eloquent appeal to the consciences of the white Americans: "When you have gotten the full story or the heroic conduct of the Negro in the Spanish-American war, have heard it from the lips of Northern soldier and Southern soldier, from ex-abolitionist and ex-masters, then decide within yourselves whether a race that is thus willing to die for its country should not be given the highest opportunity to live for its country."

The part of the speech which seems to arouse the wildest and most sensational enthusiasm was that in which I thanked the President for his recognition of the Negro in his appointments during the Spanish-American war. The President was sitting in a box at the right of the stage. When I addressed him I turned toward the box, and as I finished the sentence thanking him for his generosity, the whole audience rose and cheered again and again, waving handkerchiefs and hats and canes, until the President arose in the box and bowed his acknowledgements. At that the enthusiasm broke out again, and the demonstration was almost indescribable.

One portion of my address at Chicago seemed to have been misunderstood by the Southern press, and some of the Southern papers took occasion to criticise me rather strongly. These criticisms continued for several weeks, until I finally received a letter from the editor of the Age-Herald, published in Birmingham, Ala., asking me if I would say just what I meant by this part of the address. I replied to him in a letter which seemed to satisfy my critics. In this letter I said that I had made it a rule never to say before a Northern audience anything that I would not say before an audience in the South. I said that I did not think it was necessary for me to go into extended explanations; if my seventeen years of work in the heart of the South had not been explanation enough, I did not see how words could explain. I said that I made the same plea that I had made in my address at Atlanta, for the blotting out of race prejudice in "commercial and civil relations." I said that what is termed social recognition was a question which I never discussed, and then I quoted from my Atlanta address what I had said there in regard to that subject.

In meeting crowds of people at public gatherings, there is one type of individual that I dread. I mean the crank. I have become so accustomed to these people now that I can pick them out at a distance when I see them elbowing their way up to me. The average crank has a long beard, poorly cared for, a lean, narrow face, and wears a black coat. The front of his vest and coat are slick with grease, and his trousers bag at the knees.

In Chicago, after I had spoken at a meeting, I met one of these fellows. They usually have some process for curing all of the ills of the world at once. This Chicago specimen had a patent process by which he said Indian corn could be kept through a period of three or four years, and he felt sure that if the Negro race in the South would, as a whole, adopt his process, it would settle the whole race question. It mattered nothing that I tried to convince him that our present problem was to teach the Negroes how to produce enough corn to last them through one year. Another Chicago crank had a scheme by which he wanted me to join him in an effort to close up all the National banks in the country. If that was done, he felt sure it would put the Negro on his feet.

The number of people who stand ready to consume one's time, to no purpose, is almost countless. At one time I spoke before a large audience in

Boston in the evening. The next morning I was awakened by having a card brought to my room, and with it a message that some one was anxious to see me. Thinking that it must be something very important, I dressed hastily and went down. When I reached the hotel office I found a blank and innocent-looking individual waiting for me, who coolly remarked: "I heard you talk at a meeting last night. I rather liked your talk, and so I came in this morning to hear you talk some more."

I am often asked how it is possible for me to superintend the work at Tuskegee and at the same time be so much away from the school. In partial answer to this I would say that I think I have learned, in some degree at least, to disregard the old maxim which says, "Do not get others to do that which you can do yourself." My motto, on the other hand, is, "Do not do that which others can do as well."

One of the most encouraging signs in connection with the Tuskegee school is found in the fact that the organization is so thorough that the daily work of the school is not dependent upon the presence of any one individual. The whole executive force, including instructors and clerks, now numbers eighty-six. This force is so organized and subdivided that the machinery of the school goes on day by day like clockwork. Most of our teachers have been connected with the institutions for a number of years, and are as much interested in it as I am. In my absence, Mr. Warren Logan, the treasurer, who has been at the school seventeen years, is the executive. He is efficiently supported by Mrs. Washington, and by my faithful secretary, Mr. Emmett J. Scott, who handles the bulk of my correspondence and keeps me in daily touch with the life of the school, and who also keeps me informed of whatever takes place in the South that concerns the race. I owe more to his tact, wisdom, and hard work than I can describe.

The main executive work of the school, whether I am at Tuskegee or not, centres in what we call the executive council. This council meets twice a week, and is composed of the nine persons who are at the head of the nine departments of the school. For example: Mrs. B.K. Bruce, the Lady Principal, the widow of the late ex-senator Bruce, is a member of the council, and represents in it all that pertains to the life of the girls at the school. In addition to the executive council there is a financial committee of six, that meets every week and decides upon the expenditures for the week. Once a month, and sometimes oftener, there is a general meeting of all the instructors. Aside from these there are innumerable smaller meetings, such as that of the instructors in the Phelps Hall Bible Training School, or of the instructors in the agricultural department.

[228]

In order that I may keep in constant touch with the life of the institution, I have a system of reports so arranged that a record of the school's work reaches me every day of the year, no matter in what part of the country I am. I know by these reports even what students are excused from school, and why they are excused--whether for reasons of ill health or otherwise. Through the medium of these reports I know each day what the income of the school in money is; I know how many gallons of milk and how many pounds of butter come from the diary; what the bill of fare for the teachers and students is; whether a certain kind of meat was boiled or baked, and whether certain vegetables served in the dining room were bought from a store or procured from our own farm. Human nature I find to be very much the same the world over, and it is sometimes not hard to yield to the temptation to go to a barrel of rice that has come from the store--with the grain all prepared to go in the pot--rather than to take the time and trouble to go to the field and dig and wash one's own sweet potatoes, which might be prepared in a manner to take the place of the rice.

I am often asked how, in the midst of so much work, a large part of which is for the public, I can find time for any rest or recreation, and what kind of recreation or sports I am fond of. This is rather a difficult question to answer. I have a strong feeling that every individual owes it to himself, and to the cause which he is serving, to keep a vigorous, healthy body, with the nerves steady and strong, prepared for great efforts and prepared for disappointments and trying positions. As far as I can, I make it a rule to plan for each day's work--not merely to go through with the same routine of daily duties, but to get rid of the routine work as early in the day as possible, and then to enter upon some new or advance work. I make it a rule to clear my desk every day, before leaving my office, of all correspondence and memoranda, so that on the morrow I can begin a NEW day of work. I make it a rule never to let my work drive me, but to so master it, and keep it in such complete control, and to keep so far ahead of it, that I will be the master instead of the servant. There is a physical and mental and spiritual enjoyment that comes from a consciousness of being the absolute master of one's work, in all its details, that is very satisfactory and inspiring. My experience teachers me that, if one learns to follow this plan, he gets a freshness of body and vigour of mind out of work that goes a long way toward keeping him strong and healthy. I believe that when one can grow to the point where he loves his work, this gives him a kind of strength that is most valuable.

When I begin my work in the morning, I expect to have a successful and pleasant day of it, but at the same time I prepare myself for unpleasant and unexpected hard places. I prepared myself to hear that one of our school buildings is on fire, or has burned, or that some disagreeable accident has

[229]

occurred, or that some one has abused me in a public address or printed article, for something that I have done or omitted to do, or for something that he had heard that I had said--probably something that I had never thought of saying.

In nineteen years of continuous work I have taken but one vacation. That was two years ago, when some of my friends put the money into my hands and forced Mrs. Washington and myself to spend three months in Europe. I have said that I believe it is the duty of every one to keep his body in good condition. I try to look after the little ills, with the idea that if I take care of the little ills the big ones will not come. When I find myself unable to sleep well, I know that something is wrong. If I find any part of my system the least weak, and not performing its duty, I consult a good physician. The ability to sleep well, at any time and in any place, I find of great advantage. I have so trained myself that I can lie down for a nap of fifteen or twenty minutes, and get up refreshed in body and mind.

I have said that I make it a rule to finish up each day's work before leaving it. There is, perhaps, one exception to this. When I have an unusually difficult question to decide--one that appeals strongly to the emotions--I find it a safe rule to sleep over it for a night, or to wait until I have had an opportunity to talk it over with my wife and friends.

As to my reading; the most time I get for solid reading is when I am on the cars. Newspapers are to me a constant source of delight and recreation. The only trouble is that I read too many of them. Fiction I care little for. Frequently I have to almost force myself to read a novel that is on every one's lips. The kind of reading that I have the greatest fondness for is biography. I like to be sure that I am reading about a real man or a real thing. I think I do not go too far when I say that I have read nearly every book and magazine article that has been written about Abraham Lincoln. In literature he is my patron saint.

Out of the twelve months in a year I suppose that, on an average, I spend six months away from Tuskegee. While my being absent from the school so much unquestionably has its disadvantages, yet there are at the same time some compensations. The change of work brings a certain kind of rest. I enjoy a ride of a long distance on the cars, when I am permitted to ride where I can be comfortable. I get rest on the cars, except when the inevitable individual who seems to be on every train approaches me with the now familiar phrase: "Isn't this Booker Washington? I want to introduce myself to you." Absence from the school enables me to lose sight of the unimportant details of the work, and study it in a broader and more comprehensive manner than I could do on the grounds. This absence also brings me into contact with the best work being done in educational lines, and into contact with the best educators in the land.

But, after all this is said, the time when I get the most solid rest and recreation is when I can be at Tuskegee, and, after our evening meal is over, can sit down, as is our custom, with my wife and Portia and Baker and Davidson, my three children, and read a story, or each take turns in telling a story. To me there is nothing on earth equal to that, although what is nearly equal to it is to go with them for an hour or more, as we like to do on Sunday afternoons, into the woods, where we can live for a while near the heart of nature, where no one can disturb or vex us, surrounded by pure air, the trees, the shrubbery, the flowers, and the sweet fragrance that springs from a hundred plants, enjoying the chirp of the crickets and the songs of the birds. This is solid rest.

My garden, also, what little time I can be at Tuskegee, is another source of rest and enjoyment. Somehow I like, as often as possible, to touch nature, not something that is artificial or an imitation, but the real thing. When I can leave my office in time so that I can spend thirty or forty minutes in spading the ground, in planting seeds, in digging about the plants, I feel that I am coming into contact with something that is giving me strength for the many duties and hard places that await me out in the big world. I pity the man or woman who has never learned to enjoy nature and to get strength and inspiration out of it.

Aside from the large number of fowls and animals kept by the school, I keep individually a number of pigs and fowls of the best grades, and in raising these I take a great deal of pleasure. I think the pig is my favourite animal. Few things are more satisfactory to me than a high-grade Berkshire or Poland China pig.

Games I care little for. I have never seen a game of football. In cards I do not know one card from another. A game of old-fashioned marbles with my two boys, once in a while, is all I care for in this direction. I suppose I would care for games now if I had had any time in my youth to give to them, but that was not possible.

CHAPTER 16
EUROPE

In 1893 I was married to Miss Margaret James Murray, a native of Mississippi, and a graduate of Fisk University, in Nashville, Tenn., who had come to Tuskegee as a teacher several years before, and at the time we were married was filling the position of Lady Principal. Not only is Mrs. Washington completely one with me in the work directly connected with the school, relieving me of many burdens and perplexities, but aside from her work on the school grounds, she carries on a mothers' meeting in the town of Tuskegee, and a plantation work among the women, children, and men who live in a settlement connected with a large plantation about eight miles from Tuskegee. Both the mothers' meeting and the plantation work are carried on, not only with a view to helping those who are directly reached, but also for the purpose of furnishing object-lessons in these two kinds of work that may be followed by our students when they go out into the world for their own life-work.

Aside from these two enterprises, Mrs. Washington is also largely responsible for a woman's club at the school which brings together, twice a month, the women who live on the school grounds and those who live near, for the discussion of some important topic. She is also the President of what is known as the Federation of Southern Coloured Women's Clubs, and is Chairman of the Executive Committee of the National Federation of Coloured Women's Clubs.

Portia, the oldest of my three children, has learned dressmaking. She has unusual ability in instrumental music. Aside from her studies at Tuskegee, she has already begun to teach there.

Booker Taliaferro is my next oldest child. Young as he is, he has already nearly mastered the brickmason's trade. He began working at this trade when he was quite small, dividing his time between this and class work; and he has developed great skill in the trade and a fondness for it. He says that he is going to be an architect and brickmason. One of the most satisfactory letters that I have ever received from any one came to me from Booker last summer. When I left home for the summer, I told him that he must work at his trade half of each day, and that the other half of the day he could spend as he pleased. When I had been away from home two weeks, I received the following letter from him:

Tuskegee, Alabama.

My dear Papa: Before you left home you told me to work at my trade half of each day. I like my work so much that I want to work at my trade all day. Besides, I want to earn all the money I can, so that when I go to another school I shall have money to pay my expenses.

Your son,

Booker.

My youngest child, Earnest Davidson Washington, says that he is going to be a physician. In addition to going to school, where he studies books and has manual training, he regularly spends a portion of his time in the office of our resident physician, and has already learned to do many of the studies which pertain to a doctor's office.

The thing in my life which brings me the keenest regret is that my work in connection with public affairs keeps me for so much of the time away from my family, where, of all places in the world, I delight to be. I always envy the individual whose life-work is so laid that he can spend his evenings at home. I have sometimes thought that people who have this rare privilege do not appreciate it as they should. It is such a rest and relief to get away from crowds of people, and handshaking, and travelling, to get home, even if it be for but a very brief while.

Another thing at Tuskegee out of which I get a great deal of pleasure and satisfaction is in the meeting with our students, and teachers, and their families, in the chapel for devotional exercises every evening at half-past eight, the last thing before retiring for the night. It is an inspiring sight when one stands on the platform there and sees before him eleven or twelve hundred earnest young men and women; and one cannot but feel that it is a privilege to help to guide them to a higher and more useful life.

In the spring of 1899 there came to me what I might describe as almost the greatest surprise of my life. Some good ladies in Boston arranged a public meeting in the interests of Tuskegee, to be held in the Hollis Street Theatre. This meeting was attended by large numbers of the best people of Boston, of both races. Bishop Lawrence presided. In addition to an address made by myself, Mr. Paul Lawrence Dunbar read from his poems, and Dr. W.E.B. Du Bois read an original sketch.

Some of those who attended this meeting noticed that I seemed unusually tired, and some little time after the close of the meeting, one of the ladies who had been interested in it asked me in a casual way if I had ever been to Europe. I replied that I never had. She asked me if I had ever thought of going, and I told her no; that it was something entirely beyond me. This conversation soon passed out of my mind, but a few days afterward I was informed that some friends in Boston, including Mr. Francis J. Garrison, had raised a sum of money sufficient to pay all the expenses of Mrs. Washington and myself during a three or four months' trip to Europe. It was added with emphasis that we MUST go. A year previous to this Mr. Garrison had attempted to get me to promise to go to Europe for a summer's rest, with the understanding that he would be responsible for raising the money among his friends for the expenses of the trip. At that time such a journey seemed so entirely foreign to anything that I should ever be able to undertake that I did confess I did not give the matter very serious attention; but later Mr. Garrison joined his efforts to those of the ladies whom I have mentioned, and when their plans were made known to me Mr. Garrison not only had the route mapped out, but had, I believe, selected the steamer upon which we were to sail.

The whole thing was so sudden and so unexpected that I was completely taken off my feet. I had been at work steadily for eighteen years in connection with Tuskegee, and I had never thought of anything else but ending my life in that way. Each day the school seemed to depend upon me more largely for its daily expenses, and I told these Boston friends that, while I thanked them sincerely for their thoughtfulness and generosity, I could not go to Europe, for the reason that the school could not live financially while I was absent. They then informed me that Mr. Henry L. Higginson, and some other good friends who I know do not want their names made public, were then raising a sum of money which would be sufficient to keep the school in operation while I was away. At this point I was compelled to surrender. Every avenue of escape had been closed.

Deep down in my heart the whole thing seemed more like a dream than like reality, and for a long time it was difficult for me to make myself believe that I was actually going to Europe. I had been born and largely reared in the lowest depths of slavery, ignorance, and poverty. In my childhood I had suffered for want of a place to sleep, for lack of food, clothing, and shelter. I had not had the privilege of sitting down to a dining-table until I was quite well grown. Luxuries had always seemed to me to be something meant for white people, not for my race. I had always regarded Europe, and London, and Paris, much as I regarded heaven. And now could it be that I was actually going to Europe? Such thoughts as these were constantly with me.

Two other thoughts troubled me a good deal. I feared that people who heard that Mrs. Washington and I were going to Europe might not know all the circumstances, and might get the idea that we had become, as some might say, "stuck up," and were trying to "show off." I recalled that from my youth I had heard it said that too often, when people of my race reached any degree of success, they were inclined to unduly exalt themselves; to try and ape the wealthy, and in so doing to lose their heads. The fear that people might think this of us haunted me a good deal. Then, too, I could not see how my conscience would permit me to spare the time from my work and be happy. It seemed mean and selfish in me to be taking a vacation while others were at work, and while there was so much that needed to be done. From the time I could remember, I had always been at work, and I did not see how I could spend three or four months in doing nothing. The fact was that I did not know how to take a vacation.

Mrs. Washington had much the same difficulty in getting away, but she was anxious to go because she thought that I needed the rest. There were many important National questions bearing upon the life of the race which were being agitated at that time, and this made it all the harder for us to decide to go. We finally gave our Boston friends our promise that we would go, and then they insisted that the date of our departure be set as soon as possible. So we decided upon May 10. My good friend Mr. Garrison kindly took charge of all the details necessary for the success of the trip, and he, as well as other friends, gave us a great number of letters of introduction to people in France and England, and made other arrangements for our comfort and convenience abroad. Good-bys were said at Tuskegee, and we were in New York May 9, ready to sail the next day. Our daughter Portia, who was then studying in South Framingham, Mass., came to New York to see us off. Mr. Scott, my secretary, came with me to New York, in order that I might clear up the last bit of business before I left. Other friends also came to New York to see us off. Just before we went on board the steamer another pleasant surprise came to us in the form of a letter from two generous ladies, stating that they had decided to give us the money with which to erect a new building to be used in properly housing all our industries for girls at Tuskegee.

We were to sail on the Friesland, of the Red Star Line, and a beautiful vessel she was. We went on board just before noon, the hour of sailing. I had never before been on board a large ocean steamer, and the feeling which took possession of me when I found myself there is rather hard to describe. It was a feeling, I think, of awe mingled with delight. We were agreeably surprised to find that the captain, as well as several of the other officers, not only knew who we were, but was expecting us and gave us a pleasant greeting. There were several passengers whom we knew, including Senator Sewell, of New Jersey, and Edward Marshall, the newspaper correspondent. I had just a little fear that we would not be treated civilly by some of the passengers. This fear was based upon what I had heard other people of my race, who had crossed the ocean, say about unpleasant experiences in crossing the ocean in American vessels. But in our case, from the captain down to the most humble servant, we were treated with the greatest kindness. Nor was this kindness confined to those who were connected with the steamer; it was shown by all the passengers also. There were not a few Southern men and women on board, and they were as cordial as those from other parts of the country.

As soon as the last good-bys were said, and the steamer had cut loose from the wharf, the load of care, anxiety, and responsibility which I had carried for eighteen years began to lift itself from my shoulders at the rate, it seemed to me, of a pound a minute. It was the first time in all those years that I had felt, even in a measure, free from care; and my feeling of relief it is hard to describe on paper. Added to this was the delightful anticipation of being in Europe soon. It all seemed more like a dream than like a reality.

Mr. Garrison had thoughtfully arranged to have us have one of the most comfortable rooms on the ship. The second or third day out I began to sleep, and I think that I slept at the rate of fifteen hours a day during the remainder of the ten days' passage. Then it was that I began to understand how tired I really was. These long sleeps I kept up for a month after we landed on the other side. It was such an unusual feeling to wake up in the morning and realize that I had no engagements; did not have to take a train at a certain hour; did not have an appointment to meet some one, or to make an address, at a certain hour. How different all this was from the experiences that I have been through when travelling, when I have sometimes slept in three different beds in a single night!

When Sunday came, the captain invited me to conduct the religious services, but, not being a minister, I declined. The passengers, however, began making requests that I deliver an address to them in the dining-saloon some time during the voyage, and this I consented to do. Senator Sewell presided at this meeting. After ten days of delightful weather, during which I was not seasick for a day, we landed at the interesting old city of Antwerp, in Belgium.

The next day after we landed happened to be one of those numberless holidays which the people of those countries are in the habit of observing. It was a bright, beautiful day. Our room in the hotel faced the main public square, and the sights there--the people coming in from the country with all kinds of beautiful flowers to sell, the women coming in with their dogs drawing large, brightly polished cans filled with milk, the people streaming into the cathedral--filled me with a sense of newness that I had never before experienced.

After spending some time in Antwerp, we were invited to go with a part of a half-dozen persons on a trip through Holland. This party included Edward Marshall and some American artists who had come over on the same steamer with us. We accepted the invitation, and enjoyed the trip greatly. I think it was all the more interesting and instructive because we went for most of the way on one of the slow, old-fashioned canal-boats. This gave us an opportunity of seeing and studying the real life of the people in the country districts. We went in this way as far as Rotterdam, and later went to The Hague, where the Peace Conference was then in session, and where we were kindly received by the American representatives.

The thing that impressed itself most on me in Holland was the thoroughness of the agriculture and the excellence of the Holstein cattle. I never knew, before visiting Holland, how much it was possible for people to get out of a small plot of ground. It seemed to me that absolutely no land was wasted. It was worth a trip to Holland, too, just to get a sight of three or four hundred fine Holstein cows grazing in one of those intensely green fields.

From Holland we went to Belgium, and made a hasty trip through that country, stopping at Brussels, where we visited the battlefield of Waterloo. From Belgium we went direct to Paris, where we found that Mr. Theodore Stanton, the son of Mrs. Elizabeth Cady Stanton, had kindly provided accommodations for us. We had barely got settled in Paris before an invitation came to me from the University Club of Paris to be its guest at a banquet which was soon to be given. The other guests were ex-President Benjamin Harrison and Archbishop Ireland, who were in Paris at the time. The American Ambassador, General Horace Porter, presided at the banquet. My address on this occasion seemed to give satisfaction to those who heard it. General Harrison kindly devoted a large portion of his remarks at dinner to myself and to the influence of the work at Tuskegee on the American race question. After my address at this banquet other invitations came to me, but I declined the most of them, knowing that if I accepted them all, the object of my visit would be defeated. I did, however, consent to deliver an address in the American chapel the following Sunday morning, and at this meeting General Harrison, General Porter, and other distinguished Americans were present.

Later we received a formal call from the American Ambassador, and were invited to attend a reception at his residence. At this reception we met many

Americans, among them Justices Fuller and Harlan, of the United States Supreme Court. During our entire stay of a month in Paris, both the American Ambassador and his wife, as well as several other Americans, were very kind to us.

While in Paris we saw a good deal of the now famous American Negro painter, Mr. Henry O. Tanner, whom we had formerly known in America. It was very satisfactory to find how well known Mr. Tanner was in the field of art, and to note the high standing which all classes accorded to him. When we told some Americans that we were going to the Luxembourg Palace to see a painting by an American Negro, it was hard to convince them that a Negro had been thus honoured. I do not believe that they were really convinced of the fact until they saw the picture for themselves. My acquaintance with Mr. Tanner reenforced in my mind the truth which I am constantly trying to impress upon our students at Tuskegee--and on our people throughout the country, as far as I can reach them with my voice--that any man, regardless of colour, will be recognized and rewarded just in proportion as he learns to do something well--learns to do it better than some one else--however humble the thing may be. As I have said, I believe that my race will succeed in proportion as it learns to do a common thing in an uncommon manner; learns to do a thing so thoroughly that no one can improve upon what it has done; learns to make its services of indispensable value. This was the spirit that inspired me in my first effort at Hampton, when I was given the opportunity to sweep and dust that schoolroom. In a degree I felt that my whole future life depended upon the thoroughness with which I cleaned that room, and I was determined to do it so well that no one could find any fault with the job. Few people ever stopped, I found, when looking at his pictures, to inquire whether Mr. Tanner was a Negro painter, a French painter, or a German painter. They simply knew that he was able to produce something which the world wanted--a great painting--and the matter of his colour did not enter into their minds. When a Negro girl learns to cook, to wash dishes, to sew, or write a book, or a Negro boy learns to groom horses, or to grow sweet potatoes, or to produce butter, or to build a house, or to be able to practise medicine, as well or better than some one else, they will be rewarded regardless of race or colour. In the long run, the world is going to have the best, and any difference in race, religion, or previous history will not long keep the world from what it wants.

I think that the whole future of my race hinges on the question as to whether or not it can make itself of such indispensible value that the people in the town and the state where we reside will feel that our presence is necessary to the happiness and well-being of the community. No man who continues to add

[238]

something to the material, intellectual, and moral well-being of the place in which he lives is long left without proper reward. This is a great human law which cannot be permanently nullified.

The love of pleasure and excitement which seems in a large measure to possess the French people impressed itself upon me. I think they are more noted in this respect than is true of the people of my own race. In point of morality and moral earnestness I do not believe that the French are ahead of my own race in America. Severe competition and the great stress of life have led them to learn to do things more thoroughly and to exercise greater economy; but time, I think, will bring my race to the same point. In the matter of truth and high honour I do not believe that the average Frenchman is ahead of the American Negro; while so far as mercy and kindness to dumb animals go, I believe that my race is far ahead. In fact, when I left France, I had more faith in the future of the black man in America than I had ever possessed.

From Paris we went to London, and reached there early in July, just about the height of the London social season. Parliament was in session, and there was a great deal of gaiety. Mr. Garrison and other friends had provided us with a large number of letters of introduction, and they had also sent letters to other persons in different parts of the United Kingdom, apprising these people of our coming. Very soon after reaching London we were flooded with invitations to attend all manner of social functions, and a great many invitations came to me asking that I deliver public addresses. The most of these invitations I declined, for the reason that I wanted to rest. Neither were we able to accept more than a small proportion of the other invitations. The Rev. Dr. Brooke Herford and Mrs. Herford, whom I had known in Boston, consulted with the American Ambassador, the Hon. Joseph Choate, and arranged for me to speak at a public meeting to be held in Essex Hall. Mr. Choate kindly consented to preside. The meeting was largely attended. There were many distinguished persons present, among them several members of Parliament, including Mr. James Bryce, who spoke at the meeting. What the American Ambassador said in introducing me, as well as a synopsis of what I said, was widely published in England and in the American papers at the time. Dr. and Mrs. Herford gave Mrs. Washington and myself a reception, at which we had the privilege of meeting some of the best people in England. Throughout our stay in London Ambassador Choate was most kind and attentive to us. At the Ambassador's reception I met, for the first time, Mark Twain.

We were the guests several times of Mrs. T. Fisher Unwin, the daughter of the English statesman, Richard Cobden. It seemed as if both Mr. and Mrs. Unwin could not do enough for our comfort and happiness. Later, for nearly a week, we were the guests of the daughter of John Bright, now Mrs. Clark, of Street, England. Both Mr. and Mrs. Clark, with their daughter, visited us at Tuskegee the next year. In Birmingham, England, we were the guests for several days of Mr. Joseph Sturge, whose father was a great abolitionist and friend of Whittier and Garrison. It was a great privilege to meet throughout England those who had known and honoured the late William Lloyd Garrison, the Hon. Frederick Douglass, and other abolitionists. The English abolitionists with whom we came in contact never seemed to tire of talking about these two Americans. Before going to England I had had no proper conception of the deep interest displayed by the abolitionists of England in the cause of freedom, nor did I realize the amount of substantial help given by them.

In Bristol, England, both Mrs. Washington and I spoke at the Women's Liberal Club. I was also the principal speaker at the Commencement exercises of the Royal College for the Blind. These exercises were held in the Crystal Palace, and the presiding officer was the late Duke of Westminster, who was said to be, I believe, the richest man in England, if not in the world. The Duke, as well as his wife and their daughter, seemed to be pleased with what I said, and thanked me heartily. Through the kindness of Lady Aberdeen, my wife and I were enabled to go with a party of those who were attending the International Congress of Women, then in session in London, to see Queen Victoria, at Windsor Castle, where, afterward, we were all the guests of her Majesty at tea. In our party was Miss Susan B. Anthony, and I was deeply impressed with the fact that one did not often get an opportunity to see, during the same hour, two women so remarkable in different ways as Susan B. Anthony and Queen Victoria.

In the House of Commons, which we visited several times, we met Sir Henry M. Stanley. I talked with him about Africa and its relation to the American Negro, and after my interview with him I became more convinced than ever that there was no hope of the American Negro's improving his condition by emigrating to Africa.

On various occasions Mrs. Washington and I were the guests of Englishmen in their country homes, where, I think, one sees the Englishman at his best. In one thing, at least, I feel sure that the English are ahead of Americans, and that is, that they have learned how to get more out of life. The home life of the English seems to me to be about as perfect as anything can be. Everything moves like clockwork. I was impressed, too, with the deference that the servants show to their "masters" and "mistresses,"--terms which I suppose would not be tolerated in America. The English servant expects, as a rule, to be nothing but a servant, and so he perfects himself in the art to a degree that no class of servants in America has yet reached. In our country the servant expects to become, in a few years, a "master" himself. Which system is preferable? I will not venture an answer.

Another thing that impressed itself upon me throughout England was the high regard that all classes have for law and order, and the ease and thoroughness with which everything is done. The Englishmen, I found, took plenty of time for eating, as for everything else. I am not sure if, in the long run, they do not accomplish as much or more than rushing, nervous Americans do.

My visit to England gave me a higher regard for the nobility than I had had. I had no idea that they were so generally loved and respected by the classes, nor that I any correct conception of how much time and money they spent in works of philanthropy, and how much real heart they put into this work. My impression had been that they merely spent money freely and had a "good time."

It was hard for me to get accustomed to speaking to English audiences. The average Englishman is so serious, and is so tremendously in earnest about everything, that when I told a story that would have made an American audience roar with laughter, the Englishmen simply looked me straight in the face without even cracking a smile.

When the Englishman takes you into his heart and friendship, he binds you there as with cords of steel, and I do not believe that there are many other friendships that are so lasting or so satisfactory. Perhaps I can illustrate this point in no better way than by relating the following incident. Mrs. Washington and I were invited to attend a reception given by the Duke and Duchess of Sutherland, at Stafford House--said to be the finest house in London; I may add that I believe the Duchess of Sutherland is said to be the most beautiful woman in England. There must have been at least three hundred persons at this reception. Twice during the evening the Duchess sought us out for a conversation, and she asked me to write her when we got home, and tell her more about the work at Tuskegee. This I did. When Christmas came we were surprised and delighted to receive her photograph with her autograph on it. The correspondence has continued, and we now feel that in the Duchess of Sutherland we have one of our warmest friends.

After three months in Europe we sailed from Southampton in the steamship St. Louis. On this steamer there was a fine library that had been presented to the ship by the citizens of St. Louis, Mo. In this library I found a life of Frederick Douglass, which I began reading. I became especially interested in Mr. Douglass's description of the way he was treated on shipboard during his first or second visit to England. In this description he told how he was not permitted to enter the cabin, but had to confine himself to the deck of the ship. A few minutes after I had finished reading this description I was waited on by a committee of ladies and gentlemen with the request that I deliver an address at a concert which was to begin the following evening. And yet there are people who are bold enough to say that race feeling in America is not growing less intense! At this concert the Hon. Benjamin B. Odell, Jr., the present governor of New York, presided. I was never given a more cordial hearing anywhere. A large proportion of the passengers with Southern people. After the concert some of the passengers proposed that a subscription be raised to help the work at Tuskegee, and the money to support several scholarships was the result.

While we were in Paris I was very pleasantly surprised to receive the following invitation from the citizens of West Virginia and of the city near which I had spent my boyhood days:--

Charleston, W. Va., May 16, 1899.

Professor Booker T. Washington, Paris, France:

Dear Sir: Many of the best citizens of West Virginia have united in liberal expressions of admiration and praise of your worth and work, and desire that on your return from Europe you should favour them with your presence and with the inspiration of your words. We must sincerely indorse this move, and on behalf of the citizens of Charleston extend to your our most cordial invitation to have you come to us, that we may honour you who have done so much by your life and work to honour us.

We are,

Very truly yours,

The Common Council of the City of Charleston,

By W. Herman Smith, Mayor.

This invitation from the City Council of Charleston was accompanied by the following:--

Professor Booker T. Washington, Paris, France:

Dear Sir: We, the citizens of Charleston and West Virginia, desire to express our pride in you and the splendid career that you have thus far accomplished, and ask that we be permitted to show our pride and interest in a substantial way.

[242]

Your recent visit to your old home in our midst awoke within us the keenest regret that we were not permitted to hear you and render some substantial aid to your work, before you left for Europe.

In view of the foregoing, we earnestly invite you to share the hospitality of our city upon your return from Europe, and give us the opportunity to hear you and put ourselves in touch with your work in a way that will be most gratifying to yourself, and that we may receive the inspiration of your words and presence.

An early reply to this invitation, with an indication of the time you may reach our city, will greatly oblige,

Yours very respectfully,

The Charleston Daily Gazette, The Daily Mail-Tribune; G.W. Atkinson, Governor; E.L. Boggs, Secretary to Governor; Wm. M.O. Dawson, Secretary of State; L.M. La Follette, Auditor; J.R. Trotter, Superintendent of Schools; E.W. Wilson, ex-Governor; W.A. MacCorkle, ex-Governor; John Q. Dickinson, President Kanawha Valley Bank; L. Prichard, President Charleston National Bank; Geo. S. Couch, President Kanawha National Bank; Ed. Reid, Cashier Kanawha National Bank; Geo. S. Laidley, Superintended City Schools; L.E. McWhorter, President Board of Education; Chas. K. Payne, wholesale merchant; and many others.

This invitation, coming as it did from the City Council, the state officers, and all the substantial citizens of both races of the community where I had spent my boyhood, and from which I had gone a few years before, unknown, in poverty and ignorance, in quest of an education, not only surprised me, but almost unmanned me. I could not understand what I had done to deserve it all.

I accepted the invitation, and at the appointed day was met at the railway station at Charleston by a committee headed by ex-Governor W.A. MacCorkle, and composed of men of both races. The public reception was held in the Opera-House at Charleston. The Governor of the state, the Hon. George W. Atkinson, presided, and an address of welcome was made by ex-Governor MacCorkle. A prominent part in the reception was taken by the coloured citizens. The Opera-House was filled with citizens of both races, and among the white people were many for whom I had worked when I was a boy. The next day Governor and Mrs. Atkinson gave me a public reception at the State House, which was attended by all classes.

Not long after this the coloured people in Atlanta, Georgia, gave me a reception at which the Governor of the state presided, and a similar reception was given me in New Orleans, which was presided over by the Mayor of the city. Invitations came from many other places which I was not able to accept.

CHAPTER 17
LAST WORDS

Before going to Europe some events came into my life which were great surprises to me. In fact, my whole life has largely been one of surprises. I believe that any man's life will be filled with constant, unexpected encouragements of this kind if he makes up his mind to do his level best each day of his life--that is, tries to make each day reach as nearly as possible the high-water mark of pure, unselfish, useful living. I pity the man, black or white, who has never experienced the joy and satisfaction that come to one by reason of an effort to assist in making some one else more useful and more happy.

Six months before he died, and nearly a year after he had been stricken with paralysis, General Armstrong expressed a wish to visit Tuskegee again before he passed away. Notwithstanding the fact that he had lost the use of his limbs to such an extent that he was practically helpless, his wish was gratified, and he was brought to Tuskegee. The owners of the Tuskegee Railroad, white men living in the town, offered to run a special train, without cost, out of the main station--Chehaw, five miles away--to meet him. He arrived on the school grounds about nine o'clock in the evening. Some one had suggested that we give the General a "pine-knot torchlight reception." This plan was carried out, and the moment that his carriage entered the school grounds he began passing between two lines of lighted and waving "fat pine" wood knots held by over a thousand students and teachers. The whole thing was so novel and surprising that the General was completely overcome with happiness. He remained a guest in my home for nearly two months, and, although almost wholly without the use of voice or limb, he spent nearly every hour in devising ways and means to help the South. Time and time again he said to me, during this visit, that it was not only the duty of the country to assist in elevating the Negro of the South, but the poor white man as well. At the end of his visit I resolved anew to devote myself more earnestly than ever to the cause which was so near his heart. I said that if a man in his condition was willing to think, work, and act, I should not be wanting in furthering in every possible way the wish of his heart.

The death of General Armstrong, a few weeks later, gave me the privilege of getting acquainted with one of the finest, most unselfish, and most attractive men that I have ever come in contact with. I refer to the Rev. Dr. Hollis B.

Frissell, now the Principal of the Hampton Institute, and General Armstrong's successor. Under the clear, strong, and almost perfect leadership of Dr. Frissell, Hampton has had a career of prosperity and usefulness that is all that the General could have wished for. It seems to be the constant effort of Dr. Frissell to hide his own great personality behind that of General Armstrong--to make himself of "no reputation" for the sake of the cause.

More than once I have been asked what was the greatest surprise that ever came to me. I have little hesitation in answering that question. It was the following letter, which came to me one Sunday morning when I was sitting on the veranda of my home at Tuskegee, surrounded by my wife and three children:--

Harvard University, Cambridge, May 28, 1896.

President Booker T. Washington,

My Dear Sir: Harvard University desired to confer on you at the approaching Commencement an honorary degree; but it is our custom to confer degrees only on gentlemen who are present. Our Commencement occurs this year on June 24, and your presence would be desirable from about noon till about five o'clock in the afternoon. Would it be possible for you to be in Cambridge on that day?

Believe me, with great regard,

Very truly yours,

Charles W. Eliot.

This was a recognition that had never in the slightest manner entered into my mind, and it was hard for me to realize that I was to be honoured by a degree from the oldest and most renowned university in America. As I sat upon my veranda, with this letter in my hand, tears came into my eyes. My whole former life--my life as a slave on the plantation, my work in the coal-mine, the times when I was without food and clothing, when I made my bed under a sidewalk, my struggles for an education, the trying days I had had at Tuskegee, days when I did not know where to turn for a dollar to continue the work there, the ostracism and sometimes oppression of my race,--all this passed before me and nearly overcame me.

I had never sought or cared for what the world calls fame. I have always looked upon fame as something to be used in accomplishing good. I have often said to my friends that if I can use whatever prominence may have come to me as an instrument with which to do good, I am content to have it. I care for it only as a means to be used for doing good, just as wealth may be used. The more I come into contact with wealthy people, the more I believe that they are growing in the direction of looking upon their money simply as an instrument which God has placed in their hand for doing good with. I never go to the office of Mr. John D. Rockefeller, who more than once has been generous to Tuskegee, without being reminded of this. The close, careful, and minute investigation that he always makes in order to be sure that every dollar that he gives will do the most good--an investigation that is just as searching as if he were investing money in a business enterprise--convinces me that the growth in this direction is most encouraging.

At nine o'clock, on the morning of June 24, I met President Eliot, the Board of Overseers of Harvard University, and the other guests, at the designated place on the university grounds, for the purpose of being escorted to Sanders Theatre, where the Commencement exercises were to be held and degrees conferred. Among others invited to be present for the purpose of receiving a degree at this time were General Nelson A. Miles, Dr. Bell, the inventor of the Bell telephone, Bishop Vincent, and the Rev. Minot J. Savage. We were placed in line immediately behind the President and the Board of Overseers, and directly afterward the Governor of Massachusetts, escorted by the Lancers, arrived and took his place in the line of march by the side of President Eliot. In the line there were also various other officers and professors, clad in cap and gown. In this order we marched to Sanders Theatre, where, after the usual Commencement exercises, came the conferring of the honorary degrees. This, it seems, is always considered the most interesting feature at Harvard. It is not known, until the individuals appear, upon whom the honorary degrees are to be conferred, and those receiving these honours are cheered by the students and others in proportion to their popularity. During the conferring of the degrees excitement and enthusiasm are at the highest pitch.

When my name was called, I rose, and President Eliot, in beautiful and strong English, conferred upon me the degree of Master of Arts. After these exercises were over, those who had received honorary degrees were invited to lunch with the President. After the lunch we were formed in line again, and were escorted by the Marshal of the day, who that year happened to be Bishop William Lawrence, through the grounds, where, at different points, those who had been honoured were called by name and received the Harvard yell. This march ended at Memorial Hall, where the alumni dinner was served. To see over a thousand strong men, representing all that is best in State, Church, business, and education, with the glow and enthusiasm of college loyalty and college pride,--which has, I think, a peculiar Harvard flavour,--is a sight that does not easily fade from memory.

Among the speakers after dinner were President Eliot, Governor Roger Wolcott, General Miles, Dr. Minot J. Savage, the Hon. Henry Cabot Lodge, and myself. When I was called upon, I said, among other things:--

It would in some measure relieve my embarrassment if I could, even in a slight degree, feel myself worthy of the great honour which you do me to-day. Why you have called me from the Black Belt of the South, from among my humble people, to share in the honours of this occasion, is not for me to explain; and yet it may not be inappropriate for me to suggest that it seems to me that one of the most vital questions that touch our American life is how to bring the strong, wealthy, and learned into helpful touch with the poorest, most ignorant, and humblest, and at the same time make one appreciate the vitalizing, strengthening influence of the other. How shall we make the mansion on yon Beacon Street feel and see the need of the spirits in the lowliest cabin in Alabama cotton-fields or Louisiana sugar-bottoms? This problem Harvard University is solving, not by bringing itself down, but by bringing the masses up.

* * * * * * *

If my life in the past has meant anything in the lifting up of my people and the bringing about of better relations between your race and mine, I assure you from this day it will mean doubly more. In the economy of God there is but one standard by which an individual can succeed--there is but one for a race. This country demands that every race shall measure itself by the American standard. By it a race must rise or fall, succeed or fail, and in the last analysis mere sentiment counts for little.

During the next half-century and more, my race must continue passing through the severe American crucible. We are to be tested in our patience, our forbearance, our perseverance, our power to endure wrong, to withstand temptations, to economize, to acquire and use skill; in our ability to compete, to succeed in commerce, to disregard the superficial for the real, the appearance for the substance, to be great and yet small, learned and yet simple, high and yet the servant of all.

As this was the first time that a New England university had conferred an honorary degree upon a Negro, it was the occasion of much newspaper comment throughout the country. A correspondent of a New York Paper said:--

When the name of Booker T. Washington was called, and he arose to acknowledge and accept, there was such an outburst of applause as greeted no other name except that of the popular soldier patriot, General Miles. The

[248]

applause was not studied and stiff, sympathetic and condoling; it was enthusiasm and admiration. Every part of the audience from pit to gallery joined in, and a glow covered the cheeks of those around me, proving sincere appreciation of the rising struggle of an ex-slave and the work he has accomplished for his race.

A Boston paper said, editorially:--

In conferring the honorary degree of Master of Arts upon the Principal of Tuskegee Institute, Harvard University has honoured itself as well as the object of this distinction. The work which Professor Booker T. Washington has accomplished for the education, good citizenship, and popular enlightenment in his chosen field of labour in the South entitles him to rank with our national benefactors. The university which can claim him on its list of sons, whether in regular course or honoris causa, may be proud.

It has been mentioned that Mr. Washington is the first of his race to receive an honorary degree from a New England university. This, in itself, is a distinction. But the degree was not conferred because Mr. Washington is a coloured man, or because he was born in slavery, but because he has shown, by his work for the elevation of the people of the Black Belt of the South, a genius and a broad humanity which count for greatness in any man, whether his skin be white or black.

Another Boston paper said:--

It is Harvard which, first among New England colleges, confers an honorary degree upon a black man. No one who has followed the history of Tuskegee and its work can fail to admire the courage, persistence, and splendid common sense of Booker T. Washington.

Well may Harvard honour the ex-slave, the value of whose services, alike to his race and country, only the future can estimate.

The correspondent of the New York Times wrote:--

All the speeches were enthusiastically received, but the coloured man carried off the oratorical honours, and the applause which broke out when he had finished was vociferous and long-continued.

Soon after I began work at Tuskegee I formed a resolution, in the secret of my heart, that I would try to build up a school that would be of so much service to the country that the President of the United States would one day come to see it. This was, I confess, rather a bold resolution, and for a number of years I kept it hidden in my own thoughts, not daring to share it with any one.

In November, 1897, I made the first move in this direction, and that was in securing a visit from a member of President McKinley's Cabinet, the Hon. James Wilson, Secretary of Agriculture. He came to deliver an address at the formal opening of the Slater-Armstrong Agricultural Building, our first large building to be used for the purpose of giving training to our students in agriculture and kindred branches.

In the fall of 1898 I heard that President McKinley was likely to visit Atlanta, Georgia, for the purpose of taking part in the Peace Jubilee exercises to be held there to commemorate the successful close of the Spanish-American war. At this time I had been hard at work, together with our teachers, for eighteen years, trying to build up a school that we thought would be of service to the Nation, and I determined to make a direct effort to secure a visit from the President and his Cabinet. I went to Washington, and I was not long in the city before I found my way to the White House. When I got there I found the waiting rooms full of people, and my heart began to sink, for I feared there would not be much chance of my seeing the President that day, if at all. But, at any rate, I got an opportunity to see Mr. J. Addison Porter, the secretary to the President, and explained to him my mission. Mr. Porter kindly sent my card directly to the President, and in a few minutes word came from Mr. McKinley that he would see me.

How any man can see so many people of all kinds, with all kinds of errands, and do so much hard work, and still keep himself calm, patient, and fresh for each visitor in the way that President McKinley does, I cannot understand. When I saw the President he kindly thanked me for the work which we were doing at Tuskegee for the interests of the country. I then told him, briefly, the object of my visit. I impressed upon him the fact that a visit from the Chief Executive of the Nation would not only encourage our students and teachers, but would help the entire race. He seemed interested, but did not make a promise to go to Tuskegee, for the reason that his plans about going to Atlanta were not then fully made; but he asked me to call the matter to his attention a few weeks later.

By the middle of the following month the President had definitely decided to attend the Peace Jubilee at Atlanta. I went to Washington again and saw him, with a view of getting him to extend his trip to Tuskegee. On this second visit Mr. Charles W. Hare, a prominent white citizen of Tuskegee, kindly volunteered to accompany me, to reenforce my invitation with one from the white people of Tuskegee and the vicinity.

Just previous to my going to Washington the second time, the country had been excited, and the coloured people greatly depressed, because of several severe race riots which had occurred at different points in the South. As soon as I saw the President, I perceived that his heart was greatly burdened by reason of these race disturbances. Although there were many people waiting to see him, he detained me for some time, discussing the condition and prospects of the race. He remarked several times that he was determined to show his interest and faith in the race, not merely in words, but by acts. When I told him that I thought that at that time scarcely anything would go father in giving hope and encouragement to the race than the fact that the President of the Nation would be willing to travel one hundred and forty miles out of his way to spend a day at a Negro institution, he seemed deeply impressed.

While I was with the President, a white citizen of Atlanta, a Democrat and an ex-slaveholder, came into the room, and the President asked his opinion as to the wisdom of his going to Tuskegee. Without hesitation the Atlanta man replied that it was the proper thing for him to do. This opinion was reenforced by that friend of the race, Dr. J.L.M. Curry. The President promised that he would visit our school on the 16th of December.

When it became known that the President was going to visit our school, the white citizens of the town of Tuskegee--a mile distant from the school--were as much pleased as were our students and teachers. The white people of this town, including both men and women, began arranging to decorate the town, and to form themselves into committees for the purpose of cooperating with the officers of our school in order that the distinguished visitor might have a fitting reception. I think I never realized before this how much the white people of Tuskegee and vicinity thought of our institution. During the days when we were preparing for the President's reception, dozens of these people came to me and said that, while they did not want to push themselves into prominence, if there was anything they could do to help, or to relieve me personally, I had but to intimate it and they would be only too glad to assist. In fact, the thing that touched me almost as deeply as the visit of the President itself was the deep pride which all classes of citizens in Alabama seemed to take in our work.

The morning of December 16th brought to the little city of Tuskegee such a crowd as it had never seen before. With the President came Mrs. McKinley and all of the Cabinet officers but one; and most of them brought their wives or some members of their families. Several prominent generals came, including General Shafter and General Joseph Wheeler, who were recently returned from the Spanish-American war. There was also a host of newspaper correspondents. The Alabama Legislature was in session in Montgomery at this time. This body passed a resolution to adjourn for the purpose of visited

Tuskegee. Just before the arrival of the President's party the Legislature arrived, headed by the governor and other state officials.

The citizens of Tuskegee had decorated the town from the station to the school in a generous manner. In order to economize in the matter of time, we arranged to have the whole school pass in review before the President. Each student carried a stalk of sugar-cane with some open bolls of cotton fastened to the end of it. Following the students the work of all departments of the school passed in review, displayed on "floats" drawn by horses, mules, and oxen. On these floats we tried to exhibit not only the present work of the school, but to show the contrasts between the old methods of doing things and the new. As an example, we showed the old method of dairying in contrast with the improved methods, the old methods of tilling the soil in contrast with the new, the old methods of cooking and housekeeping in contrast with the new. These floats consumed an hour and a half of time in passing.

In his address in our large, new chapel, which the students had recently completed, the President said, among other things:--

To meet you under such pleasant auspices and to have the opportunity of a personal observation of your work is indeed most gratifying. The Tuskegee Normal and Industrial Institute is ideal in its conception, and has already a large and growing reputation in the country, and is not unknown abroad. I congratulate all who are associated in this undertaking for the good work which it is doing in the education of its students to lead lives of honour and usefulness, thus exalting the race for which it was established.

Nowhere, I think, could a more delightful location have been chosen for this unique educational experiment, which has attracted the attention and won the support even of conservative philanthropists in all sections of the country.

To speak of Tuskegee without paying special tribute to Booker T. Washington's genius and perseverance would be impossible. The inception of this noble enterprise was his, and he deserves high credit for it. His was the enthusiasm and enterprise which made its steady progress possible and established in the institution its present high standard of accomplishment. He has won a worthy reputation as one of the great leaders of his race, widely known and much respected at home and abroad as an accomplished educator, a great orator, and a true philanthropist.

The Hon. John D. Long, the Secretary of the Navy, said in part:--

I cannot make a speech to-day. My heart is too full--full of hope, admiration, and pride for my countrymen of both sections and both colours. I am filled with gratitude and admiration for your work, and from this time forward I shall have absolute confidence in your progress and in the solution of the problem in which you are engaged.

The problem, I say, has been solved. A picture has been presented to-day which should be put upon canvas with the pictures of Washington and Lincoln, and transmitted to future time and generations--a picture which the press of the country should spread broadcast over the land, a most dramatic picture, and that picture is this: The President of the United States standing on this platform; on one side the Governor of Alabama, on the other, completing the trinity, a representative of a race only a few years ago in bondage, the coloured President of the Tuskegee Normal and Industrial Institute.

God bless the President under whose majesty such a scene as that is presented to the American people. God bless the state of Alabama, which is showing that it can deal with this problem for itself. God bless the orator, philanthropist, and disciple of the Great Master--who, if he were on earth, would be doing the same work--Booker T. Washington.

Postmaster General Smith closed the address which he made with these words:--

We have witnessed many spectacles within the last few days. We have seen the magnificent grandeur and the magnificent achievements of one of the great metropolitan cities of the South. We have seen heroes of the war pass by in procession. We have seen floral parades. But I am sure my colleagues will agree with me in saying that we have witnessed no spectacle more impressive and more encouraging, more inspiring for our future, than that which we have witnessed here this morning.

Some days after the President returned to Washington I received the letter which follows:--

Executive Mansion, Washington, Dec. 23, 1899.

Dear Sir: By this mail I take pleasure in sending you engrossed copies of the souvenir of the visit of the President to your institution. These sheets bear the autographs of the President and the members of the Cabinet who accompanied him on the trip. Let me take this opportunity of congratulating you most heartily and sincerely upon the great success of the exercises provided for and entertainment furnished us under your auspices during our visit to Tuskegee. Every feature of the programme was perfectly executed and was viewed or participated in with the heartiest satisfaction by every visitor present. The unique exhibition which you gave of your pupils engaged in their industrial

[253]

vocations was not only artistic but thoroughly impressive. The tribute paid by the President and his Cabinet to your work was none too high, and forms a most encouraging augury, I think, for the future prosperity of your institution. I cannot close without assuring you that the modesty shown by yourself in the exercises was most favourably commented upon by all the members of our party.

With best wishes for the continued advance of your most useful and patriotic undertaking, kind personal regards, and the compliments of the season, believe me, always,

Very sincerely yours,

John Addison Porter,

Secretary to the President.

To President Booker T. Washington, Tuskegee Normal and Industrial Institute, Tuskegee, Ala.

Twenty years have now passed since I made the first humble effort at Tuskegee, in a broken-down shanty and an old hen-house, without owning a dollar's worth of property, and with but one teacher and thirty students. At the present time the institution owns twenty-three hundred acres of land, one thousand of which are under cultivation each year, entirely by student labour. There are now upon the grounds, counting large and small, sixty-six buildings; and all except four of these have been almost wholly erected by the labour of our students. While the students are at work upon the land and in erecting buildings, they are taught, by competent instructors, the latest methods of agriculture and the trades connected with building.

There are in constant operation at the school, in connection with thorough academic and religious training, thirty industrial departments. All of these teach industries at which our men and women can find immediate employment as soon as they leave the institution. The only difficulty now is that the demand for our graduates from both white and black people in the South is so great that we cannot supply more than one-half the persons for whom applications come to us. Neither have we the buildings nor the money for current expenses to enable us to admit to the school more than one-half the young men and women who apply to us for admission.

In our industrial teaching we keep three things in mind: first, that the student shall be so educated that he shall be enabled to meet conditions as they exist now, in the part of the South where he lives--in a word, to be able to do the

[254]

thing which the world wants done; second, that every student who graduates from the school shall have enough skill, coupled with intelligence and moral character, to enable him to make a living for himself and others; third, to send every graduate out feeling and knowing that labour is dignified and beautiful--to make each one love labour instead of trying to escape it. In addition to the agricultural training which we give to young men, and the training given to our girls in all the usual domestic employments, we now train a number of girls in agriculture each year. These girls are taught gardening, fruit-growing, dairying, bee-culture, and poultry-raising.

While the institution is in no sense denominational, we have a department known as the Phelps Hall Bible Training School, in which a number of students are prepared for the ministry and other forms of Christian work, especially work in the country districts. What is equally important, each one of the students works . . . each day at some industry, in order to get skill and the love of work, so that when he goes out from the institution he is prepared to set the people with whom he goes to labour a proper example in the matter of industry.

The value of our property is now over $700,000. If we add to this our endowment fund, which at present is $1,000,000, the value of the total property is now $1,700,000. Aside from the need for more buildings and for money for current expenses, the endowment fund should be increased to at least $3,000,000. The annual current expenses are now about $150,000. The greater part of this I collect each year by going from door to door and from house to house. All of our property is free from mortgage, and is deeded to an undenominational board of trustees who have the control of the institution.

From thirty students the number has grown to fourteen hundred, coming from twenty-seven states and territories, from Africa, Cuba, Porto Rico, Jamaica, and other foreign countries. In our departments there are one hundred and ten officers and instructors; and if we add the families of our instructors, we have a constant population upon our grounds of not far from seventeen hundred people.

I have often been asked how we keep so large a body of people together, and at the same time keep them out of mischief. There are two answers: that the men and women who come to us for an education are in earnest; and that everybody is kept busy. The following outline of our daily work will testify to this:--

5 a.m., rising bell; 5.50 a.m., warning breakfast bell; 6 a.m., breakfast bell; 6.20 a.m., breakfast over; 6.20 to 6.50 a.m., rooms are cleaned; 6.50, work bell; 7.30, morning study hours; 8.20, morning school bell; 8.25, inspection of young

men's toilet in ranks; 8.40, devotional exercises in chapel; 8.55, "five minutes with the daily news;" 9 a.m., class work begins; 12, class work closes; 12.15 p.m., dinner; 1 p.m., work bell; 1.30 p.m., class work begins; 3.30 p.m., class work ends; 5.30 p.m., bell to "knock off" work; 6 p.m., supper; 7.10 p.m., evening prayers; 7.30 p.m., evening study hours; 8.45 p.m., evening study hour closes; 9.20 p.m., warning retiring bell; 9.30 p.m., retiring bell.

We try to keep constantly in mind the fact that the worth of the school is to be judged by its graduates. Counting those who have finished the full course, together with those who have taken enough training to enable them to do reasonably good work, we can safely say that at least six thousand men and women from Tuskegee are now at work in different parts of the South; men and women who, by their own example or by direct efforts, are showing the masses of our race now to improve their material, educational, and moral and religious life. What is equally important, they are exhibiting a degree of common sense and self-control which is causing better relations to exist between the races, and is causing the Southern white man to learn to believe in the value of educating the men and women of my race. Aside from this, there is the influence that is constantly being exerted through the mothers' meeting and the plantation work conducted by Mrs. Washington.

Wherever our graduates go, the changes which soon begin to appear in the buying of land, improving homes, saving money, in education, and in high moral characters are remarkable. Whole communities are fast being revolutionized through the instrumentality of these men and women.

Ten years ago I organized at Tuskegee the first Negro Conference. This is an annual gathering which now brings to the school eight or nine hundred representative men and women of the race, who come to spend a day in finding out what the actual industrial, mental, and moral conditions of the people are, and in forming plans for improvement. Out from this central Negro Conference at Tuskegee have grown numerous state an local conferences which are doing the same kind of work. As a result of the influence of these gatherings, one delegate reported at the last annual meeting that ten families in his community had bought and paid for homes. On the day following the annual Negro Conference, there is the "Workers' Conference." This is composed of officers and teachers who are engaged in educational work in the larger institutions in the South. The Negro Conference furnishes a rare opportunity for these workers to study the real condition of the rank and file of the people.

In the summer of 1900, with the assistance of such prominent coloured men as Mr. T. Thomas Fortune, who has always upheld my hands in every effort, I organized the National Negro Business League, which held its first meeting in Boston, and brought together for the first time a large number of the coloured men who are engaged in various lines of trade or business in different parts of the United States. Thirty states were represented at our first meeting. Out of this national meeting grew state and local business leagues.

In addition to looking after the executive side of the work at Tuskegee, and raising the greater part of the money for the support of the school, I cannot seem to escape the duty of answering at least a part of the calls which come to me unsought to address Southern white audiences and audiences of my own race, as well as frequent gatherings in the North. As to how much of my time is spent in this way, the following clipping from a Buffalo (N.Y.) paper will tell. This has reference to an occasion when I spoke before the National Educational Association in that city.

Booker T. Washington, the foremost educator among the coloured people of the world, was a very busy man from the time he arrived in the city the other night from the West and registered at the Iroquois. He had hardly removed the stains of travel when it was time to partake of supper. Then he held a public levee in the parlours of the Iroquois until eight o'clock. During that time he was greeted by over two hundred eminent teachers and educators from all parts of the United States. Shortly after eight o'clock he was driven in a carriage to Music Hall, and in one hour and a half he made two ringing addresses, to as many as five thousand people, on Negro education. Then Mr. Washington was taken in charge by a delegation of coloured citizens, headed by the Rev. Mr. Watkins, and hustled off to a small informal reception, arranged in honour of the visitor by the people of his race.

Nor can I, in addition to making these addresses, escape the duty of calling the attention of the South and of the country in general, through the medium of the press, to matters that pertain to the interests of both races. This, for example, I have done in regard to the evil habit of lynching. When the Louisiana State Constitutional Convention was in session, I wrote an open letter to that body pleading for justice for the race. In all such efforts I have received warm and hearty support from the Southern newspapers, as well as from those in all other parts of the country.

Despite superficial and temporary signs which might lead one to entertain a contrary opinion, there was never a time when I felt more hopeful for the race than I do at the present. The great human law that in the end recognizes and rewards merit is everlasting and universal. The outside world does not know, neither can it appreciate, the struggle that is constantly going on in the hearts of both the Southern white people and their former slaves to free themselves from racial prejudice; and while both races are thus struggling they should have the sympathy, the support, and the forbearance of the rest of the world.

As I write the closing words of this autobiography I find myself--not by design--in the city of Richmond, Virginia: the city which only a few decades ago was the capital of the Southern Confederacy, and where, about twenty-five years ago, because of my poverty I slept night after night under a sidewalk.

This time I am in Richmond as the guest of the coloured people of the city; and came at their request to deliver an address last night to both races in the Academy of Music, the largest and finest audience room in the city. This was the first time that the coloured people had ever been permitted to use this hall. The day before I came, the City Council passed a vote to attend the meeting in a body to hear me speak. The state Legislature, including the House of Delegates and the Senate, also passed a unanimous vote to attend in a body. In the presence of hundreds of coloured people, many distinguished white citizens, the City Council, the state Legislature, and state officials, I delivered my message, which was one of hope and cheer; and from the bottom of my heart I thanked both races for this welcome back to the state that gave me birth.

THE FUTURE OF
THE AMERICAN NEGRO

Booker T. Washington

[259]

PREFACE

In giving this volume to the public, I deem it fair to say that I have yielded to the oft-repeated requests that I put in some more definite and permanent form the ideas regarding the Negro and his future which I have expressed many times on the public platform and through the public press and magazines.

I make grateful acknowledgment to the "Atlantic Monthly" and "Appleton's Popular Science Monthly" for their kindness in granting permission for the use of some part of articles which I have at various times contributed to their columns.

BOOKER T. WASHINGTON.

Tuskegee Normal and Industrial Institute,
Tuskegee, Ala., October 1, 1899.

CONTENTS

CHAPTER 1

In this volume I shall not attempt to give the origin and history of the Negro race either in Africa or in America. My attempt is to deal only with conditions that now exist and bear a relation to the Negro in America and that are likely to exist in the future. In discussing the Negro, it is always to be borne in mind that, unlike all the other inhabitants of America, he came here without his own consent; in fact, was compelled to leave his own country and become a part of another through physical force. It should also be borne in mind, in our efforts to change and improve the present condition of the Negro, that we are dealing with a race which had little necessity to labour in its native country. After being brought to America, the Negroes were forced to labour for about 250 years under circumstances which were calculated not to inspire them with love and respect for labour. This constitutes a part of the reason why I insist that it is necessary to emphasise the matter of industrial education as a means of giving the black man the foundation of a civilisation upon which he will grow and prosper. When I speak of industrial education, however, I wish it always understood that I mean, as did General Armstrong, the founder of the Hampton Institute, for thorough academic and religious training to go side by side with industrial training. Mere training of the hand without the culture of brain and heart would mean little.

The first slaves were brought into this country by the Dutch in 1619, and were landed at Jamestown, Virginia. The first cargo consisted of twenty. The census taken in 1890 shows that these twenty slaves had increased to 7,638,360. About 6,353,341 of this number were residing in the Southern States, and 1,283,029 were scattered throughout the Northern and Western States. I think I am pretty safe in predicting that the census to be taken in 1900 will show that there are not far from ten millions of people of African descent in the United States. The great majority of these, of course, reside in the Southern States. The problem is how to make these millions of Negroes self-supporting, intelligent, economical and valuable citizens, as well as how to bring about proper relations between them and the white citizens among whom they live. This is the question upon which I shall try to throw some light in the chapters which follow.

When the Negroes were first brought to America, they were owned by white people in all sections of this country, as is well known,—in the New England, the Middle, and in the Southern States. It was soon found, however, that slave labour was not remunerative in the Northern States, and for that reason by far the greater proportion of the slaves were held in the Southern States, where their labour in raising cotton, rice, and sugar-cane was more productive. The growth of the slave population in America was constant and rapid. Beginning, as I have stated, with fourteen, in 1619, the number increased at such a rate that the total number of Negroes in America in 1800 was 1,001,463. This number increased by 1860 to 3,950,000. A few people predicted that freedom would result disastrously to the Negro, as far as numerical increase was concerned; but so far the census figures have failed to bear out this prediction. On the other hand, the census of 1890 shows that the Negro population had increased from 3,950,000 in 1860 to 7,638,260 twenty-five years after the war. It is my opinion that the rate of increase in the future will be still greater than it has been from the close of the war of the Rebellion up to the present time, for the reason that the very sudden changes which took place in the life of the Negro, because of having his freedom, plunged him into many excesses that were detrimental to his physical well-being. Of course, freedom found him unprepared in clothing, in shelter and in knowledge of how to care for his body. During slavery the slave mother had little control of her own children, and did not therefore have the practice and experience of rearing children in a suitable manner. Now that the Negro is being taught in thousands of schools how to take care of his body, and in thousands of homes mothers are learning how to control their children, I believe that the rate of increase, as I have stated, will be still greater than it has been in the past. In too many cases the Negro had the idea that freedom meant merely license to do as he pleased, to work or not to work; but this erroneous idea is more and more disappearing, by reason of the education in the right direction which the Negro is constantly receiving.

During the four years that the Civil War lasted, the greater proportion of the Negroes remained in the South, and worked faithfully for the support of their masters' families, who, as a general rule, were away in the war. The self-control which the Negro exhibited during the war marks, it seems to me, one of the most important chapters in the history of the race. Notwithstanding he knew that his master was away from home, fighting a battle which, if successful, would result in his continued enslavement, yet he worked faithfully for the support of the master's family. If the Negro had yielded to the temptation and suggestion to use the torch or dagger in an attempt to destroy his master's property and family, the result would have been that the war would have been ended quickly; for the master would have returned from the battlefield to protect and defend his property and family. But the Negro to the last was faithful to the trust that had been thrust upon him, and during the four years of war in which the male members of the family were absent from their homes there is not a single instance recorded where he in any way attempted to outrage the family of the master or in any way to injure his property.

Not only is this true, but all through the years of preparation for the war and during the war itself the Negro showed himself to be an uncompromising friend to the Union. In fact, of all the charges brought against him, there is scarcely a single instance where one has been charged with being a traitor to his country. This has been true whether he has been in a state of slavery or in a state of freedom.

From 1865 to 1876 constituted what perhaps may be termed the days of Reconstruction. This was the period when the Southern States which had withdrawn from the Union were making an effort to reinstate themselves and to establish a permanent system of State government. At the close of the war both the Southern white man and the Negro found themselves in the midst of poverty. The ex-master returned from the war to find his slave property gone, his farms and other industries in a state of collapse, and the whole industrial or economic system upon which he had depended for years entirely disorganised. As we review calmly and dispassionately the period of reconstruction, we must use a great deal of sympathy and generosity. The weak point, to my mind, in the reconstruction era was that no strong force was brought to bear in the direction of preparing the Negro to become an intelligent, reliable citizen and voter. The main effort seems to have been in the direction of controlling his vote for the time being, regardless of future interests. I hardly believe that any race of people with similar preparation and similar surroundings would have acted more wisely or very differently from the way the Negro acted during the period of reconstruction.

Without experience, without preparation, and in most cases without ordinary intelligence, he was encouraged to leave the field and shop and enter politics. That under such circumstances he should have made mistakes is very natural. I do not believe that the Negro was so much at fault for entering so largely into politics, and for the mistakes that were made in too many cases, as were the unscrupulous white leaders who got the Negro's confidence and controlled his vote to further their own ends, regardless, in many cases, of the permanent welfare of the Negro. I have always considered it unfortunate that the Southern white man did not make more of an effort during the period of reconstruction to get the confidence and sympathy of the Negro, and thus have been able to keep him in close touch and sympathy in politics. It was also unfortunate that the Negro was so completely alienated from the Southern white man in all political matters. I think it would have been better for all concerned if, immediately after the close of the war, an educational and property qualification for the exercise of the franchise had been prescribed that would have applied fairly and squarely to both races, and, also, if, in educating the Negro, greater stress had been put upon training him along the lines of industry for which his services were in the greatest demand in the South. In a word, too much stress was placed upon the mere matter of voting and holding political office rather than upon the preparation for the highest citizenship. In saying what I have, I do not mean to convey the impression that the whole period of reconstruction was barren of fruitful results. While it is not a very encouraging chapter in the history of our country, I believe that this period did serve to point out many weak points in our effort to elevate the Negro, and that we are now taking advantage of the mistakes that were made. The period of reconstruction served at least to show the world that with proper preparation and with a sufficient foundation the Negro possesses the elements out of which men of the highest character and usefulness can be developed. I might name several characters who were brought before the world by reason of the reconstruction period. I give one as an example of others: Hon. Blanche K. Bruce, who had been a slave, but who held many honourable positions in the State of Mississippi, including an election to the United States Senate, where he served a full term; later he was twice appointed Register of the United States Treasury. In all these positions Mr. Bruce gave the greatest satisfaction, and not a single whisper of dishonesty or incompetency has ever been heard against him. During the period of his public life he was brought into active and daily contact with Northern and Southern white people, all of whom speak of him in the highest measure of respect and confidence.

What the Negro wants and what the country wants to do is to take advantage of all the lessons that were taught during the days of reconstruction, and apply these lessons bravely, honestly, in laying the foundation upon which the Negro can stand in the future and make himself a useful, honourable, and desirable citizen, whether he has his residence in the North, the South, or the West.

CHAPTER 2

In order that the reader may understand me and why I lay so much stress upon the importance of pushing the doctrine of industrial education for the Negro, it is necessary, first of all, to review the condition of affairs at the present time in the Southern States. For years I have had something of an opportunity to study the Negro at first-hand; and I feel that I know him pretty well,—him and his needs, his failures and his successes, his desires and the likelihood of their fulfilment. I have studied him and his relations with his white neighbours, and striven to find how these relations may be made more conducive to the general peace and welfare both of the South and of the country at large.

In the Southern part of the United States there are twenty-two millions of people who are bound to the fifty millions of the North by ties which neither can tear asunder if they would. The most intelligent in a New York community has his intelligence darkened by the ignorance of a fellow-citizen in the Mississippi bottoms. The most wealthy in New York City would be more wealthy but for the poverty of a fellow-being in the Carolina rice swamps. The most moral and religious men in Massachusetts have their religion and morality modified by the degradation of the man in the South whose religion is a mere matter of form or of emotionalism. The vote of the man in Maine that is cast for the highest and purest form of government is largely neutralised by the vote of the man in Louisiana whose ballot is stolen or cast in ignorance. Therefore, when the South is ignorant, the North is ignorant; when the South is poor, the North is poor; when the South commits crime, the nation commits crime. For the citizens of the North there is no escape; they must help raise the character of the civilisation in the South, or theirs will be lowered. No member of the white race in any part of the country can harm the weakest or meanest member of the black race without the proudest and bluest blood of the nation being degraded.

It seems to me that there never was a time in the history of the country when those interested in education should the more earnestly consider to what extent the mere acquiring of the ability to read and write, the mere acquisition of a knowledge of literature and science, makes men producers, lovers of labour, independent, honest, unselfish, and, above all, good. Call education by what name you please, if it fails to bring about these results among the masses, it falls short of its highest end. The science, the art, the literature, that fails to reach down and bring the humblest up to the enjoyment of the fullest blessings of our government, is weak, no matter how costly the buildings or apparatus used or how modern the methods of instruction employed. The study of arithmetic that does not result in making men conscientious in receiving and counting the ballots of their fellow-men is faulty. The study of art that does not result in making the strong less willing to oppress the weak means little. How I wish that from the most cultured and highly endowed university in the great North to the humblest log cabin school-house in Alabama, we could burn, as it were, into the hearts and heads of all that usefulness, that service to our brother, is the supreme end of education. Putting the thought more directly as it applies to conditions in the South, can you make the intelligence of the North affect the South in the same ratio that the ignorance of the South affects the North? Let us take a not improbable case: A great national case is to be decided, one that involves peace or war, the honour or dishonour of our nation,—yea, the very existence of the government. The North and West are divided. There are five million votes to be cast in the South; and, of this number, one-half are ignorant. Not only are one-half the voters ignorant; but, because of the ignorant votes they cast, corruption and dishonesty in a dozen forms have crept into the exercise of the political franchise to such an extent that the conscience of the intelligent class is seared in its attempts to defeat the will of the ignorant voters. Here, then, you have on the one hand an ignorant vote, on the other an intelligent vote minus a conscience. The time may not be far off when to this kind of jury we shall have to look for the votes which shall decide in a large measure the destiny of our democratic institutions.

When a great national calamity stares us in the face, we are, I fear, too much given to depending on a short "campaign of education" to do on the hustings what should have been accomplished in the school.

With this idea in view, let us examine with more care the condition of civilisation in the South, and the work to be done there before all classes will be fit for the high duties of citizenship. In reference to the Negro race, I am confronted with some embarrassment at the outset, because of the various and conflicting opinions as to what is to be its final place in our economic and political life.

[271]

Within the last thirty years—and, I might add, within the last three months,—it has been proven by eminent authority that the Negro is increasing in numbers so fast that it is only a question of a few years before he will far outnumber the white race in the South, and it has also been proven that the Negro is fast dying out, and it is only a question of a few years before he will have completely disappeared. It has also been proven that education helps the Negro and that education hurts him, that he is fast leaving the South and taking up his residence in the North and West, and that his tendency is to drift toward the low lands of the Mississippi bottoms. It has been proven that education unfits the Negro for work and that education makes him more valuable as a labourer, that he is our greatest criminal and that he is our most law-abiding citizen. In the midst of these conflicting opinions, it is hard to hit upon the truth.

But, also, in the midst of this confusion, there are a few things of which I am certain,—things which furnish a basis for thought and action. I know that whether the Negroes are increasing or decreasing, whether they are growing better or worse, whether they are valuable or valueless, that a few years ago some fourteen of them were brought into this country, and that now those fourteen are nearly ten millions. I know that, whether in slavery or freedom, they have always been loyal to the Stars and Stripes, that no school-house has been opened for them that has not been filled, that the 2,000,000 ballots that they have the right to cast are as potent for weal or woe as an equal number cast by the wisest and most influential men in America. I know that wherever Negro life touches the life of the nation it helps or it hinders, that wherever the life of the white race touches the black it makes it stronger or weaker. Further, I know that almost every other race that has tried to look the white man in the face has disappeared. I know, despite all the conflicting opinions, and with a full knowledge of all the Negroes' weaknesses, that only a few centuries ago they went into slavery in this country pagans, that they came out Christians; they went into slavery as so much property, they came out American citizens; they went into slavery without a language, they came out speaking the proud Anglo-Saxon tongue; they went into slavery with the chains clanking about their wrists, they came out with the American ballot in their hands.

I submit it to the candid and sober judgment of all men, if a race that is capable of such a test, such a transformation, is not worth saving and making a part, in reality as well as in name, of our democratic government. That the Negro may be fitted for the fullest enjoyment of the privileges and responsibilities of our citizenship, it is important that the nation be honest and candid with him, whether honesty and candour for the time being pleases or displeases him. It is with an ignorant race as it is with a child: it craves at first the superficial, the ornamental signs of progress rather than the reality. The ignorant race is tempted to jump, at one bound, to the position that it has required years of hard struggle for others to reach.

It seems to me that, as a general thing, the temptation in the past in educational and missionary work has been to do for the new people that which was done a thousand years ago, or that which is being done for a people a thousand miles away, without making a careful study of the needs and conditions of the people whom it is designed to help. The temptation is to run all people through a certain educational mould, regardless of the condition of the subject or the end to be accomplished. This has been the case too often in the South in the past, I am sure. Men have tried to use, with these simple people just freed from slavery and with no past, no inherited traditions of learning, the same methods of education which they have used in New England, with all its inherited traditions and desires. The Negro is behind the white man because he has not had the same chance, and not from any inherent difference in his nature and desires. What the race accomplishes in these first fifty years of freedom will at the end of these years, in a large measure, constitute its past. It is, indeed, a responsibility that rests upon this nation,—the foundation laying for a people of its past, present, and future at one and the same time.

One of the weakest points in connection with the present development of the race is that so many get the idea that the mere filling of the head with a knowledge of mathematics, the sciences, and literature, means success in life. Let it be understood, in every corner of the South, among the Negro youth at least, that knowledge will benefit little except as it is harnessed, except as its power is pointed in a direction that will bear upon the present needs and condition of the race. There is in the heads of the Negro youth of the South enough general and floating knowledge of chemistry, of botany, of zoölogy, of geology, of mechanics, of electricity, of mathematics, to reconstruct and develop a large part of the agricultural, mechanical, and domestic life of the race. But how much of it is brought to a focus along lines of practical work? In cities of the South like Atlanta, how many coloured mechanical engineers are there? or how many machinists? how many civil engineers? how many architects? how many house decorators? In the whole State of Georgia, where

[273]

eighty per cent. of the coloured people depend upon agriculture, how many men are there who are well grounded in the principles and practices of scientific farming? or dairy work? or fruit culture? or floriculture?

For example, not very long ago I had a conversation with a young coloured man who is a graduate of one of the prominent universities of this country. The father of this man is comparatively ignorant, but by hard work and the exercise of common sense he has become the owner of two thousand acres of land. He owns more than a score of horses, cows, and mules and swine in large numbers, and is considered a prosperous farmer. In college the son of this farmer has studied chemistry, botany, zoölogy, surveying, and political economy. In my conversation I asked this young man how many acres his father cultivated in cotton and how many in corn. With a far-off gaze up into the heavens he answered that he did not know. When I asked him the classification of the soils on his father's farm, he did not know. He did not know how many horses or cows his father owned nor of what breeds they were, and seemed surprised that he should be asked such questions. It never seemed to have entered his mind that on his father's farm was the place to make his chemistry, his mathematics, and his literature penetrate and reflect itself in every acre of land, every bushel of corn, every cow, and every pig.

Let me give other examples of this mistaken sort of education. When a mere boy, I saw a young coloured man, who had spent several years in school, sitting in a common cabin in the South, studying a French grammar. I noted the poverty, the untidiness, the want of system and thrift, that existed about the cabin, notwithstanding his knowledge of French and other academic studies.

Again, not long ago I saw a coloured minister preparing his Sunday sermon just as the New England minister prepares his sermon. But this coloured minister was in a broken-down, leaky, rented log cabin, with weeds in the yard, surrounded by evidences of poverty, filth, and want of thrift. This minister had spent some time in school studying theology. How much better it would have been to have had this minister taught the dignity of labour, taught theoretical and practical farming in connection with his theology, so that he could have added to his meagre salary, and set an example for his people in the matter of living in a decent house, and having a knowledge of correct farming! In a word, this minister should have been taught that his condition, and that of his people, was not that of a New England community; and he should

[274]

have been so trained as to meet the actual needs and conditions of the coloured people in this community, so that a foundation might be laid that would, in the future, make a community like New England communities.

Since the Civil War, no one object has been more misunderstood than that of the object and value of industrial education for the Negro. To begin with, it must be borne in mind that the condition that existed in the South immediately after the war, and that now exists, is a peculiar one, without a parallel in history. This being true, it seems to me that the wise and honest thing to do is to make a study of the actual condition and environment of the Negro, and do that which is best for him, regardless of whether the same thing has been done for another race in exactly the same way. There are those among the white race and those among the black race who assert, with a good deal of earnestness, that there is no difference between the white man and the black man in this country. This sounds very pleasant and tickles the fancy; but, when the test of hard, cold logic is applied to it, it must be acknowledged that there is a difference,—not an inherent one, not a racial one, but a difference growing out of unequal opportunities in the past.

If I may be permitted to criticise the educational work that has been done in the South, I would say that the weak point has been in the failure to recognise this difference.

Negro education, immediately after the war in most cases, was begun too nearly at the point where New England education had ended. Let me illustrate. One of the saddest sights I ever saw was the placing of a three hundred dollar rosewood piano in a country school in the South that was located in the midst of the "Black Belt." Am I arguing against the teaching of instrumental music to the Negroes in that community? Not at all; only I should have deferred those music lessons about twenty-five years. There are numbers of such pianos in thousands of New England homes. But behind the piano in the New England home there are one hundred years of toil, sacrifice, and economy; there is the small manufacturing industry, started several years ago by hand power, now grown into a great business; there is ownership in land, a comfortable home, free from debt, and a bank account. In this "Black Belt" community where this piano went, four-fifths of the people owned no land, many lived in rented one-room cabins, many were in debt for food supplies, many mortgaged their crops for the food on which to live, and not one had a bank account. In this case, how much wiser it would have been to have taught the girls in this community sewing, intelligent and economical cooking, housekeeping, something of dairying and horticulture? The boys should have been taught something of farming in connection with their common-school education, instead of awakening in them a desire for a musical instrument which resulted in their parents going into debt for a third-rate piano or organ before a home was purchased. Industrial lessons would have awakened, in this community, a desire for homes, and would have given the people the ability to free themselves from industrial slavery to the extent that most of them would have soon purchased homes. After the home and the necessaries of life were supplied could come the piano. One piano lesson in a home of one's own is worth twenty in a rented log cabin.

All that I have just written, and the various examples illustrating it, show the present helpless condition of my people in the South,—how fearfully they lack the primary training for good living and good citizenship, how much they stand in need of a solid foundation on which to build their future success. I believe, as I have many times said in my various addresses in the North and in the South, that the main reason for the existence of this curious state of affairs is the lack of practical training in the ways of life.

There is, too, a great lack of money with which to carry on the educational work in the South. I was in a county in a Southern State not long ago where there are some thirty thousand coloured people and about seven thousand whites. In this county not a single public school for Negroes had been open that year longer than three months, not a single coloured teacher had been paid more than $15 per month for his teaching. Not one of these schools was taught in a building that was worthy of the name of school-house. In this county the State or public authorities do not own a single dollar's worth of school property,—not a school-house, a blackboard, or a piece of crayon. Each coloured child had had spent on him that year for his education about fifty cents, while each child in New York or Massachusetts had had spent on him that year for education not far from $20. And yet each citizen of this county is expected to share the burdens and privileges of our democratic form of government just as intelligently and conscientiously as the citizens of New York or Boston. A vote in this county means as much to the nation as a vote in the city of Boston. Crime in this county is as truly an arrow aimed at the heart of the government as a crime committed in the streets of Boston.

[276]

A single school-house built this year in a town near Boston to shelter about three hundred pupils cost more for building alone than is spent yearly for the education, including buildings, apparatus, teachers, for the whole coloured school population of Alabama. The Commissioner of Education for the State of Georgia not long ago reported to the State legislature that in that State there were two hundred thousand children that had entered no school the year past and one hundred thousand more who were at school but a few days, making practically three hundred thousand children between six and eighteen years of age that are growing up in ignorance in one Southern State alone. The same report stated that outside of the cities and towns, while the average number of school-houses in a county was sixty, all of these sixty school-houses were worth in lump less than $2,000, and the report further added that many of the school-houses in Georgia were not fit for horse stables. I am glad to say, however, that vast improvement over this condition is being made in Georgia under the inspired leadership of State Commissioner Glenn, and in Alabama under the no less zealous leadership of Commissioner Abercrombie.

These illustrations, so far as they concern the Gulf States, are not exceptional cases; nor are they overdrawn.

Until there is industrial independence, it is hardly possible to have good living and a pure ballot in the country districts. In these States it is safe to say that not more than one black man in twenty owns the land he cultivates. Where so large a proportion of a people are dependent, live in other people's houses, eat other people's food, and wear clothes they have not paid for, it is pretty hard to expect them to live fairly and vote honestly.

I have thus far referred mainly to the Negro race. But there is another side. The longer I live and the more I study the question, the more I am convinced that it is not so much a problem as to what the white man will do with the Negro as what the Negro will do with the white man and his civilisation. In considering this side of the subject, I thank God that I have grown to the point where I can sympathise with a white man as much as I can sympathise with a black man. I have grown to the point where I can sympathise with a Southern white man as much as I can sympathise with a Northern white man.

As bearing upon the future of our civilisation, I ask of the North what of their white brethren in the South,—those who have suffered and are still suffering the consequences of American slavery, for which both North and

[277]

South were responsible? Those of the great and prosperous North still owe to their less fortunate brethren of the Caucasian race in the South, not less than to themselves, a serious and uncompleted duty. What was the task the North asked the South to perform? Returning to their destitute homes after years of war to face blasted hopes, devastation, a shattered industrial system, they asked them to add to their own burdens that of preparing in education, politics, and economics, in a few short years, for citizenship, four millions of former slaves. That the South, staggering under the burden, made blunders, and that in a measure there has been disappointment, no one need be surprised. The educators, the statesmen, the philanthropists, have imperfectly comprehended their duty toward the millions of poor whites in the South who were buffeted for two hundred years between slavery and freedom, between civilisation and degradation, who were disregarded by both master and slave. It needs no prophet to tell the character of our future civilisation when the poor white boy in the country districts of the South receives one dollar's worth of education and the boy of the same class in the North twenty dollars' worth, when one never enters a reading-room or library and the other has reading-rooms and libraries in every ward and town, when one hears lectures and sermons once in two months and the other can hear a lecture or a sermon every day in the year.

The time has come, it seems to me, when in this matter we should rise above party or race or sectionalism into the region of duty of man to man, of citizen to citizen, of Christian to Christian; and if the Negro, who has been oppressed and denied his rights in a Christian land, can help the whites of the North and South to rise, can be the inspiration of their rising, into this atmosphere of generous Christian brotherhood and self-forgetfulness, he will see in it a recompense for all that he has suffered in the past.

CHAPTER 3

In the heart of the Black Belt of the South in *ante-bellum* days there was a large estate, with palatial mansion, surrounded by a beautiful grove, in which grew flowers and shrubbery of every description. Magnificent specimens of animal life grazed in the fields, and in grain and all manner of plant growth this estate was a model. In a word, it was the highest type of the product of slave labor.

Then came the long years of war, then freedom, then the trying years of reconstruction. The master returned from the war to find the faithful slaves who had been the bulwark of this household in possession of their freedom. Then there began that social and industrial revolution in the South which it is hard for any who was not really a part of it to appreciate or understand. Gradually, day by day, this ex-master began to realise, with a feeling almost indescribable, to what an extent he and his family had grown to be dependent upon the activity and faithfulness of his slaves; began to appreciate to what an extent slavery had sapped his sinews of strength and independence, how his dependence upon slave labour had deprived him and his offspring of the benefit of technical and industrial training, and, worst of all, had unconsciously led him to see in labour drudgery and degradation instead of beauty, dignity, and civilising power. At first there was a halt in this man's life. He cursed the North and he cursed the Negro. Then there was despair, almost utter hopelessness, over his weak and childlike condition. The temptation was to forget all in drink, and to this temptation there was a gradual yielding. With the loss of physical vigour came the loss of mental grasp and pride in surroundings. There was the falling off of a piece of plaster from the walls of the house which was not replaced, then another and still another. Gradually, the window-panes began to disappear, then the door-knobs. Touches of paint and whitewash, which once helped to give life, were no more to be seen. The hinges disappeared from the gate, then a board from the fence, then others in quick succession. Weeds and unmown grass covered the once well-kept lawn. Sometimes there were servants for domestic duties, and sometimes there were none. In the absence of servants the unsatisfactory condition of the food told that it was being prepared by hands unschooled to such duties. As the years passed by, debts accumulated in every direction. The education of the children was neglected.

[279]

Lower and lower sank the industrial, financial, and spiritual condition of the household. For the first time the awful truth of Scripture, "Whatsoever a man soweth, that shall he also reap," seemed to dawn upon him with a reality that it is hard for mortal to appreciate. Within a few months the whole mistake of slavery seemed to have concentrated itself upon this household. And this was one of many.

We have seen how the ending of slavery and the beginning of freedom produced not only a shock, but a stand-still, and in many cases a collapse, that lasted several years in the life of many white men. If the sudden change thus affected the white man, should this not teach us that we should have more sympathy than has been shown in many cases with the Negro in connection with his new and changed life? That they made many mistakes, plunged into excesses, undertook responsibilities for which they were not fitted, in many cases took liberty to mean license, is not to be wondered at. It is my opinion that the next forty years are going to show by many per cent. a higher degree of progress in the life of the Negro along all lines than has been shown during the first thirty years of his life. Certainly, the first thirty years of the Negro's life was one of experiment; and consequently, under such conditions, he was not able to settle down to real, earnest, hard common sense efforts to better his condition. While this was true in a great many cases, on the other hand a large proportion of the race, even from the first, saw what was needed for their new life, and began to settle down to lead an industrious, frugal existence, and to educate their children and in every way prepare themselves for the responsibilities of American citizenship.

The wonder is that the Negro has made as few mistakes as he has, when we consider all the surrounding circumstances. Columns of figures have been gleaned from the census reports within the last quarter of a century to show the great amount of crime committed by the Negro in excess of that committed by other races. No one will deny the fact that the proportion of crime by the present generation of Negroes is seriously large, but I believe that any other race with the Negro's history and present environment would have shown about the same criminal record.

Another consideration which we must always bear in mind in considering the Negro is that he had practically no home life in slavery; that is, the mother and father did not have the responsibility, and consequently the experience, of training their own children. The matter of child training was left to the master and mistress. Consequently, it has only been within the last thirty years that the Negro parents have had the actual responsibility and experience of training their own children. That they have made some mistakes in thus training them is not to be wondered at. Many families scattered over all parts of the United States have not yet been able to bring themselves together. When the Negro parents shall have had thirty or forty additional years in which to found homes and get experience in the training of their children, I believe that we will find that the amount of crime will be considerably less than it is now shown to be.

In too large a measure the Negro race began its development at the wrong end, simply because neither white nor black understood the case; and no wonder, for there had never been such a case in the history of the world.

To show where this primary mistake has led in its evil results, I wish to produce some examples showing plainly how prone we have been to make our education formal, superficial, instead of making it meet the needs of conditions.

In order to emphasise the matter more fully, I repeat, at least eighty per cent. of the coloured people in the South are found in the rural districts, and they are dependent on agriculture in some form for their support. Notwithstanding that we have practically a whole race dependent upon agriculture, and notwithstanding that thirty years have passed since our freedom, aside from what has been done at Hampton and Tuskegee and one or two other institutions, but very little has been attempted by State or philanthropy in the way of educating the race in this one industry upon which its very existence depends. Boys have been taken from the farms and educated in law, theology, Hebrew and Greek,—educated in everything else except the very subject that they should know most about. I question whether among all the educated coloured people in the United States you can find six, if we except those from the institutions named, who have received anything like a thorough training in agriculture. It would have seemed that, since self-support, industrial independence, is the first condition for lifting up any race, that education in theoretical and practical agriculture, horticulture, dairying, and stock-raising, should have occupied the first place in our system.

Some time ago, when we decided to make tailoring a part of our training at the Tuskegee Institute, I was amazed to find that it was almost impossible to find in the whole country an educated coloured man who could teach the making of clothing. We could find them by the score who could teach astronomy, theology, grammar, or Latin, but almost none who could instruct in the making of clothing, something that has to be used by every one of us every day in the year. How often has my heart been made to sink as I have gone through the South and into the homes of people, and found women who could converse intelligently on Grecian history, who had studied geometry, could analyse the most complex sentences, and yet could not analyse the poorly cooked and still more poorly served corn bread and fat meat that they and their families were eating three times a day! It is little trouble to find girls who can locate Pekin or the Desert of Sahara on an artificial globe, but seldom can you find one who can locate on an actual dinner table the proper place for the carving knife and fork or the meat and vegetables.

A short time ago, in one of the Southern cities, a coloured man died who had received training as a skilled mechanic during the days of slavery. Later by his skill and industry he built up a great business as a house contractor and builder. In this same city there are 35,000 coloured people, among them young men who have been well educated in the languages and in literature; but not a single one could be found who had been so trained in mechanical and architectural drawing that he could carry on the business which this ex-slave had built up, and so it was soon scattered to the wind. Aside from the work done in the institutions that I have mentioned, you can find almost no coloured men who have been trained in the principles of architecture, notwithstanding the fact that a vast majority of our race are without homes. Here, then, are the three prime conditions for growth, for civilisation,—food, clothing, shelter; and yet we have been the slaves of forms and customs to such an extent that we have failed in a large measure to look matters squarely in the face and meet actual needs.

It may well be asked by one who has not carefully considered the matter: "What has become of all those skilled farm-hands that used to be on the old plantations? Where are those wonderful cooks we hear about, where those exquisitely trained house servants, those cabinet makers, and the jacks-of-all-trades that were the pride of the South?" This is easily answered,—they are mostly dead. The survivors are too old to work. "But did they not train their children?" is the natural question. Alas! the answer is "no." Their skill was so commonplace to them, and to their former masters, that

[282]

neither thought of it as being a hard-earned or desirable accomplishment: it was natural, like breathing. Their children would have it as a matter of course. What their children needed was education. So they went out into the world, the ambitious ones, and got education, and forgot the necessity of the ordinary training to live.

God for two hundred and fifty years, in my opinion, prepared the way for the redemption of the Negro through industrial development. First, he made the Southern white man do business with the Negro for two hundred and fifty years in a way that no one else has done business with him. If a Southern white man wanted a house or a bridge built, he consulted a Negro mechanic about the plan and about the actual building of the house or bridge. If he wanted a suit of clothes or a pair of shoes made, it was to the Negro tailor or shoemaker that he talked. Secondly, every large slave plantation in the South was, in a limited sense, an industrial school. On these plantations there were scores of young coloured men and women who were constantly being trained, not alone as common farmers, but as carpenters, blacksmiths, wheelwrights, plasterers, brick masons, engineers, bridge-builders, cooks, dressmakers, housekeepers, etc. I would be the last to apologise for the curse of slavery; but I am simply stating facts. This training was crude and was given for selfish purposes, and did not answer the highest ends, because there was the absence of brain training in connection with that of the hand. Nevertheless, this business contact with the Southern white man, and the industrial training received on these plantations, put the Negro at the close of the war into possession of all the common and skilled labour in the South. For nearly twenty years after the war, except in one or two cases, the value of the industrial training given by the Negroes' former masters on the plantations and elsewhere was overlooked. Negro men and women were educated in literature, mathematics, and the sciences, with no thought of what had taken place on these plantations for two and a half centuries. After twenty years, those who were trained as mechanics, etc., during slavery began to disappear by death; and gradually we awoke to the fact that we had no one to take their places. We had scores of young men learned in Greek, but few in carpentry or mechanical or architectural drawing. We had trained many in Latin, but almost none as engineers, bridge-builders, and machinists. Numbers were taken from the farm and educated, but were educated in everything else except agriculture. Hence they had no sympathy with farm life, and did not return to it.

[283]

This last that I have been saying is practically a repetition of what I have said in the preceding paragraph; but, to emphasise it,—and this point is one of the most important I wish to impress on the reader,—it is well to repeat, to say the same thing twice. Oh, if only more who had the shaping of the education of the Negro could have, thirty years ago, realised, and made others realise, where the forgetting of the years of manual training and the sudden acquiring of education were going to lead the Negro race, what a saving it would have been! How much less my race would have had to answer for, as well as the white!

But it is too late to cry over what might have been. It is time to make up, as soon as possible, for this mistake,—time for both races to acknowledge it, and go forth on the course that, it seems to me, all must now see to be the right one,—industrial education.

As an example of what a well-trained and educated Negro may now do, and how ready to acknowledge him a Southern white man may be, let me return once more to the plantation I spoke of in the first part of this chapter. As the years went by, the night seemed to grow darker, so that all seemed hopeless and lost. At this point relief and strength came from an unexpected source. This Southern white man's idea of Negro education had been that it merely meant a parrot-like absorption of Anglo-Saxon civilisation, with a special tendency to imitate the weaker elements of the white man's character; that it meant merely the high hat, kid gloves, a showy walking cane, patent leather shoes, and all the rest of it. To this ex-master it seemed impossible that the education of the Negro could produce any other results. And so, last of all, did he expect help or encouragement from an educated black man; but it was just from this source that help came. Soon after the process of decay began in this white man's estate, the education of a certain black man began, and began on a logical, sensible basis. It was an education that would fit him to see and appreciate the physical and moral conditions that existed in his own family and neighbourhood, and, in the present generation, would fit him to apply himself to their relief. By chance this educated Negro strayed into the employ of this white man. His employer soon learned that this Negro not only had a knowledge of science, mathematics, and literature in his head, but in his hands as well. This black man applied his knowledge of agricultural chemistry to the redemption of the soil; and soon the washes and gulleys began to disappear, and the waste places began to bloom. New and improved machinery in a few months began to

[284]

rob labour of its toil and drudgery. The animals were given systematic and kindly attention. Fences were repaired and rebuilt. Whitewash and paint were made to do duty. Everywhere order slowly began to replace confusion; hope, despair; and profits, losses. As he observed, day by day, new life and strength being imparted to every department of his property, this white son of the South began revising his own creed regarding the wisdom of educating Negroes.

Hitherto his creed regarding the value of an educated Negro had been rather a plain and simple one, and read: "The only end that could be accomplished by educating a black man was to enable him to talk properly to a mule; and the Negro's education did great injustice to the mule, since the language tended to confuse him and make him balky."

We need not continue the story, except to add that to-day the grasp of the hand of this ex-slaveholder, and the listening to his hearty words of gratitude and commendation for the education of the Negro, are enough to compensate those who have given and those who have worked and sacrificed for the elevation of my people through all of these years. If we are patient, wise, unselfish, and courageous, such examples will multiply as the years go by.

Before closing this chapter,—which, I think, has clearly shown that there is at present a very distinct lack of industrial training in the South among the Negroes,—I wish to say a few words in regard to certain objections, or rather misunderstandings, which have from time to time arisen in regard to the matter.

Many have had the thought that industrial training was meant to make the Negro work, much as he worked during the days of slavery. This is far from my idea of it. If this training has any value for the Negro, as it has for the white man, it consists in teaching the Negro how rather not to work, but how to make the forces of nature—air, water, horse-power, steam, and electric power—work for him, how to lift labour up out of toil and drudgery into that which is dignified and beautiful. The Negro in the South works, and he works hard; but his lack of skill, coupled with ignorance, causes him too often to do his work in the most costly and shiftless manner, and this has kept him near the bottom of the ladder in the business world. I repeat that industrial education teaches the Negro how not to drudge in his work. Let him who doubts this contrast the Negro in the South toiling through a field of oats with an old-fashioned reaper with the white man on a modern farm in the West, sitting upon a modern "harvester," behind

[285]

two spirited horses, with an umbrella over him, using a machine that cuts and binds the oats at the same time,—doing four times as much work as the black man with one half the labour. Let us give the black man so much skill and brains that he can cut oats like the white man, then he can compete with him. The Negro works in cotton, and has no trouble so long as his labour is confined to the lower forms of work,—the planting, the picking, and the ginning; but, when the Negro attempts to follow the bale of cotton up through the higher stages, through the mill where it is made into the finer fabrics, where the larger profit appears, he is told that he is not wanted.

The Negro can work in wood and iron; and no one objects so long as he confines his work to the felling of trees and sawing of boards, to the digging of iron ore and making of pig iron. But, when the Negro attempts to follow this tree into the factory where it is made into desks and chairs and railway coaches, or when he attempts to follow the pig iron into the factory where it is made into knife-blades and watch-springs, the Negro's trouble begins. And what is the objection? Simply that the Negro lacks the skill, coupled with brains, necessary to compete with the white man, or that, when white men refuse to work with coloured men, enough skilled and educated coloured men cannot be found able to superintend and man every part of any one large industry; and hence, for these reasons, they are constantly being barred out. The Negro must become, in a larger measure, an intelligent producer as well as a consumer. There should be a more vital and practical connection between the Negro's educated brain and his opportunity of earning his daily living.

A very weak argument often used against pushing industrial training for the Negro is that the Southern white man favours it, and, therefore, it is not best for the Negro. Although I was born a slave, I am thankful that I am able so far to rid myself of prejudice as to be able to accept a good thing, whether it comes from a black man or a white man, a Southern man or a Northern man. Industrial education will not only help the Negro directly in the matter of industrial development, but also in bringing about more satisfactory relations between him and the Southern white man. For the sake of the Negro and the Southern white man there are many things in the relation of the two races that must soon be changed. We cannot depend wholly upon abuse or condemnation of the Southern white man to bring about these changes. Each race must be educated to see matters in a broad, high, generous, Christian spirit: we must bring the two races together, not estrange them. The Negro

[286]

must live for all time by the side of the Southern white man. The man is unwise who does not cultivate in every manly way the friendship and good will of his next-door neighbour, whether he be black or white. I repeat that industrial training will help cement the friendship of the two races. The history of the world proves that trade, commerce, is the forerunner of peace and civilisation as between races and nations. The Jew, who was once in about the same position that the Negro is to-day, has now recognition, because he has entwined himself about America in a business and industrial sense. Say or think what we will, it is the tangible or visible element that is going to tell largely during the next twenty years in the solution of the race problem.

CHAPTER 4

One of the main problems as regards the education of the Negro is how to have him use his education to the best advantage after he has secured it. In saying this, I do not want to be understood as implying that the problem of simple ignorance among the masses has been settled in the South; for this is far from true. The amount of ignorance still prevailing among the Negroes, especially in the rural districts, is very large and serious. But I repeat, we must go farther if we would secure the best results and most gratifying returns in public good for the money spent than merely to put academic education in the Negro's head with the idea that this will settle everything.

In his present condition it is important, in seeking after what he terms the ideal, that the Negro should not neglect to prepare himself to take advantage of the opportunities that are right about his door. If he lets these opportunities slip, I fear they will never be his again. In saying this, I mean always that the Negro should have the most thorough mental and religious training; for without it no race can succeed. Because of his past history and environment and present condition it is important that he be carefully guided for years to come in the proper use of his education. Much valuable time has been lost and money spent in vain, because too many have not been educated with the idea of fitting them to do well the things which they could get to do. Because of the lack of proper direction of the Negro's education, some good friends of his, North and South, have not taken that interest in it that they otherwise would have taken. In too many cases where merely literary education alone has been given the Negro youth, it has resulted in an exaggerated estimate of his importance in the world, and an increase of wants which his education has not fitted him to supply.

But, in discussing this subject, one is often met with the question, Should not the Negro be encouraged to prepare himself for any station in life that any other race fills? I would say, Yes; but the surest way for the Negro to reach the highest positions is to prepare himself to fill well at the present time the basic occupations. This will give him a foundation upon which to stand while securing what is called the more exalted positions. The Negro has the right to study law; but success will come to the race sooner if it produces intelligent, thrifty farmers, mechanics, and housekeepers to support the lawyers. The want of proper direction of the use of the Negro's education results in tempting too many to live mainly by their wits, without producing anything that is of real value to the world. Let me quote examples of this.

Hayti, Santo Domingo, and Liberia, although among the richest countries in natural resources in the world, are discouraging examples of what must happen to any people who lack industrial or technical training. It is said that in Liberia there are no wagons, wheelbarrows, or public roads, showing very plainly that there is a painful absence of public spirit and thrift. What is true of Liberia is also true in a measure of the republics of Hayti and Santo Domingo. The people have not yet learned the lesson of turning their education toward the cultivation of the soil and the making of the simplest implements for agricultural and other forms of labour.

Much would have been done toward laying a sound foundation for general prosperity if some attention had been spent in this direction. General education itself has no bearing on the subject at issue, because, while there is no well-established public school system in either of these countries, yet large numbers of men of both Hayti and Santo Domingo have been educated in France for generations. This is especially true of Hayti. The education has been altogether in the direction of *belles lettres*, however, and practically little in the direction of industrial and scientific education.

It is a matter of common knowledge that Hayti has to send abroad even to secure engineers for her men-of-war, for plans for her bridges and other work requiring technical knowledge and skill. I should very much regret to see any such condition obtain in any large measure as regards the coloured people in the South, and yet this will be our fate if industrial education is much longer neglected. We have spent much time in the South in educating men and women in letters alone, too, and must now turn our attention more than ever toward educating them so as to supply their wants and needs. It is more lamentable to see educated people unable to support themselves than to see uneducated people in the same condition. Ambition all along this line must be stimulated.

If educated men and women of the race will see and acknowledge the necessity of practical industrial training and go to work with a zeal and

[289]

determination, their example will be followed by others, who are now without ambition of any kind.

The race cannot hope to come into its own until the young coloured men and women make up their minds to assist in the general development along these lines. The elder men and women trained in the hard school of slavery, and who so long possessed all of the labour, skilled and unskilled, of the South, are dying out; their places must be filled by their children, or we shall lose our hold upon these occupations. Leaders in these occupations are needed now more than ever.

It is not enough that the idea be inculcated that coloured people should get book learning; along with it they should be taught that book education and industrial development must go hand in hand. No race which fails to do this can ever hope to succeed. Phillips Brooks gave expression to the sentiment: "One generation gathers the material, and the next generation builds the palaces." As I understand it, he wished to inculcate the idea that one generation lays the foundation for succeeding generations. The rough affairs of life very largely fall to the earlier generation, while the next one has the privilege of dealing with the higher and more æsthetic things of life. This is true of all generations, of all peoples; and, unless the foundation is deeply laid, it is impossible for the succeeding one to have a career in any way approaching success. As regards the coloured men of the South, as regards the coloured men of the United States, this is the generation which, in a large measure, must gather the material with which to lay the foundation for future success.

Some time ago it was my misfortune to see a Negro sixty-five years old living in poverty and filth. I was disgusted, and said to him, "If you are worthy of your freedom, you would surely have changed your condition during the thirty years of freedom which you have enjoyed." He answered: "I do want to change. I want to do something for my wife and children; but I do not know how,—I do not know what to do." I looked into his lean and haggard face, and realised more deeply than ever before the absolute need of captains of industry among the great masses of the coloured people.

It is possible for a race or an individual to have mental development and yet be so handicapped by custom, prejudice, and lack of employment as to dwarf and discourage the whole life. This is the condition that prevails among the race in many of the large cities of the North; and it is to prevent this same

[290]

condition in the South that I plead with all the earnestness of my heart. Mental development alone will not give us what we want, but mental development tied to hand and heart training will be the salvation of the Negro.

In many respects the next twenty years are going to be the most serious in the history of the race. Within this period it will be largely decided whether the Negro will be able to retain the hold which he now has upon the industries of the South or whether his place will be filled by white people from a distance. The only way he can prevent the industrial occupations slipping from him in all parts of the South, as they have already in certain parts, is for all educators, ministers, and friends of the race to unite in pushing forward in a whole-souled manner the industrial or business development of the Negro, whether in school or out of school. Four times as many young men and women of the race should be receiving industrial training. Just now the Negro is in a position to feel and appreciate the need of this in a way that no one else can. No one can fully appreciate what I am saying who has not walked the streets of a Northern city day after day seeking employment, only to find every door closed against him on account of his colour, except in menial service. It is to prevent the same thing taking place in the South that I plead. We may argue that mental development will take care of all this. Mental development is a good thing. Gold is also a good thing, but gold is worthless without an opportunity to make itself touch the world of trade. Education increases greatly an individual's wants. It is cruel in many cases to increase the wants of the black youth by mental development alone without, at the same time, increasing his ability to supply these increased wants in occupations in which he can find employment.

The place made vacant by the death of the old coloured man who was trained as a carpenter during slavery, and who since the war had been the leading contractor and builder in the Southern town, had to be filled. No young coloured carpenter capable of filling his place could be found. The result was that his place was filled by a white mechanic from the North, or from Europe, or from elsewhere. What is true of carpentry and house-building in this case is true, in a degree, in every skilled occupation; and it is becoming true of common labour. I do not mean to say that all of the skilled labour has been taken out of the Negro's hands; but I do mean to say that in no part of the South is he so strong in the matter of skilled labour as he was twenty years ago, except possibly in the country districts and the smaller towns. In the more northern of the Southern cities, such as Richmond and Baltimore, the change is

[291]

most apparent; and it is being felt in every Southern city. Wherever the Negro has lost ground industrially in the South, it is not because there is prejudice against him as a skilled labourer on the part of the native Southern white man; the Southern white man generally prefers to do business with the Negro mechanic rather than with a white one, because he is accustomed to do business with the Negro in this respect. There is almost no prejudice against the Negro in the South in matters of business, so far as the native whites are concerned; and here is the entering wedge for the solution of the race problem. But too often, where the white mechanic or factory operative from the North gets a hold, the trades-union soon follows, and the Negro is crowded to the wall.

But what is the remedy for this condition? First, it is most important that the Negro and his white friends honestly face the facts as they are; otherwise the time will not be very far distant when the Negro of the South will be crowded to the ragged edge of industrial life as he is in the North. There is still time to repair the damage and to reclaim what we have lost.

I stated in the beginning that industrial education for the Negro has been misunderstood. This has been chiefly because some have gotten the idea that industrial development was opposed to the Negro's higher mental development. This has little or nothing to do with the subject under discussion; we should no longer permit such an idea to aid in depriving the Negro of the legacy in the form of skilled labour that was purchased by his forefathers at the price of two hundred and fifty years of slavery. I would say to the black boy what I would say to the white boy, Get all the mental development that your time and pocket-book will allow of,—the more, the better; but the time has come when a larger proportion—not all, for we need professional men and women—of the educated coloured men and women should give themselves to industrial or business life. The professional class will be helped in so far as the rank and file have an industrial foundation, so that they can pay for professional service. Whether they receive the training of the hand while pursuing their academic training or after their academic training is finished, or whether they will get their literary training in an industrial school or college, are questions which each individual must decide for himself. No matter how or where educated, the educated men and women must come to the rescue of the race in the effort to get and hold its industrial footing. I would not have the standard of mental development lowered one whit; for, with the Negro, as with all races,

[292]

mental strength is the basis of all progress. But I would have a large measure of this mental strength reach the Negroes' actual needs through the medium of the hand. Just now the need is not so much for the common carpenters, brick masons, farmers, and laundry women as for industrial leaders who, in addition to their practical knowledge, can draw plans, make estimates, take contracts; those who understand the latest methods of truck-gardening and the science underlying practical agriculture; those who understand machinery to the extent that they can operate steam and electric laundries, so that our women can hold on to the laundry work in the South, that is so fast drifting into the hands of others in the large cities and towns.

Having tried to show in previous chapters to what a condition the lack of practical training has brought matters in the South, and by the examples in this chapter where this state of things may go if allowed to run its course, I wish now to show what practical training, even in its infancy among us, has already accomplished.

I noticed, when I first went to Tuskegee to start the Tuskegee Normal and Industrial Institute, that some of the white people about there rather looked doubtfully at me; and I thought I could get their influence by telling them how much algebra and history and science and all those things I had in my head, but they treated me about the same as they did before. They didn't seem to care about the algebra, history, and science that were in my head only. Those people never even began to have confidence in me until we commenced to build a large three-story brick building, and then another and another, until now we have forty buildings which have been erected largely by the labour of our students; and to-day we have the respect and confidence of all the white people in that section.

There is an unmistakable influence that comes over a white man when he sees a black man living in a two-story brick house that has been paid for. I need not stop to explain. It is the tangible evidence of prosperity. You know Thomas doubted the Saviour after he had risen from the dead; and the Lord said to Thomas, "Reach hither thy finger, and behold my hands; and reach hither thy hand, and thrust it into my side." The tangible evidence convinced Thomas.

We began, soon after going to Tuskegee, the manufacture of bricks. We also started a wheelwright establishment and the manufacture of good

[293]

wagons and buggies; and the white people came to our institution for that kind of work. We also put in a printing plant, and did job printing for the white people as well as for the blacks.

By having something that these people wanted, we came into contact with them, and our interest became interlinked with their interest, until to-day we have no warmer friends anywhere in the country than we have among the white people of Tuskegee. We have found by experience that the best way to get on well with people is to have something that they want, and that is why we emphasise this Christian Industrial Education.

Not long ago I heard a conversation among three white men something like this. Two of them were berating the Negro, saying the Negro was shiftless and lazy, and all that sort of thing. The third man listened to their remarks for some time in silence, and then he said: "I don't know what your experience has been; but there is a 'nigger' down our way who owns a good house and lot with about fifty acres of ground. His house is well furnished, and he has got some splendid horses and cattle. He is intelligent and has a bank account. I don't know how the 'niggers' are in your community, but Tobe Jones is a gentleman. Once, when I was hard up, I went to Tobe Jones and borrowed fifty dollars; and he hasn't asked me for it yet. I don't know what kind of 'niggers' you have down your way, but Tobe Jones is a gentleman."

Now what we want to do is to multiply and place in every community these Tobe Joneses; and, just in so far as we can place them throughout the South this race question will disappear.

Suppose there was a black man who had business for the railroads to the amount of ten thousand dollars a year. Do you suppose that, when that black man takes his family aboard the train, they are going to put him into a Jim Crow car and run the risk of losing that ten thousand dollars a year? No, they will put on a Pullman palace car for him.

Some time ago a certain coloured man was passing through the streets of one of the little Southern towns, and he chanced to meet two white men on the street. It happened that this coloured man owns two or three houses and lots, has a good education and a comfortable bank account. One of the white men turned to the other, and said: "By Gosh! It is all I can do to keep from calling that 'nigger' Mister." That's the point we want to get to.

[294]

Nothing else so soon brings about right relations between the two races in the South as the commercial progress of the Negro. Friction between the races will pass away as the black man, by reason of his skill, intelligence, and character, can produce something that the white man wants or respects in the commercial world. This is another reason why at Tuskegee we push industrial training. We find that as every year we put into a Southern community coloured men who can start a brickyard, a saw-mill, a tin-shop, or a printing-office,—men who produce something that makes the white man partly dependent upon the Negro instead of all the dependence being on the other side,—a change for the better takes place in the relations of the races. It is through the dairy farm, the truck-garden, the trades, the commercial life, largely, that the Negro is to find his way to respect and confidence.

What is the permanent value of the Hampton and Tuskegee system of training to the South, in a broader sense? In connection with this, it is well to bear in mind that slavery unconsciously taught the white man that labour with the hands was something fit for the Negro only, and something for the white man to come into contact with just as little as possible. It is true that there was a large class of poor white people who laboured with the hands, but they did it because they were not able to secure Negroes to work for them; and these poor whites were constantly trying to imitate the slaveholding class in escaping labour, as they, too, regarded it as anything but elevating. But the Negro, in turn, looked down upon the poor whites with a certain contempt because they had to work. The Negro, it is to be borne in mind, worked under constant protest, because he felt that his labour was being unjustly requited; and he spent almost as much effort in planning how to escape work as in learning how to work. Labour with him was a badge of degradation. The white man was held up before him as the highest type of civilisation, but the Negro noted that this highest type of civilisation himself did little labour with the hand. Hence he argued that, the less work he did, the more nearly he would be like the white man. Then, in addition to these influences, the slave system discouraged labour-saving machinery. To use labour-saving machinery, intelligence was required; and intelligence and slavery were not on friendly terms. Hence the Negro always associated labour with toil, drudgery, something to be escaped. When the Negro first became free, his idea of education was that it was something that would soon put him in the same position as regards work that his recent master had occupied. Out of these conditions grew the habit of

[295]

putting off till to-morrow and the day after the duty that should be done promptly to-day. The leaky house was not repaired while the sun shone, for then the rain did not come through. While the rain was falling, no one cared to expose himself to stop the rain. The plough, on the same principle, was left where the last furrow was run, to rot and rust in the field during the winter. There was no need to repair the wooden chimney that was exposed to the fire, because water could be thrown on it when it was on fire. There was no need to trouble about the payment of a debt to-day, because it could be paid as well next week or next year. Besides these conditions, the whole South at the close of the war was without proper food, clothing, and shelter,—was in need of habits of thrift and economy and of something laid up for a rainy day.

To me it seemed perfectly plain that here was a condition of things that could not be met by the ordinary process of education. At Tuskegee we became convinced that the thing to do was to make a careful, systematic study of the condition and needs of the South, especially the Black Belt, and to bend our efforts in the direction of meeting these needs, whether we were following a well-beaten track or were hewing out a new path to meet conditions probably without a parallel in the world. After eighteen years of experience and observation, what is the result? Gradually, but surely, we find that all through the South the disposition to look upon labour as a disgrace is on the wane; and the parents who themselves sought to escape work are so anxious to give their children training in intelligent labour that every institution which gives training in the handicrafts is crowded, and many (among them Tuskegee) have to refuse admission to hundreds of applicants. The influence of Hampton and Tuskegee is shown again by the fact that almost every little school at the remotest cross-road is anxious to be known as an industrial school, or, as some of the coloured people call it, an "industrous" school.

The social lines that were once sharply drawn between those who laboured with the hands and those who did not are disappearing. Those who formerly sought to escape labour, now when they see that brains and skill rob labour of the toil and drudgery once associated with it, instead of trying to avoid it, are willing to pay to be taught how to engage in it. The South is beginning to see labour raised up, dignified and beautified, and in this sees its salvation. In proportion as the love of labour grows, the large idle class, which has long been one of the curses of the South, disappears. As people become absorbed in their own affairs, they have less time to attend to everybody's else business.

The South is still an undeveloped and unsettled country, and for the next half-century and more the greater part of the energy of the masses will be needed to develop its material resources. Any force that brings the rank and file of the people to have a greater love of industry is therefore especially valuable. This result industrial education is surely bringing about. It stimulates production and increases trade,—trade between the races; and in this new and engrossing relation both forget the past. The white man respects the vote of a coloured man who does ten thousand dollars' worth of business; and, the more business the coloured man has, the more careful he is how he votes.

Immediately after the war there was a large class of Southern people who feared that the opening of the free schools to the freedmen and the poor whites—the education of the head alone—would result merely in increasing the class who sought to escape labour, and that the South would soon be overrun by the idle and vicious. But, as the results of industrial combined with academic training begin to show themselves in hundreds of communities that have been lifted up, these former prejudices against education are being removed. Many of those who a few years ago opposed Negro education are now among its warmest advocates.

This industrial training, emphasising, as it does, the idea of economic production, is gradually bringing the South to the point where it is feeding itself. After the war, what profit the South made out of the cotton crop it spent outside of the South to purchase food supplies,—meat, bread, canned vegetables, and the like,—but the improved methods of agriculture are fast changing this custom. With the newer methods of labour, which teach promptness and system and emphasise the worth of the beautiful, the moral value of the well-painted house, the fence with every paling and nail in its place, is bringing to bear upon the South an influence that is making it a new country in industry, education, and religion.

It seems to me I cannot do better than to close this chapter on the needs of the Southern Negro than by quoting from a talk given to the students at Tuskegee:—

"I want to be a little more specific in showing you what you have to do and how you must do it.

[297]

"One trouble with us is—and the same is true of any young people, no matter of what race or condition—we have too many stepping-stones. We step all the time, from one thing to another. You find a young man who is learning to make bricks; and, if you ask him what he intends to do after learning the trade, in too many cases he will answer, 'Oh, I am simply working at this trade as a stepping-stone to something higher.' You see a young man working at the brick-mason's trade, and he will be apt to say the same thing. And young women learning to be milliners and dressmakers will tell you the same. All are stepping to something higher. And so we always go on, stepping somewhere, never getting hold of anything thoroughly. Now we must stop this stepping business, having so many stepping-stones. Instead, we have got to take hold of these important industries, and stick to them until we master them thoroughly. There is no nation so thorough in their education as the Germans. Why? Simply because the German takes hold of a thing, and sticks to it until he masters it. Into it he puts brains and thought from morning to night. He reads all the best books and journals bearing on that particular study, and he feels that nobody else knows so much about it as he does.

"Take any of the industries I have mentioned, that of brick-making, for example. Any one working at that trade should determine to learn all there is to be known about making bricks; read all the papers and journals bearing upon the trade; learn not only to make common hand-bricks, but pressed bricks, fire-bricks,—in short, the finest and best bricks there are to be made. And, when you have learned all you can by reading and talking with other people, you should travel from one city to another, and learn how the best bricks are made. And then, when you go into business for yourself, you will make a reputation for being the best brick-maker in the community; and in this way you will put yourself on your feet, and become a helpful and useful citizen. When a young man does this, goes out into one of these Southern cities and makes a reputation for himself, that person wins a reputation that is going to give him a standing and position. And, when the children of that successful brick-maker come along, they will be able to take a higher position in life. The grandchildren will be able to take a still higher position. And it will be traced back to that grandfather who, by his great success as a brick-maker, laid a foundation that was of the right kind.

"What I have said about these two trades can be applied with equal force to the trades followed by women. Take the matter of millinery. There is no good reason why there should not be, in each principal city in the South, at least three or four competent coloured women in charge of millinery establishments. But what is the trouble?

"Instead of making the most of our opportunities in this industry, the temptation, in too many cases, is to be music-teachers, teachers of elocution, or something else that few of the race at present have any money to pay for, or the opportunity to earn money to pay for, simply because there is no foundation. But, when more coloured people succeed in the more fundamental occupations, they will then be able to make better provision for their children in what are termed the higher walks of life.

"And, now, what I have said about these important industries is especially true of the important industry of agriculture. We are living in a country where, if we are going to succeed at all, we are going to do so largely by what we raise out of the soil. The people in those backward countries I have told you about have failed to give attention to the cultivation of the soil, to the invention and use of improved agricultural implements and machinery. Without this no people can succeed. No race which fails to put brains into agriculture can succeed; and, if you want to realize the truth of this statement, go with me into the back districts of some of our Southern States, and you will find many people in poverty, and yet they are surrounded by a rich country.

"A race, like an individual, has got to have a reputation. Such a reputation goes a long way toward helping a race or an individual; and, when we have succeeded in getting such a reputation, we shall find that a great many of the discouraging features of our life will melt away.

"Reputation is what people think we are, and a great deal depends on that. When a race gets a reputation along certain lines, a great many things which now seem complex, difficult to attain, and are most discouraging, will disappear.

"When you say that an engine is a Corliss engine, people understand that that engine is a perfect piece of mechanical work,—perfect as far as human skill and ingenuity can make it perfect. You say a car is a Pullman car. That is all; but what does it mean? It means that the builder of that car got a reputation at the outset for thorough, perfect work, for turning out everything in first-class shape. And so with a race. You cannot keep back very long a race

[299]

that has the reputation for doing perfect work in everything that it undertakes. And then we have got to get a reputation for economy. Nobody cares to associate with an individual in business or otherwise who has a reputation for being a trifling spendthrift, who spends his money for things that he can very easily get along without, who spends his money for clothing, gewgaws, superficialities, and other things, when he has not got the necessaries of life. We want to give the race a reputation for being frugal and saving in everything. Then we want to get a reputation for being industrious. Now, remember these three things: Get a reputation for being skilled. It will not do for a few here and there to have it: the race must have the reputation. Get a reputation for being so skilful, so industrious, that you will not leave a job until it is as nearly perfect as any one can make it. And then we want to make a reputation for the race for being honest,—honest at all times and under all circumstances. A few individuals here and there have it, a few communities have it; but the race as a mass must get it.

"You recall that story of Abraham Lincoln, how, when he was postmaster at a small village, he had left on his hands $1.50 which the government did not call for. Carefully wrapping up this money in a handkerchief, he kept it for ten years. Finally, one day, the government agent called for this amount; and it was promptly handed over to him by Abraham Lincoln, who told him that during all those ten years he had never touched a cent of that money. He made it a principle of his life never to use other people's money. That trait of his character helped him along to the Presidency. The race wants to get a reputation for being strictly honest in all its dealings and transactions,—honest in handling money, honest in all its dealings with its fellow-men.

"And then we want to get a reputation for being thoughtful. This I want to emphasise more than anything else. We want to get a reputation for doing things without being told to do them every time. If you have work to do, think about it so constantly, investigate and read about it so thoroughly, that you will always be finding ways and means of improving that work. The average person going to work becomes a regular machine, never giving the matter of improving the methods of his work a thought. He is never at his work before the appointed time, and is sure to stop the minute the hour is up. The world is looking for the person who is thoughtful, who will say at the close of work hours: 'Is there not something else I can do for you? Can I not stay a little later, and help you?'

[300]

"Moreover, it is with a race as it is with an individual: it must respect itself if it would win the respect of others. There must be a certain amount of unity about a race, there must be a great amount of pride about a race, there must be a great deal of faith on the part of a race in itself. An individual cannot succeed unless he has about him a certain amount of pride,—enough pride to make him aspire to the highest and best things in life. An individual cannot succeed unless that individual has a great amount of faith in himself.

"A person who goes at an undertaking with the feeling that he cannot succeed is likely to fail. On the other hand, the individual who goes at an undertaking, feeling that he can succeed, is the individual who in nine cases out of ten does succeed. But, whenever you find an individual that is ashamed of his race, trying to get away from his race, apologising for being a member of his race, then you find a weak individual. Where you find a race that is ashamed of itself, that is apologising for itself, there you will find a weak, vacillating race. Let us no longer have to apologise for our race in these or other matters. Let us think seriously and work seriously: then, as a race, we shall be thought of seriously, and, therefore, seriously respected."

CHAPTER 5

In this chapter I wish to show how, at Tuskegee, we are trying to work out the plan of industrial training, and trust I shall be pardoned the seeming egotism if I preface the sketch with a few words, by way of example, as to the expansion of my own life and how I came to undertake the work at Tuskegee.

My earliest recollection is of a small one-room log hut on a slave plantation in Virginia. After the close of the war, while working in the coal mines of West Virginia for the support of my mother, I heard, in some accidental way, of the Hampton Institute. When I learned that it was an institution where a black boy could study, could have a chance to work for his board, and at the same time be taught how to work and to realise the dignity of labor, I resolved to go there. Bidding my mother good-by, I started out one morning to find my way to Hampton, although I was almost penniless and had no definite idea as to where Hampton was. By walking, begging rides, and paying for a portion of the journey on the steam-cars, I finally succeeded in reaching the city of Richmond; Virginia. I was without money or friends. I slept on a sidewalk; and by working on a vessel the next day I earned money enough to continue my way to the institute, where I arrived with a capital of fifty cents. At Hampton I found the opportunity—in the way of buildings, teachers, and industries provided by the generous—to get training in the classroom and by practical touch with industrial life,—to learn thrift, economy, and push. I was surrounded by an atmosphere of business, Christian influence, and spirit of self-help, that seemed to have awakened every faculty in me, and caused me for the first time to realise what it meant to be a man instead of a piece of property.

While there, I resolved, when I had finished the course of training, I would go into the Far South, into the Black Belt of the South, and give my life to providing the same kind of opportunity for self-reliance, self-awakening, that I had found provided for me at Hampton.

My work began at Tuskegee, Alabama, in 1881, in a small shanty church, with one teacher and thirty students, without a dollar's worth of property. The spirit of work and of industrial thrift, with aid from the State and generosity from the North, have enabled us to develop an institution which now has about one thousand students, gathered from twenty-three States, and eighty-eight instructors. Counting students, instructors, and their families, we have a resident population upon the school grounds of about twelve hundred persons.

The institution owns two thousand three hundred acres of land, seven hundred of which are cultivated by student labor. There are six hundred head of live-stock, including horses, mules, cows, hogs, and sheep. There are over forty vehicles that have been made, and are now used, by the school. Training is given in twenty-six industries. There is work in wood, in iron, in leather, in tin; and all forms of domestic economy are engaged in. Students are taught mechanical and architectural drawing, receive training as agriculturists, dairymen, masons, carpenters, contractors, builders, as machinists, electricians, printers, dressmakers, and milliners, and in other directions.

The value of the property is $300,000. There are forty-two buildings, counting large and small, all of which, with the exception of four, have been erected by the labour of the students.

Since this work started, there has been collected and spent for its founding and support $800,000. The annual expense is now not far from $75,000. In a humble, simple manner the effort has been to place a great object-lesson in the heart of the South for the elevation of the coloured people, where there should be, in a high sense, that union of head, heart, and hand which has been the foundation of the greatness of all races since the world began.

What is the object of all this outlay? It must be first borne in mind that we have in the South a peculiar and unprecedented state of things. The cardinal needs among the eight million coloured people in the South, most of whom are to be found on the plantations, may be stated as food, clothing, shelter, education, proper habits, and a settlement of race relations. These millions of coloured people of the South cannot be reached directly by any missionary agent; but they can be reached by sending out among them strong, selected young men and women, with the proper training of head, hand, and heart, who will live among them and show them how to lift themselves up.

The problem that the Tuskegee Institute keeps before itself constantly is how to prepare these leaders. From the outset, in connection with religious and academic training, it has emphasised industrial, or hand, training as a means of finding the way out of present conditions. First, we have found the industrial teaching useful in giving the student a chance to work out a portion of his expenses while in school. Second, the school furnishes labour that has an economic value and at the same time gives the student a chance to acquire knowledge and skill while performing the labour. Most of all, we find the industrial system valuable in teaching economy, thrift, and the dignity of labour and in giving moral backbone to students. The fact that a student goes into the world conscious of his power to build a house or a wagon or to make a set of harness gives him a certain confidence and moral independence that he would not possess without such training.

A more detailed example of our methods at Tuskegee may be of interest. For example, we cultivate by student labour seven hundred acres of land. The object is not only to cultivate the land in a way to make it pay our boarding department, but at the same time to teach the students, in addition to the practical work, something of the chemistry of the soil, the best methods of drainage, dairying, cultivation of fruit, the care of live-stock and tools, and scores of other lessons needed by people whose main dependence is on agriculture.

Friends some time ago provided means for the erection of a large new chapel at Tuskegee. Our students made the bricks for this chapel. A large part of the timber was sawed by the students at our saw-mill, the plans were drawn by our teacher of architectural and mechanical drawing, and students did the brick-masonry, the plastering, the painting, the carpentry work, the tinning, the slating, and made most of the furniture. Practically, the whole chapel was built and furnished by student labour. Now the school has this building for permanent use, and the students have a knowledge of the trades employed in its construction.

While the young men do the kinds of work I have mentioned, young women to a large extent make, mend, and laundry the clothing of the young men. They also receive instruction in dairying, horticulture, and other valuable industries.

One of the objections sometimes urged against industrial education for the Negro is that it aims merely to teach him to work on the same plan that he worked on when in slavery. This is far from being the object at Tuskegee. At the

[304]

head of each of the twenty-six industrial divisions we have an intelligent and competent instructor, just as we have in our history classes, so that the student is taught not only practical brick-masonry, for example, but also the underlying principles of that industry, the mathematics and the mechanical and architectural drawing. Or he is taught how to become master of the forces of nature, so that, instead of cultivating corn in the old way, he can use a corn cultivator that lays off the furrows, drops the corn into them, and covers it; and in this way he can do more work than three men by the old process of corn planting, while at the same time much of the toil is eliminated and labour is dignified. In a word, the constant aim is to show the student how to put brains into every process of labour, how to bring his knowledge of mathematics and the sciences in farming, carpentry, forging, foundry work, how to dispense as soon as possible with the old form of *ante-bellum* labour. In the erection of the chapel referred to, instead of letting the money which was given to us go into outside hands, we made it accomplish three objects: first, it provided the chapel; second, it gave the students a chance to get a practical knowledge of the trades connected with the building; and, third, it enabled them to earn something toward the payment of their board while receiving academic and industrial training.

Having been fortified at Tuskegee by education of mind, skill of hand, Christian character, ideas of thrift, economy, and push, and a spirit of independence, the student is sent out to become a centre of influence and light in showing the masses of our people in the Black Belt of the South how to lift themselves up. Can this be done? I give but one or two examples. Ten years ago a young coloured man came to the institute from one of the large plantation districts. He studied in the class-room a portion of the time, and received practical and theoretical training on the farm the remainder of the time. Having finished his course at Tuskegee, he returned to his plantation home, which was in a county where the coloured people outnumbered the whites six to one, as is true of many of the counties in the Black Belt of the South. He found the Negroes in debt. Ever since the war they had been mortgaging their crops for the food on which to live while the crops were growing. The majority of them were living from hand-to-mouth on rented land, in small one-room log cabins, and attempting to pay a rate of interest on their advances that ranged from fifteen to forty per cent. per annum. The school had been taught in a wreck of a log cabin, with no apparatus, and had never been in session longer than three months out of twelve. He found the people, as many as eight or ten persons, of all ages and conditions and of both sexes, huddled together and living in one-room cabins year after year, and with a minister whose only aim was to work upon the emotions. One can imagine something of the moral and religious state of the community.

But the remedy! In spite of the evil the Negro got the habit of work from slavery. The rank and file of the race, especially those on the Southern plantations, work hard; but the trouble is that what they earn gets away from them in high rents, crop mortgages, whiskey, snuff, cheap jewelry, and the like. The young man just referred to had been trained at Tuskegee, as most of our graduates are, to meet just this condition of things. He took the three months' public school as a nucleus for his work. Then he organized the older people into a club, or conference, that held meetings every week. In these meetings he taught the people, in a plain, simple manner, how to save their money, how to farm in a better way, how to sacrifice,—to live on bread and potatoes, if necessary, till they could get out of debt, and begin the buying of lands.

Soon a large proportion of the people were in a condition to make contracts for the buying of homes (land is very cheap in the South) and to live without mortgaging their crops. Not only this; under the guidance and leadership of this teacher, the first year that he was among them they learned how and built, by contributions in money and labour, a neat, comfortable school-house that replaced the wreck of a log cabin formerly used. The following year the weekly meetings were continued, and two months were added to the original three months of school. The next year two more months were added. The improvement has gone on until these people have every year an eight months' school.

I wish my readers could have the chance that I have had of going into this community. I wish they could look into the faces of the people, and see them beaming with hope and delight. I wish they could see the two or three room cottages that have taken the place of the usual one-room cabin, see the well-cultivated farms and the religious life of the people that now means something more than the name. The teacher has a good cottage and well-kept farm that serve as models. In a word, a complete revolution has been wrought in the industrial, educational, and religious life of this whole community by reason of the fact that they have had this leader, this guide and object-lesson, to show them how to take the money and effort that had hitherto been scattered to the wind in mortgages and high rents, in whiskey and gewgaws, and how to concentrate it in the direction of their own uplifting. One community on its feet presents an object-lesson for the adjoining communities, and soon improvements show themselves in other places.

Another student, who received academic and industrial training at Tuskegee, established himself, three years ago, as a blacksmith and wheelwright in a community; and, in addition to the influence of his successful business enterprise, he is fast making the same kind of changes in the life of the people about him that I have just recounted. It would be easy for me to fill many pages describing the influence of the Tuskegee graduates in every part of the South. We keep it constantly in the minds of our students and graduates that the industrial or material condition of the masses of our people must be improved, as well as the intellectual, before there can be any permanent change in their moral and religious life. We find it a pretty hard thing to make a good Christian of a hungry man. No matter how much our people "get happy" and "shout" in church, if they go home at night from church hungry, they are tempted to find something to eat before morning. This is a principle of human nature, and is not confined alone to the Negro. The Negro has within him immense power for self-uplifting, but for years it will be necessary to guide him and stimulate his energies.

The recognition of this power led us to organise, five years ago, what is known as the Tuskegee Negro Conference,—a gathering that meets every February, and is composed of about eight hundred representatives, coloured men and women, from all sections of the Black Belt. They come in ox-carts, mule-carts, buggies, on muleback and horseback, on foot, by railroad. Some travel all night in order to be present. The matters considered at the conference are those that the coloured people have it in their own power to control,—such as the evils of the mortgage system, the one-room cabin, buying on credit, the importance of owning a home and of putting money in the bank, how to build school-houses and prolong the school term, and to improve their moral and religious condition. As a single example of the results, one delegate reported that since the conference was started, seven years ago, eleven people in his neighbourhood had bought homes, fourteen had gotten out of debt, and a number had stopped mortgaging their crops. Moreover, a school-house had been built by the people themselves, and the school term had been extended from three to six months; and, with a look of triumph, he exclaimed, "We's done libin' in de ashes."

Besides this Negro Conference for the masses of the people, we now have a gathering at the same time known as the Tuskegee Workers' Conference, composed of the officers and instructors of the leading coloured schools in the South. After listening to the story of the conditions and needs from the people themselves, the Workers' Conference finds much food for thought and discussion. Let me repeat, from its beginning, this institution has kept in mind the giving of thorough mental and religious training, along with such industrial training as would enable the student to appreciate the dignity of labour and become self-supporting and valuable as a producing factor, keeping in mind the occupations open in the South to the average man of the race.

This institution has now reached the point where it can begin to judge of the value of its work as seen in its graduates. Some years ago we noted the fact, for example, that there was quite a movement in many parts of the South to organise and start dairies. Soon after this, we opened a dairy school where a number of young men could receive training in the best and most scientific methods of dairying. At present we have calls, mainly from Southern white men, for twice as many dairymen as we are able to supply. The reports indicate that our young men are giving the highest satisfaction, and are fast changing and improving the dairy product in the communities where they labour. I have used the dairy industry simply as an example. What I have said of this industry is true in a larger or less degree of the others.

I cannot but believe, and my daily observation and experience confirm me in it, that, as we continue placing men and women of intelligence, religion, modesty, conscience, and skill in every community in the South, who will prove by actual results their value to the community, this will constitute the solution for many of the present political and sociological difficulties. It is with this larger and more comprehensive view of improving present conditions and laying the foundation wisely that the Tuskegee Normal and Industrial Institute is training men and women as teachers and industrial leaders.

Over four hundred students have finished the course of training at this institution, and are now scattered throughout the South, doing good work. A recent investigation shows that about 3,000 students who have taken only a partial course are doing commendable work. One young man, who was able to

[308]

remain in school but two years, has been teaching in one community for ten years. During this time he has built a new school-house, extended the school term from three to seven months, and has bought a nice farm upon which he has erected a neat cottage. The example of this young man has inspired many of the coloured people in this community to follow his example in some degree; and this is one of many such examples.

Wherever our graduates and ex-students go, they teach by precept and example the necessary lesson of thrift, economy, and property-getting, and friendship between the races.

CHAPTER 6

It has become apparent that the effort to put the rank and file of the coloured people into a position to exercise the right of franchise has not been the success that was expected in those portions of our country where the Negro is found in large numbers. Either the Negro was not prepared for any such wholesale exercise of the ballot as our recent amendments to the Constitution contemplated or the American people were not prepared to assist and encourage him to use the ballot. In either case the result has been the same.

On an important occasion in the life of the Master, when it fell to him to pronounce judgment on two courses of action, these memorable words fell from his lips: "And Mary hath chosen the better part." This was the supreme test in the case of an individual. It is the highest test in the case of a race or a nation. Let us apply this test to the American Negro.

In the life of our Republic, when he has had the opportunity to choose, has it been the better or worse part? When in the childhood of this nation the Negro was asked to submit to slavery or choose death and extinction, as did the aborigines, he chose the better part, that which perpetuated the race.

When, in 1776, the Negro was asked to decide between British oppression and American independence, we find him choosing the better part; and Crispus Attucks, a Negro, was the first to shed his blood on State Street, Boston, that the white American might enjoy liberty forever, though his race remained in slavery. When, in 1814, at New Orleans, the test of patriotism came again, we find the Negro choosing the better part, General Andrew Jackson himself testifying that no heart was more loyal and no arm was more strong and useful in defence of righteousness.

When the long and memorable struggle came between union and separation, when he knew that victory meant freedom, and defeat his continued enslavement, although enlisting by the thousands, as opportunity presented itself, to fight in honourable combat for the cause of the Union and liberty, yet, when the suggestion and the temptation came to burn the home and massacre wife and children during the absence of the master in battle, and thus insure his liberty, we find him choosing the better part, and for four long years protecting and supporting the helpless, defenceless ones intrusted to his care.

When, during our war with Spain, the safety and honour of the Republic were threatened by a foreign foe, when the wail and anguish of the oppressed from a distant isle reached our ears, we find the Negro forgetting his own wrongs, forgetting the laws and customs that discriminate against him in his own country, and again choosing the better part. And, if any one would know how he acquitted himself in the field at Santiago, let him apply for answer to Shafter and Roosevelt and Wheeler. Let them tell how the Negro faced death and laid down his life in defence of honour and humanity. When the full story of the heroic conduct of the Negro in the Spanish-American War has been heard from the lips of Northern soldier and Southern soldier, from ex-abolitionist and ex-master, then shall the country decide whether a race that is thus willing to die for its country should not be given the highest opportunity to live for its country.

In the midst of all the complaints of suffering in the camp and field during the Spanish-American War, suffering from fever and hunger, where is the official or citizen that has heard a word of complaint from the lips of a black soldier? The only request that came from the Negro soldier was that he might be permitted to replace the white soldier when heat and malaria began to decimate the ranks of the white regiments, and to occupy at the same time the post of greater danger.

But, when all this is said, it remains true that the efforts on the part of his friends and the part of himself to share actively in the control of State and local government in America have not been a success in all sections. What are the causes of this partial failure, and what lessons has it taught that we may use in regard to the future treatment of the Negro in America?

In my mind there is no doubt but that we made a mistake at the beginning of our freedom of putting the emphasis on the wrong end. Politics and the holding of office were too largely emphasised, almost to the exclusion of every other interest.

I believe the past and present teach but one lesson,—to the Negro's friends and to the Negro himself,—that there is but one way out, that there is but one hope of solution; and that is for the Negro in every part of America to

[311]

resolve from henceforth that he will throw aside every non-essential and cling only to essential,—that his pillar of fire by night and pillar of cloud by day shall be property, economy, education, and Christian character. To us just now these are the wheat, all else the chaff. The individual or race that owns the property, pays the taxes, possesses the intelligence and substantial character, is the one which is going to exercise the greatest control in government, whether he lives in the North or whether he lives in the South.

I have often been asked the cause of and the cure for the riots that have taken place recently in North Carolina and South Carolina.[6] I am not at all sure that what I shall say will answer these questions in a satisfactory way, nor shall I attempt to narrow my expressions to a mere recital of what has taken place in these two States. I prefer to discuss the problem in a broader manner.

In the first place, in politics I am a Republican, but have always refrained from activity in party politics, and expect to pursue this policy in the future. So in this connection I shall refrain, as I always have done, from entering upon any discussion of mere party politics. What I shall say of politics will bear upon the race problem and the civilisation of the South in the larger sense. In no case would I permit my political relations to stand in the way of my speaking and acting in the manner that I believe would be for the permanent interest of my race and the whole South.

In 1873 the Negro in the South had reached the point of greatest activity and influence in public life, so far as the mere holding of elective office was concerned. From that date those who have kept up with the history of the South have noticed that the Negro has steadily lost in the number of elective offices held. In saying this, I do not mean that the Negro has gone backward in the real and more fundamental things of life. On the contrary, he has gone forward faster than has been true of any other race in history, under anything like similar circumstances.

If we can answer the question as to why the Negro has lost ground in the matter of holding elective office in the South, perhaps we shall find that our reply will prove to be our answer also as to the cause of the recent riots in North Carolina and South Carolina. Before beginning a discussion of the question I

---

[6] November, 1898.

[312]

have asked, I wish to say that this change in the political influence of the Negro has continued from year to year, notwithstanding the fact that for a long time he was protected, politically, by force of federal arms and the most rigid federal laws, and still more effectively, perhaps, by the voice and influence in the halls of legislation of such advocates of the rights of the Negro race as Thaddeus Stevens, Charles Sumner, Benjamin F. Butler, James M. Ashley, Oliver P. Morton, Carl Schurz, and Roscoe Conkling, and on the stump and through the public press by those great and powerful Negroes, Frederick Douglass, John M. Langston, Blanche K. Bruce, John R. Lynch, P. B. S. Pinchback, Robert Browne Elliot, T. Thomas Fortune, and many others; but the Negro has continued for twenty years to have fewer representatives in the State and national legislatures. The reduction has continued until now it is at the point where, with few exceptions, he is without representatives in the law-making bodies of the State and of the nation.

Now let us find, if we can, a cause for this. The Negro is fond of saying that his present condition is due to the fact that the State and federal courts have not sustained the laws passed for the protection of the rights of his people; but I think we shall have to go deeper than this, because I believe that all agree that court decisions, as a rule, represent the public opinion of the community or nation creating and sustaining the court.

At the beginning of his freedom it was unfortunate that those of the white race who won the political confidence of the Negro were not, with few exceptions, men of such high character as would lead them to assist him in laying a firm foundation for his development. Their main purpose appears to have been, for selfish ends in too many instances, merely to control his vote. The history of the reconstruction era will show that this was unfortunate for all the parties in interest.

It would have been better, from any point of view, if the native Southern white man had taken the Negro, at the beginning of his freedom, into his political confidence, and exercised an influence and control over him before his political affections were alienated.

The average Southern white man has an idea to-day that, if the Negro were permitted to get any political power, all the mistakes of the reconstruction period would be repeated. He forgets or ignores the fact that thirty years of acquiring education and property and character have produced a higher type of black man than existed thirty years ago.

But, to be more specific, for all practical purposes, there are two political parties in the South,—a black man's party and a white man's party. In saying this, I do not mean that all white men are Democrats; for there are some white men in the South of the highest character who are Republicans, and there are a few Negroes in the South of the highest character who are Democrats. It is the general understanding that all white men are Democrats or the equivalent, and that all black men are Republicans. So long as the colour line is the dividing line in politics, so long will there be trouble.

The white man feels that he owns most of the property, furnishes the Negro most of his employment, thinks he pays most of the taxes, and has had years of experience in government. There is no mistaking the fact that the feeling which has heretofore governed the Negro—that, to be manly and stand by his race, he must oppose the Southern white man with his vote—has had much to do with intensifying the opposition of the Southern white man to him.

The Southern white man says that it is unreasonable for the Negro to come to him, in a large measure, for his clothes, board, shelter, and education, and for his politics to go to men a thousand miles away. He very properly argues that, when the Negro votes, he should try to consult the interests of his employer, just as the Pennsylvania employee tries to vote for the interests of his employer. Further, that much of the education which has been given the Negro has been defective, in not preparing him to love labour and to earn his living at some special industry, and has, in too many cases, resulted in tempting him to live by his wits as a political creature or by trusting to his "influence" as a political time-server.

Then, there is no mistaking the fact, that much opposition to the Negro in politics is due to the circumstance that the Southern white man has not become accustomed to seeing the Negro exercise political power either as a voter or as an office-holder. Again, we want to bear it in mind that the South has not yet reached the point where there is that strict regard for the enforcement of the law against either black or white men that there is in many of our Northern and Western States. This laxity in the enforcement of the laws in general, and especially of criminal laws, makes such outbreaks as those in North Carolina and South Carolina of easy occurrence.

[314]

Then there is one other consideration which must not be overlooked. It is the common opinion of almost every black man and almost every white man that nearly everybody who has had anything to do with the making of laws bearing upon the protection of the Negro's vote has proceeded on the theory that all the black men for all time will vote the Republican ticket and that all the white men in the South will vote the Democratic ticket. In a word, all seem to have taken it for granted that the two races are always going to oppose each other in their voting.

In all the foregoing statements I have not attempted to define my own views or position, but simply to describe conditions as I have observed them, that might throw light upon the cause of our political troubles. As to my own position, I do not favour the Negro's giving up anything which is fundamental and which has been guaranteed to him by the Constitution of the United States. It is not best for him to relinquish any of his rights; nor would his doing so be best for the Southern white man. Every law placed in the Constitution of the United States was placed there to encourage and stimulate the highest citizenship. If the Negro is not stimulated and encouraged by just State and national laws to become the highest type of citizen, the result will be worse for the Southern white man than for the Negro. Take the State of South Carolina, for example, where nearly two-thirds of the population are Negroes. Unless these Negroes are encouraged by just election laws to become tax-payers and intelligent producers, the white people of South Carolina will have an eternal millstone about their necks.

In an open letter to the State Constitutional Convention of Louisiana, I wrote:

"I am no politician. On the other hand, I have always advised my race to give attention to acquiring property, intelligence, and character, as the necessary bases of good citizenship, rather than to mere political agitation. But the question upon which I write is out of the region of ordinary politics. It affects the civilisation of two races, not for to-day alone, but for a very long time to come.

"Since the war, no State has had such an opportunity to settle, for all time, the race question, so far as it concerns politics, as is now given to Louisiana. Will your convention set an example to the world in this respect? Will Louisiana take such high and just grounds in respect to the Negro that no one can doubt that the South is as good a friend to him as he possesses elsewhere? In all this, gentlemen of the convention, I am not pleading for the Negro alone, but for the morals, the higher life, of the white man as well.

"The Negro agrees with you that it is necessary to the salvation of the South that restrictions be put upon the ballot. I know that you have two serious problems before you; ignorant and corrupt government, on the one hand; and, on the other, a way to restrict the ballot so that control will be in the hands of the intelligent, without regard to race. With the sincerest sympathy with you in your efforts to find a good way out of the difficulty, I want to suggest that no State in the South can make a law that will provide an opportunity or temptation for an ignorant white man to vote, and withhold the opportunity or temptation from an ignorant coloured man, without injuring both men. No State can make a law that can thus be executed without dwarfing, for all time, the morals of the white man in the South. Any law controlling the ballot that is not absolutely just and fair to both races will work more permanent injury to the whites than to the blacks.

"The Negro does not object to an educational and property test, but let the law be so clear that no one clothed with State authority will be tempted to perjure and degrade himself by putting one interpretation upon it for the white man and another for the black man. Study the history of the South, and you will find that, where there has been the most dishonesty in the matter of voting, there you will find to-day the lowest moral condition of both races. First, there was the temptation to act wrongly with the Negro's ballot. From this it was an easy step to act dishonestly with the white man's ballot, to the carrying of concealed weapons, to the murder of a Negro, and then to the murder of a white man, and then to lynching. I entreat you not to pass a law that will prove an eternal millstone about the necks of your children. No man can have respect for the government and officers of the law when he knows, deep down in his heart, that the exercise of the franchise is tainted with fraud.

"The road that the South has been compelled to travel during the last thirty years has been strewn with thorns and thistles. It has been as one groping through the long darkness into the light. The time is not far distant when the world will begin to appreciate the real character of the burden that was imposed upon the South in giving the franchise to four millions of ignorant and impoverished ex-slaves. No people was ever before given such a problem to

[316]

solve. History has blazed no path through the wilderness that could be followed. For thirty years we have wandered in the wilderness. We are now beginning to get out. But there is only one road out; and all makeshifts, expedients, profit and loss calculations, but lead into swamps, quicksands, quagmires, and jungles. There is a highway that will lead both races out into the pure, beautiful sunshine, where there will be nothing to hide and nothing to explain, where both races can grow strong and true and useful in every fibre of their being. I believe that your convention will find this highway, that it will enact a fundamental law that will be absolutely just and fair to white and black alike.

"I beg of you, further, that in the degree that you close the ballot-box against the ignorant you will open the school-house. More than one-half of the population of your State are Negroes. No State can long prosper when a large part of its citizenship is in ignorance and poverty, and has no interest in the government. I beg of you that you do not treat us as an alien people. We are not aliens. You know us. You know that we have cleared your forests, tilled your fields, nursed your children, and protected your families. There is an attachment between us that few understand. While I do not presume to be able to advise you, yet it is in my heart to say that, if your convention would do something that would prevent for all time strained relations between the two races, and would permanently settle the matter of political relations in one Southern State at least, let the very best educational opportunities be provided for both races; and add to this an election law that shall be incapable of unjust discrimination, at the same time providing that, in proportion as the ignorant secure education, property, and character, they will be given the right of citizenship. Any other course will take from one-half your citizens interest in the State, and hope and ambition to become intelligent producers and tax-payers, and useful and virtuous citizens. Any other course will tie the white citizens of Louisiana to a body of death.

"The Negroes are not unmindful of the fact that the poverty of the State prevents it from doing all that it desires for public education; yet I believe that you will agree with me that ignorance is more costly to the State than education, that it will cost Louisiana more not to educate the Negroes than it will to educate them. In connection with a generous provision for public schools, I believe that nothing will so help my own people in your State as provision at some institution for the highest academic and normal training, in connection with thorough training in agriculture, mechanics, and domestic economy.

[317]

First-class training in agriculture, horticulture, dairying, stock-raising, the mechanical arts, and domestic economy, would make us intelligent producers, and not only help us to contribute our honest share as tax-payers, but would result in retaining much money in the State that now goes outside for that which can be as well produced at home. An institution which will give this training of the hand, along with the highest mental culture, would soon convince our people that their salvation is largely in the ownership of property and in industrial and business development, rather than in mere political agitation.

"The highest test of the civilisation of any race is in its willingness to extend a helping hand to the less fortunate. A race, like an individual, lifts itself up by lifting others up. Surely, no people ever had a greater chance to exhibit the highest Christian fortitude and magnanimity than is now presented to the people of Louisiana. It requires little wisdom or statesmanship to repress, to crush out, to retard the hopes and aspirations of a people; but the highest and most profound statesmanship is shown in guiding and stimulating a people, so that every fibre in the body and soul shall be made to contribute in the highest degree to the usefulness and ability of the State. It is along this line that I pray God the thoughts and activities of your convention may be guided."

As to such outbreaks as have recently occurred in North Carolina and South Carolina, the remedy will not be reached by the Southern white man merely depriving the Negro of his rights and privileges. This method is but superficial, irritating, and must, in the nature of things, be short-lived. The statesman, to cure an evil, resorts to enlightenment, to stimulation; the politician, to repression. I have just remarked that I favour the giving up of nothing that is guaranteed to us by the Constitution of the United States, or that is fundamental to our citizenship. While I hold to these views as strongly as any one, I differ with some as to the method of securing the permanent and peaceful enjoyment of all the privileges guaranteed to us by our fundamental law.

In finding a remedy, we must recognise the world-wide fact that the Negro must be led to see and feel that he must make every effort possible, in every way possible, to secure the friendship, the confidence, the co-operation of his white neighbour in the South. To do this, it is not necessary for the Negro to become a truckler or a trimmer. The Southern white man has no respect for a Negro who does not act from principle. In some way the Southern white man must be led to see that it is to his interest to turn his attention more and more to the making of laws that will, in the truest sense, elevate the Negro. At the present moment, in many cases, when one attempts to get the Negro to co-operate with the Southern white man, he asks the question, "Can the people who force me to ride in a Jim Crow car, and pay first-class fare, be my best friends?" In answering such questions, the Southern white man, as well as the Negro, has a duty to perform. In the exercise of his political rights I should advise the Negro to be temperate and modest, and more and more to do his own thinking.

I believe the permanent cure for our present evils will come through a property and educational test for voting that shall apply honestly and fairly to both races. This will cut off the large mass of ignorant voters of both races that is now proving so demoralising a factor in the politics of the Southern States.

But, most of all, it will come through industrial development of the Negro. Industrial education makes an intelligent producer of the Negro, who becomes of immediate value to the community rather than one who yields to the temptation to live merely by politics or other parasitical employments. It will make him soon become a property-holder; and, when a citizen becomes a holder of property, he becomes a conservative and thoughtful voter. He will more carefully consider the measures and individuals to be voted for. In proportion as he increases his property interests, he becomes important as a tax-payer.

There is little trouble between the Negro and the white man in matters of education; and, when it comes to his business development, the black man has implicit faith in the advice of the Southern white man. When he gets into trouble in the courts, which requires a bond to be given, in nine cases out of ten, he goes to a Southern white man for advice and assistance. Every one who has lived in the South knows that, in many of the church troubles among the coloured people, the ministers and other church officers apply to the nearest white minister for assistance and instruction. When by reason of mutual concession we reach the point where we shall consult the Southern white man about our politics as we now consult him about our business, legal, and religious matters, there will be a change for the better in the situation.

The object-lesson of a thousand Negroes in every county in the South who own neat and comfortable homes, possessing skill, industry, and thrift, with money in the bank, and are large tax-payers co-operating with the white men in the South in every manly way for the development of their own communities and counties, will go a long way, in a few years, toward changing the present status of the Negro as a citizen, as well as the attitude of the whites toward the blacks.

As the Negro grows in industrial and business directions, he will divide in his politics on economic issues, just as the white man in other parts of the country now divides his vote. As the South grows in business prosperity it will divide its vote on economic issues, just as other sections of the country divide their vote. When we can enact laws that result in honestly cutting off the large ignorant and non-tax-paying vote, and when we can bring both races to the point where they will co-operate with each other in politics, as they do now in matters of business, religion, and education, the problem will be in a large measure solved, and political outbreaks will cease.

CHAPTER 7

One of the great questions which Christian education must face in the South is the proper adjustment of the new relations of the two races. It is a question which must be faced calmly, quietly, dispassionately; and the time has now come to rise above party, above race, above colour, above sectionalism, into the region of duty of man to man, of American to American, of Christian to Christian.

I remember not long ago, when about five hundred coloured people sailed from the port of Savannah bound for Liberia, that the news was flashed all over the country, "The Negro has made up his mind to return to his own country," and that, "in this was the solution of the race problem in the South." But these short-sighted people forgot the fact that before breakfast that morning about five hundred more Negro children were born in the South alone.

And then, once in a while, somebody is so bold as to predict that the Negro will be absorbed by the white race. Let us look at this phase of the question for a moment. It is a fact that, if a person is known to have one per cent. of African blood in his veins, he ceases to be a white man. The ninety-nine per cent. of Caucasian blood does not weigh by the side of the one per cent. of African blood. The white blood counts for nothing. The person is a Negro every time. So it will be a very difficult task for the white man to absorb the Negro.

Somebody else conceived the idea of colonising the coloured people, of getting territory where nobody lived, putting the coloured people there, and letting them be a nation all by themselves. There are two objections to that. First, you would have to build one wall to keep the coloured people in, and another wall to keep the white people out. If you were to build ten walls around Africa to-day you could not keep the white people out, especially as long as there was a hope of finding gold there.

I have always had the highest respect for those of our race who, in trying to find a solution for our Southern problem, advised a return of the race to Africa, and because of my respect for those who have thus advised, especially Bishop Henry M. Turner, I have tried to make a careful and unbiassed study of the question, during a recent sojourn in Europe, to see what opportunities presented themselves in Africa for self-development and self-government.

I am free to say that I see no way out of the Negro's present condition in the South by returning to Africa. Aside from other insurmountable obstacles, there is no place in Africa for him to go where his condition would be improved. All Europe—especially England, France, and Germany—has been running a mad race for the last twenty years, to see which could gobble up the greater part of Africa; and there is practically nothing left. Old King Cetewayo put it pretty well when he said, "First come missionary, then come rum, then come traders, then come army"; and Cecil Rhodes has expressed the prevailing sentiment more recently in these words, "I would rather have land than 'niggers.'" And Cecil Rhodes is directly responsible for the killing of thousands of black natives in South Africa, that he might secure their land.

In a talk with Henry M. Stanley, the explorer, he told me that he knew no place in Africa where the Negroes of the United States might go to advantage; but I want to be more specific. Let us see how Africa has been divided, and then decide whether there is a place left for us. On the Mediterranean coast of Africa, Morocco is an independent State, Algeria is a French possession, Tunis is a French protectorate, Tripoli is a province of the Ottoman Empire, Egypt is a province of Turkey. On the Atlantic coast, Sahara is a French protectorate, Adrar is claimed by Spain, Senegambia is a French trading settlement, Gambia is a British crown colony, Sierra Leone is a British crown colony. Liberia is a republic of freed Negroes, Gold Coast and Ashanti are British colonies and British protectorates, Togoland is a German protectorate, Dahomey is a kingdom subject to French influence, Slave Coast is a British colony and British protectorate, Niger Coast is a British protectorate, the Cameroons are trading settlements protected by Germany, French Congo is a French protectorate, Congo Free State is an international African Association, Angola and Benguela are Portuguese protectorates, and the inland countries are controlled as follows: The Niger States, Masina, etc., are under French protection; Land Gandu is under British protection, administered by the Royal Haussan Niger Company.

South Africa is controlled as follows: Damara and Namaqua Land are German protectorates, Cape Colony is a British colony, Basutoland is a Crown colony, Bechuanaland is a British protectorate, Natal is a British colony,

Zululand is a British protectorate, Orange Free State is independent, the South African Republic is independent, and the Zambesi is administered by the British South African Company. Lourence Marques is a Portuguese possession.

East Africa has also been disposed of in the following manner: Mozambique is a Portuguese possession, British Central Africa is a British protectorate, German East Africa is in the German sphere of influence, Zanzibar is a sultanate under British protection, British East Africa is a British protectorate, Somaliland is under British and Italian protection, Abyssinia is independent. East Soudan (including Nubia, Kordofan, Darfur, and Wadai) is in the British sphere of influence. It will be noted that, when one of these European countries cannot get direct control over any section of Africa, it at once gives it out to the world that the country wanted is in the "sphere of its influence,"—a very convenient term. If we are to go to Africa, and be under the control of another government, I think we should prefer to take our chances in the "sphere of influence" of the United States.

All this shows pretty conclusively that a return to Africa for the Negro is out of the question, even provided that a majority of the Negroes wished to go back, which they do not. The adjustment of the relations of the two races must take place here; and it is taking place slowly, but surely. As the Negro is educated to make homes and to respect himself, the white man will in turn respect him.

It has been urged that the Negro has inherent in him certain traits of character that will prevent his ever reaching the standard of civilisation set by the whites, and taking his place among them as an equal. It may be some time before the Negro race as a whole can stand comparison with the white in all respects,—it would be most remarkable, considering the past, if it were not so; but the idea that his objectionable traits and weaknesses are fundamental, I think, is a mistake. For, although there are elements of weakness about the Negro race, there are also many evidences of strength.

It is an encouraging sign, however, when an individual grows to the point where he can hold himself up for personal analysis and study. It is equally encouraging for a race to be able to study itself,—to measure its weakness and strength. It is not helpful to a race to be continually praised and have its weakness overlooked, neither is it the most helpful thing to have its faults alone

[323]

continually dwelt upon. What is needed is downright, straightforward honesty in both directions; and this is not always to be obtained.

There is little question that one of the Negroes' weak points is physical. Especially is this true regarding those who live in the large cities, North and South. But in almost every case this physical weakness can be traced to ignorant violation of the laws of health or to vicious habits. The Negro, who during slavery lived on the large plantations in the South, surrounded by restraints, at the close of the war came to the cities, and in many cases found the freedom and temptations of the city too much for him. The transition was too sudden.

When we consider what it meant to have four millions of people slaves to-day and freemen to-morrow, the wonder is that the race has not suffered more physically than it has. I do not believe that statistics can be so marshalled as to prove that the Negro as a race is physically or numerically on the decline. On the other hand, the Negro as a race is increasing in numbers by a larger percentage than is true of the French nation. While the death-rate is large in the cities, the birth-rate is also large; and it is to be borne in mind that eighty-five per cent. of these people in the Gulf States are in the country districts and smaller towns, and there the increase is along healthy and normal lines. As the Negro becomes educated, the high death-rate in the cities will disappear. For proof of this, I have only to mention that a few years ago no coloured man could get insurance in the large first-class insurance companies. Now there are few of these companies which do not seek the insurance of educated coloured men. In the North and South the physical intoxication that was the result of sudden freedom is giving way to an encouraging, sobering process; and, as this continues, the high death-rate will disappear even, in the large cities.

Another element of weakness which shows itself in the present stage of the civilisation of the Negro is his lack of ability to form a purpose and stick to it through a series of years, if need be,—years that involve discouragement as well as encouragement,—till the end shall be reached. Of course there are brilliant exceptions to this rule; but there is no question that here is an element of weakness, and the same, I think, would be true of any race with the Negro's history.

Few of the resolutions which are made in conventions, etc., are remembered and put into practice six months after the warmth and enthusiasm

[324]

of the debating hall have disappeared. This, I know, is an element of the white man's weakness, but it is the Negro I am discussing, not the white man. Individually, the Negro is strong. Collectively, he is weak. This is not to be wondered at. The ability to succeed in organised bodies is one of the highest points in civilisation. There are scores of coloured men who can succeed in any line of business as individuals, or will discuss any subject in a most intelligent manner, yet who, when they attempt to act in an organised body, are utter failures.

But the weakness of the Negro which is most frequently held up to the public gaze is that of his moral character. No one who wants to be honest and at the same time benefit the race will deny that here is where the strengthening is to be done. It has become universally accepted that the family is the foundation, the bulwark, of any race. It should be remembered, sorrowfully withal, that it was the constant tendency of slavery to destroy the family life. All through two hundred and fifty years of slavery, one of the chief objects was to increase the number of slaves; and to this end almost all thought of morality was lost sight of, so that the Negro has had only about thirty years in which to develop a family life; while the Anglo-Saxon rate, with which he is constantly being compared, has had thousands of years of training in home life. The Negro felt all through the years of bondage that he was being forcibly and unjustly deprived of the fruits of his labour. Hence he felt that anything he could get from the white man in return for this labour justly belonged to him. Since this was true, we must be patient in trying to teach him a different code of morals.

From the nature of things, all through slavery it was life in the future world that was emphasised in religious teaching rather than life in this world. In his religious meetings in *ante-bellum* days the Negro was prevented from discussing many points of practical religion which related to this world; and the white minister, who was his spiritual guide, found it more convenient to talk about heaven than earth, so very naturally that to-day in his religious meeting it is the Negro's feelings which are worked upon mostly, and it is description of the glories of heaven that occupy most of the time of his sermon.

Having touched upon some of the weak points of the Negro, what are his strong characteristics? The Negro in America is different from most people for whom missionary effort is made, in that he works. He is not ashamed or afraid of work. When hard, constant work is required, ask any Southern white

[325]

man, and he will tell you that in this the Negro has no superior. He is not given to strikes or to lockouts. He not only works himself, but he is unwilling to prevent other people from working.

Of the forty buildings of various kinds and sizes on the grounds of the Tuskegee Normal and Industrial Institute, in Alabama, as I have stated before, almost all of them are the results of the labour performed by the students while securing their academic education. One day the student is in his history class. The next day the same student, equally happy, with his trowel and in overalls, is working on a brick wall.

While at present the Negro may lack that tenacious mental grasp which enables one to pursue a scientific or mathematical investigation through a series of years, he has that delicate, mental feeling which enables him to succeed in oratory, music, etc.

While I have spoken of the Negro's moral weakness, I hope it will be kept in mind that in his original state his is an honest race. It was slavery that corrupted him in this respect. But in morals he also has his strong points.

Few have ever found the Negro guilty of betraying a trust. There are almost no instances in which the Negro betrayed either a Federal or a Confederate soldier who confided in him. There are few instances where the Negro has been entrusted with valuables when he has not been faithful. This country has never had a more loyal citizen. He has never proven himself a rebel. Should the Southern States, which so long held him in slavery, be invaded by a foreign foe, the Negro would be among the first to come to the rescue.

Perhaps the most encouraging thing in connection with the lifting up of the Negro in this country is the fact that he knows that he is down and wants to get up, he knows that he is ignorant and wants to get light. He fills every school-house and every church which is opened for him. He is willing to follow leaders, when he is once convinced that the leaders have his best interest at heart.

Under the constant influence of the Christian education which began thirty-five years ago, his religion is every year becoming less emotional and more rational and practical, though I, for one, hope that he will always retain in a large degree the emotional element in religion.

[326]

During the two hundred and fifty years that the Negro spent in slavery he had little cause or incentive to accumulate money or property. Thirty-five years ago this was something which he had to begin to learn. While the great bulk of the race is still without money and property, yet the signs of thrift are evident on every hand. Especially is this noticeable in the large number of neat little homes which are owned by these people on the outer edges of the towns and cities in the South.

I wish to give an example of the sort of thing the Negro has to contend with, however, in his efforts to lift himself up.

Not long ago a mother, a black mother, who lived in one of our Northern States, had heard it whispered around in her community for years that the Negro was lazy, shiftless, and would not work. So, when her only boy grew to sufficient size, at considerable expense and great self-sacrifice, she had her boy thoroughly taught the machinist's trade. A job was secured in a neighbouring shop. With dinner bucket in hand and spurred on by the prayers of the now happy-hearted mother, the boy entered the shop to begin his first day's work. What happened? Every one of the twenty white men threw down his tools, and deliberately walked out, swearing that he would not give a black man an opportunity to earn an honest living. Another shop was tried with the same result, and still another, the result ever the same. To-day this once promising, ambitious black man is a wreck,—a confirmed drunkard,—with no hope, no ambition. I ask, Who blasted the life of this young man? On whose hands does his lifeblood rest? The present system of education, or rather want of education, is responsible.

Public schools and colleges should turn out men who will throw open the doors of industry, so that all men, everywhere, regardless of colour, shall have the same opportunity to earn a dollar that they now have to spend it. I know of a good many kinds of cowardice and prejudice, but I know none equal to this. I know not which is the worst,—the slaveholder who perforce compelled his slave to work without compensation or the man who, by force and strikes, compels his neighbour to refrain from working for compensation.

The Negro will be on a different footing in this country when it becomes common to associate the possession of wealth with a black skin. It is not within the province of human nature that the man who is intelligent and virtuous, and owns and cultivates the best farm in his county, is the largest

[327]

tax-payer, shall very long be denied proper respect and consideration. Those who would help the Negro most effectually during the next fifty years can do so by assisting in his development along scientific and industrial lines in connection with the broadest mental and religious culture.

From the results of the war with Spain let us learn this, that God has been teaching the Spanish nation a terrible lesson. What is it? Simply this, that no nation can disregard the interest of any portion of its members without that nation becoming weak and corrupt. The penalty may be long delayed. God has been teaching Spain that for every one of her subjects that she has left in ignorance, poverty, and crime the price must be paid; and, if it has not been paid with the very heart of the nation, it must be paid with the proudest and bluest blood of her sons and with treasure that is beyond computation. From this spectacle I pray God that America will learn a lesson in respect to the ten million Negroes in this country.

The Negroes in the United States are, in most of the elements of civilisation, weak. Providence has placed them here not without a purpose. One object, in my opinion, is that the stronger race may imbibe a lesson from the weaker in patience, forbearance, and childlike yet supreme trust in the God of the Universe. This race has been placed here that the white man might have a great opportunity of lifting himself by lifting it up.

Out from the Negro colleges and industrial schools in the South there are going forth each year thousands of young men and women into dark and secluded corners, into lonely log school-houses, amidst poverty and ignorance; and though, when they go forth, no drums beat, no banners fly, no friends cheer, yet they are fighting the battles of this country just as truly and bravely as those who go forth to do battle against a foreign enemy.

If they are encouraged and properly supported in their work of educating the masses in the industries, in economy, and in morals, as well as mentally, they will, before many years, get the race upon such an intellectual, industrial, and financial footing that it will be able to enjoy without much trouble all the rights inherent in American citizenship.

Now, if we wish to bring the race to a point where it should be, where it will be strong, and grow and prosper, we have got to, in every way possible, encourage it. We can do this in no better way than by cultivating that amount of

[328]

faith in the race which will make us patronise its own enterprises wherever those enterprises are worth patronising. I do not believe much in the advice that is often given that we should patronise the enterprises of our race without regard to the worth of those enterprises. I believe that the best way to bring the race to the point where it will compare with other races is to let it understand that, whenever it enters into any line of business, it will be patronised just in proportion as it makes that business as successful, as useful, as is true of any business enterprise conducted by any other race. The race that would grow strong and powerful must have the element of hero-worship in it that will, in the largest degree, make it honour its great men, the men who have succeeded in that race. I think we should be ashamed of the coloured man or woman who would not venerate the name of Frederick Douglass. No race that would not look upon such a man with honour and respect and pride could ever hope to enjoy the respect of any other race. I speak of this, not that I want my people to regard themselves in a narrow, bigoted sense, because there is nothing so hurtful to an individual or to a race as to get into the habit of feeling that there is no good except in its own race, but because I wish that it may have reasonable pride in all that is honourable in its history. Whenever you hear a coloured man say that he hates the people of the other race, there, in most instances, you will find a weak, narrow-minded coloured man. And, whenever you find a white man who expresses the same sentiment toward the people of other races, there, too, in almost every case, you will find a narrow-minded, prejudiced white man.

That person is the broadest, strongest, and most useful who sees something to love and admire in all races, no matter what their colour.

If the Negro race wishes to grow strong, it must learn to respect itself, not to be ashamed. It must learn that it will only grow in proportion as its members have confidence in it, in proportion as they believe that it is a coming race.

We have reached a period when educated Negroes should give more attention to the history of their race; should devote more time to finding out the true history of the race, and in collecting in some museum the relics that mark its progress. It is true of all races of culture and refinement and civilisation that they have gathered in some place the relics which mark the progress of their civilisation, which show how they lived from period to period. We should have so much pride that we would spend more time in looking into the history of the

[329]

race, more effort and money in perpetuating in some durable form its achievements, so that from year to year, instead of looking back with regret, we can point to our children the rough path through which we grew strong and great.

We have a very bright and striking example in the history of the Jews in this and other countries. There is, perhaps, no race that has suffered so much, not so much in America as in some of the countries in Europe. But these people have clung together. They have had a certain amount of unity, pride, and love of race; and, as the years go on, they will be more and more influential in this country,—a country where they were once despised, and looked upon with scorn and derision. It is largely because the Jewish race has had faith in itself. Unless the Negro learns more and more to imitate the Jew in these matters, to have faith in himself, he cannot expect to have any high degree of success.

I wish to speak upon another subject which largely concerns the welfare of both races, especially in the South,—lynching. It is an unpleasant subject; but I feel that I should be omitting some part of my duty to both races did I not say something on the subject.

For a number of years the South has appealed to the North and to federal authorities, through the public press, from the public platform, and most eloquently through the late Henry W. Grady, to leave the whole matter of the rights and protection of the Negro to the South, declaring that it would see to it that the Negro would be made secure in his citizenship. During the last half-dozen years the whole country, from the President down, has been inclined more than ever to pursue this policy, leaving the whole matter of the destiny of the Negro to the Negro himself and to the Southern white people, among whom the great bulk of Negroes live.

By the present policy of non-interference on the part of the North and the federal government the South is given a sacred trust. How will she execute this trust? The world is waiting and watching to see. The question must be answered largely by the protection it gives to the life of the Negro and the provisions that are made for his development in the organic laws of the State. I fear that but few people in the South realise to what an extent the habit of lynching, or the taking of life without due process of law, has taken hold of us,

[330]

and is hurting us, not only in the eyes of the world, but in our own moral and material growth.

Lynching was instituted some years ago with the idea of punishing and checking criminal assaults upon women. Let us examine the facts, and see where it has already led us and is likely further to carry us, if we do not rid ourselves of the evil. Many good people in the South, and also out of the South, have gotten the idea that lynching is resorted to for one crime only. I have the facts from an authoritative source. During last year one hundred and twenty-seven persons were lynched in the United States. Of this number, one hundred and eighteen were executed in the South and nine in the North and West. Of the total number lynched, one hundred and two were Negroes, twenty-three were whites, and two Indians. Now, let every one interested in the South, his country, and the cause of humanity, note this fact,—that only twenty-four of the entire number were charged in any way with the crime of rape; that is, twenty-four out of one hundred and twenty-seven cases of lynching. Sixty-one of the remaining cases were for murder, thirteen for being suspected of murder, six for theft, etc. During one week last spring, when I kept a careful record, thirteen Negroes were lynched in three of our Southern States; and not one was even charged with rape. All of these thirteen were accused of murder or house-burning; but in neither case were the men allowed to go before a court, so that their innocence or guilt might be proven.

When we get to the point where four-fifths of the people lynched in our country in one year are for some crime other than rape, we can no longer plead and explain that we lynch for one crime alone.

Let us take another year, that of 1892, for example, when 241 persons were lynched in the whole United States. Of this number 36 were lynched in Northern and Western States, and 205 in our Southern States; 160 were Negroes, 5 of these being women. The facts show that, out of the 241 lynched, only 57 were even charged with rape or attempted rape, leaving in this year alone 184 persons who were lynched for other causes than that of rape.

If it were necessary, I could produce figures for other years. Within a period of six years about 900 persons have been lynched in our Southern States. This is but a few hundred short of the total number of soldiers who lost their lives in Cuba during the Spanish-American War. If we would realise still more fully how far this unfortunate evil is leading us on, note the classes of crime during a few months for which the local papers and the Associated Press say that lynching has been inflicted. They include "murder," "rioting," "incendiarism," "robbery," "larceny," "self-defence," "insulting women," "alleged stock-poisoning," "malpractice," "alleged barn-burning," "suspected robbery," "race prejudice," "attempted murder," "horse-stealing," "mistaken identity," etc.

The evil has so grown that we are now at the point where not only blacks are lynched in the South, but white men as well. Not only this, but within the last six years at least a half-dozen coloured women have been lynched. And there are a few cases where Negroes have lynched members of their own race. What is to be the end of all this? Furthermore, every lynching drives hundreds of Negroes out of the farming districts of the South, where they make the best living and where their services are of greatest value to the country, into the already over-crowded cities.

I know that some argue that the crime of lynching Negroes is not confined to the South. This is true; and no one can excuse such a crime as the shooting of innocent black men in Illinois, who were guilty of nothing, except seeking labour. But my words just now are to the South, where my home is and a part of which I am. Let other sections act as they will; I want to see our beautiful Southland free from this terrible evil of lynching. Lynching does not stop crime. In the vicinity in the South where a coloured man was alleged recently to have committed the most terrible crime ever charged against a member of my race, but a few weeks previously five coloured men had been lynched for supposed incendiarism. If lynching was a cure for crime, surely the lynching of those five would have prevented another Negro from committing a most heinous crime a few weeks later.

We might as well face the facts bravely and wisely. Since the beginning of the world crime has been committed in all civilised and uncivilised countries, and a certain percentage of it will always be committed both in the North and in the South; but I believe that the crime of rape can be stopped. In proportion to the numbers and intelligence of the population of the South, there exists little more crime than in several other sections of the country; but, because of the lynching evil, we are constantly advertising ourselves to the world as a lawless people. We cannot disregard the teachings of the civilised world for eighteen hundred years, that the only way to punish crime is by law. When we leave this anchorage chaos begins.

[332]

I am not pleading for the Negro alone. Lynching injures, hardens, and blunts the moral sensibilities of the young and tender manhood of the South. Never shall I forget the remark by a little nine-year-old white boy, with blue eyes and flaxen hair. The little fellow said to his mother, after he had returned from a lynching: "I have seen a man hanged; now I wish I could see one burned." Rather than hear such a remark from one of my little boys, I would prefer to see him in his grave. This is not all. Every community guilty of lynching says in so many words to the governor, to the legislature, to the sheriff, to the jury, and to the judge: "We have no faith in you and no respect for you. We have no respect for the law which we helped to make."

In the South, at the present time, there is less excuse for not permitting the law to take its course where a Negro is to be tried than anywhere else in the world; for, almost without exception, the governors, the sheriffs, the judges, the juries, and the lawyers are all white men, and they can be trusted, as a rule, to do their duty. Otherwise, it is needless to tax the people to support these officers. If our present laws are not sufficient properly to punish crime, let the laws be changed; but that the punishment may be by lawfully constituted authorities is the plea I make. The history of the world proves that where the law is most strictly enforced there is the least crime: where people take the administration of the law into their own hands there is the most crime.

But there is still another side. The white man in the South has not only a serious duty and responsibility, but the Negro has a duty and responsibility in this matter. In speaking of my own people, I want to be equally frank; but I speak with the greatest kindness. There is too much crime among them. The figures for a given period show that in the United States thirty per cent. of the crime committed is by Negroes, while we constitute only about twelve per cent. of the entire population. This proportion holds good not only in the South, but also in Northern States and cities.

No race that is so largely ignorant and so recently out of slavery could, perhaps, show a better record, but we must face these plain facts. He is most kind to the Negro who tells him of his faults as well as of his virtues. A large percentage of the crime among us grows out of the idleness of our young men and women. It is for this reason that I have tried to insist upon some industry being taught in connection with their course of literary training. It is vitally important now that every parent, every teacher and minister of the gospel,

[333]

should teach with unusual emphasis morality and obedience to the law. At the fireside, in the school-room, in the Sunday-school, from the pulpit, and in the Negro press, there should be such a sentiment created regarding the committing of crime against women that no such crime could be charged against any member of the race. Let it be understood, for all time, that no one guilty of rape can find sympathy or shelter with us, and that none will be more active than we in bringing to justice, through the proper authorities, those guilty of crime. Let the criminal and vicious element of the race have, at all times, our most severe condemnation. Let a strict line be drawn between the virtuous and the criminal. I condemn, with all the indignation of my soul, any beast in human form guilty of assaulting a woman. I am sure I voice the sentiment of the thoughtful of my race in this condemnation.

We should not, as a race, become discouraged. We are making progress. No race has ever gotten upon its feet without discouragements and struggles.

I should be a great hypocrite and a coward if I did not add that which my daily experience has taught me to be true; namely, that the Negro has among many of the Southern whites as good friends as he has anywhere in the world. These friends have not forsaken us. They will not do so. Neither will our friends in the North. If we make ourselves intelligent, industrious, economical, and virtuous, of value to the community in which we live, we can and will work out our salvation right here in the South. In every community, by means of organised effort, we should seek, in a manly and honourable way, the confidence, the co-operation, the sympathy, of the best white people in the South and in our respective communities. With the best white people and the best black people standing together, in favour of law and order and justice, I believe that the safety and happiness of both races will be made secure.

We are one in this country. The question of the highest citizenship and the complete education of all concerns nearly ten millions of my people and sixty millions of the white race. When one race is strong, the other is strong; when one is weak, the other is weak. There is no power that can separate our destiny. Unjust laws and customs which exist in many places injure the white man and inconvenience the Negro. No race can wrong another race, simply because it has the power to do so, without being permanently injured in its own morals. The Negro can endure the temporary inconvenience, but the injury to

[334]

the white man is permanent. It is for the white man to save himself from this degradation that I plead. If a white man steals a Negro's ballot, it is the white man who is permanently injured. Physical death comes to the one Negro lynched in a county; but death of the morals—death of the soul—comes to those responsible for the lynching.

Those who fought and died on the battlefield for the freedom of the slaves performed their duty heroically and well, but a duty remains to those left. The mere fiat of law cannot make an ignorant voter an intelligent voter, cannot make a dependent man an independent man, cannot make one citizen respect another. These results will come to the Negro, as to all races, by beginning at the bottom and gradually working up to the highest possibilities of his nature.

In the economy of God there is but one standard by which an individual can succeed: there is but one for a race. This country expects that every race shall measure itself by the American standard. During the next half-century, and more, the Negro must continue passing through the severe American crucible. He is to be tested in his patience, his forbearance, his perseverance, his power to endure wrong,—to withstand temptations, to economise, to acquire and use skill,—his ability to compete, to succeed in commerce, to disregard the superficial for the real, the appearance for the substance, to be great and yet small, learned and yet simple, high and yet the servant of all. This,—this is the passport to all that is best in the life of our Republic; and the Negro must possess it or be barred out.

In working out his own destiny, while the main burden of activity must be with the Negro, he will need in the years to come, as he has needed in the past, the help, the encouragement, the guidance, that the strong can give the weak. Thus helped, those of both races in the South will soon throw off the shackles of racial and sectional prejudice, and rise above the clouds of ignorance, narrowness, and selfishness into that atmosphere, that pure sunshine, where it will be the highest ambition to serve man, our brother, regardless of race or previous condition.

[335]

CHAPTER 8

Before ending this volume, I have deemed it wise and fitting to sum up in the following chapter all that I have attempted to say in the previous chapters, and to speak at the same time a little more definitely about the Negro's future and his relation to the white race.

All attempts to settle the question of the Negro in the South by his removal from this country have so far failed, and I think that they are likely to fail. The next census will probably show that we have about ten millions of Negroes in the United States. About eight millions of these are in the Southern States. We have almost a nation within a nation. The Negro population within the United States lacks but two millions of being as large as the whole population of Mexico. It is nearly twice as large as the population of the Dominion of Canada. It is equal to the combined population of Switzerland, Greece, Honduras, Nicaragua, Cuba, Uruguay, Santo Domingo, Paraguay, and Costa Rica. When we consider, in connection with these facts, that the race has doubled itself since its freedom, and is still increasing, it hardly seems possible for any one to consider seriously any scheme of emigration from America as a method of solution of our vexed race problem. At most, even if the government were to provide the means, but a few hundred thousand could be transported each year. The yearly increase in population would more than overbalance the number transplanted. Even if it did not, the time required to get rid of the Negro by this method would perhaps be fifty or seventy-five years. The idea is chimerical.

Some have advised that the Negro leave the South and take up his residence in the Northern States. I question whether this would leave him any better off than he is in the South, when all things are considered. It has been my privilege to study the condition of our people in nearly every part of America; and I say, without hesitation, that, with some exceptional cases, the Negro is at his best in the Southern States. While he enjoys certain privileges in the North that he does not have in the South, when it comes to the matter of securing property, enjoying business opportunities and employment, the South presents a far better opportunity than the North. Few coloured men from the South are as yet able to stand up against the severe and increasing competition that

[336]

exists in the North, to say nothing of the unfriendly influence of labour organisations, which in some way prevents black men in the North, as a rule, from securing employment in skilled labour occupations.

Another point of great danger for the coloured man who goes North is in the matter of morals, owing to the numerous temptations by which he finds himself surrounded. He has more ways in which he can spend money than in the South, but fewer avenues of employment are open to him. The fact that at the North the Negro is confined to almost one line of employment often tends to discourage and demoralise the strongest who go from the South, and to make them an easy prey to temptation. A few years ago I made an examination into the condition of a settlement of Negroes who left the South and went to Kansas about twenty years ago, when there was a good deal of excitement in the South concerning emigration to the West. This settlement, I found, was much below the standard of that of a similar number of our people in the South. The only conclusion, therefore, it seems to me, which any one can reach, is that the Negroes, as a mass, are to remain in the Southern States. As a race, they do not want to leave the South, and the Southern white people do not want them to leave. We must therefore find some basis of settlement that will be constitutional, just, manly, that will be fair to both races in the South and to the whole country. This cannot be done in a day, a year, or any short period of time. We can, it seems to me, with the present light, decide upon a reasonably safe method of solving the problem, and turn our strength and effort in that direction. In doing this, I would not have the Negro deprived of any privilege guaranteed to him by the Constitution of the United States. It is not best for the Negro that he relinquish any of his constitutional rights. It is not best for the Southern white man that he should.

In order that we may, without loss of time or effort, concentrate our forces in a wise direction, I suggest what seems to me and many others the wisest policy to be pursued. I have reached these conclusions by reason of my own observations and experience, after eighteen years of direct contact with the leading and influential coloured and white men in most parts of our country. But I wish first to mention some elements of danger in the present situation, which all who desire the permanent welfare of both races in the South should carefully consider.

[337]

First.—There is danger that a certain class of impatient extremists among the Negroes, who have little knowledge of the actual conditions in the South, may do the entire race injury by attempting to advise their brethren in the South to resort to armed resistance or the use of the torch, in order to secure justice. All intelligent and well-considered discussion of any important question or condemnation of any wrong, both in the North and the South, from the public platform and through the press, is to be commended and encouraged; but ill-considered, incendiary utterances from black men in the North will tend to add to the burdens of our people in the South rather than relieve them.

Second.—Another danger in the South, which should be guarded against, is that the whole white South, including the wide, conservative, law-abiding element, may find itself represented before the bar of public opinion by the mob, or lawless element, which gives expression to its feelings and tendency in a manner that advertises the South throughout the world. Too often those who have no sympathy with such disregard of law are either silent or fail to speak in a sufficiently emphatic manner to offset, in any large degree, the unfortunate reputation which the lawless have too often made for many portions of the South.

Third.—No race or people ever got upon its feet without severe and constant struggle, often in the face of the greatest discouragement. While passing through the present trying period of its history, there is danger that a large and valuable element of the Negro race may become discouraged in the effort to better its condition. Every possible influence should be exerted to prevent this.

Fourth.—There is a possibility that harm may be done to the South and to the Negro by exaggerated newspaper articles which are written near the scene or in the midst of specially aggravating occurrences. Often these reports are written by newspaper men, who give the impression that there is a race conflict throughout the South, and that all Southern white people are opposed to the Negro's progress, overlooking the fact that, while in some sections there is trouble, in most parts of the South there is, nevertheless, a very large measure of peace, good will, and mutual helpfulness. In this same relation much can be done to retard the progress of the Negro by a certain class of Southern white people, who, in the midst of excitement, speak or write in a manner that gives the impression that all Negroes are lawless, untrustworthy, and shiftless. As an example, a Southern writer said not long ago, in a communication to the New York *Independent*: "Even in small towns the husband cannot venture to leave his wife alone for an hour at night. At no time, in no place, is the white woman safe from insults and assaults of these creatures." These statements, I presume, represented the feelings and the conditions that existed at the time they were written in one community or county in the South. But thousands of Southern white men and women would be ready to testify that this is not the condition throughout the South, nor throughout any one State.

Fifth.—Under the next head I would mention that, owing to the lack of school opportunities for the Negro in the rural districts of the South, there is danger that ignorance and idleness may increase to the extent of giving the Negro race a reputation for crime, and that immorality may eat its way into the moral fibre of the race, so as to retard its progress for many years. In judging the Negro in this regard, we must not be too harsh. We must remember that it has only been within the last thirty-four years that the black father and mother have had the responsibility, and consequently the experience, of training their own children. That they have not reached perfection in one generation, with the obstacles that the parents have been compelled to overcome, is not to be wondered at.

Sixth.—As a final source of danger to be guarded against, I would mention my fear that some of the white people of the South may be led to feel that the way to settle the race problem is to repress the aspirations of the Negro by legislation of a kind that confers certain legal or political privileges upon an ignorant and poor white man and withholds the same privileges from a black man in the same condition. Such legislation injures and retards the progress of both races. It is an injustice to the poor white man, because it takes from him incentive to secure education and property as prerequisites for voting. He feels that, because he is a white man, regardless of his possessions, a way will be found for him to vote. I would label all such measures, "Laws to keep the poor white man in ignorance and poverty."

As the Talladega *News Reporter*, a Democratic newspaper of Alabama, recently said: "But it is a weak cry when the white man asks odds on intelligence over the Negro. When nature has already so handicapped the African in the race for knowledge, the cry of the boasted Anglo-Saxon for still

[339]

further odds seems babyish. What wonder that the world looks on in surprise, if not disgust. It cannot help but say, if our contention be true that the Negro is an inferior race, that the odds ought to be on the other side, if any are to be given. And why not? No, the thing to do—the only thing that will stand the test of time—is to do right, exactly right, let come what will. And that right thing, as it seems to me, is to place a fair educational qualification before every citizen,—one that is self-testing, and not dependent on the wishes of weak men, letting all who pass the test stand in the proud ranks of American voters, whose votes shall be counted as cast, and whose sovereign will shall be maintained as law by all the powers that be. Nothing short of this will do. Every exemption, on whatsoever ground, is an outrage that can only rob some legitimate voter of his rights."

Such laws as have been made—as an example, in Mississippi—with the "understanding" clause hold out a temptation for the election officer to perjure and degrade himself by too often deciding that the ignorant white man does understand the Constitution when it is read to him and that the ignorant black man does not. By such a law the State not only commits a wrong against its black citizens; it injures the morals of its white citizens by conferring such a power upon any white man who may happen to be a judge of elections.

Such laws are hurtful, again, because they keep alive in the heart of the black man the feeling that the white man means to oppress him. The only safe way out is to set a high standard as a test of citizenship, and require blacks and whites alike to come up to it. When this is done, both will have a higher respect for the election laws and those who make them. I do not believe that, with his centuries of advantage over the Negro in the opportunity to acquire property and education as prerequisites for voting, the average white man in the South desires that any special law be passed to give him advantage over the Negro, who has had only a little more than thirty years in which to prepare himself for citizenship. In this relation another point of danger is that the Negro has been made to feel that it is his duty to oppose continually the Southern white man in politics, even in matters where no principle is involved, and that he is only loyal to his own race and acting in a manly way when he is opposing him. Such a policy has proved most hurtful to both races. Where it is a matter of principle, where a question of right or wrong is involved, I would advise the Negro to stand by principle at all hazards. A Southern white man has no respect for or confidence in a Negro who acts merely for policy's sake; but

[340]

there are many cases—and the number is growing—where the Negro has nothing to gain and much to lose by opposing the Southern white man in many matters that relate to government.

Under these six heads I believe I have stated some of the main points which all high-minded white men and black men, North and South, will agree need our most earnest and thoughtful consideration, if we would hasten, and not hinder, the progress of our country.

As to the policy that should be pursued in a larger sense,—on this subject I claim to possess no superior wisdom or unusual insight. I may be wrong; I may be in some degree right.

In the future, more than in the past, we want to impress upon the Negro the importance of identifying himself more closely with the interests of the South,—the importance of making himself part of the South and at home in it. Heretofore, for reasons which were natural and for which no one is especially to blame, the coloured people have been too much like a foreign nation residing in the midst of another nation. If William Lloyd Garrison, Wendell Phillips, and George L. Stearns were alive to-day, I feel sure that each one of them would advise the Negroes to identify their interests as far as possible with those of the Southern white man, always with the understanding that this should be done where no question of right and wrong is involved. In no other way, it seems to me, can we get a foundation for peace and progress. He who advises against this policy will advise the Negro to do that which no people in history who have succeeded have done. The white man, North or South, who advises the Negro against it advises him to do that which he himself has not done. The bed-rock upon which every individual rests his chances of success in life is securing the friendship, the confidence, the respect, of his next-door neighbour of the little community in which he lives. Almost the whole problem of the Negro in the South rests itself upon the fact as to whether the Negro can make himself of such indispensable service to his neighbour and the community that no one can fill his place better in the body politic. There is at present no other safe course for the black man to pursue. If the Negro in the South has a friend in his white neighbour and a still larger number of friends in his community, he has a protection and a guarantee of his rights that will be more potent and more lasting than any our Federal Congress or any outside power can confer.

[341]

In a recent editorial the London *Times*, in discussing affairs in the Transvaal, South Africa, where Englishmen have been denied certain privileges by the Boers, says: "England is too sagacious not to prefer a gradual reform from within, even should it be less rapid than most of us might wish, to the most sweeping redress of grievances imposed from without. Our object is to obtain fair play for the outlanders, but the best way to do it is to enable them to help themselves." This policy, I think, is equally safe when applied to conditions in the South. The foreigner who comes to America, as soon as possible, identifies himself in business, education, politics, and sympathy with the community in which he settles. As I have said, we have a conspicuous example of this in the case of the Jews. Also, the Negro in Cuba has practically settled the race question there, because he has made himself a part of Cuba in thought and action.

What I have tried to indicate cannot be accomplished by any sudden revolution of methods, but it does seem that the tendency more and more should be in this direction. If a practical example is wanted in the direction that I favour, I will mention one. The North sends thousands of dollars into the South each year, for the education of the Negro. The teachers in most of the academic schools of the South are supported by the North, or Northern men and women of the highest Christian culture and most unselfish devotion. The Negro owes them a debt of gratitude which can never be paid. The various missionary societies in the North have done a work which, in a large degree, has been the salvation of the South; and the result will appear in future generations more than in this. We have now reached the point in the South where, I believe, great good could be accomplished by changing the attitude of the white people toward the Negro and of the Negro toward the whites, if a few white teachers of high character would take an active interest in the work of these high schools. Can this be done? Yes. The medical school connected with Shaw University at Raleigh, North Carolina, has from the first had as instructors and professors, almost exclusively, Southern white doctors, who reside in Raleigh; and they have given the highest satisfaction. This gives the people of Raleigh the feeling that this is their school, and not something located in, but not a part of, the South. In Augusta, Georgia, the Payne Institute, one of the best colleges for our people, is officered and taught almost wholly by Southern white men and women. The Presbyterian Theological School at Tuscaloosa, Alabama, has all Southern white men as instructors. Some time ago, at the

[342]

Calhoun School in Alabama, one of the leading white men in the county was given an important position in the school. Since then the feeling of the white people in the county has greatly changed toward the school.

We must admit the stern fact that at present the Negro, through no choice of his own, is living among another race which is far ahead of him in education, property, experience, and favourable condition; further, that the Negro's present condition makes him dependent upon the white people for most of the things necessary to sustain life, as well as for his common school education. In all history, those who have possessed the property and intelligence have exercised the greatest control in government, regardless of colour, race, or geographical location. This being the case, how can the black man in the South improve his present condition? And does the Southern white man want him to improve it?

The Negro in the South has it within his power, if he properly utilises the forces at hand, to make of himself such a valuable factor in the life of the South that he will not have to seek privileges, they will be freely conferred upon him. To bring this about, the Negro must begin at the bottom and lay a sure foundation, and not be lured by any temptation into trying to rise on a false foundation. While the Negro is laying this foundation he will need help, sympathy, and simple justice. Progress by any other method will be but temporary and superficial, and the latter end of it will be worse than the beginning. American slavery was a great curse to both races, and I would be the last to apologise for it; but, in the presence of God, I believe that slavery laid the foundation for the solution of the problem that is now before us in the South. During slavery the Negro was taught every trade, every industry, that constitutes the foundation for making a living. Now, if on this foundation—laid in rather a crude way, it is true, but a foundation, nevertheless—we can gradually build and improve, the future for us is bright. Let me be more specific. Agriculture is, or has been, the basic industry of nearly every race or nation that has succeeded. The Negro got a knowledge of this during slavery. Hence, in a large measure, he is in possession of this industry in the South to-day. The Negro can buy land in the South, as a rule, wherever the white man can buy it, and at very low prices. Now, since the bulk of our people already have a foundation in agriculture, they are at their best when living in the country, engaged in agricultural pursuits. Plainly, then, the best thing, the logical thing, is to turn the larger part of our strength in a direction that will make the Negro among the most skilled agricultural people in the world. The man who has learned to do something better than any one else, has learned to do a common thing in an uncommon manner, is the man who has a power and influence that no adverse circumstances can take from him. The Negro who can make himself so conspicuous as a successful farmer, a large tax-payer, a wise helper of his fellow-men, as to be placed in a position of trust and honour, whether the position be political or otherwise, by natural selection, is a hundred-fold more secure in that position than one placed there by mere outside force or pressure. I know a Negro, Hon. Isaiah T. Montgomery, in Mississippi, who is mayor of a town. It is true that this town, at present, is composed almost wholly of Negroes. Mr. Montgomery is mayor of this town because his genius, thrift, and foresight have created the town; and he is held and supported in his office by a charter, granted by the State of Mississippi, and by the vote and public sentiment of the community in which he lives.

Let us help the Negro by every means possible to acquire such an education in farming, dairying, stock-raising, horticulture, etc., as will enable him to become a model in these respects and place him near the top in these industries, and the race problem would in a large part be settled, or at least stripped of many of its most perplexing elements. This policy would also tend to keep the Negro in the country and smaller towns, where he succeeds best, and stop the influx into the large cities, where he does not succeed so well. The race, like the individual, that produces something of superior worth that has a common human interest, makes a permanent place for itself, and is bound to be recognised.

At a county fair in the South not long ago I saw a Negro awarded the first prize by a jury of white men, over white competitors, for the production of the best specimen of Indian corn. Every white man at this fair seemed to be pleased and proud of the achievement of this Negro, because it was apparent that he had done something that would add to the wealth and comfort of the people of both races in that county. At the Tuskegee Normal and Industrial Institute in Alabama we have a department devoted to training men in the science of agriculture; but what we are doing is small when compared with what should be done at Tuskegee and at other educational centres. In a material sense the South is still an undeveloped country. While race prejudice is strongly exhibited in many directions, in the matter of business, of commercial and industrial development, there is very little obstacle in the Negro's way. A Negro who produces or has for sale something that the community wants finds customers among white people as well as black people. A Negro can borrow money at the bank with equal security as readily as a white man can. A bank in Birmingham, Alabama, that has now existed ten years, is officered and controlled wholly by Negroes. This bank has white borrowers and white depositors. A graduate of the Tuskegee Institute keeps a well-appointed grocery store in Tuskegee, and he tells me that he sells about as many goods to the one race as to the other. What I have said of the opening that awaits the Negro in the direction of agriculture is almost equally true of mechanics, manufacturing, and all the domestic arts. The field is before him and right about him. Will he occupy it? Will he "cast down his bucket where he is"? Will his friends North and South encourage him and prepare him to occupy it? Every city in the South, for example, would give support to a first-class architect or house-builder or contractor of our race. The architect and contractor would not only receive support, but, through his example, numbers of young coloured men would learn such trades as carpentry, brick-masonry, plastering, painting, etc., and the race would be put into a position to hold on to many of the industries which it is now in danger of losing, because in too many cases brains, skill, and dignity are not imparted to the common occupations of life that are about his very door. Any individual or race that does not fit itself to occupy in the best manner the field or service that is right about it will sooner or later be asked to move on, and let some one else occupy it.

But it is asked, Would you confine the Negro to agriculture, mechanics, and domestic arts, etc.? Not at all; but along the lines that I have mentioned is where the stress should be laid just now and for many years to come. We will need and must have many teachers and ministers, some doctors and lawyers and statesmen; but these professional men will have a constituency or a foundation from which to draw support just in proportion as the race prospers along the economic lines that I have mentioned. During the first fifty or one hundred years of the life of any people are not the economic occupations always given the greater attention? This is not only the historic, but, I think, the common-sense view. If this generation will lay the material foundation, it will be the quickest and surest way for the succeeding generation to succeed in the cultivation of the fine arts, and to surround itself even with some of the luxuries of life, if desired. What the race now most needs, in my opinion, is a whole army of men and women well trained to lead and at the same time infuse themselves into agriculture, mechanics, domestic employment, and business. As to the mental training that these educated leaders should be equipped with, I should say, Give them all the mental training and culture that the circumstances of individuals will allow,—the more, the better. No race can permanently succeed until its mind is awakened and strengthened by the ripest thought. But I would constantly have it kept in the thoughts of those who are educated in books that a large proportion of those who are educated should be so trained in hand that they can bring this mental strength and knowledge to bear upon the physical conditions in the South which I have tried to emphasise.

Frederick Douglass, of sainted memory, once, in addressing his race, used these words: "We are to prove that we can better our own condition. One way to do this is to accumulate property. This may sound to you like a new gospel. You have been accustomed to hear that money is the root of all evil, etc. On the other hand, property—money, if you please—will purchase for us the only condition by which any people can rise to the dignity of genuine manhood; for without property there can be no leisure, without leisure there can be no thought, without thought there can be no invention, without invention there can be no progress."

The Negro should be taught that material development is not an end, but simply a means to an end. As Professor W. E. B. DuBois puts it, "The idea should not be simply to make men carpenters, but to make carpenters men." The Negro has a highly religious temperament; but what he needs more and more is to be convinced of the importance of weaving his religion and morality into the practical affairs of daily life. Equally as much does he need to be taught to put so much intelligence into his labour that he will see dignity and beauty in the occupation, and love it for its own sake. The Negro needs to be taught that more of the religion that manifests itself in his happiness in the prayer-meeting should be made practical in the performance of his daily task. The man who owns a home and is in the possession of the elements by which he is sure of making a daily living has a great aid to a moral and religious life. What bearing will all this have upon the Negro's place in the South as a citizen and in the enjoyment of the privileges which our government confers?

To state in detail just what place the black man will occupy in the South as a citizen, when he has developed in the direction named, is beyond

[346]

the wisdom of any one. Much will depend upon the sense of justice which can be kept alive in the breast of the American people. Almost as much will depend upon the good sense of the Negro himself. That question, I confess, does not give me the most concern just now. The important and pressing question is, Will the Negro with his own help and that of his friends take advantage of the opportunities that now surround him? When he has done this, I believe that, speaking of his future in general terms, he will be treated with justice, will be given the protection of the law, and will be given the recognition in a large measure which his usefulness and ability warrant. If, fifty years ago, any one had predicted that the Negro would have received the recognition and honour which individuals have already received, he would have been laughed at as an idle dreamer. Time, patience, and constant achievement are great factors in the rise of a race.

I do not believe that the world ever takes a race seriously, in its desire to enter into the control of the government of a nation in any large degree, until a large number of individuals, members of that race, have demonstrated, beyond question, their ability to control and develop individual business enterprises. When a number of Negroes rise to the point where they own and operate the most successful farms, are among the largest tax-payers in their county, are moral and intelligent, I do not believe that in many portions of the South such men need long be denied the right of saying by their votes how they prefer their property to be taxed and in choosing those who are to make and administer the laws.

In a certain town in the South, recently, I was on the street in company with the most prominent Negro in the town. While we were together, the mayor of the town sought out the black man, and said, "Next week we are going to vote on the question of issuing bonds to secure water-works for this town; you must be sure to vote on the day of election." The mayor did not suggest whether he must vote "yes" or "no"; he knew from the very fact that this Negro man owned nearly a block of the most valuable property in the town that he would cast a safe, wise vote on this important proposition. This white man knew that, because of this Negro's property interests in the city, he would cast his vote in the way he thought would benefit every white and black citizen in the town, and not be controlled by influences a thousand miles away. But a short time ago I read letters from nearly every prominent white man in Birmingham, Alabama, asking that the Rev. W. R. Pettiford, a Negro, be appointed to a certain important federal office. What is the explanation of this? Mr. Pettiford for nine years has been the president of the Negro bank in Birmingham to which I have alluded. During these nine years these white citizens have had the opportunity of seeing that Mr. Pettiford could manage successfully a private business, and that he had proven himself a conservative, thoughtful citizen; and they were willing to trust him in a public office. Such individual examples will have to be multiplied until they become the rule rather than the exception. While we are multiplying these examples, the Negro must keep a strong and courageous heart. He cannot improve his condition by any short-cut course or by artificial methods. Above all, he must not be deluded into the temptation of believing that his condition can be permanently improved by a mere battledore and shuttlecock of words or by any process of mere mental gymnastics or oratory alone. What is desired, along with a logical defence of his cause, are deeds, results,—multiplied results,—in the direction of building himself up, so as to leave no doubt in the minds of any one of his ability to succeed.

An important question often asked is, Does the white man in the South want the Negro to improve his present condition? I say, "Yes." From the Montgomery (Alabama) *Daily Advertiser* I clip the following in reference to the closing of a coloured school in a town in Alabama:—

"Eufaula, May 25, 1899.

"The closing exercises of the city coloured public school were held at St. Luke's A. M. E. Church last night, and were witnessed by a large gathering, including many white. The recitations by the pupils were excellent, and the music was also an interesting feature. Rev. R. T. Pollard delivered the address, which was quite an able one; and the certificates were presented by Professor T. L. McCoy, white, of the Sanford Street School. The success of the exercises reflects great credit on Professor S. M. Murphy, the principal, who enjoys a deservedly good reputation as a capable and efficient educator."

I quote this report, not because it is the exception, but because such marks of interest in the education of the Negro on the part of the Southern white people can be seen almost every day in the local papers. Why should white people, by their presence, words, and many other things, encourage the black man to get education, if they do not desire him to improve his condition?

[348]

The Payne Institute in Augusta, Georgia, an excellent institution, to which I have already referred, is supported almost wholly by the Southern white Methodist church. The Southern white Presbyterians support a theological school at Tuscaloosa, Alabama, for Negroes. For a number of years the Southern white Baptists have contributed toward Negro education. Other denominations have done the same. If these people do not want the Negro educated to a high standard, there is no reason why they should act the hypocrite in these matters.

As barbarous as some of the lynchings in the South have been, Southern white men here and there, as well as newspapers, have spoken out strongly against lynching. I quote from the address of the Rev. Mr. Vance, of Nashville, Tennessee, delivered before the National Sunday School Union in Atlanta, not long since, as an example:—

"And yet, as I stand here to-night, a Southerner speaking for my section, and addressing an audience from all sections, there is one foul blot upon the fair fame of the South, at the bare mention of which the heart turns sick and the cheek is crimsoned with shame. I want to lift my voice to-night in loud and long and indignant protest against the awful horror of mob violence, which the other day reached the climax of its madness and infamy in a deed as black and brutal and barbarous as can be found in the annals of human crime.

"I have a right to speak on the subject, and I propose to be heard. The time has come for every lover of the South to set the might of an angered and resolute manhood against the shame and peril of the lynch demon. These people, whose fiendish glee taunts their victim as his flesh crackles in the flames, do not represent the South. I have not a syllable of apology for the sickening crime they meant to avenge. But it is high time we were learning that lawlessness is no remedy for crime. For one, I dare to believe that the people of my section are able to cope with crime, however treacherous and defiant, through their courts of justice; and I plead for the masterful sway of a righteous and exalted public sentiment that shall class lynch law in the category with crime."

It is a notable and praiseworthy fact that no Negro educated in any of our larger institutions of learning in the South has been charged with any of the recent crimes connected with assaults upon females.

[349]

If we go on making progress in the directions that I have tried to indicate, more and more the South will be drawn to one course. As I have already said, it is not for the best interests of the white race of the South that the Negro be deprived of any privilege guaranteed him by the Constitution of the United States. This would put upon the South a burden under which no government could stand and prosper. Every article in our federal Constitution was placed there with a view of stimulating and encouraging the highest type of citizenship. To permanently tax the Negro without giving him the right to vote as fast as he qualifies himself in education and property for voting would work the alienation of the affections of the Negro from the States in which he lives, and would be the reversal of the fundamental principles of government for which our States have stood. In other ways than this the injury would be as great to the white man as to the Negro. Taxation without the hope of becoming a voter would take away from one-third the citizens of the Gulf States their interest in government and their stimulant to become tax-payers or to secure education, and thus be able and willing to bear their share of the cost of education and government, which now weighs so heavily upon the white tax-payers of the South. The more the Negro is stimulated and encouraged, the sooner will he be able to bear a larger share of the burdens of the South. We have recently had before us an example, in the case of Spain, of a government that left a large portion of its citizens in ignorance, and neglected their highest interests.

As I have said elsewhere, there is no escape through law of man or God from the inevitable:—

"The laws of changeless justice bind Oppressor with opprest; And, close as sin and suffering joined, We march to fate abreast."

"Nearly sixteen millions of hands will aid you in pulling the load upward or they will pull against you the load downward. We shall constitute one-third and more of the ignorance and crime of the South or one-third its intelligence and progress. We shall contribute one-third to the business and industrial prosperity of the South or we shall prove a veritable body of death, stagnating, depressing, retarding, every effort to advance the body politic."

My own feeling is that the South will gradually reach the point where it will see the wisdom and the justice of enacting an educational or property qualification, or both, for voting, that shall be made to apply honestly to both races. The industrial development of the Negro in connection with education

[350]

and Christian character will help to hasten this end. When this is done, we shall have a foundation, in my opinion, upon which to build a government that is honest and that will be in a high degree satisfactory to both races.

I do not suffer myself to take too optimistic a view of the conditions in the South. The problem is a large and serious one, and will require the patient help, sympathy, and advice of our most patriotic citizens, North and South, for years to come. But I believe that, if the principles which I have tried to indicate are followed, a solution of the question will come. So long as the Negro is permitted to get education, acquire property, and secure employment, and is treated with respect in the business or commercial world,—as is now true in the greater part of the South,—I shall have the greatest faith in his working out his own destiny in our Southern States. The education and preparing for citizenship of nearly eight millions of people is a tremendous task, and every lover of humanity should count it a privilege to help in the solution of a great problem for which our whole country is responsible.

APPENDIX

THE HISTORY OF SLAVERY

By Booker T. Washington

1

It was one hot summer's day in the month of August 1619, as the story goes, that a Dutch man-of-war entered the mouth of the James River, in what is now the State of Virginia, and, coming in with the tide, dropped anchor opposite the little settlement of Jamestown. Ships were rare enough to be remembered in that day, even when there was nothing especially remarkable about them, as there was about this one. But this particular ship was so interesting at the time, and so important because of what followed in the wake of its coming, that it has not been forgotten to this day. The reason for this is that it brought the first slaves to the first English settlement in the New World. It is with the coming of these first African slaves to Jamestown that the story of slavery, so far as our own country is concerned, begins.

Although the coming of the first slave ship to what is now the United States is still remembered, the name of the ship and almost everything else concerning the vessel and its strange merchandise has been forgotten. Almost all that is known about it is told in the diary of John Rolfe, who will be remembered as the man who married the Indian girl, Pocahontas. He says, "A Dutch man-of-war that sold us twenty Negars came to Jamestown late in August, 1619." An old record has preserved some of the names of those first twenty slaves, and from other sources it is known that the ship sailed from Flushing, Holland. But that is almost all that is definitely known about the first slave ship and the first slaves that were brought from Africa to the United States.

The first slaves landed in Virginia were not, by any means, the first slaves that were brought to the New World. Fifty years before Columbus landed on the island of San Salvador, the first African slaves were brought from the West Coast of Africa to Spain, and we know from historical references and records that Negro slavery had become firmly established in Spain before Columbus made his first voyage. It was, therefore, natural enough that the Spanish explorers and adventurers, following close upon the heels of Columbus in search of gold, should bring their Negro servants with them.

[355]

It seems likely, from all that we can learn, that a few Negroes were sent out to the West Indies as early as 1501, only eleven years after the discovery of America and one hundred and twenty years before the first cargo of slaves was landed in Jamestown. Four years later, in a letter dated September 15, 1505, written by King Ferdinand to one of his officials in Hispaniola, which we now call Hayti, he says among other things: "I will send you more Negro slaves as you request. I think there be an hundred."

Thus early was Negro slavery introduced into the New World and what do you suppose was the reason, or rather the excuse, for bringing black men to America at this time?

It was to save from slavery the native Indians. A good priest by the name of Las Casas, who accompanied the first Spanish explorers and conquerors, found that the native people, the Indians, were fast dying out under the cruel tasks put upon them by their Spanish conquerors. Unaccustomed to labor, they could not endure the hardships of working in the mines. The Negroes, on the contrary, had, in many cases, been slaves in their own country, and had been accustomed to labor. At the same time it was said that one Negro could do the work of four Indians. So it was that this good man, out of pity for the enslaved Americans, proposed that the black people of Africa should be brought over to take their places.

Thus the traffic in African slaves began, and in the course of the next three hundred years many millions of black people were carried across the ocean and settled in slave colonies in the New World. They were brought to America, first of all, to work in the mines, and afterwards more of them were brought to do the almost equally difficult pioneer work on the plantations. Thus, in all hard labor of clearing and draining the land, building roads and opening up the New World to cultivation and to civilization, the black man did his part.

It has been estimated that no less than 12,000,000 slaves were transplanted from Africa to America to supply the demand for labor in the West Indies, in South America and in the United States, during the centuries that the white people of Europe were seeking to establish their civilization in the Western World.

Perhaps as many as 12,000,000 more, who were taken in the wars and raids in Africa, died on the way to the coast, or in the terrible "middle

[356]

passage," as the journey from the coast of Africa to that of America was called. Many of those captured and sold in Africa, who did not die on the high seas in the crowded and stifling hold of the ships into which they were thrust, did not survive what was known as the "seasoning process," after they were landed in America.

Roughly speaking, it is safe to say that not less than 24,000,000 human beings were snatched from their homes in Africa and sold into slavery, to help in building up the world in which we live today in America.

Although African slavery was introduced into America at first in order to save from extinction the native people of the West Indies, who were not strong enough to endure the hardships of slavery, it is sad to recall that the slavery of the Negro did not serve to preserve the Indian, for it was but a comparatively few years after the Spaniards landed in the West Indies before nearly all the native tribes had been swept away. There are today in the West Indies only a few remnants of the Indians whom Columbus met when he first landed in America.

The black man, on the other hand, in spite of the hardships he has endured, has not only survived but has greatly increased in numbers. So greatly has the black man increased that in the West Indies today the black population far outnumbers all other races represented among the inhabitants. Altogether, it is estimated there are now about 24,591,000 Negroes in North and South America and the West Indies. Of this number 10,000,000 are in the United States.

2

The story of the first American voyage to Africa to obtain slaves of which there is any definite record, is that of a certain Captain Smith, commanding the ship, Rainbowe, and sailing from Boston. Captain Smith had sailed to Madeira with a cargo of salt fish and staves and, on the way home, he touched on the coast of Guinea for slaves. There happened to be very few slaves for sale at the moment and on this account, Captain Smith, together with the masters of some London slave ships already on the ground, conspired together to pick a quarrel with some of the natives, so as to have an excuse to attack their village and carry off the prisoners made as slaves. Captain Smith's share of the booty was two slaves with whom he returned to Boston.

It happened, however, that when he reached home he got into a quarrel with the ship's owners over the proceeds of the voyage, and, in the lawsuits which resulted, the story of the manner in which the slaves were obtained was told in court. Thereupon one of the magistrates charged Captain Smith with a "threefold offence—murder, man-stealing and Sabboth breaking." He was acquitted of all three charges on the ground that these crimes were committed in Africa, but, as a result of the trial, the slaves were returned to their homes.

This story is interesting, for one reason because it shows that, in the early days of the slave trade, the barter and sale of Negro slaves, so long as it was conducted in an honest and orderly way, according to the accepted customs and manners of trade, was not considered a wrong or wicked business.

At first the slave traders purchased slaves only from the native chiefs. These slaves were generally prisoners who had been taken in the tribal wars. In some cases they were men or women who had been sold for debt. There were, also, other ways in which one black man in Africa might hold another in slavery.

Very soon, however, the ordinary sources of supply of slaves was not sufficient to meet the demand of the American trade. Then traders became less scrupulous. They began buying from any one who had a man or woman for sale. This encouraged kidnapping. Not infrequently the man who brought a gang of slaves to the coast to be sold would himself be kidnapped and sold by other men before he could return home. Sometimes the traders, after they had purchased a gang or a "coffle" of slaves, as they were called, would invite the traders on board ship in order to entertain them. Then, after they were under the influence of liquor, they would put chains upon them and carry them away with the very slaves the traders themselves a few hours before had sold.

As time went on, and the demand for slave labor increased, the men engaged in this cruel traffic became hardened to its cruelty and the West Coast of Africa became one vast hunting ground. Men and women were tracked and hunted as if they were wild beasts. It grew so bad at length that the conscience of the civilized world was aroused. Then, one by one, the nations of the world began to prohibit the traffic. England, which had formerly been one of the nations most deeply involved in this evil business, now became the leader in the attempt to put a stop to it.

The importation of slaves was prohibited in the United States in 1808, but that did not put an end to the importation of slaves. For, after the invention of the cotton gin at the close of the eighteenth century by Eli Whitney, a Connecticut school master, slaves were needed more than ever, to plant and till and pick the cotton which had now become much more valuable than before.

Although it was no longer lawful to import slaves, they were smuggled into the country. As late as 1860 the famous yacht, Wanderer, which had at one time been owned by a member of the New York Yacht Club, brought into the United States 450 slaves, and it has been estimated that as many as 15,000 slaves were smuggled into the different Southern ports in the year 1858.

At this time it had become the custom to gather great numbers of slaves at different points along the coast of Africa, in what were called barracoons. These were nothing more or less than strong stockades made by planting trees close together in the ground so as to form a strong enclosure from which there was no escape. In these barracoons slaves captured in the interior were held until they were ready to be shipped.

Swift sailing vessels, which travelled so fast that, once they escaped the vigilance of the war ships stationed along the coast, they could never be overtaken, were used to carry the slaves from the coast of Africa to that of America.

These vessels would hover about in the neighborhood of one of these slave barracoons until the coast was clear; then swiftly the living cargo would be hurried aboard, and the vessel would put on all sail and make all possible haste to put itself and its human freight beyond the reach of the police ships.

Usually these slave ships were provided with a lower, or what was called a "slave deck," beneath the ordinary deck of the ship. In some instances, in order to escape suspicion, the ship would have no permanent slave deck but such a deck would be hastily arranged after the vessel arrived in the neighborhood of one of the slave barracoons. In such cases the ordinary cargo would be put in the bottom of the ship and then, above this and from three to five feet beneath the ordinary deck, a second deck would be hastily improvised. Here as many slaves would be stowed away as could be possibly crowded into the narrow space.

It is only necessary to read the descriptions of the methods by which this traffic was carried on to understand the horrible suffering to which the slaves were subjected during this middle passage. In many instances, when brought out on deck for a little air, the slaves had to be chained to keep them from jumping overboard.

Sometimes a pestilence would break out on one of these ships and the whole cargo, consisting of three or four hundred slaves, would be lost. It is said that the yellow fever was brought to America by slaves. There are instances, also, where the captain of a slave ship jettisoned, that is to say, threw over-board, a whole ship-load of slaves to escape being caught by the ships that were pursuing him.

When a slave ship reached the shore of America there were snug harbors at various points along the coast into which one of these swift sailing vessels could always hide until its cargo of slaves had been discharged. The island upon which the present city of Galveston is built was once a refuge for slave pirates and slave smugglers. The coast of Louisiana is full of shallow bays, which reach far into the land, and they were a favorite resort for slave smugglers. Here was the hiding place of the Barataria pirates who were long famous as slave smugglers.

Mobile Bay was one of the points at which a slave cargo was occasionally landed. It is said that the hull of the very last slave ship, the Lawrence, which was captured and burned by the Federal troops during the first year of the Civil War, may still be seen hidden away in the swamps and marshes east of Mobile.

There is still living in the suburbs of Mobile a little colony of Africans who were brought over on this last slave ship. When they were released by the Federal officers they settled here. It is said that there are old men living in this settlement who still speak an African language, but their children have all grown up to be good Americans.

[360]

Once a ship load of slaves was landed on the American coast, they were immediately divided and scattered in every direction. Some were taken to one plantation, others to another, and so on until all were disposed of. Soon they were so thoroughly intermingled with the great body of slaves that all trace of them was lost. At least it was rare that anyone ever did trace the cargo of slaves after it was once landed, although slave ships were frequently captured on the high seas.

When slavers were captured red-handed on the high seas by the United States or English navies, an effort was made to return the slaves to their homes in Africa. As this was not practical the English government established at Sierra Leone, on the west coast of Africa, a station to which they sent all liberated slaves. It was in this manner, that what is now one of the most thriving English colonies on the west coast of Africa was started.

The story of the slave trade is one of the darkest chapters in the history of the Western World, for though it began in the comparatively harmless way already described, it grew steadily worse until in its last stages even those familiar with slavery in its worst form came to look upon it with shame.

And yet, in spite of all the suffering that it entailed, and in spite of its degrading effect upon the people who engaged in it, we can see, as we look back upon it now, that some good has come out of it. It served, for one thing, to bring a large number of the savage people of Africa into closer contact with the enlightenment and civilization of the Western World. In the end, it aroused in the minds of some of the best people in Europe and America a new interest in Africa and led hundreds of good Christian people to give up the security of their comfortable homes and give their lives to the task of uplifting and educating the neglected races of the Dark Continent.

Among the first and greatest of those who gave their lives for this purpose was the missionary, David Livingstone, who did more than anyone else to arouse the world to the iniquities of the African slave trade.

[361]

Although, slavery was introduced into Virginia as early as 1619 it was not until nearly one hundred years later that African slaves began to be brought into the English colonies in any very large numbers. For nearly a century the bulk of the rough labor in the field and in the forest was performed, not by Negro slaves, but by white bond servants, who were imported from England and sold like other merchandise in the markets of the colonies.

In 1673, for example, the average price of a bond servant in the colonies, so the historian Bancroft tells us, was ten pounds. At this same time a Negro slave was worth twenty-five pounds.

It was often that the almshouses and prisons of England were emptied in order to furnish laborers for America. It should be remembered, however, that many of the persons who were sent out as bond servants to America were political prisoners, and some of these were persons of quality.

When there was a civil war in England the victorious party frequently disposed of its prisoners by sending them to the colonies as bond servants, or even as slaves. Thousands of Irish Catholics were sent over to America in this way, and it is said that the hardships which these unfortunate bondsmen suffered on the voyage was hardly less than those endured by the African slaves.

It should be remembered, also, in the case of these white bond servants, as in that of the Negro slaves, the sale of human beings began innocently enough. At the time the English colonies were planted in America there was comparatively little free labor anywhere, and especially was this true of farm labor.

The freedom and independence which seem now to be the natural rights of everyone were enjoyed by very few among the masses of the laboring people in Europe one hundred or two hundred years ago. At that time nearly everyone who worked with his hands was bound, in one way or another, to a master who had control over his actions to an extent which amounted to something like servitude. But it was to the man on the soil and in the country that freedom has everywhere come most slowly. In fact, it was not until the middle of the last century that the complete emancipation of the serfs took place in Western Europe. It was not until 1861, two years before Abraham Lincoln's Emancipation Proclamation set the American Negroes free, that the Russian serfs were emancipated.

It is necessary to remember these facts if we wish to understand how it came about that the slavery of the black man and the servitude of the white man came to be established in this country.

When the first bond servants were sent to America it was not intended that they should be transferred and sold from one owner to another. It was merely intended that they should be bound to labor for the man who paid their passage money until that sum had been repaid. Gradually, however, in their eagerness to obtain labor, people lost sight of the fact that the merchandise they were selling was human beings. It was not long, therefore, before the bond servant was rated among the other property, the horses, the sheep and the cattle, in the inventories of the estate, and he could be disposed of by will and deed along with the remainder of the stock on the plantation.

At first the only legal distinction between the bond servant and the Negro slave was that the one was a servant for a period of years and the other was a servant for life. In the long run, however, this distinction made a great difference. In the first place, as the number of these bond servants who became free increased there grew up in the colonies a considerable body of citizens who had known the trials and hardships of servitude. These people naturally sympathized with those of their own class and this created a sentiment against white servitude.

The case of the Negro, however, was different. He was a man of a different race and he was doomed to perpetual servitude. The result was, as time went on, it came to be regarded as the natural vocation and destiny of the man with the black skin to be the servant and the slave of the white man.

One thing that helped to fix the status of the black man, and which finally resulted in the passing away of white servitude in favor of Negro slavery, was the fact that the Negro was better fitted to perform the hard pioneer work which the time demanded. Particularly was this true in the more Southern colonies, like Georgia and the Carolinas.

[363]

In South Carolina an effort had been made to reestablish serfdom as it had existed in England one hundred years before. In Georgia, it was at first hoped, by prohibiting slavery to establish a system of free labor. In both instances the effort failed and, after a very few years, Negro slavery was as firmly established in Georgia as it had been in the neighboring state of South Carolina.

Still later, efforts were made to establish white servitude in Louisiana and large numbers of German "redemptioners," as they were called, were brought over for this purpose. In a very few years these colonists had been swept away by disease.

In one of the reports setting forth "the true state" of the colony of Georgia it was said that, "hardly one-half of the servants of working people were able to do their masters or themselves the least labor: and the yearly sickness of each servant, generally speaking, cost his master as much as would have maintained a Negro for four years."

With the introduction of rice planting the necessity of employing Africans was doubled, because, as it was said, "white servants would have exhausted their strength in clearing a spot for their own graves."

Thus it came about that Negro slavery grew up on the mainland to replace the servitude of the white man, just as it had grown up in the West Indies to take the place of the slavery of the native Indians.

It most not be assumed, however, that the Negro slaves, because they were better able than the white man to stand the hardships of labor in the New World, did not suffer from the effects of the work they were compelled to do. The truth is that so many of them died that the stock of slaves had to be continually replenished. In some parts of the country it was even said of the slave, as one hears it sometimes said of horses, that it paid to work them to death. It was a rule on some of the plantations that the stock of slaves was to be renewed every seven years.

One of the effects of the passing away of white servitude was to make the distance between the free white man and the black slave seem greater than ever. There grew up in the minds of white people, and, to a certain extent, in the minds of black people, the notion that slavery was the natural condition of the Negro just as freedom was the natural condition of the white man. People

[364]

began to feel that the black man did not have the same human feelings as the white man; that his pains and his sorrows were somehow not as real and did not have to be considered in the same way that one would consider these same feelings in a white man. All this sentiment of the one race for the other entered into the system of slavery and made it what it became finally before it was abolished as a result of the Civil War.

What this system really was can not be best shown by any account of the cruelties that were sometimes practiced upon slaves, because these cruelties were not practiced by the best masters and were not supported by public sentiment.

The best expression of the innate wrong of slavery will be found in the decision of a Chief Justice of South Carolina in the case of a man who had been tried for beating his slave. In this decision, which affirmed the right of the master to inflict any kind of punishment upon a slave, short of death, it is stated that, in the whole history of slavery there has been no prosecution of a master for punishing his slave.

It had been said in the course of the trial of this case that the relations of the master and slave were like those of parent and child. Justice Ruffin, in delivering the decision, said that this was not so. The object of a parent in training his son, for example, was to fit him to live the life of a free man, and, as a means to that end, he gave him moral and intellectual instruction. There was, said the Justice, no sense in addressing moral instruction to a slave. He said:

"The end is the profit of the master, his security, and the public safety; the subject, one doomed in his own person and his posterity to live without knowledge and without the capacity to make anything his own, and to toil that another may reap the fruit. What moral consideration shall be addressed to such a being to convince him, what it is impossible but that the most stupid must feel and know can never be true—that he is thus to labor upon a principle of natural duty or for the sake of his own personal happiness. Such services can only be expected from one who has no will of his own, who surrenders his will in implicit obedience to that of another. Such obedience is the consequence only of uncontrolled authority over the body. There is nothing else which can operate to produce the effect. The power of the master must be absolute to render the submission of the slave perfect."

[365]

In making this decision Justice Ruffin did not attempt to justify the rule he had laid down on moral grounds. "As a principle of right," he said, "every person must repudiate it, but in the actual condition of things it must be so; there is no remedy. This discipline belongs to the state of slavery. It constitutes the curse of slavery both to the bond and free portion of our population."

Thus it is clear that at the bottom of slavery is the idea that one man's evil is or can be some other man's good.

4

Although there was much of evil connected with slavery, much that tended to weaken the master as well as to injure the slave, there was also a brighter, kindlier side to the life of the slave which is not always understood.

There was, for example, a great deal of difference between the life of a slave on a plantation in Virginia, where master and slaves grew up together as members of one household, and the life of a slave on a similar plantation further South. In either case a large plantation was always a little kingdom in itself, and in this little kingdom the black man and the white man frequently learned to live together on terms of intimacy and friendship such as would scarcely have been possible under other conditions.

On one of these large plantations there were usually several types, or one might almost say castes, among the slaves. There were first of all the house servants, many of whom had grown up from childhood in the "Big House" or mansion of the master. These servants usually became in time very much attached to their masters and their master's children and were often regarded as much a part of the household as any other member of the family. It was to this class that the old servants belonged, of whom so many interesting stories are told, illustrating the devotion of the slaves to their masters.

One of the stories that has been repeated in more than one Southern family relates how the old Southern servant followed his master to war; watched over and cared for him faithfully during all the hardships of the campaign, and

[366]

finally, when that master had fallen in battle, carried him back to his home to be buried.

There are many instances, also, of which one does not so often hear, in which the friendship and devotion of the old servants to their master's family continued after the Civil War was over and slavery was abolished. Not infrequently these old slaves continued to work for their masters in freedom much as they had done in slavery. Sometimes when the master's family became poor, the former slave secretly supported them.

There is a story of one man who had agreed before the war broke out to buy his freedom from his master for a certain sum. After freedom came he continued to make the payments just the same until the entire sum was paid, because he knew his master's family was poor and needed the money.

Another class of slaves on the big plantation was composed of the artisans and skilled workmen of every kind, for every one of these large plantations was organized, as nearly as possible, so as to provide for every want of its inhabitants.

Beneath this class of skilled laborers there were the field hands, who did all the common work under the direction of an overseer, sometimes with the help of Negro "drivers."

In addition to all the others there was usually on every large plantation a slave preacher, who might at the same time be a trusted employee of one kind or another. He was at any rate a natural leader among his own people, and often a man of great influence and authority among the slaves, and was frequently a sort of intermediary between them and their master.

The conditions of slavery were harder, as a rule, on the big plantations farther South. These regions were usually peopled by a class of enterprising persons who had come, perhaps, from Virginia or some of the older slave states. They had removed to the new country in order to find virgin soil, on which large fortunes were made in raising cotton.

In these regions, especially where the slaves were left in charge of an overseer, whose sole function was to make the plantation pay, the slaves came to be treated a great deal more like the mules and the rest of the stock on the

[367]

plantation. They were treated as if their whole reason for existence consisted in the ability of their owners to use them to make corn, cotton and sugar.

In spite of the bad reputation which the plantations in the far South had among the slaves of Virginia, and in spite of the horror which all the slaves in the border states had of being "sold South," there were many plantations like those of Joseph and Jefferson Davis, the President of the Southern Confederacy and his brother, where the relations between the master and slave were as happy as one could ask or expect, under the circumstances.

The history of the Davis family and of the two great plantations, the "Hurricane" and the "Brierfield," which they owned in Mississippi, is typical. In 1818 Joseph Davis, who was the elder brother of Jefferson, and at that time a young lawyer in Vicksburg, took his father's slaves and went down the river to a place now called Davis' Bend. He was attracted thither by the rich bottom land, which was frequently overflowed by the spring floods of the Mississippi.

At this time there were no steamboats on the Mississippi and the country was wild and lonely. In a few years, with the aid of his slaves, Mr. Davis succeeded in building up a plantation of about 5,000 acres, which soon became known as one of the largest and richest in the whole State of Mississippi, where there were many large and rich plantations.

Some years after the settlement at Davis' Bend, Joseph Davis was joined by his brother Jefferson, who lived for several years on the adjoining plantation, known as the "Brierfields."

Joseph Davis had peculiar notions about the government of his slaves. It was a maxim with him that, "the less people are governed, the more submissive they will be to control."

This idea he attempted to carry out in the government of his slaves. Thus he instituted on the plantation a certain measure of self-government. For example, his plantation, like that of his brother Jefferson, was turned over, so far as its agricultural operations were concerned, almost wholly into the hands of one of his slaves. Under the direction of this man the land was surveyed, the levees constructed and the buildings erected. This same man was allowed to conduct a store of his own. He bought and sold goods, not only among the hands on the plantation, but among the hands on other plantations. Sometimes

[368]

Mr. Davis himself was several hundred dollars in debt to him for goods purchased.

Mr. Davis also instituted a jury system for the trial of minor offences committed by his slaves. In a court thus constituted a jury of slaves passed judgment on their fellows, Mr. Davis reserving for himself, however, the pardoning power. When a slave could do better for himself at some other form of work than day labor he was allowed the liberty to do so, giving in money, or other equivalent, the worth of ordinary service in the field. There was at one time a school on the plantation, taught by a poor white man, in which the white children from the Big House as well as some of the children of the more favorite slaves went to school together.

In this novel and statesman-like way Joseph Davis sought to carry out his notion of making the plantation, as near as possible under the circumstances, a little self-governing community. After freedom came it was Joseph Davis' plan to keep all his former slaves on the plantation and, as they grew in intelligence and ability to care for themselves, to make them its owners. To this end he sold the plantation to the man who had been his overseer. This man, with his two sons, all of whom had formerly been slaves on the plantation, continued for a number of years to carry on the work of the plantation until, as the result of losses, due to overflow, it became apparent they would not be able to pay the heavy interest charges which the purchase of the place had entailed and were thus forced to give up the experiment.

It is a mistake to assume that life for the slave on the plantation was always one of unremitting labor. In a humble way the slaves had their seasons of rejoicing and festivity. There were the usual weekly meetings in the plantation churches, where they had sermons, sometimes by a white minister, but more often by one of their own number. It was here that those beautiful old plantation melodies sprang up, in which the slaves poured out, in rude but picturesque language and in simple plaintive melodies, what lay deepest and heaviest on their hearts.

Sometimes at night, around the fireside, they listened to those quaint and homely stories which have been preserved in classic form in the Tales of Uncle Remus.

"Hog-killing" was a sort of annual festival among the slaves, and the occasional cornshuckings were always a joyous event in which both master and servants, each in their separate ways, took part.

These cornshucking bees took place during the last of November or the first of December, and were a sort of prelude to the festivities of the Christmas season. After all the corn had been gathered it would be piled up in the shape of a great mound. Then invitations would be sent around by the master of one of the large plantations to the neighboring plantations, inviting them and their slaves to be present on a certain night. In response to these invitations as many as one or two hundred men, women and children would come together.

After all were assembled around the pile of corn some one, who had already gained a reputation as a leader in singing, would climb on top of the mound and begin at once, in a clear loud voice, to sing. He sang a song of the cornshucking season, making up the words very largely as he went along. All the others gathered at the base of the mound and joined of course in the chorus. The whole proceeding had a good deal of the flavor of the campmeeting and some of the music was weird and wild.

One of the songs that used to be sung on occasions like this ran about as follows:

Massa's niggers am slick and fat, Oh! Oh! Oh! Shine just like a new beaver hat, Oh! Oh! Oh!

Refrain:—

Turn out here and shuck dis corn, Oh! Oh! Oh! Biggest pile o' corn seen since I was born, Oh! Oh! Oh!

Jones's niggers am lean an' po'; Oh! Oh! Oh! Don't know whether dey get 'nough to eat or no, Oh! Oh! Oh!

Refrain:—

Turn out here and shuck dis corn; Oh! Oh! Oh! Biggest pile o' corn seen since I was born, Oh! Oh! Oh!

[370]

Half the charm of Southern life was made by the presence of the Negro. The homes that had no Negro servants were dreary by contrast with those that did.

The native quality of the Negro, his natural sympathy, cheerfulness and good humor, and above all his fidelity to his master and his master's children, helped to make slavery, for both white man and black man, a very much more tolerable institution than it would otherwise have been.

Almost all that has been said of slavery, whether good or bad, is probably true as far as it goes. The institution had its heartless and its human side, and, since slavery is no more, it is perhaps better to close this story with this brighter and more cheerful view.